Sally Trench's Book

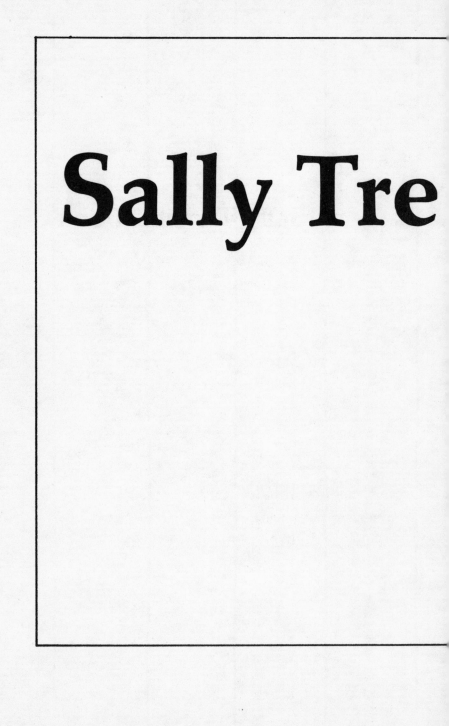

Sally Tre

nch's Book

Sally Trench

HV
4548
L7
T7

STEIN AND DAY/*Publishers*/New York

To

Christopher, Put and my parents, who have
had to bear the brunt of my escapades, and to
all those who have given me their unfailing
support in this work.

ACKNOWLEDGEMENTS

I would like to express my appreciation to those in charge of Waterloo Station waiting room where, whilst 'on the road', I sat and typed this manuscript without being moved on!

I would also like to thank Paddy, the Dobbie, Vick and Gorham families, who kept their homes permanently open to me.

Photographs between pp. 64–65 by Christa Feiler.

FOREWORD

SALLY Trench blew into my life in this way.

Last year, some nuns I knew spoke to me about her in glowing terms. They had expelled her from school some five years earlier when she was about sixteen, but it was a case of the ugly duckling for now she was doing wonderful work among the down-and-outs. However, they were anxious about the state of her soul. With all this good work she was doing, was she still keeping close to God?

At that time I was editing a little magazine, so I wrote to Sally asking for an article. She sent me one, and I sent her a cheque and asked her to come round to discuss one or two points in what she had written.

This was sheer jesuitry, of course, but it worked and she came along and we got acquainted and I was able to set the nuns' minds at rest.

But Sally seemed almost too good to be true, and although I believed her story I wanted to see for myself. So one evening last January we set out together to look up some of her friends.

We drove over London Bridge, turned north-east and, after passing through some narrow streets, found ourselves alongside an acre of derelict land, the site of bomb damage twenty-five years ago.

With torches in our hands we made our way across mud and the débris of bricks and concrete to a group of nine or ten men sitting round a fire.

When they saw Sally they stood up and shouted greetings. As we came up, she introduced me, "A friend I've brought along." I shook hands with the men on my side of the fire. They called me 'Father' or 'Reverend'.

We stayed there about half an hour. Sally laughed and talked with them all, handing round cigarettes and asking if anyone had any cuts or wounds she could attend to. One man had fallen into the fire while drunk and his hands were badly burned. She treated them and bandaged them up.

Meanwhile, sitting on a rusty petrol drum, I talked with those near me.

There was Henry, who seemed very drunk and kept asking me about the patron saint of thieves. He came from the Shetland Isles. Sally was pleased with his condition because he was drunk on surgical spirits, which was better than being drunk on meths.

Then there was a man from Longford who never smiled or joked and kept telling me of what clothes he needed. He fought shy of talking about Longford.

Jock came from Aberdeen and reproached Sally for not having brought him the trousers she had promised him. She said that she had not promised to bring them *that* night, but that she would soon.

Then there was Pat who talked nostalgically about Dublin. He was very friendly and more than half drunk. He soon disappeared to go begging.

When we got up to go, they made me promise that I'd be back soon. It was all most pathetic, although I had seen them at their best: it was a warm, fine night, the ground was not too wet, and they were all relatively sober. A week or so before, some boys had burst in on them and beaten them up. So Sally had found them another site with a camouflaged entrance, where they went for sleeping. We went there now.

It was another open bombed site, even worse than the first, with great chunks of masonry lying around. Sally told me to beware of rats, as she had twice been bitten there and had had to get some anti-tetanus treatment in hospital. As we threaded our way through the débris, she pointed to a corner of the site and said, "I found a man dead there one day."

She had covered the entrance to this site with a moveable piece of corrugated iron, and another piece concealed the entrance to a

8

fragment of a house that was still standing. She was very proud of this as she had fixed the roof (or what was left of it) herself. We looked in the one room there was: we saw a litter of bits and pieces of sacking and filthy blanket, with bottles and broken glass here and there. And the smell!

To see our next hide-out, we had to crawl on hands and knees through openings about two feet high; perhaps it had been an air-raid shelter of sorts. Again there was the litter of sacking and rags, and always the bottles, broken and unbroken.

Our next call was at a three-storey derelict house. Like the two previous places, this one was empty. The occupants (and Sally told me there would be thirty people sleeping there) were out procuring their meths or whatever was their addiction. Again, there was all the filth, the rags, the bottles, the smell.

Sally told me that there were more than a hundred such places she could take me to, but I was already beginning to feel that I'd had enough. So we went to just one more place.

It was a derelict cellar, quite the ultimate in squalor. Here we found an old man with an ulcerous foot. He was already on Sally's 'panel', and she dressed the wound for him. We chatted for a while and then bade him good night and left. (The pathos of that 'good night'! It nearly made one weep. How many years would it have been since he had known a good night?)

Sally then drove me home. I gave her a pair of trousers for Jock and some other clothes, and while I went off to bed she set out on her nightly round.

Sally's is an unusual apostolate – unusual, perhaps, because most of us are too calculating and uncommitted in the living of our faith.

Her apostolate is unusual, but it is authentically Christian. Her book shows this. Many people will say that it can't be true. But it is. She is no twentieth-century beatnik playing the compassion game. She is a Christian, in love with Christ and with her fellow-men. And her apostolate to them has a long tradition. How many

9

of the saints have seen and helped Christ in the poor and under-privileged! St Francis of Assisi, St Elizabeth of Hungary, St Vincent de Paul! Sally too has caught sight of what they saw.

And while we pray that God may look after her and keep her humble and go on using her to help His poor, we can also pray for ourselves: that we too may see Him in the socially inadequate – that we may see Him and have the courage to help Him.

Hugh S. Thwaites, S.J.
4th September, 1967

St George's,
Sansome Place,
Worcester.

CHAPTER ONE

It was surrounded by a high wall and barbed wire. There was one entrance and one exit. The grounds were well kept and the many match-box buildings were of a clinical appearance. It looked like a prison; and in its corridors, behind those formidable walls, I could feel the sense of foreboding that hangs round our penal institutions. When I was told where I was, I felt as if I had been kicked in the stomach. I was in a mental hospital.

I lay in my bed stunned by the news, all sorts of imaginative thoughts flashing across my mind.

"Why couldn't you walk when the ambulance men brought you in?" The staff nurse was standing over me writing down a list of all the gear I had brought in.

"I don't know," I feebly replied, and as an afterthought, "I suppose because I'm so tired." I had forgotten that I had been carried in.

"Right, I've emptied your haversack and I think I've got all the items down. I've taken your money and your passport to put in the office. Will you sign here?" I could have been signing my death warrant for all I cared. God, I felt tired.

The staff nurse was talking again: "I'll bring you a cup of hot chocolate and then you can sleep. The doctor will be seeing you in the morning."

"Go to hell," I thought, "just leave me alone." She did, but not for long.

"Here you are, drink this up, it'll do you good." Obediently I drank it. "Sleep well." She seemed to drift from sight. Dear God, I was tired.

It was morning, and the daily bustle of the ward penetrated my sleep. I did not want to open my eyes. I had no wish to face reality, the stigma of my surroundings, the endless day ahead.

"Hello, you awake?" a pimply face bent over me. "Got a

fag?" she continued. "I'm Christine. Got a fag?" I shook my head. She wrapped her dressing gown around her and walked away, obviously uninterested now that she had learnt I had not brought any cigarettes in with me. I glanced at my watch. It was only 7.30 a.m. I groaned and buried my face in the pillow. How I ached, as if every limb had been torn from me, and my head felt like a lump of lead.

"Everyone up. Mrs Forbes, your turn to do the floor. Doris, get up and go and wash; get out of that bed at once." It reminded me of my old boarding school. "You must be Sally Trench. You can stay in bed." The sister moved on to the next bed. "Time to get up, Nula." She shook the dormant body beside me. "Nurse, will you see that Mrs Forbes washes herself?" Patients and nurses scuttled past and only Sister's voice was to be heard. I dozed fitfully.

"Wake up, Miss Trench, here's your breakfast. Shall I put your pillows up for you?" I raised myself on to my elbows and tried to sit up; only then did I realise how weak I was. The nurse helped. "There you are, dear. Eat that up and you'll feel better." She smiled kindly and patted my shoulder reassuringly. I ate my porridge slowly, assimilating my present environment. I was in a ward with thirty empty beds; no, the one at the far end was not empty for I could see a bulge under the blankets. A nurse in a blue pin-stripe uniform came through the door.

"Where is everyone?" I asked.

"Having breakfast in the refectory."

Well at least we're allowed up, I thought. What did it matter anyway? I lay back exhausted. Someone entered. I shut my eyes and feigned sleep. Thoughts on the past year flooded back to me: the fighting of the past six weeks to keep the cause alive; the desperation of the last two weeks and my own sudden collapse twenty-four hours ago. I heard weeping – or did I? Yes, coming from my left. I hauled myself into a sitting position. "Can I help?"

A young girl looked up, not much older than myself I would

12

have thought, with straight black hair draping over her red cardigan. Tears were spilling down her clear pale face. "No, it's nothing."

I smiled. "I always say that but it's never true."

"It's the sister, she has it in for me; if it's not one thing, it's another." Again she wept into her handkerchief.

"Come over here and talk to me. I feel just as miserable as you, you know. No one's spoken to me yet apart from the staff." She came and sat on my bed. "My name's Sally. I was brought in last night."

"I know. I'm Nula. I've been here two weeks."

I felt a little lost for conversation, for I did not want to be tactless enough to ask her what she was here for. "What's this place like – a mad house?"

"No, and don't let anyone tell you it is," she burst out. "They might be mad over in the main buildings, but not in here."

"Well, I'm not mad; a crazy mixed-up kid perhaps, but not mad."

"What happened to you to get you in here, then?"

"Collapse from overwork and exhaustion basically. I think they call it a nervous breakdown."

"That all? That's nothing. You should see some of the cranks here. Some of them have been here years. At least they don't lock you up in this ward, you're free to come and go within reason."

"What! no padded cells?" I joked, and regretted it instantaneously.

"There, over the other side with the lock-up wards." I fell silent.

"What's your work anyway, or are you still at school?"

"Social worker," I replied, and quickly changed the subject. "Will I be allowed up or will I be kept in bed?"

"Oh, they'll let you up when they're ready, or they might keep you under sedation if you're violent. Or they might do what they did to Dot, give you deep sleep treatment. It depends how bad you are."

13

"Nothing wrong with me that sleep won't cure." I tried to sound convincing. We were interrupted by a nurse calling Nula for her medicine. "See you later," she called quite cheerfully as she left.

Well, I'd helped her forget her tears, but she had left me in a state of apprehension. Patients seemed to drift in and out throughout the morning; females of all description, fat, thin, old and young, each one with a haunted look, each one with her own problem. Some of the more pathetic figures rested on their beds, whilst others just wandered up the ward staring vacantly into the distance and then back again. Christine padded over to me. I noticed she had a cigarette hanging from the corner of her lips.

"Hello, won't they allow you up either? They've kept me in bed for the past four days. It's not my fault. You see, I told my doctor I was going to do away with myself and he's just waiting for me to do it now."

"Nonsense! You're letting your imagination run away with you. He just wants you to get well. How long have you been here?"

"About a year now." I tried to hide my horror. "I don't mind really, it's just my little girl, you know what it is? You see I'm sick up top." She pointed to her head and continued, "If only I hadn't told my doctor. He's waiting for me to do it now."

I was glad that we were interrupted by the doctor. "Go back to bed, Christine." She obeyed meekly. "Miss Trench?" He peered at me through thick-rimmed spectacles, and gave me a quick bow. He was an Indian of very slight build, with a pleasant face. In silence he began to examine me. "There's nothing really wrong with me," I assured him.

He straightened himself and politely replied, "If there wasn't anything wrong with you, Miss Trench, you wouldn't be here and nor would I." I decided not to say another word.

Having scratched my toes, peered into my mouth and pressed my tummy, he seemed fairly satisfied. "You stay in bed today and sleep. Tomorrow you get up, and we will talk." How ghastly, I thought.

"Talk about what?"

"Your troubles, your work and why you are here." I groaned inwardly.

"I haven't any troubles now; they're all over . . . and . . . so is my work."

"We will talk." Another quick bow and he was gone. So I was going to have a talk to him? Like hell I was. As if he could understand. I felt very lonely, as if I had been torn naked from the world. I had. My world had been smashed yesterday when everything I had believed in, worked for and fought for had collapsed under the hand of a misguided idealist.

"Hi, you look miserable. It's no good thinking in here." It was Nula.

"Just meditating. The doctor said I've got to stay in bed today and have a talk with him tomorrow."

"That's the usual procedure. You're all right, you've nothing to hide." I glanced at her questioningly. "You're not a potential suicide like me." Proudly she waved her wrists in front of me. "Sixteen stitches in one, and eighteen in the other."

I stared at the two slashes cruelly red against her lily-white skin. "With a razor," she confirmed. "Second time I've tried, but luck hasn't been on my side." How brazen she was.

I spoke quietly, "Nula, don't every try it again; truly it's not a way out."

"I won't be able to as long as they keep me here. Anyway, what do you care? You can't understand. You don't know what it's like to have a couple of kids and nowhere to sleep them, let alone who their fathers are. Christ, the times I've sat up all night wondering where the next slice of bread's going to come from and whether I'm going to have to sell myself to another man tomorrow night. Kid, you haven't met life yet." She spoke with bitterness and hatred.

"Nula, I may not have suffered your experiences, but I have

15

seen life. I know the smell of the unwanted homeless, and the neglected and helpless. Before now I have sat with dirty and drunk men, infested with bugs, who are dying, in order to hold their hands so that they might realise there is someone in this world who cares whether they live or die. I've held down junkies when they've been frantic for a fix and I've held up alcoholics whilst they've vomited into the gutter. I do know the disgust and horror of losing one's self-respect and I also know hiding from it is not the answer." She was staring at me, incredulous. I shrugged my shoulders and wished I had not said anything. "Forget it — just remember, running from yourself won't solve your problems." I yawned and closed my eyes. "I'm going to catch up on some of that much needed sleep; see you later." She took the hint and left.

Next morning I roused myself with the rest of the patients. I was entering the wash room when I heard a scream. "Don't touch me, don't touch me!" In the corner, clinging to the wall in apparent fear of her life, was a middle-aged woman with short-cropped grey hair. Grinning at her nearby was a young coloured girl. "Don't touch me, don't touch me!" the screams continued.

"Shut up, Olive," came a voice from behind one of the shower curtains.

A nurse arrived. "Now, dear, no one is going to touch you. Go back to the ward." Olive pressed herself further against the wall. "I can't while she's standing there; I'll touch her." The nurse led me aside, and the intimidated Olive shrank by. I noticed through my mirror that the girl opposite was furtively watching me. I could not understand why until she took the towel from round her neck. Two ugly rope marks indented her skin. Another potential suicide!

I had breakfast on Nula's table and then lined up with the other patients for my medicine. "Come and join us after in the sitting room?" Nula called. A few minutes later I was being introduced to Dot and Rita.

"What's the date today?" No one seemed to know.

"Anyone heard the news?" No one had.

16

"Well, whose turn is it today for a chin-wag with the doctor?" No one knew and no one really cared. They puffed away at their cigarettes.

"Can you go out if you want to?" I broke the silence.

"If you have the doc's permission."

"What do you do all day?"

"Nothing."

"Is there any organised group therapy?"

"Yes." This was hard work, but I persevered.

"When's lunch?" It was an incongruous question, having only just finished breakfast. No one seemed inclined to answer. The coloured girl came up behind Dot and extended her hand for a cigarette. "Don't touch me, don't touch me," Dot shouted jokingly. Everyone laughed. I looked round the room and saw Olive sitting alone tearfully watching Dot's act.

"Lay off, Dot." Nula said it for me and rose to wander over to talk kindly to Olive. Suddenly, for the first time since I had arrived, I could have wept. Here, shut away from the rest of the world were people, all worthwhile and in their own way with something to offer, yet unable to play their part because they could not face or overcome their problem. What a waste!

"Miss Trench, the doctor will see you in room 12," a nurse called. My heart leapt into my mouth. "Good luck," someone called. "It's down the corridor on the left."

"Come in." The doctor relaxed in an armchair behind a desk. "Sit down. I hope you slept well last night?"

"Yes thanks."

"Now tell me all about yourself."

"Where do you want me to start?"

"At the beginning."

"Er . . . yes, of course. I was born in Woking . . . you want me to go back that far?"

"Yes, yes, that's the beginning isn't it?" I grunted. In for a penny, in for a pound! I gave him my life history, at least as much of it as I was prepared to give him, with some additional

17

fabrications put in here and there for good measure. "And that's it so far," I concluded. I wondered how perceptive he was.

"Mmm!" he sat twiddling his pencil, watching me. "And what do you intend to do when you leave here?"

"Who knows? When can I leave?"

"When you like — you're a voluntary patient. I advise you to stay a week and rest, but you can discharge yourself whenever you wish." This piece of news brightened me no end. "Meanwhile I should think about your future and put the past behind you. I can put you in touch with our social worker if you like, she might be able to help you."

"No thanks, I can stand on my own two feet. I'll see you around then."

I closed the door behind me. So I was free to go when I liked. What a difference it made to my outlook! I made my way back to the sitting room, and as I passed the sister's office, I saw a thin lady carrying two cases talking to the nurse. "Sister said I'd never cope. She was right. I've come back." I heard the nurse's reply also: "Well, we thought you would, dear, so we kept your bed vacant."

For five days more I stayed as a voluntary patient, observing, listening and helping. The time came when I knew that I was fit enough to leave, so I collected my haversack and belongings and said my farewells and stepped once again into the world. What the future held, I did not know, but I cared as I had never cared before. The past year's experience had given me a wealth of knowledge and understanding of human nature, but the past week in hospital had managed to give me more than I could have ever asked for. Now the time had come to start again and use this wealth. No longer was I a naive do-gooder, a kid with a big heart, but a real person with a job to do. How very different from eighteen months ago when I, as a rebellious teenager, decided to make my stamp on the world. Wrapped in my own self-importance, I thought it was in my power to help everyone less fortunate than myself. I learnt from my mistakes the hard way!

CHAPTER TWO

I HAD always been a presumptuous child. I was the sort of ghastly kid that everyone dreaded having, the kind that if you said, "Don't speak to strange men", would go in search of strangers to talk to, and the more weird and strange they were the better. A proper St Trinian's pupil!

My interest in the 'social inadequate' developed from my hero-worshipping of tramps. How I envied their way of life, so free and wild, a world of their own. I loved to listen to their tales as much as I loved to tell my own, truth or fiction! When I left boarding school I went in search of a lost cause, determined to play a role in society. I found it on Waterloo Station.

I was coming home very late one night from the country, feeling weary and looking forward to a warm bed. Against a background noise of chamber music intermingled with the groans and sneezings of the engines, I passed the ticket office into the main hall. "Oh, I beg your pardon!" I swung round to see who I had bumped into. She was an old lady, so wrapped up in moth-eaten scarves that her face was hardly visible. She wore a dress down to her ankles and a man's sweater, three times too big for her. She had no stockings, but a pair of disintegrating slippers covered part of her feet. She stood hunched over her brown paper parcels; I do not think she had noticed the impact as I had collided with her, not to mention my apology. I walked on. I noticed scruffy men bedded down under newspapers on the benches, others slouched dejectedly in the corners. They were all dirty and un-shaven, a few of the lucky ones had overcoats to protect them against the winter nights, the rest just sat shivering. How easy it was to walk past. How easy it was to sympathise from a dis-tance. How easy it was to pass by on the other side of the road like the Levite in the New Testament.

I stopped and turned back. I parked myself in the middle of a bench between two of the scruffiest men. All at once my Good Samaritan intentions left me and I became nervous. The men had not batted an eyelid. I could smell the alcohol. I fumbled in my pockets for cigarettes and, as I lit one, the two men seemed to wake up. One lurched sideways and leaned against me. I was really frightened. "Go' any to spare?" he slurred. I lit one and handed it to him and repeated the gesture for the bloke on my other side. The man was becoming heavy. If I edged away he might take offence, so I did the only thing possible. I took him by the shoulders and straightened him.

"Want any help, Missy?" A large West Indian, with his hands on his hips, a hat pushed to one side, and a most amiable grin on his round face, swayed before me. "You don't belong here, Missy, not a high-class filly like you," he reprimanded gently.

"I'm not a permanent, just passing through," I said hastily.

"Just visiting? You're too pretty to be amongst us dirty drunks. You're not one of us. Go home."

"I will. I just thought they might like a cigarette. What will happen to them? Will they go home?" He threw back his head and laughed.

"Home? Man they got no home. This is their bedroom for tonight." He bent down to me. "Now you go home yourself, Missy, and don't you worry about us. Go home and thank the good Lord you got a home to go to."

The background music had stopped, the engines were bedded down and the station porters were calling out their final farewells. The vast station, an active terminus during the day, was silent save for the periodical cooing of a sleepless pigeon. The homeless, neglected and unwanted shivered under their newspapers. I shoved the packet of cigarettes into the West Indian's hands and did as I was told. I left the cold and hungry dossers to the night. But when I lay in my warm bed with my dog at my feet and a glass of hot chocolate in my hand, I did thank the kind Lord for having blessed me with a family and a home.

The following morning I was exercising my Afghan hound in

the park when I came across a similar character to those of the previous night. He was prodding around in the litter bins in search of scraps. I smiled at him as I passed, and said "good morning". He gave an inaudible grunt, picked up a dog-end and shuffled off in the opposite direction. I wondered where he had spent the night.

Just after midnight I dressed quickly in my jeans and placed the thermos flask of coffee that I had made that evening in my haversack. The dog wagged his tail with excitement. "Not this time," I whispered, "And don't you dare bark when I come back." I patted him. Despondently, he jumped back on to my bed and watched me open the window and climb out on the window-sill. I wished that our stairs did not creak and that my father was not such a light sleeper. But he was, and the stairs did creak abominably, so there was only the drain-pipe left. By the time I had reached the bottom and climbed down the wall, I was a nervous wreck. A car had passed with its headlights on, and a courting couple had inconveniently halted under the tree where I had intended to descend, so I had been forced to deviate from the route I had worked out in daylight. Trembling, I opened the garage and felt for my bicycle. It was as I had left it. I closed the door gently behind me and crossed to the other side of the road and waited. I expected the lights to come on in the house as father discovered his beloved daughter was not in bed. A full ten minutes I waited. I was in the clear, no one had heard me. Relieved, I bicycled over to Waterloo Station.

It was as cold and silent as the other night. Underneath the newspapers were the same grey debauched faces. I lowered my haversack and poured out the coffee. Someone had woken up, another was stirring. I handed them the hot cups. Along the line of benches, the bodies shifted and haggard faces appeared. I refilled the cups and passed them down the line. I placed cigar-ettes between icy-mauve lips and poured out more hot coffee for grabbing hands. When I ran dry, I went over to the hot drinks machine and bought more and rationed it to half a cup per man. Cigarettes were being divided also.

The big clock struck two, and as it did so a general move took place. Dossers staggered to their feet, their eyes still closed, and wandered off; they were still asleep as they walked into the telephone booths or down the station where they could not be seen. Some, on hearing the move, automatically rolled off the benches, still snoring, picked themselves up and sauntered behind closed bookstalls where they stood up asleep, hanging on to the bars or the grill. At first I was nonplussed, but I soon discovered the reason for it. In the distance I saw the blue uniforms. Quickly I collected up my pieces and hid myself in the shadows of the arches. I had a front-stall view! There were two of them, and between them they woke every man up. They were polite until the man proved obstreperous or difficult, then they just hauled him to his feet and shoved him towards the exit. Some they escorted off the premises, others they dragged away roughly. The more respectable-looking citizens they asked to see their tickets, for there were a few who were staying the night to catch the first trains at dawn. If they failed to produce a ticket, they were removed too. I was to learn later that this was a regular two-hourly feature throughout the night. Part of the routine for the law-boys, but a purely symbolic gesture, for they later stood by and watched the same faces reappear and did not bother to move them on till two hours later. I retreated to my bike, passing sleeping men still on their feet, but the general drift back to the benches had begun.

My routine with the dossers on Waterloo Station became a regular shift. I learnt to sleep till two, be at the station by three and home by four. Even my nerves were becoming nerveless! The drain-pipe climb was a piece of cake! The lads at the station became as accustomed to the whiff of hot coffee in their sleep, as they did to the two-hourly move-on.

Only once my luck ran out. I was perched on the window-sill adjusting my haversack before commencing my now fairly agile descent. There was quite a wind blowing, and the trees were whispering in chorus beneath a quarter-moon. My eyes were accustomed to the dark shapes around me and my ears always alert for unfamiliar sounds. Down the drain-pipe on to the terrace, a few steps and over a ledge, along the garage roof and over the wall. I jumped on to the pavement. I saw little and heard less. I rubbed my grubby hands and took off my gym shoes in the shadow of the garage.

"Quite a circus act, that!" Out of the same shadows loomed a policeman. "Well, any more tricks tonight?"

I tried to appear calm and dignified. "Hello, officer. You must have thought that a bit odd?"

He drew himself up to his full height, "To say the least."

"Oh, please. Don't think the worst. I do it regularly." Somehow that did not sound the right thing to say.

"I'm sure you do. A different house each time, no doubt?"

"Oh, no. Never. I do live there, you know."

"You live there," he affirmed agreeably. "And because there are no doors to your house, unlike every other house, you have a drain-pipe. Right?"

"I didn't want to wake my parents and our stairs creak." It all sounded most unconvincing.

"Any way of identifying yourself?"

I dug into my pockets and went through my haversack and produced a filthy handkerchief and a purse.

"What's all this?" He had tipped my ten packets of cigarettes out followed by the bottles and flasks of coffee. "Not thinking of coming home for a while, or are you just a chain smoker?"

I recited the narrative of my night vigils at the station.

"It all sounds very good and Christian, if it's true, though highly improper for a young girl like you. And how do you get to the other side of the Embankment at this time of night?" Of course, how stupid of me, that was proof in itself. I produced the garage key from my purse and showed him my bike. "How's that for evidence?" We parted the best of friends, and on many

23

occasions after that meeting I used to wave to him from my drain-pipe as he walked his beat. I also arranged with him that he should pass the word around to his colleagues should he be taken off night duty. I never again had police trouble and was often greeted by some strange policeman who addressed me by my Christian name. My friends and neighbours were often to raise an eyebrow at this!

I found my time was so scarce, not to mention busy, during my hour at the station, that I never managed to get to know the characters and the stories behind them till some months later. The most pathetic case I discovered was Jane, the lady I collided with that first night. For ten years, Jane had been dividing her time between Victoria and Waterloo Stations. During the day she hung around the platforms and pigeons at Victoria until it closed down at night, when she would drift over to Waterloo to pass the long nights. She possessed nothing but her brown paper parcels which contained anything she could beg or pick out of litter bins, and the worn thin clothes she stood up in. Another was Bulldog, so named because of his squashed-in features and flabby jowls. He suffered from what is now commonly termed 'war neurosis', but what is better known as shell-shock. He had periodic hallucinations and thought the Germans were after him and every time an engine in the station blew steam, he used to dive under a bench under the impression that it was a grenade exploding. Then there was Baldy, for whom I had a very soft spot. Baldy joined the school of drunks and dossers on the station because he refused to live in any of the large hostels with all their rules and regulations. He was a little man whom the wind could have blown away any time, but he was tough and hardy despite his looks, and the most even-tempered man I have ever met. He was seventy-four and had served in both world wars. There was very little Baldy had not done in his life, and he had become wise with his experiences. How wasted he was, living as a dosser whom no one noticed as they charged by to catch their après-work trains to take them home to a family, a warm house and a cooked meal.

But after all, these people had become part of the scenery, they were there every night without fail. Fragile, sick, with no one to care for them, least of all love them. It was easy not to notice them. Some had been kipping out in the cold for years, others had just come down to London to try their luck in the Great Metropolis and had no money and nowhere to stay, so the station became their bedroom too.

Over the months I came to realise that social inadequacy was a problem that was becoming more and more pressing: the number of down-and-outs seemed to be increasing, even in this day of the Welfare State. There were a mere handful who were professionally concerned with their care, and there were others, admittedly, whose occupations were unconnected with the problem and who interested themselves on a part-time basis. But it was all too clear that there were too few prepared to assist them. Perhaps it was fear that held them back. Indeed these were people we would prefer not to know, drifters, dossers, down-and-outs, call them what you will. But I could not escape from the fact that they were homeless and rootless, unwanted and very much alone. They were too afraid of the organised social services, and too nervous to live long in the big hostels with all the regimentations and quarrels found there, so they drifted on to Waterloo Station, or in and out of prison and hospital, just to find a bed. They were the rejects with nothing to live for. They were the people who could not, or would not, be helped by the Welfare State, because they were unable to face the demands, pressures and responsibilities of our society. One did not know them, often one did not even see them, but they were there, waiting for death to relieve them of their living hell.

I began to realise that my coffee trips were futile – they only brought temporary relief whereas these people needed something more permanent with more individual care and attention. But the needs of these outcasts were insufficiently met or even understood by the public. To give them practical help needed money, time and professional skills. Of which I had none. My own

25

inadequacy to assist them haunted me, so I went in search of others who felt the same. I found people kind and sympathetic, but not prepared to stick their necks out and become involved. What was so frustrating, most of the objections they offered were reasonable. After all, the down-and-out was an unattractive figure. He was pitiful and, at the same time, inspired a sense of disgust and exasperation in any self-respecting person, that he could drift so far from any contact with responsibility. Was an unhappy childhood, a broken home, war neurosis, or any other commonly cited cause, enough to bring a man to that point of degradation? Who were we to judge? Whatever the cause, I felt it was society's responsibility to help break their pattern since they did rely on us as their fellow-men. Thus I was determined to reinstate the rejected from their no-man's-land, not on a temporary basis but permanently. How I was intending to do this I had no idea, and after a short space of time I realised that it would not be with the support of my family or friends who so strongly disapproved.

CHAPTER THREE

IT was by the hand of fate that I was walking up Ladbroke Grove, an indigent area of London, one evening when I came across a down-and-out sprawled in the gutter. He was groaning quietly as if in pain. People just walked past as if they had not seen him. I knelt down beside him and turned him on to his back. I could not see his face for dirt. "What's the trouble?"

"They hit me."

"Who?"

"Them blokes." I could see no one apart from the occasional passer-by.

"Where do you live?"

"Golborne."

"Where's that?"

"Up that road there."

"Do you think you can stand? Have a bash and I'll help you back."

Together we stumbled to our feet, hanging on to each other, and with his arm round my neck we began to walk leisurely back – to Golborne. Crammed tightly in the middle of a row of shops, just off the Portobello Road, behind a vegetable and fruit stall, was the Golborne Centre. We pushed open the unlatched front door and walked in. I was staggered, we were standing in a church. It was a large drab room with a pulpit at one end looking down on rows of shabby chairs and cigarette ends and up at a false roof stretching across to hide what was once a circular gallery. My companion led me to the spiral staircase. It was an ancient one, of wrought iron, just wide enough for one man to ascend at a time. We climbed into the gallery. It was packed with two-tier bunks and narrow steel lockers. I clung to a bunk looking down at the false roof which, though safe enough, had a precarious feel to it. I helped the old man on to his bed and he lay

there huddled in equally old blankets. I descended the spiral staircase even more gingerly than I had climbed it and went in search
of someone.

I found a tiny kitchen with two old gas stoves in it but no
people. It was partitioned off from the church, and from it I could
hear talking in the next partitioned room. As I entered, the smell
of tobacco was overpowering and visibility very poor. I was in
a fair-sized room, filthy and bleak, but warm. Crippled tables
and chairs stood around on which were hunched vagrants, delinquents, ex-convicts and inadequates. A battered television set
at the other end was the only other piece of furniture. No one
looked up as I made my way through dog-ends and dinner scraps
on the bare wooden floor. I sat myself beside a young man with
shoulder-length hair. His features were sharp and his eyes cold
and narrow; a dangerous friend to make, I thought.

"Hello. Like a cigarette?" I gave him a friendly smile. His eyes
narrowed to almost closing; from his pocket he pulled some loose
tobacco and began to roll his own. I put mine away. He watched
me suspiciously.

"I brought back one of your chaps," I explained. He continued
rolling his cigarette, watching me like a hawk.

"I took him upstairs to his bunk." Pause. "I hope that's all
right?" He put the cigarette between his lips and slowly went
through his pockets, never taking his eyes off me. He produced
a lighter and flicked it alight. Instead of lighting his cigarette, he
enlarged the flame. I felt his shifty eyes burning behind that
flame. I sat, cold with fear, wondering what his next move was
going to be. Suddenly he stuck the lighter under my nose. I
threw my head back to avoid the heat, and with clenched fists
banged his arm on to the table. It was an automatic reaction. Fear
gripped me for his face was red with rage. He spat the cigarette
out and rolled his eyes and laughed. "You're not f... bad," he
commented.

"Thank you," I said dryly, not sharing the joke. "You're not
bad at making friends yourself." I found myself saying this

28

angrily before I could check myself. He glanced at me and burst into more laughter.

"You should 'ave seen your face; right green you were."

"Now that we're talking, who's in charge here?" I inquired.

"Depends 'ow you look on it, don't it? No one's in charge of me."

"Well, who runs the place then?"

"The Guv'." Patience was never my virtue.

"And who's the Guv'?"

"Peake, the Right Reverend Peake."

"Where would I find him?"

"Gone 'ome."

"Well, who's in charge while he's away?" He grinned at me and I noticed his front teeth were missing.

"Dunno."

The door swung open and a tall grey-bearded man entered. He saw me and came over. "Can I help you?"

"Well, actually I just brought back one of your lads. I found him in Ladbroke Grove. Apparently, there was a fight."

"That was good of you. Thanks. Would you like to come into the office?" I rose to follow him.

"Thank you for nothin'. Goodbye." The young man I had been talking to threw back his chair and pushed in front of me and out the door in a temper. Grey beard turned to me: "Don't take any notice of Bob, he's got a temperament like a yo-yo!"

In the office I learnt from Dave (he told me his name later) that the Reverend Peake, a Nonconformist minister, had turned his church into a doss-house some years previously, and could now sleep anything up to fifty men. He offered them the draughty protection of his church and three square meals a day; it was not a lot, but a castle compared with the Embankment or the gutter. At first the minister slept them in the gallery among the pews, and they used to hang their washing across the church and over the pulpit; by their very presence, three-quarters of his congregation, who considered that this was carrying practical Christianity to unreasonable lengths, refused to come to his services. But the project grew, and the pews made way for bunks and lockers. After many visits to Golborne, I realised that outwardly it seemed to offer considerably less than many of the more orthodox establishments in the way of material comfort, and I wondered why so many sought refuge at the Centre. For two reasons perhaps. One a practical consideration. In the centres set up by the local authorities, the homeless man had to present himself early in the evening if he was to be fortunate enough to secure himself a bed for the night. In the morning he was expected to help with the cleaning and other essential chores, and then he was told to leave. He has nowhere to go during the day and so just waits till five or six o'clock in the evening, when he will again be queueing at the same centre, or, having wandered too far from it, will be in search of a warm spot where he can sleep out the night. However, at Golborne, such a man was taken in and could stay indefinitely, leave when he liked and could consider himself a resident free to come and go in a small community. The other reason lay in the minister himself. His aim was to rekindle in each of his men some sense of their own dignity and importance. It was the individual, warm concern for the residents' well-being which raised Golborne high above any of the other centres for dossers.

There were the usual disappointments, naturally; a young homeless boy would spend three weeks there, helping with the chores without ever being asked, friendly and popular, and then suddenly disappear only to be found later in hospital suffering from an overdose. It was a base for many of the toughest criminal types. Some stayed for a few days, others for weeks. And some stayed longer, as helpers.

Golborne became another place for me to visit in the winter evenings. I used to frequent it two or three times a week to wash up the dinner plates or just to talk to the boys. With the young delinquents I was able to trace a pattern after a while. Most of them had been in trouble in their teens, and so were familiar with the Juvenile Courts and probation officers when they left school.

They took a job, but after a few months they became bored and restless. The advantages of a regular wage packet became insufficient compensation for the hours they put in, and there was no additional stimulus to hold them there, so they left. They drifted from one job to another; and from employment to unemployment; and were soon in trouble with the police again. Heavy drinking or drug-taking became part of their long-established social pattern. It all provided an escape from boredom. Soon they ran out of money and pilfering became their next excitement. It always ended in Borstal or prison.

My relationship with the lads took some months to establish. Some of them clearly looked upon me as a rather amusing curiosity and teased me incessantly about the way I spoke. This worried me at first and I thought it might prove a difficult barrier to cross, but I felt it was better than putting on a phoney accent which they might distrust. The more intelligent were perceptive enough to realise that I did not quite fit, and were highly suspicious. My presence, though, made no difference to the way they behaved. The language was well punctuated with the usual swear words and adjectives and as often as not, someone came out with a string of abuse just to see how I would react.

Having made a casual acquaintance with the boys, my problem became how to transform this superficial and fleeting relationship into one of greater depth and permanency without becoming too intimate. Gaining their acceptance was always the first step, but gaining their trust proved a very difficult second! Throughout my visits I concentrated on keeping the atmosphere personal and informal. On the whole the response was relaxed, but occasionally I met with abruptness and suspicion and a generally inflexible attitude; with this type it was not easy to communicate friendship.

One of these was Bob. Having been accepted by him as a regular visitor, I began to encourage him to talk factually about himself, especially about his home and family, to establish a relaxed and informal atmosphere. He was the eldest of five from a poor working-class family. His mother was a semi-invalid and his father also suffered from poor health. He was a strict authoritarian and Bob had resented the restrictions put on him. Whilst at school, when he was not playing truant, he produced inadequate work and lacked any kind of concentration. With another boy he became a peripheral member of a large and quite notorious group of youths involved in anti-social activities. He left school at fifteen and found a factory job. He found this both unpleasant and boring, and was eventually sacked. By now he had developed an ugly temper which he enjoyed losing; fighting was a regular outlet for his emotions. A couple of youth clubs were unable to cope with him and his own friends were transient. He worked up considerable hostility against any kind of authority. At sixteen he walked out of home never to return and roamed around England obtaining the odd job on a fair ground or on a building site. The rest of his time he spent in coffee bars or pubs. He resented anyone who had money, and his own philosophy was that money was the be-all and end-all of everything, with the implication that with remuneration one can do anything, everything. His attitude towards sex lacked respect: sexual intercourse was regarded as a matter of course at the first opportunity in any relationship. Later I was to discover that he had a wife somewhere and three children, though he swore only one was his. Since he left home he had been in and out of prison for pilfering and violence; when I met him he had just been discharged, having completed a four-year sentence for knifing a policeman. His attitude towards prison was particularly light-hearted, in fact he claimed to enjoy being 'inside', and it was a kindness on society's part to return him to prison, since the strain of living outside was so painful and intense.

I was to encounter many like Bob later. It became quite clear to me that repeated punishment was having less and less effect on the ex-convict and was serving almost the exact opposite purpose to that presumably intended, for it was neither deterring nor reforming him. It seemed to me axiomatic that the more often a man offended and went back to prison, the more clearly he was showing a need for care and understanding. Prison only covered behavioural or personality maladjustments with a layer of 'institutional neurosis', officially described as 'prisonisation'. Prison conditioned these men so that they were almost totally incapable of living outside. Was this because we set them standards that they were incapable of attaining and then followed it up by punishing them? Or was it that because their disabilities did not manifest themselves in physical symptoms or in any recognisable form, they drew no understanding or acceptance? I did not know the cause and I was equally unsure of the answers.

I persisted with my relationship with Bob despite the obvious suspicion and hostility. He refused to meet me in Golborne and so we met in a café in the Portobello Road at a prearranged time. This refusal was a self-recognition of his disreputable environment. Often he never turned up, or when he did, his behaviour was rude and insulting. I felt he was trying me and waiting to hear the familiar threat, "I'm not going to have anything more to do with you," but on these occasions I managed to hold my tongue and ignore him, which as often as not infuriated him more. Patience and perseverance over many months eventually proved their worth, though failure and success were relative concepts and I spent little time in considering them. When we did not meet in the coffee bar, we met in the pub where he would boast about how much drink he could take.

It took many meetings before he began to ask me for my help and advice. At first I was very cautious with my answers—I put out feelers. I tried not to dictate or deprive him of the right to self-determination, because I felt this would not help him to come to terms with himself or to develop a sense of responsibility towards his own affairs. When he consulted me about his problems I made no attempt to provide a ready-made solution or to pass moral judgement on the rights or wrongs of the situation. I tried to show him the involvements of his problems and the consequences of any action he might be contemplating. With Bob, I learnt that asking the right question was more important than knowing the right answer and more useful than any lecturing and moralising.

The first visible breakthrough came ten months after he left prison and five months after our first meeting at Golborne. I was sitting in Johnny's Café waiting for him; a couple of Teds were on the next table taking the micky out of me by referring to my 'posh' clothes and 'upper class' smell when Bob came in looking rather sheepish. He was smartly dressed and, for the first time, shaved. But what took my breath away was the haircut. No longer did he look a troglodyte but a well-groomed young man. I wished that he had some false teeth, because the ugly gap when he smiled rather spoilt the effect.

"Bob, what a vast improvement!" I encouraged.

"I could take you anywhere now, couldn't I?"

"Indeed you could. To the best hotel."

"Yeah — Sal, I want to get a job."

"Good. Anything in mind?" I wanted to sound pleased but not enthusiastic, in case I frightened him off the idea.

"Well, I 'ad a job in a baker's once. I've got a mate who's said 'e'll fix me up workin' beside 'im in a bakery."

"Sounds admirable. Looking as you do, you'd get any job you applied for, but that sounds a splendid idea." I wanted to ask when he was thinking of starting, but I refrained. I was glad I had.

"My mate thinks 'e can get me in on Monday. You think that's all right? And when I get a bit of lolly I'll take you out."

"That would be lovely, I'll look forward to that. Meanwhile here's a packet of cigarettes." It gave him the opening he wanted.

"Er . . . Sal, could you lend me a quid to see me over?"

"Okay, as long as it doesn't all go on drink." I knew it would, but it did not worry me. I had given him a small amount previous to this and it had been lavishly spent in the pub, but I felt that our relationship was not established enough to refuse him his demand without an almighty scene and a final break-up.

34

Bob took the job in the bakery, and twice a week I met him after work, in the pub. Initially, the mere fact of having a job boosted his ego, not to mention the wages. Expansively, he insisted on taking me out for meals, and often we went to the cinema. Once or twice I brought along a girl friend so that he would become accustomed to having females around him without having to think of going to bed with them. On our outings he was always the gentleman, well-mannered and protective, yet he was still very moody and very quick-tempered. Drink was still his downfall and he was always ready to take on anyone who was prepared to fight. If someone refused to fight him he went into tantrums like a spoilt child, though next morning when he had sobered up, he would have forgotten all about it.

The second barrier was broken three months after he had taken his bakery job.

"Sal, will yer 'elp me?"

"If I can. What's the trouble?"

"I want to go home and see my old lady again." This took the wind out of my sails.

"Splendid! But why do you want my help?"

"Well, I don't think my old man'll have me in the house, having not been in touch in the last five years like, and I was wonderin' like if you could go and see them first?"

"Why not go together one day?" I felt it would be better if he managed this step alone, with me just behind him to support him.

"Would you do that then?"

"Of course. Where do they live?"

"West Byfleet, near Woking in Surrey. We can get a Green Line bus all the way. When can you get off from work?"

"Next Thursday?" I said, glancing through my diary.

"Okay. Meet you at Hammersmith at ten-thirty."

"It's a date." I was about to say it was time I went when he thrust ten pounds into my hand. "What's this for?"

"Keep it for me, will you? Stop me spendin' it on booze."

"As you wish. Why not start a post office account?"

35

"No," he answered defiantly. "You keep it. I trust you."

"All right if that's what you want."

I departed with mixed feelings. Had I been too gullible? Did he really have parents out at West Byfleet? Or was he just wanting to get me out into the country? After all, Dave of Golborne had often said about Bob that I was playing with fire – was I? To date it had all been too good to be true; was there any evil intent behind his improvements? Was I just another sucker?

I was at the bus stop on Thursday as agreed. Together, we travelled to West Byfleet. Alone we crossed a canal bridge towards a row of council houses. We stopped outside one of them. Bob's confidence deserted him. "You go and face the old man first," he urged.

Leaving him at the front gate, I walked up the path not knowing quite what to expect. Having tapped on the front door with no result, I edged it open. I was standing in a minute kitchen.

"Come in, dear, what can I do for you? I'm through here."

I looked into the adjoining room and saw a vast figure bulging over a chair; despite her size, her face was haggard and lined, a face that had tasted poverty and suffering.

"I'm sorry to disturb you; my name's Sally. You must be Mrs H. Could I talk to you for a minute?" I noticed another figure in the corner. He was long and lanky like Bob but his features were softer; his eyes were tired and his expression was one of weary resignation. He greeted me suspiciously.

"I'll be quite frank with you," I began. "I've come down about your son, Bob. I've been seeing a lot of him lately and he's doing very well for himself. He's in a good job now." There was no reaction.

"I thought 'e was in prison," his father said eventually.

"No, he's been out nearly a year now and is really making a go of it."

"Believe that when I see it!"

"As a matter of fact you can. Bob's outside." There was a silence and Mr H. turned as white as a sheet. "If you turn him

36

away, you could be doing as much damage as signing a court order. You might be causing irreparable damage. Let him prove himself as he has done to me," I exhorted. Mrs H. glanced nervously across at her husband who was in turn clenching his fists with anger.

"He's spent four years paying his debts," I went on hastily, "he's squared it up, now he's wanting to square it up with you. Give him that chance. He is your son."

"Let me see the boy, Dad. It's been a long time," Mrs H. burst out.

He stared at her astonished. "Since when did you concern yourself about your eldest?" She began to cry. I sat like a stuffed rabbit feeling utterly helpless while they argued. Words were useless when fighting bitterness.

"Let me see 'im. You don't have to," Mrs H. wept.

"Stop your crying." He sat puffing his pipe; only the monotonous tick of the clock broke the silence. "Well, since he's here, he'd better come in," he said gruffly.

Outside, Bob was like an excited child, hopping from one foot to the other.

"Come on," I said, "they're waiting for you." He followed behind as I led him into the drawing room. His father got to his feet and they faced each other like a couple of angry bulls. Mrs H. broke it.

"Hello, son."

"Hello, Ma." Silence and then Bob put out his hand to his father.

"Hello, Dad. Sorry I haven't written." His father made no move to reciprocate the gesture. I saw Bob's ears go red, and his eyes began to narrow. His mother caught her breath, and I bit my lip. They were both too big for me to hold from fighting. Then the man took the pipe from his lips and laid it down on the mantelpiece. Grudgingly he extended his hand. I breathed again. "You'll stay to lunch, won't you?" he said.

Bob began to visit them once a month, both men making great

37

efforts to accept each other as they were. Whenever he went down there, he always took a large cake that he baked for the family. The ice had been broken, and each visit became easier and more enjoyable for them all. I prided myself on my success. A few months later I was to receive a jolt. It was just another lesson I was to learn.

Bob was very demanding on both time and emotion. He expected me to give him all my attention and became extremely jealous if I lavished any interest on anyone else. Having been so successful with him so far, and brought about what I thought was a 'drastic cure', I rather sat back preening myself. I was so confident that I had him at my fingertips that I became careless.

I had met up with another social worker called Duncan who was a male nurse in a mental home. He was interested in my work at Golborne and asked me to take him along to see it. I agreed. It was thoughtless of me and a very grave mistake. After work we made our way to the Portobello Road, and as I passed Johnny's Café I noticed Bob out of the corner of my eye. His eyes were narrowed on Duncan. Even then I was blind to the danger signals. Knowing well that if Bob wanted to see me he would come out to make his presence known, I walked on to the Centre. We passed the evening talking to the 'boys' and washing up the dinner plates; half-way through, Bob came in. Without acknowledging me he went and sat at the far table. I smiled at him from where I was sitting, but only received a scowl, so I made no further attempt to communicate with him. I think possibly that was another mistake too.

At eleven Duncan and I said our farewells to Dave and began to amble towards the tube station in Ladbroke Grove. Suddenly Bob and one of his mates appeared from nowhere. They blocked our path and Bob began to scream with rage, "You f... hypocrite. You bloody bitch." From the wallet I had given him he extracted my letters to him and tore them into little pieces and threw them at us. I quickened the pace. They followed right behind. We bought two tickets and started down the stairs, Bob still shouting after me. A few people turned to see where the filthy language was coming from. Something hit me on the shoulder. It was the diary I had given Bob. It fell to the ground, and with his mate Pete on his heels he came up to us. Silently I began to pray, for I realised Bob meant business. "Pick it up," he ordered me. I took no notice. He grabbed me by the coat. Duncan made as if to defend me, but Pete threw him back by the seat. "Pick it up!" I stared in disgust at him. He spat in my face and let me go. I said nothing but took out a handkerchief and wiped my face. He went on shouting obscene language at me again and threatened to knock Duncan's head off.

A train came in and its doors slid open. Duncan and I, relieved, boarded, but to my horror so did Bob and Pete. I looked around; there were a few girls opposite us and a couple of men at the other end. I scanned Bob's waist line for a bulge. As far as I could see he had no knife on him, but his fists were clenched, and his face was full of hatred. After a while, he began to tremble and then it was over before I realised it. He had Duncan, who was half his size, on his feet and was beating him round the head. The girls opposite screamed and rushed to the other end of the tube, and to my utter disgust so did the men. Suddenly I saw red and in my fury threw all caution to the wind. Head down, I bulldozed my way between the two grappling men. I had no inhibitions about how I fought. I went for Bob like a cat, kicking, biting and punching. I felt Pete pounce on me. Somehow I threw him off. We were drawing into a station. "Duncan, get off!" I screamed. I felt that I could handle them better without him, and that if he remained they would really hurt him. He hesitated and the doors were closing. "Duncan, do as you're told, get off." It was not the time to act the heroic cavalier. I saw him crawl on to the platform; how hurt he was, I did not know. I was pushed back into my seat. I heard Bob giving Pete directions to disembark at the next station and wait for the next train, hoping that Duncan was on it, and that if he himself had not returned in two hours' time to Golborne, he was to come with some of the lads over to

St John's Wood and look my address up in the telephone book and raid the house.

I wondered who he thought was going to call the police. The compartment had emptied, and we were now alone. I was too empty and deflated to talk. I guessed that now that Duncan had gone, and now that he had let off steam, Bob would not touch me. My main worry now was to get rid of him before we reached St John's Wood and I reached home, so that he would not know where I lived. At the stop before St John's Wood I got out, Bob followed. I began to walk slowly, taking the long way round, keeping to the main roads as a precaution. He followed a few yards behind.

"Come and talk. Don't follow me like a shadow."I stopped to allow him to catch up, but he refused and stood still. I shrugged my shoulders and walked on. It was cold and I began to shiver. I wondered if Duncan had had the sense to go a different way home or if he was in hospital or at the police station.

"Shall we walk a bit faster? It's a bit chilly." I explained my movements in case he became suspicious of my intentions. A police car drove by; I pretended I had not seen it.

"Go on, call 'em," he shouted at me. I took no notice.

"Go on, you want me back in nick. Why don't you call 'em?"

"I can't now anyway. They've gone; and even if I could, I wouldn't."

"You bein' soft on me? Don't waste it, mate." I walked on. Whatever happened, I would not be the one to call the police. If I did I knew he would be sent back to prison because of his previous records of violence. It would ruin everything that he had built. We were passing some road works now, just coming into St John's Wood, and I was working out where I was going to tramp next — anywhere but home. Suddenly something hard zoomed past me, grazing my head. It was a workman's oil lantern. As it crashed to the ground, Bob hit me on the back of my neck. I fell to the ground and lay there pretending I was unconscious. The fact that he had hit me was far more painful to me than the actual blow. The pavement was hard and cold, and I found it rather boring lying there, so I groaned myself to apparent consciousness and got to my feet. Bob was leaning against a wall seemingly unconcerned. "Still not goin' to call the cops?" he asked.

"Nope, not now, not never; so I should stop wasting your time trying to make me. I'm going home. I'm tired." Determinedly I marched away.

Eventually, at the end of our road, I turned to Bob. "I live down here. I only hope my father hasn't called the police himself to search for me. I suggest you go back to Golborne and stop your friends coming out here. I hope you've enjoyed your evening, I haven't. In fact I've been sickened by the whole affair. You must be proud of yourself. I'll see you next Monday at the usual time, but let's not have another demonstration like this. Good night."

I turned my back and went into the house. As I was opening the front door, I heard the telephone ring. Well, this would wake them if they were not already awake. I heard my brother's voice: "No, she's not in. I haven't a clue where she is, and at this time of night, I don't really care. Good night." He slammed the receiver down, and muttering under his breath, went back to bed. Thank heavens he had answered it and not my father. Quietly I slipped upstairs. It was wonderful to be safely in bed. Only then was I aware of how frightened I had been.

My door burst open and all six foot two inches of my brother blocked the aperture. "What the hell are you up to? Don't your bloody friends sleep? According to this one on now, it's a matter of life and death. I told him to ring back in the morning, but he said it's urgent. Get him off the bloody line will you, so I can get some sleep." Fuming, he bounced out. I made my way to the telephone wondering what had happened now.

It was Pete, ringing from St John's Wood Station. Bob had not turned up at the specified time, and Pete and his mates had come to find out why. I managed with difficulty to persuade them that I had not split to the cops, that as far as I knew Bob should be back at Golborne by now. With a final threat that, if he wasn't there I would 'know all about it', Pete rang off.

I retired to bed with my heart in my mouth. Somehow I dozed off. But every now and then I went to the window and drew my curtains back. There was nothing to see, and the morning arrived without further mishap. But with it came questions and abuses from my brother, and much explaining to my parents for the late hour I had come in. I lied my way clear.

The next time I saw Bob he was subdued with shame but could not bring himself to apologise, nor even mention it; I was thankful that I had remained impassive to his dares and threats, for it saved our relationship as well as his freedom. From that episode I learnt to think in terms of prevention rather than cure. With a year behind me at Golborne I had proved that sympathy, understanding and genuine concern for an individual's condition, in contrast to the cynicism and despair which were so characteristic of many, was half the battle in adjusting the delinquent. Bob loved and respected me far more after that dreadful night than he had done before. In fact, when I went into a hospital a few weeks later with a bad back, a nurse said a very strange thing to me. "That man was out there again. I told him he could come in and see you, but he seemed a bit bashful."

"What man?" I asked, staggered.

"Hasn't anyone told you? There's a man who comes along at eight every evening and catches one of the nurses going off to find out how you are. He's fairly tall, without any front teeth and rather grubby looking. He sits at the bottom of the stairs eating his sandwiches waiting for one of us off the ward." I laughed.

"That's Bob. Do tell him to come up next time you see him."

The following morning she came and saw me. "I did as you asked, but he was quite adamant about it. He said he thought he might let you down amongst your posh visitors so he sends his love and asked me to give you this." She handed me a transistor radio. "Oh, yes, and he says, don't worry, he didn't nick it!" The nurse's eyebrows went up, but she made no further comment.

CHAPTER FOUR

ONE evening when I biked over to Golborne, just before the Bob episode, I bumped into Dave going out. He was wearing a suit, which was unusual.

"Hello, hello, and who's the lucky bird, Dave?"

"Don't be daft," he replied self-consciously, "I'm going to a meeting. I've got to give a talk on Golborne."

"Sounds good publicity. Who to?"

"Simons?"

"Who are Simons?"

"From the Simon Community."

"What is the Simon Community?"

"It's a community of our sort of lads here."

"Why Simon?"

"After Simon of Cyrene, who helped carry the cross of our Lord."

"Ugh! Religious?"

"No, undenominational like us, though the founder is a Roman Catholic, I believe. Look, why don't you come along to the meeting with me instead of asking all these questions, and see for yourself? You can help me out with the talk, too."

I had nothing to lose, so I agreed. Little did I know the extent to which I was committing myself.

The meeting was held in a large terraced house just off the Harrow Road. I was introduced to the owner, Helen Jacobs, as she sat buttering sandwiches and making coffee. One by one strangers came in to whom I was politely introduced. About fifteen had arrived when the chairman opened the meeting in front of a glowing fire, spread-eagled in an armchair. "The Central London Group's minutes for the last meeting, please, Miss Dixon." I was told later that the Companions of Simon were divided into area Groups. Most of the meeting was double-dutch to me, but the interval was first class – plenty of tasty grub and stacks of coffee. Dave contributed his piece after the interval, and I filled in a few gaps that he left out. The meeting came to a close and more food and more coffee was produced. It was an excellent evening.

As we left Dave said, "You know, you ought to go and visit a Simon house. You'd find it most interesting. Go and see their house in Camden Town. It's called St Joseph's."

The following evening I paid a call on St Joseph's. It was one of many shabby terraced houses running geometrically east to west. The exterior looked decayed and ready for demolition. The door was open, so I boldly walked in. My first fleeting impression was that it reminded me of Piccadilly Circus; there was a congestion of bodies in a rather dark and dingy corridor. The wallpaper was peeling off, and the floors unswept. Young men swaggered around in creased Italian-cut suits and winkle-picker shoes, whilst the older folk wore grubby and worn clothes that were either too small or too big for them. Most of them were unshaved and obviously took no care of their appearance whatsoever. No one had taken any notice of my entrance, so casually, with an air of 'I belong here too', I nosed around.

The small kitchen was a continuation of the corridor, where a couple of boys were busy washing up. To its right I found the dining room where a group of men sat mournfully staring at the cluttered table. I received an occasional hostile glance, but no one questioned me or greeted me. I found the front room was an office where another group of men were sitting on either the beds or the desk or wherever they could place themselves in comfort. A few were on the floor.

"Can I help you, Miss?" a tall, balding man asked.

I introduced myself. He shook my hand. "I'm Len Green and I run the joint in a sort of way."

The door burst open, and in came a paunchy young man with receding hair. He wore thick-rimmed glasses which gave him

44

the appearance of an academic. He had a certain air of confidence about him, and was wearing a good-looking sports coat. Somehow I knew he was not a down-and-out.

"Everything all right, Len?" He had a pleasant-sounding voice.

"Yup, except the Berkshire probation officers have asked us if we'd take in an epileptic grave-digger. And the grocers say if they don't get paid within the next two days, we'll have to go somewhere else for our groceries."

"What, another?"

"Yes, and this is Sally from Golborne. She's just come to sus. the joint."

"An enemy in the camp! How are you? I'm Pat Egan, supposedly the bursar, but since we have no money to burse I fall short of this rank." I liked him. "Have you seen round the place yet?"

"I've only just come."

"Well, allow me to give you a conducted tour. Incidentally, have you eaten, because I haven't. Len, what's cooking?"

"You're too late Pat, it's all been eaten. Though there's plenty of bread and cheese." Pat turned up his nose with distaste.

"Check, be a good lad and pop down the road and buy two lots of fish and chips." A middle-aged lanky body unwound himself from the bed and, talking to himself, sauntered out. "Right; coffee?" There was a murmur of approval at his suggestion. We went out into the kitchen where we could talk more quietly without interruption.

That evening, over the fish and chips, I learnt a lot about the Simon Community. The more Pat talked, the more I liked what I heard. Here, at last, was what I had been in search of for all these months. "Our philosophy is complete permissiveness and tolerance for the next man," Pat explained in a somewhat pontificating manner. "His past means nothing to us; we are only interested in his future. To accept people as they are, and not as they were. To forgive and forget." I knew Simon was

45

for me, because we shared the same vision and the same principles. But I never realised just then how much I was to become involved.

The Simon Community, generally referred to as 'Simon', was a new experimental venture in care for the social inadequate. It was founded in the autumn of 1963 by Anton Wallich Clifford, on the ideal that condemning men and women to homelessness, prison or mental hospitals for whatever they had done, or failed to do, was not the answer to the problems of our society or of the individuals themselves.

It was a ten-year-old dream before Anton was able to sow the first seeds of Simon. In those days he was just a progressive probation officer in London who recognised the increasing problem of social inadequacy. Thus it was that in 1961 he helped found the Voluntary Hostels Conference (now the National Association of Voluntary Hostels) as a 'front-line' movement to further this recognition and to assist the acute problem of accommodation and care arising directly from the social isolation and apathy of the misfit. He watched with marked interest the pioneers such as Merfyn Turner and Austin Williams, of Norman House and St Martin of Tours respectively, establish themselves, and other similar units get off the ground. But there were still too few to meet the increasing demand made on them and, moreover, their effectiveness was confined to an upper stratum of homeless offenders and patients. By statistics, Anton proved that for the hard core of severely socially crippled men and women — the persistent recidivists, the hospital 'social problems' — short-term work or care was failing. Also he felt very strongly that the existing statutory services were ineffectual, and tended to aggravate rather than diminish the problem by increasing the feeling of rejection; he was sure that many could be helped to live relatively useful lives, without offending or demanding from society, provided they were given a protected environment, with unpressurised, long-term care and individual attention.

To meet this challenge, and to spearhead the mission to the misfit, the Simon Community Trust was created under Anton's directorship and was registered with the Charity Commissioners; soon Simon was to make a home for hundreds, as opposed to a temporary haven or just another doss-house. It was to care for the inadequate, the alcoholic, the drug addict, the ex-convict, the meths drinker, the mentally disturbed and the homeless. Simon was to welcome home the rejects of our society, the forgotten bundles of humanity.

But the road to Simon was not just being a concerned social worker. It took hard work, courage and, above all, faith. In November 1962, Anton had to make the decision of his life. Either to remain in the square orthodox world of our stodgy middle-class society, living well and comfortably as a middle-aged bachelor, with a secure office job with plenty of future; or to make a definite break from society and security and join the undesirable world of the unwanted. He put away his bowler hat and umbrella and quietly departed from the affluent society he was used to. Clad in shoddy clothes he moved to Southampton to assist Father Pat Murphy-O'Connor to open Dismas House, a half-way house for discharged prisoners. Here for two years, whilst initiating Simon, he worked amongst the criminals of our time, and made contact with the undesirables whom he felt could have a place in his brain-child.

Meanwhile, he and his trustees, who represented a very influential cross-section of well-known personalities, continued to solicit prayer, support and financial help towards the ultimate object of launching a country estate for his future community. The dream almost came true when negotiations were in progress to buy an estate in Sussex which would accommodate fifty people. Capital of £14,000 had been raised by way of guarantee, and Christian Action had promised help. Initially the plan envisaged a home farm, a half-way house, an alcoholic lodge and a system of family cottages. But Anton's plans were halted after the local press had given adverse publicity to his ideas of starting a community in the district for down-and-outs. The local council fought him and won.

A year later, in May 1964, quietly and inconspicuously, the Simon Community opened St Joseph's, a House of Hospitality, in North West London. It started with three contacts Anton had brought up from Dismas House, and from that first day the doors were kept open twenty-four hours a day. Between the three of them, articles were written, posters were painted, people were notified and house-to-house begging organised. This all-out drive on promotion by Anton and his trustees brought Simon into the public eye, and support, both practical and financial, rapidly grew. Anton and Sidney B.S., treasurer and a trustee, attended one-night stands at public meetings all over the country. They talked as they had never talked before, inspiring and enthralling their audiences with the ideals and needs of Simon. In a very short period of time, its methods and philosophy were proved to be acceptable for the social misfit, and qualified social workers were recommending their problem clients to us.

The essential feature of St Joe's was the permissive regime and high degree of tolerance. There were no rules; the men were allowed to come and go as they liked, and were not required to get up or go to bed at any fixed hour. During the day it was hoped that some would be willing to do some of the essential chores. If not, then they did not get done. Meals were continuous as long as the cook was prepared to supply them to anyone who wanted to eat, though bread and cheese, being the easiest to prepare, was the staple diet. Yet sometimes I have known the cook to get up in the middle of the night when he has heard some poor cold tramp come in. Conversation and discussions about community business were often held with the inmates for, by doing so, Anton felt it gave an air of belonging and a feeling of participation, which in turn gave a sense of 'home'. As a member was never asked to leave, it gave him an additional sense of security, so essential to people who have experienced years of rejection and who had finally rejected society themselves.

48

Another of Anton's philosophies was that to persist in the ethic that work was the only respectable way of living was merely creating further conflicts. He felt strongly that members who wanted to work should wait until they were absolutely ready, otherwise they would only relapse, which would give them a further sense of failure. He encouraged them by telling them they were doing a good job working for each other, and in keeping a self-contained community. This proved true, for in time they began to take an active responsibility for each other, and by doing so they began to interact in the group in a positive and out-going way. As this developed they began to lose their apathy and also their identification with their former life. With the security came self-confidence and eventually a new equilibrium was found. This was important, for they must regain their own self-respect before they could modify their behaviour. Again this is where Anton's philosophy differed from that of the other organisations; he felt that the best way of helping them was to meet them on their own level, and not expect them to meet him on his terms and standards. Thus it was that Joe's was never particularly spruced up, but just rough-and-ready like the inmates.

The Simon houses became a kind of pipe-line. From the permissive and rather dirty reception centres of St Joe's and St Antony's at Rochester, the boys were automatically moved to Simonrise at Rochester. Here a higher standard of living was exercised. In contrast to the bare wooden table with a meal of bread and cheese for anyone who should wander in at St Joe's, the inmates of Simonrise sat down to two-course meals from off table cloths. No one went to Simonrise from off the street, they had to pass through St Joe's or St Antony's first. From Simonrise, they moved on to Simonwell, a farm purposely situated in a very rural part of Kent. Here a very ordered family life was maintained. Meals were excellent and always to time. They enjoyed inviting guests down, guests whom they could entertain in their own home, and it brought them in touch with the 'world'. During the day everyone had a job to do in the house or on the farm. It was interesting to find that those who had progressed up this pipe-line and were now well instated at the farm, were critical of the state of St Joe's and St Antony's. They felt it lowered the tone of Simon! This was a good sign – they were taking an interest in their fellow-men and so becoming viable members of a community. It was interesting to see that they had forgotten that at one stage they had been part of St Joe's. In this way they had raised their own standards without actually realising it.

Anton was Simon's only full-time trained social worker. He took his own lads who had come up from skid-row level and completed the pipe-line of houses, and trained them to run the new houses. For instance a young epileptic ex-convict was house leader at St Joe's, whilst an alcoholic ran St Antony's and a homosexual kept the peace at the farm; a highly reputed safe-breaker who had once 'cased a joint' and got away with £30,000, was in charge of Simonrise. This was another of Anton's controversial ideas: he believed in creating the situation by putting them in a house and leaving the 'group' to help itself as a group of individuals. Thus the drug addict was looking after the alcoholic, and the alcoholic looking after the epileptic.

So it was that when I landed on the scene, Simon had a self-contained community with four viable houses catering for up to twenty-five occupants in each. In each house there were the hard-core Simon workers who had previously passed through the mill and, instead of returning to society, lived on in Simon in voluntary poverty and shared the same cramped conditions and insecurity of the down-and-out, only receiving one pound pocket money a week and keep. Thus the caring and the cared for were living together on an equal footing.

Brian is one of the many success stories in Simon. At the age of two his mother put him in a children's home because she could not be bothered to look after him (his father had walked out some time ago). He was brought up in this children's home

50

until the age of fifteen, school-leaving time, when his mother suddenly turned up and demanded him back. She packed him off to work every day to bring in the rent money. Being so unsettled and resenting his mother's behaviour, he drifted from one job to another. For fun he made abusive anonymous telephone calls to people. He was picked up and put on probation for three years. A year later he was picked up again for carrying a stolen butcher's knife on him — further probation. Months later he pinched a bicycle and when the police charged him he tried to lie his way out. He was put temporarily in a mental home and then moved to a rehabilitation centre. On his release he began making more anonymous telephone calls, and made small amounts of money by breaking and entering private houses. He was caught and sent to Borstal. He took up his old ways on discharge and was returned to prison.

He drifted to Simon after his third prison discharge. By chance there was no one prepared to cook in Joe's at the time, and Brian was offered the position. Like the others he moved to Simonrise and thence to the farm, where he was given a taste of being deputy house leader. Anton brought him back to St Joe's to become Assistant Organising Secretary to the Companions. When Simon House, the office in the city, was opened, he was promoted to office manager and became Anton's right hand man. With specialised care and attention, Anton had managed to produce the best out of this boy. But the story does not end here, for Brian was not a Simon hard-core member because he was still drawing his £3 10s. a week National Assistance Board money. The community hard-core members were not registered with N.A.B., as they were classed as working in the community, which paid their stamps and pocket money. But the day did come when Brian, on his own volition, came to Anton and asked if he could become a hard-core Simon worker and like the other workers just draw one pound.

Of course, Anton had his failures too. John, an alcoholic, an ex-commissioned officer in the Army, and from a well-to-do

Irish family, was at one time in charge of one of our houses. For six months he ran the house brilliantly, keeping it in order and maintaining a happy atmosphere among the men, which is an incredibly difficult combination when one is dealing with mal-adjusted people with personality conflicts. Suddenly, for no apparent reason, he broke. With thirty-six pounds of the house's petty cash money, he walked out. We did nothing about it. We did not call in the police or go in search of him, despite knowing his hide-outs. We just hoped and prayed he would come back to us in one piece. We waited for news.

Two weeks later we received a telephone call from Bow Street magistrates' court; a probation officer there, knowing he was one of our lads, gave us the tip-off that he was coming up in front of the court that day on a charge of being drunk and disorderly. We dashed over and bailed him out. We took him back to St Joe's where we dried him out. We never mentioned the missing money. Why should we? It was over, and he had spent it, so what would have been the purpose? Obviously he was ashamed of himself and more so because we were prepared to have him back and not reject him for his failure. It was wonderful having him back, but it always was when we received a lost sheep back to the fold. In time John regained his self-respect and dignity, and his old confidence returned. Within three months he was back as house leader, running it smoothly and honestly. Often we were to lose money or things, but this was of little importance. We were dealing with failures, the throw-outs of other organisations, the 'impossible' cases and the 'no hope' cases — we never expected success.

To relieve the forlornness, failure and desperation afflicting someone unwanted for years, warmth and understanding and sympathy were as essential to a Simon Home as a roof, four walls and a bed. Usually the house leader could provide this, having moved through the same sufferings and experiences himself. Of course, Anton was always on call for advice or to deal with any house emergency that was beyond the control of the house leader.

Anton, himself, was peripatetic. He moved around the houses, staying sometimes just overnight, sometimes for a week. But he was in constant touch with the other houses. One day he was in Rochester when the house leader rang up to say one of the boys had gone berserk and, having smashed all the windows on the second floor, had now locked himself in the lavatory. Anton, the only man knowing the case history of the culprit, was the only one in the position to deal with him. Whether he could be talked down, threatened or blackmailed out, or whether sheer force was the only answer, only Anton knew. Of course the house leaders got to know the characters they were looking after fairly well after a time, and often learnt to deal with them when they became difficult without having to contact Anton. The latter liked them on the whole to deal with the situation themselves for it forced them to face their responsibility and use their initiative and thus sharpened the 'conception of self'.

Simon was providing a service of accommodation and security and a therapeutic environment for those who fell beneath the Statutes. Simon was solving the problem of the down-and-out. Many said that this was already being done by the Welfare State; this Simon did not deny, but the existing provision the Welfare State made for this type of person was not adequate and not the right kind of treatment. Simon, being a small and flexible organisation, was attempting to create a more 'tolerating' environment for society's deviants. When I came into Simon it was not old enough for me to draw any real conclusions about its methods, but at least I found it was trying to solve the problem of meeting the needs of the misfit in society, and these were the people I cared about.

I had an excellent job that I really enjoyed when I decided to go full-time into Simon and subsequently into social work. I was earning nearly £900 a year, plus a travelling allowance, and thus I was able to buy plenty of food and cigarettes for my dossers. I made the decision after my first meeting with Anton; in fact it was strange how we were thrown together to enable me to make it.

I was now visiting St Joe's regularly, but Anton was away in Naples seeing Father Borelli's work, so I had never met him. One evening I appeared at St Joe's straight from work, looking rather smart, only to find cameramen occupying the rooms. I grabbed Check. "What's going on here, are you making a film?" "Nah, Sal, blooming television people," he grumbled.

I settled down out of the way to watch as they interviewed Pat. At the end Pat turned to me and said, "Sal, be a sport and go and give Kim his pills — here's the key to the medicine chest. Don't let him con you into giving him more than two." As I went out I heard Tim, the producer, enquire about me. When I returned, Pat called me over. "How would you like to appear on television? Tim here thinks it would add a bit of glamour!" I was very chuffed at the idea.

And so it was that I appeared on television talking about the Simon Community, without having ever met its founder and director. Anton managed to return from Naples just in time to see the programme; simultaneously I landed in hospital with my old back injury. Anton saw the programme at his mother's home, and as soon as it was finished he was on the telephone to Pat, enquiring about this young dynamic girl who had spoken with such sincerity and enthusiasm. Directly he made preparations to return to London to meet me.

As he walked up the ward, out of visiting hours, I recognised him from his photographs. I was thrilled to meet this great man. He plonked himself on my bed and from the very beginning I felt as if I had known him all my life. He sat with me for over an hour, we swapped stories and experiences and giggled together like a couple of schoolchildren; one would not have thought there were twenty years between us, the way we gassed and shared the same wonderful vision. I think he was as impressed with me as I was with him. I thought the world of him in just that one meeting. He had great ideas for me, and when he had finished reading some of my articles, insisted that I became a sub-editor to his monthly paper. He left me with my imagination reeling with ideas and prospects for the two of us working together.

It was three months before I was in circulation again, and the first action I took was to give in my notice at my job; the second was to appear at Anton's office to tell him I had come to work for him full-time. That afternoon we discussed plans for expanding the Simon Community, we discussed the administrative affairs, the community problems, we discussed everything under the sun. It was extraordinary how similar our approach to the social problems of the country were; we were on the same wave-length throughout. That night I skipped all the way home, so happy that my dreams of really helping these people, not just by giving them coffee and fags every night, but by providing a roof and a home, had come true. Once back at home, I was brought back to reality with a bump as I plucked up courage to tell my parents I had thrown my job in, to work voluntarily with Anton amongst dossers and criminals. To give father his due, he took it fairly well, though I know he disapproved. I expected a rocket, but fortunately he was too caught up in his own work and problems to really digest the full meaning of it. Later we were to have many rows about it, eventually ending in disaster by my walking out and causing my parents a great amount of unhappiness. So I came into the Simon Community as a fully-fledged worker, as Anton's personal assistant and eventually his co-director.

For the first month I went everywhere with him; whether it was to do a food run to one of the houses, to do a 'skipper' on a bomb-site, to edit the monthly paper Simonstar, or to go and visit a man in prison. I learnt how to deal with people and to love them despite their failings and faults. As a team we worked well; he passed down his knowledge and in return I gave him young fresh ideas. If we could have remained detached it might have worked; yet the Simon Community could not have worked on an impersonal, uninvolved basis, for we relied on personal contact and identification. At the beginning we went from strength to

55

strength and Anton and I shared the privilege of shouldering the many burdens; as his confidence grew in me he gave me more work. Soon I was touring the country giving lectures, or if he was away on tour I would remain at the office and hold the fort that end, coping with house troubles, administrative problems and publicity. Because of Anton's complete faith in my ability to cope, he made it clear to all our hundred-odd inmates that in his absence I was in control. This could have proved terribly awkward as I was still a teenager, still wet behind the ears, but thankfully I won the confidence of the house leaders who trusted Anton's judgement implicitly. Whatever Anton said went without question, and when he was absent my leadership was never disputed.

I have never worked so hard in all my life as I did for Anton and his cause, and I loved every minute of it. Often we only managed a couple of hours sleep a night, other times we just worked on, not knowing whether it was night or day. We drove ourselves on and on, completely hypnotised by our vision of having a self-contained and self-supporting community. Our work was not in vain, for after two years of existence, Simon had six viable houses in operation and a fully-staffed office in the City. We still refused to have any trained social workers in, and each house and the office were all manned by the lads themselves. Anton had succeeded towards half his ambition, we were a self-contained community, but alas! we were hardly self-supporting. Neither of us being accountants, nor particularly efficient in administration, we had no idea how much money we were losing. Anton never wanted to be stuck behind an office desk and was the first to admit he was pretty useless there, but since there was no one else apart from me, he took his share of the burden. Nevertheless, it did not stop us from doing a night's 'skipper' on Waterloo Station. Having changed from our office clothes into our dosser's outfits we would make our way to the station, our pockets filled with cigarettes for the lads, and sit amongst them on the benches talking to them, finding out their problems and needs. There was one memorable occasion when both Anton and

I, with little Neil, were thrown off the station as suspicious characters! It was a great joke amongst the lads for months!

Our real work on the 'coal-face' took place in Simonlight. This was in Cable Street, Stepney, known as London's 'Little Harlem'. It was a shelter in a row of gutted houses and dingy cafés, linked to the bomb-sites of the East End. During the day, the crumbling street was like a graveyard. At night it came to life. Prostitutes appeared, and negroes, half stoned, waited in the doorways for their friends; and when the rain fell social derelicts, having brewed their lethal drinks, crawled from their bomb-sites to hug the shadow of the walls. We opened Simonlight to them. It was dirty but warm; no questions were asked, instead we handed them a bowl of soup or a cup of tea and a slice of bread. We slept them anywhere and everywhere; we welcomed them with their bottle of meths or 'jake'. To many it was the first real home they had ever known. At the weekends we slept up to a hundred; they sprawled on top of each other in their clothes and boots, lying on soiled mattresses. Their faces flushed and fiery red with meths, they lay there with their bottles at their sides. The sweet sickening stench would sting our nostrils at first until we grew immune to it. Often we would go out in the middle of the night and fetch those unable to walk without aid, and carry them back. All night, hungry and thirsty men knocked on the door for a slice of bread and soup. No one was refused. Other nights we would go out with soup to the bomb-sites and feed them, or down to the caves and into the drains by the docks. Anton was happiest here amongst the men on the bomb-sites. He was a good listener and they appreciated that. Often we found ourselves bringing back the same wreck as the night before, and we always went through the same procedure with them. First we would have to feed them, mostly on Complan, because they could not hold down solids after drinking 'jake' all day. Then we would wash them down and tend their burns and injuries before carrying them to the basement where we would put them in the 'pit' to sleep it off.

The first man I ever felt I had done something worthwhile for was C. For four months I had performed this ritual of going out and looking for him and every time had helped him back to Simonlight and fed him Complan with a teaspoon; every morning after soup he shuffled out in search of more drink, and I knew I would be looking for him again that night. When he left next morning, he never smiled or said thank you, and often I would feel despondent, and that I was wasting my time. Then one day I picked C. up and he was very ill; the meths was burning him up fast. I got him back to our shelter and for two days I sat with him as he died. I held his hand, hoping that at one minute or another he would become conscious enough to realise that he was not alone and that someone cared. I fed him regularly and bathed down his sweating body and I prayed. When he rallied two days later, I was still there and he knew it. His eyes were weak as the result of the meths so he could not see me, but his grip on my hand tightened. For the first time since I had known him he smiled and said, "Girl, yer the first person who's loved me." I wept many a tear when a few days later he died. Yet amongst these boys death was not a tragedy but a relief.

Anton and Simon were synonymous. Without Anton there would be no Simon and when, as the months went on, Anton became tired and ill, it was to affect everyone in the community. Having worn out his body and exhausted his mind, he looked for spiritual aid. He became moody and discouraged, and with my own exhaustion I was of little help to him. Despite the increasing pressures and lack of financial support, he bulldozed on; it was not in his nature to give up, he believed in being positive and not negative. Therefore when things looked bad he would push on in faith, 'relying on small miracles' as he called it! I admired his faith, but disapproved of its impracticability, which was to lead Simon into eventual curtailment.

Simon, still a babe-in-arms, had grown too rapidly and had tried to run before it could walk; we ran out of money and came into debt. At the same time Anton became ill and had to have a rest; it was fantastic that he had endured the two-and-a-half years at such a pace without a break. On his return he arrived at the office looking very grim, and I never saw him so ruthless as I did that evening when he announced that four of the houses and the office were to be closed, including the much needed Simonlight. The thought of throwing out all these men who needed us broke my heart into shreds as it must have done his. It was a brave action on Anton's part if it was necessary, but I could not condone it. It was as if we had given life to these boys and now were snatching it away from them. The time had come to leave Simon and Anton.

I walked miles in utter misery, not knowing where I was going, and not caring; my heart was torn apart and ached for the many lads who would have to suffer because of this curtailment. I felt as rejected as they would do when they found themselves back on the streets, homeless. It seemed so unfair, I felt, and unnecessary. I walked and walked and walked until I dropped; and when I woke up, I was in that mental hospital.

When I left the hospital a week later, with my haversack on my back, determined to begin again and learn from my mistakes, I had no idea where I was going to go or what I was going to do with myself. From Epsom I walked to London, trying to sort out my thoughts. Somehow I could not bring myself to go home, not as a failure. I had too much pride to face my highly successful father; it was against all my principles to go and sponge off friends and I did not want to answer questions anyway. Eventually I went to a friend of a friend, whom I hardly knew, and she very kindly put me up till I had sorted myself out.

I knew the best action I could take was to find a job and some digs. But my heart had always ruled my head and I knew my place was with the down-and-outs, so back I went to the bombsites in the East End. I was given the welcome of my life, they were so glad to see me. I did a 'skipper' that night with them. It was the first of many, and one I will never forget because it was the night that I decided to dig to the root of the problem of meths drinkers. They had all gone to sleep and I was keeping the wood fire going, sitting on an old milk crate. I was mentally reminiscing, going over the facts and figures of all the case histories I knew. Nearly every problem went back to childhood or to the war. It went back to when they were on alcohol or drugs; and then I remembered passing through Trafalgar Square a few days before and seeing debauched young, desperately young faces, who had the same haunted look in their eyes. I cogitated quietly.

"What yer thinkin'?" a voice asked. It was one of the lads.

"Hi! I didn't know you were awake. I was just thinking that meths drinkers are an advanced version of alcoholics and junkies."

"Yeah, that about sums us up."

"So really, to prevent the problem, one has to catch the kids?"

"Yeah, the teenagers are the ones, if yer lookin' for prevention rather than cure."

"Those kids in Trafalgar Square?"

"Yup, anywhere in the West End yer'll find 'em."

"I might go down there some time and take a sniff."

"Yer'll do well; all yer have to do is become a beatnik."

"Become a beatnik?"

"Yeah, yer could do it."

"That's an idea."

"Well, I'm goin' to kip."

"Good night."

"Good night, luv."

CHAPTER FIVE

"Will you come to bed with with me tonight?" a pouting faced youth with blond shoulder-length hair asked me. His eyes were lethargic and looked as if they had just been sprinkled with tomato ketchup. His speech was slow and indifferent.

"No thank you," I answered. He screwed up his nose in disgust and wandered aimlessly away. I leant against the bar and watched Mother Hubbard con her second pint of beer off another long-haired youth. Her own hair was like straw, and the colour of her nicotined fingers. Her weather-beaten face was stamped with age and exposure. From her pocket she drew a soiled rag and wiped the froth from her lips before straightening her crushed felt hat and hitching up the petticoat that hung equally soiled, below a tatty brown dress. Mother Hubbard had nothing but what she was standing up in or what she could con out of the junkies surrounding her. Drugs or drink opened up the highway to hopelessness for her, as for everyone in the vicinity. Despite the notices behind the bar that anyone seen peddling drugs would be reported to the police, both pills and hash were being bargained for. Listless, thin-armed youths shuffled around; similar seedy specimens of the human race shambled in, their faces puffed with drugged slumber. Beneath ragged beards and swollen lips, haunted ghost-like faces flinched in the agony of rage and shame. With shaking hands they tried to light their cigarettes. I held a steady match up for them and they looked at it in a kind of dull amazement. Night after night, day after day, week after week, month after month, they staggered groggily in having just had their evening fixes. This was their black cul-de-sac, a place where they accepted they would walk for evermore.

"Hi, man, what's your trouble? Not got a derry for tonight?" an underfed and overdosed frail youth asked me.

"Oh, I'm okay tonight: a friend's putting me up. What about you?"

"I'm all right, man; I've been kipping down in the sewers under Piccadilly these past months. Sharing it with five of my mates."

"Comfortable?"

"Can't complain, really. Surroundings a bit crude mind you."

I hoped he was going to expand on his unusual living quarters, but old Mother Hubbard interrupted; she pointed to her empty glass and I shrugged my shoulders sympathetically. "No dole?" she whispered expectantly. I shook my head. "Oh!" she sighed, "Yer ain't got no money either. Not even enough fer another drink?" I shook my head again. "Oh!" was all she replied. She moved across to a group of youths standing by the juke box. A few minutes later she had returned with some silver and bought her third pint of brown ale. I noted she left nearly half of it in the bottle, thus only half filling her own glass. I was wondering at this when she pushed the bottle towards me. "Ere, 'ave this," she said. This, I was to learn, was the most wonderful characteristic in all down-and-outs. Amongst their own kind, share and share alike. I was very touched, not to say conscience-ridden as I clutched the pound note in my pocket.

When I first rolled up in my denim jeans and polo-neck sweater beneath a matching denim shirt, with long straight hair hanging limply over my shoulders plus the traditional 'eye-concealing' fringe, I was no different from numerous other females there — or males! What with both sexes wearing elaborate rings and bracelets it only provided further complications in discriminating one from the other, though as often as not the men wore earrings in the form of crucifixes whilst the girls just had gold rings.

At first conversation was non-existent, and for over two weeks I spent every evening there without a word passing my lips, whilst conspicuous glances passed among them. Yet it was obvious that I was receiving the same treatment that every unknown face was given: a greeting of hostility in case I might be a social worker or some kind of religious preacher who might attempt to 'guide' or 'help' them. I discovered they were averse to any kind of patronising and equally reluctant to committing themselves to friendship. I found that as long as I was undemanding, they were prepared to give me a chance and talk to me. At the same time, having skirted various cafés and their dingy havens, I realised that fear of launching out into an unknown relationship or of rebuffal played a predominant part in their hostility. For months I patronised the addicts' hideouts and was given the cold shoulder; if I spoke without having been spoken to first, they turned their backs and walked away. It was made perfectly clear that I was not one of them. When I passed a group of youths talking they would fall silent until I was well out of ear-shot. If one of them was trying to con a drink out of someone, they never tried me. I was out on a limb and was made to feel so. This Coventry applied by all the youngsters was very hurtful, and often when I was out of sight I would burst into tears and pray for the guts and perseverance to return the following evening. It was not easy and I dreaded the slow, uncommunicative passing of time.

It was Doc Livingstone, universally so called by the beats because of his roamings, who broke the barrier. But he censored me for a week before deciding to accept me. He was a small, skinny man with a long face covered by a thin beard and side whiskers. He permanently wore an old pair of trousers under tails with a decorated ribbon suspended round his neck and a silver medallion attached to it, with 'Doc Livingstone' inscribed on it. He regarded himself as an 'old class' of beat:

"Twizzle and I are the old type you know," he said, "very few of them around now. Sure we're unconventional and have rejected society; sure we do strange things and look odd and are scruffy, but we're no part of these new pseudo-beats. We have misbehaved in a public place and were always polite. We have to suffer the reputation of these new creeps. You know I came in this coffee bar last week and the manageress threw us out because she thought we were some of those that had messed her around a few days previous — just because we look like them, we're taken for them. Sure we've stolen food and things in our time, but not like these new beats who take what they can from anyone, rich or poor. When Twizzle and I were in Manchester we used to walk out to the outskirts where the wealthy live and pinch from them. After all, these businessmen must have trodden on other people's toes to get their position and money, so we just kind of tread on theirs by swiping the occasional bottle of milk. But we never took anything from those who couldn't afford to give. And everything we had we shared. Twizzle would give his last cig. to me, and when I met him in Nottingham he gave me his last two-shilling bit because I hadn't eaten for three days. And I did the same when he came to London, but these new beats have no code of living. The best conners survive, the others fall by the wayside. You know, a sixteen-year-old kid came to London last week with twenty quid in her pocket. I had a tanner and bought her some food 'cause I thought she'd need her money and I suggested she put it into the post office. She was going to do it the next morning, but when I found her later that night those bastards had conned every penny from her and pinched her hand-grip. No wonder crime is on the increase when innocent new-comers are toughened in this way. Twizzle and I are the old type of beat, unconventional and scruffy, but sincere and reliable." In time I found this to be almost true.

Having been initially accepted and identified as one of them, I decided to press my point further and so I hit the road. With my pack on my back and a couple of blankets I trudged down to Trafalgar Square where some would be either in the toilets giving themselves fixes or in the National Gallery where as long as they were quiet they could sit undisturbed, though the attendants soon made a rule that no one could sit for more than twenty minutes at a time, so when the lads were moved from one room they just went and parked themselves in another. Some, if they had conned enough money, would spend the day in coffee bars or news

A ramp character

Late Night Special at the Orange Street Mission

Morning on the ramp

Afternoon in Trafalgar Square

On the ramp

Night on the ramp

theatres where they were able to sleep. Charing Cross Station buffet was a popular meeting point, and very rarely did I put my head round the doors and not see a couple of beats I knew. On Sunday nights all the beats in the district flocked to a Mission behind Trafalgar Square which opened for them and dished out free food and tea. Some of the kids who turned up could not have been more than fifteen, probably having just run away from home and come down south to seek the bright lights of London. The majority of those over eighteen were on the run from Borstal or the police, or had just come out of prison. Each and every person had a reason for hiding up in this underworld of iniquity. Yet little was kept secret between themselves, in fact, many of their devious activities were a source of boasting.`

I remember Pinkie once saying to me: "We're getting engaged after Christmas."

"Oh, well done, good for you. Who's the lucky chap?"

"Riki, she lives up over Holloway way." I glanced at her dead-serious face and wondered if I was being pulled as a sucker.

"Don't look so confused," she continued. "Didn't you know I'm a lesbian and so's Riki? We'll be married in the spring. Would you like to come?"

"Surely! But looking on the practical side, who would marry you both?"

"Oh, Vicar will, he marries all the beats." I was taken aback.

"Do you mean he would marry two girls? I don't believe it."

"Of course he will; he has done in the past."

"What parish does he come from?" I innocently asked. A great hoot of laughter from Pinkie told me I had said something stupid.

"Oh, don't be so naive, love, he's only called Vicar because he does marry us; he's just one of the beats like you and me." I fell into dumbfounded silence. There seemed little point in saying it wasn't valid, because matrimony to beats was like a dog with his bone — having enjoyed it, it was buried, and occasionally dug up thereafter.

65

Once on the road, I was taught how to con money from people. The usual story was that I had found a kid crying and on asking him the trouble, he had told me he had spent all his money and hadn't enough to get home, so I had generously given him half-a-crown only to discover later it was my last one! Could they possibly help me out? When travelling on the buses, we would search our pockets only to find we had left the money behind! We would give false names and addresses. On tubes we never bought tickets and at our destination swore that we had embarked one station before so only ended up paying fourpence. Pickpocketing was another trade I was taught. The 'dip', or 'buzzer' as he is known, is a craftsman in his own right, who often works with a gang. The 'stalls' jostle their victim or by mistake barge into him and thus knock his hat off; the victim bends down to pick it up leaving his hip pockets exposed to sensitive fingers. Another favourite is for a dip to board a bus, get half-way up and then apparently realise that he is on the wrong route. As he struggles down through the passengers following him, he is ideally placed for fingering through inside pockets. Cinemas, race meetings and football matches are good hunting grounds. Christmas shopping crowds prove lucrative also! And armloads of parcels means good opportunities for shoving and hustling.

Peddling drugs discreetly is often carried out in a crowd. Often the peddlers work in pairs, like a young twenty-year-old boy I knew, who, with his girl-friend, hung around Waterloo Station. He was the peddler and the addicts approached him, but as they left the station they would bump into his girl-friend at the other end. She was the carrier, so that should he be picked up he would be as clean as a whistle.

One evening a youth took me back to his 'pad' which he was sharing with two other boys and three girls. We entered a room which was bare save for three mattresses, a gas ring and four syringes. They all sat there holding each other's hands and as the evening progressed and the fixes began to wear off, they fell upon each other kissing and fondling the other's body; the sexual orgy that followed sickened me. Some drugs stimulate the sexual organs, and then it can be extra dangerous if not fatal, as on one occasion when I paid an unscheduled call upon Trix.

Trix had been a heroin addict for five years and was registered as such. She lived in a room in Hackney, though she spent most of her time in the West End. I climbed the concrete staircase and walked into her room without knocking, thinking she would be out with Bill. In the dim light I caught sight of Trix sitting on an upturned packing case. The room had an air of musty, stodgy decorum. Curtains of machine lace hung, dust-coloured, over a broken window. There was a foul odour, a vague mixture of alcohol and stale flesh. As I entered, a young negress in her underclothes, sullenly smoking a cigarette, disappeared into the opposite room. Trix, hunched on the packing case, had not heard my entrance for she was still busy with her hands. I trod warily across the rough planks, crudely laid. From the nails in the crumbling walls hung bits of desiccated photographs. I heard a car outside change gear as it passed. Suddenly Trix looked up, and for an instant we stared eye to eye. Under the faded electric light bulb something glowed in her hands. She sat motionless, her mouth a little open. Blood was trickling from her wrist. Between her long fingers was a piece of glass. I sprang forward, plucking at her. She surged to her feet, flinging her arms backwards for balance. Head down, my body arched, I went for her. She reeled backwards, thrusting out her hand with the piece of glass. I caught her bloody wrist. She struggled and flicked the glass towards my eyes. I ducked, but not far enough. I thudded against the wall as she hit me on the cheek. It made a dry, flat sound. She stumbled backwards, wailing, and jerkingly staggered out of the room towards the stairs. Blood from the gashes in my forehead crossed my field of vision as I sat rigid opposite the open door. With the palm of my hand I wiped the blood aside for a second before the stream continued. I spun downstairs after her. As I whirled out of the hallway, I saw her leaping at me with a brick. I lurched twisting in the air, grabbing the glass from her.

67

I felt it strike me solidly on the temple. I rocked sideways trying to regain my balance but my head was spinning and the floor was rising. I saw her legs running into space before I hit the floor unconscious.

After a brief spell in hospital I went back to see Trix. She was giving herself a fix in the arm where the telling gash was healing. The veins down her arm were burnt out and now lay mauve and rotted. She greeted me cordially, and only when the evening was nearly over did she mention our fight. "Sorry abaht that do the other night. I'd 'a' been all right if Bill'd been here."

"Well, I have no desire to go through that a second time, so don't let's have any repercussions, okay?"

"Okay, man! Don't go on. It were just a feelin' I had at the time."

I realised the reason for that feeling was the absence of Bill, and quite suddenly it came to me that the simple failure of people to make contact with one another was often the cause of such human problems. What a paradox! We can bounce messages off the moon and send space probes to Mars, yet we are finding it more difficult as each day passes to communicate with the minds and hearts of those we love. Love is the climate in which all living things flourish. This language of love is designed to crack the shell of isolation by effective channels of communication. It is a universal language that is sadly neglected. Love is like gratitude, not much good unless you can show it. No doubt these addicts had relations who nominally loved them, but for these lone wolves it must be a tender understanding and a personal care, not just verbal concern. They needed compassion, not condemnation.

I was able to give compassion, not pity, and because of this giving it became a reciprocal action. They loved me in return. They began to love me so much that they asked me to fix them. At first I refused because I did not want to be part of it, I did not want to be involved. But I was involved and I was part of it. I was identified as one of them. So gritting my teeth so that I

68

should not be sick, I began to give fixes. I had been fixing Stuart, a registered addict, for some weeks with ten grains, when it occurred to me that I might try cutting it down without him knowing. Over a period of three months I had cut him down to five grains without him noticing. I hoped there would be a time that I would be just injecting water into him. But as I learnt to deal with these drug addicts and look after them, I arrived at the opinion that a true addict is unable to come off without hospital-isation. Many a time a youth has wept his heart out on my shoulder because he is unable to give it up without a drug to take its place. Yet the majority who are fortunate enough to receive hospitalisation return straight to drugs on their release. There-fore there are two actions necessary to help the addicts and control addiction. The addicted must receive medical aid, and the source must be stopped. Until the peddlers are exterminated, drug addic-tion will be on the up-and-up not only amongst the young, but amongst all ages and classes. I don't blame the young for their idiocy, I blame the hard, calculating peddler who provides the ammunition for them to destroy themselves with — and they do.

CHAPTER SIX

DARKNESS had fallen and the steady rain had changed to a mere drizzle. Black shadows frowned over the deserted streets as tattered clouds were driven in scattered formation across the sky. My clothes hung coldly to my back. I walked faster across the slumbering City. The chill wind was freezing my face and numbing my fingers. I passed an old nightwatchman, sitting solemnly in his canvas box, staring at the glow of the brazier and the line of red lights that surrounded the road works. I called a cheerful greeting as I passed, which he acknowledged with a grunt. I crossed the vast empty bus terminus, my steps amplified in the eerie silence. Deserted buses stood in neat rows, their windows glazed and reflective. I continued down drenched streets where rivulets scuttled down steps and whirlpools gushed round gratings. Past grey uniform buildings and a graveyard where the rain pattered mournfully upon the tombs — upon the just and unjust alike. Everywhere was filled with the raw night air, damp, dark and cold.

I came to a junction and turned left, leaving the Whitechapel Road behind me. I wondered if they would be here. The wet breeze blew my hair over my face in a kind of mockery. I was nearly there. Just past these abandoned derelict buildings, carcasses of 'home', and beyond that creeping wall. The stillness spread like a blanket into the distance. I approached the ramp as softly as I could, and advanced from behind the sodden wall. There was a dull red glow of a wood fire. Beside it cowered figures with hands outstretched to meet the grateful warmth. With limbs huddled together and heads bowed, they bent over the fitful light. In the smouldering embers these stricken figures sat the nights out, amongst the ashes and dust and debris of the bomb-site. The figures neither spoke nor turned to look at me. Quietly I moved across to one of the stooping figures who clasped a bottle; gently I unlocked his fingers and the glass smashed to pieces as it hit the ground, echoing across the night. The stooping figure rocked forward and I grabbed him as he was about to fall into the embers. His clothes were soaked. Little by little, with an intense effort, he lifted his head and looked at me. His eyes were red and glazed.

"Hello, Benghazi! It's all right, it's only me, Sally. How are you?"

He stared expressionlessly at my face. His lips began to move, but no sound came from them in reply. I dug into my pockets and produced a packet of squashed cigarettes. I lit one for him and placed it between his swollen lips. I looked around to see how many of the regulars were here tonight. I counted eleven heads in all, that was including the three prostrate bodies lying over by the wall. I recognised seven faces by name. Some had lived on this bomb-site for seventeen years, some were newcomers. Others who had once lived here had passed away, their guts and stomach burnt dry by methylated spirits or eau-de-cologne. Some just died of exposure; a few so drunk, fell into the fire and were burnt to death, and the occasional one was killed by some angry drunkard. They lived animals' lives with a law of their own. How I longed for a lighted room, bright fires and cheerful faces, the music of happy voices, words of love and welcome and warm hearts. It was a night to be home, asleep by a warm hearth.

I glanced across at the heaped bodies of Canada, Hank, Steela Horse, Jock and Paddy. Their faces, concealed behind knotted stubble and stale old grime, were muffled under flea-ridden overcoats. Benghazi suddenly rocked forward again and I put out a supportive hand. He seemed to pull himself to consciousness as he felt my grip and smiled at me in recognition, revealing a few discoloured fangs scattered around in his mouth. He gave me his hand in friendship. It was rough and very dirty, his gritty fingernails were jagged and yellow. He was unwholesome and animal-like. Each night I met him he seemed to grow weaker and more feeble and care-worn. The mask of death that

71

I had seen so many times before, was about to claim another victim.

Canada turned over and stretched out for a bottle beside him. "It's empty, Canada. You're wasting your time," I told him. He fixed his eyes on me, eyes that were drunk and strained. With trembling hands he picked the bottle up and put it to his lips, then threw it down with disgust. A look of persecution crossed his face. I went over to him and sat myself down on an old petrol tin that someone had once drunk out of. Benghazi watched my movements like a devoted dog.

"How are things?" I asked gently.

Canada scratched his wiry hair infested with lice, and fixed his eyes once again on me. "Ow, Sal. Wheeeel. Vrrry wheeeel." I gave him a cigarette.

Jock, having heard voices, came to. " 'Ello, Sal," he greeted me and put his hand out for a cigarette. I threw him one.

"You dry tonight, Jock?" I tried to hide my surprise.

"Ay. Ain't got much option. Came out of nick this morning."

"I thought I hadn't seen you around lately. Actually I heard you'd joined another school of meths drinkers down by the Elephant and Castle."

"Ay, and we all got picked up by the cops. They gave me a month."

"And what's the score now, or shouldn't I ask?"

"Ahrr! Dunno. Try and stay dry, I suppose. Git m'self a job tomorrow. Try Covent Garden in the morning — or Spitalfields."

"Well, good luck." I knew that if I probed further he would clam up. "A few new faces round here tonight. Who's that bloke?"

"That's Gypsy Bill. Used to be a cell mate of mine. We've done time together, like. 'E's a good enough bloke, a bit keen on using 'is fists, mind. 'E's a good friend," he repeated thoughtfully.

Canada turned to Jock and waved a trembling hand. "Passsh de botttttle," he rolled out in his drunken, stinking stupor.

"No, laddie, this one's empty. Try Benghazi. 'E 'ad some."

72

I butted in. "No, he hasn't. I had a look earlier."

Jock stumbled to his feet and bent over Steela Horse. He kicked him awake. "Horse! Horse! Canada wants some jake." There was a muffled grunt of agreement; Jock took the bottle that he was clasping tightly to his chest, and handed it to the tottering Canada. "Sit down b'fore yer fall down," Jock cried and pushed him over. He crashed on top of Benghazi and the two of them rolled in the mud, grappling for the bottle.

Meanwhile Paddy was whimpering by the almost dead fire. I was about to get up and see what the matter was when Jock put a restraining hand on me. "Ye canna do anythin' for 'im, Sal. 'E won't last the night out, I don't think." I looked at the writhing body, the haggard face looking mauve in the spark-light of the embers. The eyes were sunken and black and the open mouth gasping for breath. Bile dribbled down his chin. I had seen it all before. I closed my eyes and prayed. I forced myself to my feet and went and knelt beside him. I took his ice-cold languid hand and rubbed it. For a second he opened his puffed eyes and gave me a glassy stare. I smiled caringly at him. I knew there was nothing I could do, I knew that he was beyond medical help. I smiled again and grasped his hand. As long as he knows he's not alone, that someone cares, that was all I wanted to transmit to him in my smile. It was so little and cost me nothing, and yet could mean the whole world to a dying man.

A few hours later, everyone had drifted back to sleep. The fire and Paddy had died together. I looked around at his mates; many of them would be joining him soon, and they did not care. They had nothing left in life to live for. They had hit 'rock bottom'. For them, time was timeless; only the bottle counted. Methylated spirits was their passport to oblivion — finally their passport to death. How can they sleep, I thought, Paddy was one of them. But they were used to it. I remember Canada telling me one day when he was dry that during the cold winter of 1963 the police were picking up six dead men a week off the bomb-sites. I felt the chill run down my spine. I felt so small, so inadequate.

73

I blamed myself, I blamed society, I blamed the world. Whose fault was it that these men were forsaken? Fellow-mankind. Let moralists and philosophers say what they like, but it is questionable that a guilty person could have suffered such misery as I did that night, being innocent. I wept tears, not for Paddy, for he had been released from his torture, not for his pathetic animal-like buddies, but for me and my family and friends; that we regarded ourselves as Christians and yet allowed a man, a young man at that, to pass away unnoticed. Here today and gone tomorrow, who cared? No one. I sat, alone, penitent. The rain seemed to pour down more hopelessly and more heavily than ever. The puddles became deeper and dirtier. The men, in their mighty ocean of solitude, slept on. Time itself seemed to have grown dull and old, as if day was unable to displace the melancholy night. I began to shiver with cold, it was so wet.

Stiffly I rose from beside Paddy and went in search of wood to re-start the fire. I combed the surrounding bomb-sites, but it was all too damp. When I returned to the ramp, Jock was awake.

"So Paddy never made it," he sighed.

"No, you were right. What should we do with him?"

"In the morning, ye'd better go to the police station and report it. They'll deal with the body, they're used to it."

"Will he get a burial?" I asked.

"Only if someone'll cough up to pay." He got to his feet. "God! I'm bloody well soaked through. I'm not stayin' here any longer." He stepped over Canada and Benghazi, smashing the bottle as he went.

"Where are you going?" I called after him.

"Plenty of derries round here with warm fires, d'ye no' ken them?"

"I know the one in Fairfax Street, where Big Michael hangs out."

"Och! there's a nearer one than that. Come along and see for yourself." I glanced at my human derelicts lying in the mud;

when dawn came they would be out scavenging the gutters for their breakfast.

"Comin', lassie?" Jock called back at me. I left them to the approaching dawn and followed him.

Back on the road, lorries with their loads began to rattle past, and the first commuters slunk out of their houses. Exhausted with discomfort and sick from exposure, the crude spirit drinkers and the ordinary dossers lay amongst the thrown-out debris, glaring at the intruders, cursing at their life and their world. Beyond the sunrise, people were truly living; living and not existing from day to day, from hour to hour with questions of how to fill their bellies, how to keep warm, how to live. Whilst they squatted amongst rubble, empty bottles and trodden cigarette butts, watching the world dispassionately, trying to divert their minds from the crucifixion of living.

"What's the matter? Has Paddy's death upset ye?" Jock was saying.

"No, Jock, just thinking. A mistake, I know, so don't say it."

"Noo, I wouldna'. D' ye know Bignall Street at all?"

"It's off Cannon Street isn't it?"

"Ay. There's a wee derry there that'll give us shelter for the night, what little there is left." We came to another bomb-site and clambered over a wall and made our way through the rubble towards a row of houses on the far side. We found a gap in the fence that surrounded the buildings and climbed over falling stone. One of the houses was roofless, and one side of the wall had collapsed. We came to the third dilapidated ruin and entered it through a gap in the wall where once had stood a door. "Careful!" Jock warned, pointing to a missing step in the cob-ridden staircase. My eyes were growing accustomed to the dark, but it was the smell that made me want to turn tail; it was sweet and sickly and desperately strong. I stopped on the decaying landing and leaned against the wall. The smell was everywhere.

"What's the matter?" Jock called as he ascended the second staircase. "No' feelin' too good?"

75

"I'm all right, Jock. It's just that ghastly smell."

"Och! that's meths. The lads are up here. Come and meet them."

I climbed after him, passing a large hole in the wall where the wind and rain were driving in. Suddenly I heard the quiet murmur of voices. As I entered the room a bright fire leapt cheerfully in the hearth, making friendly shadows on the wall. In the corner was an iron bed on which lay three cramped figures. Before the fire sat another three on the dusty floor, their twisted faces grinning in welcome. The rest of the room was empty; it was dark and murky, full of dust and rust and rotting with wood-worm. Someone handed me a bottle, the stink became unbearable. I thought I was going to be sick. Speechless, grinding my teeth for self-control, I handed it back to greedy hands. "Sit down, Sal. Ye'll feel better if ye get some kip," Jock urged. I joined him on the floor by the fire. " 'Ere, have my donkey jacket for yer head." He put it down as a pillow for me to use. I was grateful for it. I lay listening to the drunken wanderings of the men as they passed the bottle round. It was difficult to distinguish what they were actually saying, but as far as I could gather they were talking about the war. This, I was to discover, was the predominant topic of conversation amongst the meths drinkers because that was the last time they felt they had been real men.

I must have dozed off, for when I came round the three figures that had been on the bed had gone. "Kip well?" Jock asked as he put more wood on the fire.

"Yes, thanks, I must have been tired. Where is everyone?"

"Och! they've gone off to work."

"But would they get a job in that condition? Surely not?"

"They weren't on meths, you know. They were just dossers without any place to go and no money for a bed and breakfast."

"If they work, they must have some money, come off it!" I replied.

"Ay, they get a wage, but they spend it in the pub during the evening."

"What, the whole lot? Anyway, what kind of work do they do?"

"Casual labour; paid by the hour so it don't make no difference to the employer if they don't turn up ever again. Mostly they try the caterin' firms, or the younger ones try the building sites or Covent Garden."

"And how do these blokes get their money?" I pointed to the three unconscious bodies on the floor.

"Pinch it, or con it. Or a few of them stagger into a hardware store and demand a bottle of meths. The chap's only too pleased to give it to them — it's cheaper than having your shop smashed to pieces, and they can do a lot of damage before the police arrive."

"Personally I'm surprised the police don't arrest them from the ramp."

"Och, they don't want us infesting up their cells, spewing everywhere. Ye see, we're more trouble than we're worth, really. As long as they know where to put their finger on us any time they want, they're happy to let us go."

"But couldn't you get help from the Welfare State like other people?"

"Don't be daft, lassie."

I tried to visualise hundreds of Benghazis pouring into the local authority centre, bringing with them the stench of dirt and surrounded by the peculiar and nauseating aura created by poverty, crime and self-destructive compulsions. Would I, too, see them as inferior and representing merely a job of work of the least inspiring and most exacting kind? Would I shout at them and drive them into a pattern which would make that job as easy as possible? Would I despise them and resent them as a blot on my life and society, and a waste of time, effort and money? Would I make them the unhappy products of the cruelty, ignorance and regimentation of these so-called places of refuge?

"You see, Sal," one of them told me once, "we're unclean. No one wants to touch us. Sure, we get given advice and occasionally help in order to try and break the vicious circle we're in, but you should see the non-existent conviction with which they offer it! It's like putting a penny in the slot machine and we're expected to play the tune. We try, but Rome wasn't built in a day. You can't take us out of one environment and dump us in another, expecting us to fall in with your standards and ways of living. It all takes time and patience, and no one in this day and age has either."

"Well lassie, I'll be off to find myself a job. What are ye goin' to do? Ye can stay here if ye want, they'll no worry ye." Jock rose and dusted down his ragged trousers.

"No, I'll be pushing on, thanks, Jock."

"Will ye be back tonight on the ramp?"

"Maybe. I'm not quite sure what the day holds for me yet. Anyway, I'll be around, so I'll see you. Good luck with the job."

We shook hands and went our different ways. The rain had stopped, and the tradesmen's doors were open. Smoke rose from the chimneys, and traffic rumbled by. I walked towards the City in solitary meditation. What was the answer to this problem? Obviously the authorities did not have the right approach, and only created resentment. The answer must lie in making the men believe in themselves. Without faith in themselves, and without having somebody who truly cares whether they live or die, how can they be expected to rise above this depression? Was it not possible for one to say, I love this man, and by doing so, rekindle in him a sense of his own dignity and a love in himself, that he might regain his self-respect? Love, respect, call it what you will, was the vital spark which was missing from these broken personalities who sought shelter. There were thousands of such men now; tomorrow there might be millions. They did not advertise their presence, but they were there, waiting to be released from the torture of living. They were people who had failed to find a proper place in our society and who rejected all our standards, perhaps through misfortune or perhaps through choice. The majority, though, were afflicted with some difficulty or inade-

78

quacy of personality which contributed to this destitution. I felt sure the only answer was in love.

I turned into the police station to report the death of an unknown citizen of the name of Paddy. *Love* — take away love and there was no more life.

CHAPTER SEVEN

I BEGAN to devote my days to mixing with the beats and my nights to the dossers and crude spirit drinkers. I bummed around with my grotty long-haired friends around Trafalgar Square. If we had conned enough money we would sit in Lyons with a cup of tea which we would pass between us drawing out the time as much as possible until we were thrown out. On to the National Gallery, where we would sit and doze till we were asked to leave, and so to the Square post office where we would lounge around on the ground, having scanned it for dog-ends. Eventually the police would be called in and once again we would be moved on, so across to Charing Cross Station where we would con a few shillings and cigarettes and return to another Lyons. This was the cycle of the day till the pubs opened.

I became bored and frustrated. I had successfully identified myself with the beats, but had now come to a dead end. I was being of no practical help apart from assisting with the occasional fix. In contrast, my nights were too short for all the work I had to fit in. With money I conned during the day I bought loaves of bread and cheese and cigarettes to take round to my dossers in the evenings. When the pubs closed at eleven and the beats dispersed to derries or night clubs or just to walk the road till morning, I collected from Charing Cross left luggage department the food I had bought previously. I moved into the waiting room where I began to butter the bread and fill the sandwiches. Onlookers watched me with disbelief. This task completed, I went down to a tea stall on the Embankment where long-distance lorry-drivers stopped during the night to freshen up. Here I bought eight cups of tea and instead of drinking them poured them into a thermos flask which I carried (in time I got to know the Italian gentleman behind the stall, and filling my flask with free tea became his contribution towards my work). About midnight I commenced my rounds: Waterloo Station, Elephant and Castle, back along the Embankment where dossers slept on the benches, down the alleyways of Fleet Street where they would huddle in doorways, a brisk walk across the deserted City to Stepney. I had usually finished by five, and after a quick kip I was back in Trafalgar Square at eleven, conning unsuspecting sightseers.

Initially I had offered the beats, like the dossers, an uncritical, undemanding and tolerant attitude and a readiness to understand their problems. With the dossers I had proved it was possible to progress to more demanding relationships and towards more positive goals. In contrast, when dealing with the beats there was a hard core of resistance which I seemed unable to break through. Certainly I had fulfilled a role as one of them, but despite all the tolerance and understanding I gave, I was unable to penetrate their tough shells. I was an intellectual beat in their eyes, and was accordingly treated with greater respect and eventually labelled 'Sally the Christian'. Anyone else tagged as this was automatically despised and spat upon, yet they accepted me and admired me for it. But obviously not enough to follow my example. Yet this was not entirely true, as time proved.

I met Twizzle and Brazil Nut in the post office. French Jean and American Charlie were sitting with them; from their heavy eyelids and dilated pupils I gathered they had just had a fix.

"Seen Doc Livingstone? He's missing. No one's seen him since he took sixteen people out to Stanmore to a party," Twizzle said.

"He's probably stoned, man; he'll be okay," I replied.

"No, man; there weren't no party there. He did it as a joke."

"Well, they've probably killed him then. I would have, if he'd done that to me," I assured him, but Twizzle still looked unhappy.

"I think he's been nicked. He would have been back by now, otherwise."

The low, drugged drawl of American Charlie interrupted. "I'm goin' to the Duke. Comin'?"

We went. En route we conned some money, though Brazil

Nut had plenty – her crazy mixed-up father sends her fifty pounds every month to pay for her to have English lessons. The beats spent it for her on alcohol and drugs. Halfway through the evening Twizzle, French Jean and myself ran out of cash, so we left the pub and wandered into Soho. "We'll get more if we split up. Sally, you cover Greek Street, and Frenchie, you do Wardour Street, I'll do Dean Street. Meet you back here in fifteen minutes," Twizzle instructed. "Try the spades and the Chinese blokes, Sally; they're easier meat and usually quite generous. See yer." The tall, lank figure of Twizzle loped off in the direction of Dean Street, whilst French Jean, with his shoulders hunched, limped grotesquely, for effect, towards Wardour Street.

On the corner of Greek Street, I pretended to look at the cinema advertisements; from experience I knew that I would be approached without having to attract anyone's attention. A young Indian brushed past me, his hand knocking me slightly. I felt repulsed, but forcing a friendly smile I turned to him.

"You come with me," he said, highly delighted with his catch.

"Very kind of you, but I must make a telephone call. You couldn't lend me a tanner?" I enquired. He began to delve into his pocket.

"You come with me after telephone call?" He produced the sixpence.

"Well, no, I won't if you don't mind." I put my hand out for the money.

"You no come with me, you get no sixpence." Angrily he stumped away. Quietly to myself I let out a string of abuse.

Two other similar conditioned offers were made before a West Indian spade tossed me a shilling on request. I extracted four cigarettes from a sympathetic Malayan boy and a Bounty Bar to eat from a sailor. Six football supporters wrapped in red and white scarves and bobble hats and corresponding rosettes gaily sauntered towards me. "You couldn't help me out with a shilling for some breakfast tomorrow morning?" I asked.

One of them turned to his friends. "Now lads, here we have

a damsel in distress. Unless you give her some money she'll have to go without her breakfast tomorrow."

A red-faced man, matching the red stripes of his scarf replied, "Well, lassie, what can you do for it? Sing, dance perhaps?"

I felt myself turn the same colour. "I've got no voice."

"Gentlemen, I beg you for mercy," one of them cried out. "Into your pockets and see what fruits you have." Everyone emptied their pockets.

The first speaker took over. "Two pennies each towards this most excellent cause." He took off his bobble cap and everyone threw their money in.

"Thank you gentlemen, I will remember you as I scoff bacon and eggs tomorrow."

"A delightful idea, fair maiden." The first speaker bent low and kissed my hand. "Adios amigos." With merry laughter they continued down the road.

Fifteen minutes later the three of us met and were pooling our gains. Between us we had conned fourteen shillings and five-pence. "I'm hungry; what about some fish and chips?" French Jean suggested. As we were ambling round Soho, our hands sticky with vinegar and grease, we were discussing where we were going to sleep the night.

"I slept in the Alphabet last night," Twizzle was saying.

"Bit noisy wasn't it?" I remarked, remembering that when I was there the juke box never stopped till closing time at seven in the morning.

"Yeah, yer get used to it. I slept right through last night, never heard a sound."

"Last time I tried it, people kept walking over me," French Jean said.

"Yeah, well whadderyer expect when yer sleep on the dance floor? I go and park myself on the platform where the juke box is; yer less likely to be kicked there. Anyway that's where I'm kipping tonight; at least it's warm," Twizzle confirmed.

"I'll come," Frenchie replied. "You'll have to give me five bob to get in, otherwise I'll have to con it. Where're you kipping, Sally?"

"I'm not, at least not yet. I've got some work to do." They stood still and gazed at me in horror.

"Work? What do yer do a crazy thing like that for?"

"Not what you mean by work, I don't get paid for it. It's voluntary. I go round the dossers and meths drinkers and give them food."

"You must be mad," they cried simultaneously. I made no comment.

"Yer scatty, man." Conversation waned and then, "Whadder-yer do it for?"

"Because they're people like us with no money, no food and no home, and many of them are too old, too ill or are too disabled to help themselves. You're all right, Twizzle, you're compara-tively young and agile and able to look after yourself. The public are fairly tolerant towards your conning them and the aimless way you all bum around. They make excuses for your youth and immaturity that they won't make for the old dirty dossers."

"But yer said yerself, they're so dirty an' horrible."

"Give yourself twenty years, Twizzle, and you'll be one of them." He lapsed into silence. He had nothing to say for himself. We walked on.

Frenchie broke the silence: "Whereabouts do you meet them?"

"They're all over London, but time being limited I usually concentrate on the East End and Waterloo Station area."

"Whadderyer actually do for 'em?" Twizzle asked, forgetting his sulks.

"Well, I take them food and cigarettes and hot tea. Occasion-ally I get given the odd piece of clothing for them which I take along. But more important to them is a friendly smile which does not cost me a penny." I withheld myself from adding that it would not cost them anything either.

"I dunno why yer want to bother yerself with 'em," Twizzle commented.

84

"Perhaps because no one else is prepared to; I've always been a supporter of lost causes," I mused. "I'm a sentimentalist."

"Yer just daft. Yer wastin' yer money. They don't appreciate it."

"I'd rather spend it on that, which will keep them alive, than drugs and alcohol which will only lead to your own destruction." My two comrades had nothing to reply. "Well, I'm going to see if I can borrow a car for tonight. I'll see you tomorrow in the Square."

"Borrow? You mean take one. I'll do it for you if yer want."

"No, I do actually mean borrow. I have a friend who occasionally lends me one. It saves a lot of time and a lot of walking."

"Okay, man, see yer tomorrow." I was turning to leave them both when Twizzle called after me, "Hey, want any 'elp tonight?"

I could not believe my ears. Trying not to sound too eager I replied, "Twizzle, I could always do with help, however little."

He looked at Frenchie. Their eyes met. "Come on, Frenchie, wot abaht it?"

"No, what's the point of all three of us being mad," he replied.

"Just this once, Frenchie," Twizzle pleaded. I kept quiet, not wanting to appear to influence them either way. "Whassa matter? Yellow?"

"You accusing me of being yellow? Get lost, man."

"Prove it then. Come with us." Twizzle set the challenge.

"Okay, man, I'll come for the lark and show you I'm not yellow." It was settled. I promised to meet them at the Duke at ten-thirty after I had fetched the car.

As I drove to pick them up, I was so inflated with my own egoism that should I have had a halo I would not have fitted into the car. I felt I had broken through to them at last. I checked myself as my thoughts ran away with me on what future help they could give me. "Slow down, Sally, or you'll be pressurising them too much and all your good will be undone," I murmured

85

to myself. I made a promise that after tonight I would never mention to them the possibility of helping me further. It must be their idea and come from within themselves. As I turned the corner to the Duke, I was disillusioned. There was no sign of Twizzle or Frenchie. I waited till the pub emptied at closing time, optimistically, but in vain. At midnight, with still no sign of them, I left for Waterloo Station.

"Hi, Sally, over 'ere," Twizzle called across to me next morning in the Square. " 'Ere, 'ave a drag?" He handed me a soggy cigarette. I was tired after a hectic night with my dossers. There had been a fight, and one of them had had his teeth knocked out and because he was bleeding so much I had escorted him to hospital and sat up half the night with him in Casualty.

"How are things, Twizzle?" On purpose I avoided discussing the previous night. "Did you sleep at the Alphabet after all?"

"Yea, with Frenchie and God. 'Ere Sal, sorry about last night. We went conning after yer left and forgot about time."

"Forget it, Twizzle, it didn't matter," I said as casually as I could, feeling my anger brewing up inside me.

"Tell yer what, man, we'll come another night. Okay?"

"Okay, I go every night. Just give the word," I said pointedly. Creeping Jesus arrived and the conversation switched to sex.

The next time I had offers of help was on Christmas Eve. There was a group of us on the steps of St Martin's Church. A tramp shuffled by and waved to me. "Do you know him?" Doc Livingstone enquired.

"Yes, he has a derry over in Elephant and Castle that I visit."

"Yea, Twizzle was telling me about you looking after these dossers. I think it's a great idea. Jolly good luck to you, and if you ever want our help, of course, just let us know."

I drew a deep breath and took the plunge. "As a matter of fact, I need some support tomorrow night, if you're not doing anything. I've got four families cooking and baking food for me, but no one to help dish it out."

"Sure, we'll help. Lads," he said, turning to his group, "tomorrow evening we're going to help Sally give out Christmas dinners to the poor old boys on Waterloo Station. Where do you want us to meet?"

"I should think platform one at about nine-thirty. If you can bring any cigarettes without having to steal them, I'd be most grateful."

"Right, lassie, we'll see what we can do."

"Don't worry if you can't; I've bought a thousand," I added.

"Where did you get the money from for those?" Scouse asked.

"I've been working in the post office these past two weeks as a Christmas recruit. Sorting and delivering."

"So that you could buy food and cigarettes for your boys?" Doc was obviously impressed with my motives for working.

"Partly, and to buy presents for my family," I admitted. They looked at me as if I was an apparition. Doc spoke for them:

"I admire you, Sally. You're not one of these people that stand up on a soap-box saying what's it's like to have Christ in you and how easy it is to be saved. You don't go around calling yourself a Christian and the next minute sticking a knife in the other fellow's back, if you know what I mean, like these preaching bastards we sometimes have to listen to. I was staying with one a few weeks ago. He told me Christ was inside him, yet when he asked one of the lads to get some coal and he didn't, he swore abuses at him and told him he was an idle swine and a bad influence on the rest of us, and then he threw him out on to the street. Was that being a Christian?"

"It's not for me to say, Doc. All I know from my own experience, is that to be a practising Christian is the hardest life-long task one can ever set oneself. And believe me no human being can help you; that's what makes it so difficult."

"Yer got quite a brain, ain't yer?" Sloppy Terrence contributed.

"I've learnt from bitter experience. Nothing else can teach you. As it comes from the Almighty above, it goes back to the Almighty above."

87

"You really do believe we are the instruments of God, don't you?" Doc said.

"Absolutely, Doc."

"I don't believe in all this religion," Scouse interrupted, crossly.

"Dear Scouse, this is nothing to do with religion. This is to do with believing in Christ and following his trail from Bethlehem to Calvary in the way that he lived and loved. It doesn't mean going to church, taking the sacraments, going to prayer meetings. It's far more simple than that, and a hundred times more difficult – being a Christian is simply being Christ-like."

"I wouldn't know anything about that."

"Don't worry, Scouse, I'm still suffering from birth pangs myself."

He got up and dusted down his jeans, and said: "I'm off conning; see yer at Duke's tonight." The group seemed to split up, but Doc turned to me before leaving. "We'll be outside platform one tomorrow at nine-thirty, so don't you worry, lassie." We shook hands warmly. "Happy Christmas to you, Doc, and thanks."

I spent that Christmas Day driving from Bournemouth to Petersfield to Guildford to London, collecting the food I had been promised from the various scattered sources. Fortunately my mother had lent me her van for this food run, otherwise I would have been in dire trouble. By nine o'clock on Christmas night I had acquired over a hundred mince pies and home-made sausage rolls, cakes and sandwiches, biscuits and four giant sized flasks of tea. My little van was crammed with goodies and exuding delicious smells as I drove into a trainless Waterloo Station. Parking the van, I walked to platform one where I was not only to meet the beats but also the Dobbie family, who were insistent upon giving up part of their own family festivities to come and help me.

I was fifteen minutes early, so I began to wander round the station seeing how many we would have to feed. I had reached the other end when I was startled to hear myself summoned over the loud-speaker to the station-master's office. I began to worry. What had happened now? The station-master was standing outside for me. "You Miss Sally Trench? Good, your boy-friend's on the other end of my telephone. Will you kindly make your conversation brief, I'm not a social Answerphone." I grabbed the receiver apologising profusely. "Hello, Sally here. Who's that?"

I recognised Doc's voice on the other end. "Me, Twizzle and company. Look, Sally, we're stuck out at Crystal Palace and we've just discovered there's no transport running and we can't get out to help you." I smiled to myself.

"Never mind, Doc, I'll manage. What are you doing out at Crystal Palace?"

"We're staying here with Brother Karl. Look, we really are very sorry. Truly we had every intention of coming. You do believe me, don't you?"

"Yes, of course, Doc. Honestly it doesn't matter."

"No, well, I don't like letting you down, and I did say we would be there."

"Forget it, Doc; it's quite unimportant. Nothing's going to come to a stop because you can't make it. Anyway I have got some others coming."

"Well, Twizzle's just had an idea. If you've got the car, why not come and get us? We would love to help." I hesitated before replying.

"I don't think so, Doc. I'll be running round all night picking the dossers up to take them to a bomb-site where I'm organising a party. I don't think it's worth-while adding to the mileage by coming out to pick you up, and I would have to do two loads because I can only fit four in the van."

"Oh! All right then." He sounded disappointed. "Happy Christmas to you, lassie, and I'm sorry to have let you down like this."

"Happy Christmas to you all, and don't think about it again."

"Okay. Scouse and Twizzle say Happy New Year."

I put the receiver down and turned to face a puzzled station-master.

"Did I hear you say you're organising a dossers' party tonight?"

"Yes, that's right. Like to come?" He laughed.

"That's very kind of you, Miss Trench, but I'm glad to have met you. I think it's a grand idea and it's nice to know that there's someone who cares what happens to these people." Jovially we shook hands and exchanged greetings. I returned to platform one to await the arrival of the others.

Our Christmas party was a great success. Having fed those at Waterloo Station, we drove along the Embankment picking up the lonely figures who were straying into the Christmas night. In two loads we arrived at the party bomb-site. We filed out of the cars with boxes of food and gigantic flasks of piping hot tea. I left them there whilst I drove round to the meths cellars in search of more. I found them wrapped in old newspapers amongst the bottles and thrown out debris; they squatted together for warmth, trying to divert their minds from their misery. Over the road drifted the sound of gay music and corks popping. It was the time to sing, drink, dance and be merry.

"Hi! You look cold," I sympathised. They opened their eyes wearily. "If you like, I'll take you to a place where you can have some food and hot drinks." Again they opened their eyes; their faces were hollow and expressionless and I felt as if I was looking right through their eyes. They were living bodies, but dead souls.

The music from across the way broke into the Gay Gordons and the high pitched whoopees became louder. I bent down and one by one got them to their feet. "Trust me, and I'll bring you back here after if you like." I took one by the hand and led him to the car. The others followed.

As we drew up at the bomb-site a large fire was blazing. Silhouetted against the leaping flames were my unwanted friends. The Dobbies were passing the food round; the lads, sitting on upturned petrol cans and buckets, were talking and laughing. One of them, clasping a bottle of eau-de-cologne which he had been drinking, rose and gave a voluble welcome to the new arrivals; seats were found for them on dustbin lids. Mrs Dobbie and I ladled out the tea while Colonel Dobbie was kept busy passing the sausage rolls and mince pies. Charles, the son, produced a trumpet and began to play 'Silent Night', and they began to sing. It was a wonderful sight. As the stars shone bright and midnight struck, voices that perhaps had not sung for ten years, accompanied the carol the trumpet blew. It did not go unheard, for through the darkness their voices echoed across the Stepney bomb-sites and more figures appeared. Some Germans and Norwegians heard us from their mission-hostel a mile and a half away, and followed the music till they found us. They had been going to bed after the evening's celebrations when they heard us start up and just had to come and investigate. So they too joined in singing the carols in their native tongues. Smiles that I had never seen before on certain faces appeared. Cold, despairing eyes became filled with warmth and light. Haunted faces lost their creases and hunched shoulders straightened as they sang aloud, and laughed from the depths of their hearts. It was real and it was wonderful.

It must have been about three in the morning. It was all over. How I hated myself dropping them back at their respective spots to walk the night out, to become the 'unknown citizen' again. Around the fire we had shared a feeling, a feeling of belonging to one another, a feeling of need. It had brought us together as one family. Now I blamed myself for giving them to the cold night and a blanket of loneliness. At the time I knew I had no choice but to return them to their chasm of nonentity, yet now as I drove home to a warm bed I could not clear my conscience of the responsibility of picking them off the road and throwing them back on to it. "God, why am I so powerless to help?" I whispered. His answer came seconds later as I fell asleep at the wheel. Fortunately the road was clear, and as the car swung across to the other side I woke with a start. I was only human, too.

CHAPTER EIGHT

ON Boxing Day I visited Singer in the London Hospital. Singer was an old friend. I had known him nearly a year. We had first met on the ramp where he had sat with his mates brewing up 'jake', a mixture of lemonade and methylated spirits. Simon had just opened its night shelter in Cable Street, and we were out searching the ramp for customers. Singer was one of our first. They came back with us to our newly painted shelter where the inevitable Simon cup of tea awaited them. With Tommy McGeachy, Singer and Benghazi gathered almost nightly in our meths pit where they would doss down with their bottles on mattresses on the floor. When they woke in the morning they were welcomed upstairs for a hot meal. In our Simon shelter they could live without questions, pressures or money. Money for food was our big problem, but we managed to get round this by scavenging. Every morning we went to the Spitalfields fruit and vegetable market where we got on to our hands and knees and hunted for thrown-away scraps — bruised potatoes, battered turnips, broken stalks of rhubarb, lettuce and cabbage leaves. Under the contemptuous gaze of the market porters and lorrymen we challenged the mongrel dogs for the scraps. We turned them into vast bowls of soup for the lads.

As time went on, Singer, noticing our efforts to supply food, offered to help. He dried out of his own accord and started to work for us. Eventually I transferred him to the Simon Central Office to help me during the day. For two months he was a tower of strength in the office, organising the jumble that came in, supplying me with hot chocolate and meals, and enjoying every minute of the fifteen-hour work-day I enforced on him.

During that time he told me a little about himself. He was an Irishman and during the war had been in the Commandos, fighting the Japs in Malaya. He was modest about his army career, but from the hair-raising stories he narrated, he was no coward. I discovered that his downfall had been fighting, and that he had just come out of prison having done five years for manslaughter. He was amusing to listen to, and I enjoyed the short breaks I had with him listening to his horrific stories. Unfortunately, one night when he left the office he never came home. Apparently he came across an old friend who had taken him for a drink, and within days he was back on the ramp drinking meths. Just before Christmas, when he was very drunk, he fell into the ramp fire. He was found in it twenty-four hours later, his left leg burnt right through. It was amputated. I visited him as regularly as I could manage and I had promised to go and see him on Boxing Day.

"Hi, Singer! And what have you done to the nurses this time?" He grinned gleefully.

" 'Ello, Sal darling." He hauled me down and smothered a kiss on my cheek. "I'm leavin' Thursday, yer know." I appeared surprised though I did know, for Sister had told me some weeks previously.

"Don't blame them, Singer, they've had to put up with you two months now. It's quite a strain you know." He chuckled quietly. "Are they moving you to Roehampton for a wooden leg?"

"Nah, Tooting, to a alcoholic ward. Don't wanta go wivout Betty." Betty was his meths-drinking girl-friend.

"Why don't you try and persuade them to take Betty with you?" I suggested. He brightened at this. "Would you like me to have a chat with Sister about this?"

"Would yer, Sal darling? Yer know how it is, we've been together for sixteen years. She and Tommy were my best mates. Yer remember Tommy McGeachy?" Indeed I remembered him. Thomas had been the undisputed leader of the group that used the ramp and Running Water bomb-sites. I remembered the care he took of his men, the trouble he took supervising their living arrangements. Stoking the ramp fire, frying the fish heads for them, patching the holes of the shelter with cardboard. He was arrested stealing two legs of pork for them, and died in Brixton Prison two days later. Alone. Away from them. But they did not forget him. Neither could I. He was a bum and he knew it. He was a saintly sinner, who cared more for others than he did for himself. In looking after them he had a string of convictions for petty offences. He had bummed in the States and Australia and had been on the jake for eighteen years, yet always remained quiet and courteous. He was an incorrigible rogue, but his quiet consideration and kindness left their mark on every soul. For this his subjects made him king. For this we revered him, and sorely missed him. It was on a drizzly June morning that, attended by a Catholic Prison Chaplain, mourned by one Anglican Brother and a Simon, Thomas was laid to rest; no fuss, no commotion. A pauper's grave, for he died alone in prison. There was a wreath from 'his boys' – they had managed to steal enough money for that.

"Yes, Singer, of course I remember . . ."

"He was the most courageous man I've ever met." True praise from Singer.

"I also remember the time you came down to the Simon shelter and as you came in you took off your hat and blood poured down your head."

"Yeah, some f. . . bastard had clobbered me one. Oh, we've had a good time. Remember all the cups of chocolate I made to keep yer awake through the night?"

"Dear Singer, I couldn't have done without you then." We continued to reminisce until it was time for me to go.

"Promise me yer'll see Sister about Betty coming to Tooting." I promised, and also agreed to come over to see him. This I did. We managed to get Betty over there too, thanks to the co-operation of the Welfare people in the London Hospital. But all was not well, for I found him in a locked ward. He was sitting by his bed with his peg-leg, grinning sheepishly.

94

"And now what have you done, Singer? Can't trust you an inch out of my sight, can I?"

"Yeah, I've lost me parole." He had escaped into town one evening and met a friend who gave him some purple hearts, and with a couple of drinks inside him, he was well away. He giggled as he continued, "And then seemingly I threw me crutches away and hopped up the High Street, and kept falling down on me stub. Of course, I can't remember nothing about it. I just woke up next morning when everyone was out, looking for me crutches." He broke into more guffaws.

"Singer, it's not funny; it was thoroughly irresponsible of you and you ought to be ashamed of yourself." He was hooting with laughter.

"Yer should 'ave seen their faces, Sal. They tell me I threatened to kill one of the staff . . ."

"Well, I'm sorry I can't share the joke. In fact I think I've wasted my time coming to see you. Damned if I'm going to make the effort, when you have no intention of trying." I rose stiffly, and Singer was pulling me back.

"Oh, Sal, don't be like that. I'm sorry, but yer know it's hell in 'ere and I ain't had a proper drink for months." His eyes were solemn and pleading like a naughty school-boy trying to talk his way out of a beating. "Honest, Sal, I won't touch another. Believe me, I won't let yer down."

"While you're locked up like this you won't have much chance," I replied.

A week after this episode I met some of the beats down at the Mission in Orange Street, where every Sunday night we were all given free food and free cups of tea. The same faces were there every week — to con, to grab, to take as much as they could. This Sunday was no exception, and I was there too!

"Hi yer, Kiddo. 'Ow's life been treating yer?" It was God. I could never quite bring myself to call him by this name, it repulsed me and his looks just made me want to vomit.

"Hello, there, how's yourself? Fine, though I wish it wasn't so cold."

"*Ciao,* lassie, have a good Christmas?" It was Doc.

"Yes, you missed a terrific party."

"Hi there, Sal," Jimmy was shouting across the crowded room. I waved to him. I saw Scots Geordie and Brazil Nut forcing their way through a crowd towards me. "Got a fag, Sal?" he asked when they reached me. I produced one for him and gave one to Brazil Nut. She was looking tired and sick, her hair was unbrushed and greasy, and her face was dirty. I wondered what she had been given to make her so drowsy. The music started up, and we found ourselves some chairs. A great cheer arose as the food was produced, and as soon as a plate was put on the table it was emptied before I had even put out my hand. The sandwiches were stuffed into their pockets or under the table cloth, the plate was removed and then they were shouting again. "Here, over here Missy, we haven't had any here." Another plate was put in front of them, and again the food had vanished and they were attracting another person pretending they had not had any yet.

"Sal, can I have a word with you, it won't take a minute?" Doc was saying.

"Sure, Doc, what's the trouble?" It was hard to hear oneself talk above the taunts and jeers of the beats as an evangelist gave his testimony of how he had been saved by God.

"Well, Sal, we were wondering if you were going on your rounds tonight and if we could come?"

"As a matter of fact I am, and I also have the use of the car, so there would be no walking. Sure, I'd love to have your company. We'll leave here when it closes, about ten-thirty."

Doc gave me the thumbs-up sign and returned to his table where he sat with Twizzle and Carlos. "Third time lucky," I said to myself.

"Wot d' yer say, Sally?" It was Keith, the registered drug addict.

"Hello, Keith, nice to see you. Where's Denise?"

"She's gone to scrounge some more food off the evangelists. Sal, we were wanting to talk to you. You being a Christian an' all that . . . Well, we wondered if you could put us up and a few of the others. Freddie and Scouse and Jimmy were wanting to join us."

"Join us where?" I thought I knew what he was hinting at.

"Well, Sal, it's like this; we feel you can help us, and we want to come over to you."

"Come over where?" I asked cautiously.

"Well, we know you haven't got a place but . . . well . . . we wondered if you'd get one for us. We'd do anything you tell us. We'd take it from you, because if you preach to us we know you mean it."

I took a deep breath. "Keith, you want me to get a flat for you all, so that you can come off the road?"

"Yeah, that's it. And Jimmy suggested we could look after your dossers, while you went out to work." He had it all tied up. "You see, Sally, I couldn't work to start with 'cause I'm on the junk, and Scouse couldn't 'cause he's on the run like Jimmy, but we'd do anything in the flat you wanted. Honest, we'll pull our weight."

I was silent, not because I had not anything to say, but because he had 'jumped my gun'! I had been turning such an idea over in my mind for some time, but I knew that before I could start such a project I would have to find myself some kind of permanent employment. It had been with this in mind that a few days previously I had approached Task Force for a job. I had intended to wait a month for my first pay before pursuing the idea or even mentioning it to any of the boys, but now that Task Force had agreed to take me, and Keith was standing before me, I felt that four weeks was too far off. "Let me think about it, Keith. I don't promise anything, but I might be able to do something in that line for you."

Doc and Twizzle were waiting for me.

" 'Ave yer got the car?" Twizzle asked.

"Yes, why?"

"I was thinking; we could earn ourselves a bit of bread."

"How?"

"Well, you have the car with the engine running, while I go up to a spade and ask if he'd like a dirty woman for the night for ten shillings. He's bound to say yes, and when he gives me the money I make for yer car at the double."

"No thanks, Twizzle, I don't want a brick through it. It's not mine."

I took them to all my usual hide-outs and across the bomb-sites, and we spent twenty minutes talking to the lads on the ramp. Doc and Twizzle were nervous at first, for they had heard the rather frightening reputation of Cable Street and how people were beaten up in the East End. As we drove back to Trafalgar Square at two in the morning Doc was saying, "You know, Sal, I've been on the road for eight years all over the world, and I've never seen anything quite like what I've seen tonight. I thought I'd seen everything, but I'll never forget tonight. God, I wish all the beats could have seen this, they would bloody well realise how lucky they are. It would shatter them, don't you think, Twizzle?" Twizzle was himself shattered and was speechless.

"Sal, what do you need to help you in your work?" Doc went on.

"Volunteers to start with. Money, food, blankets, candles — you've seen the needs yourself tonight without me having to tell you."

"I'll get you those things, Sal."

"Well, thanks, but don't do a Robin Hood for me — no stealing, please," I exhorted.

"No, I have friends. When's the next time you're going?"

"When I can next afford it. Probably in the middle of the week."

"I'll be in the Lamb and Flag. Come and get me, will you?"

"Okay." I was thrilled. If only he could take it over from me eventually, and organise a proper group to take over the responsibility for them; to make sure they had enough food and clothing. To take the sick ones to the doctor and to help the really elderly ones to get firewood and other fuel; to patch up the holes in their walls and to find more suitable seats for the ramp. If only I could bring about a closer link between the young beats and the old dossers. If only I could present it in the form of a challenge. At least I could supply them with the opportunity, and enthuse and encourage them to befriend these lonely neglected people. If only I could harness the hidden good-will the beats gave to one another. It would reinstate a sense of purpose into their lives in place of the aimless boredom among both the young and old. There would be a sense of being wanted and needed. If only I could awaken that dormant desire to be of service; if only I could give them an urge to help other people. Preaching was not the answer, only example. If I could have them living with me, observing me, following me, wanting of their own free will to be and do the same things as me, then give them the reins and fall into the background only to be there as an adviser should they want it. Was it in my power? No, but it was in God's power.

Over the next week I prayed about it and thought about it. I knew I was not earning enough money to support them all, but this seemed the least of my worries. I had not in fact come to any definite decision about the flat when one of the beats came up to me to tell me that Chicko was missing and that the latest rumour was that she had taken an overdose. I combed the hospitals for her only to find I was out of luck — though as I did not know what name she would have given and I just wandered through the wards until I got myself thrown out, I did not do too badly. I searched five hospitals before giving up. I met her next Sunday at Orange Street. She was on heroin. When she saw me, she blushed with shame. "Don't give me it, Sal; I'm on main-line stuff."

"I won't give it you, love; you know you're being a fool. I can't help you unless you're prepared to help yourself."

99

"No, I get too much of a kick out of it, so f... off."

"Okay, love," a leather-jacketed kid grinned at Chicko's language.

"Who's your boy-friend?" I asked.

"That's Tiny. He's just come over from Ireland. Been here ten days."

"Hi! Nice to meet you." I offered him my hand; he looked at Chicko to see whether she approved or not.

"Ah! Go ahead, Sal's all right. She won't preach unless there's real cause."

"So Chicko's showing you the ropes. You're in good hands but don't follow her on to main-line stuff."

Chicko giggled. "You're too late, Sal, he's on it. I gave him a fix yesterday."

"Well, I hope you're proud of yourself, love. See you, take care."

I shoved my way through a crowd of beats and up the stairs to the street. I felt sick. He could not have been more than fifteen, and within ten days of being in London, he was fixing. If only I had a flat now, I could whisk him away. For three hours I trudged the streets aimlessly. I was tormented with my own inability to do anything about it. I knew then and there I would have to make a decision whether to postpone acquiring a flat until I was more financially secure and more fully planned for the event, or to start looking now and muddle my way through. I decided upon the latter, for my sins.

The following night I came across Tiger on the verge of suicide. She was frightened; she knew the police were looking for her, and this prevented her from walking the streets with her chums. A Greek was paying her five pounds a night to stay in his room, and I knew she was earning every penny of it! She was sick and lonely, having lost her self-respect, and did not know where to turn. "I don't want to live another day, Sal, not like this. What can I do though, he pays me well, and I daren't

100

be on the streets at the moment?" The poor kid grasped my jacket, pleading with me. I felt sick and frightened for her.

"Look, Tiger, if I can get you in somewhere will you go?"

"Yeah, if you promise they won't give me away."

"I promise. Now I'll take you over by car. We'll have to walk over to fetch it. It's not very far." She began to hesitate.

"Where yer taking me then?"

"Guildford. I have a friend who'll look after you, and she won't split."

"Nah, I'm not going out of London." She shrugged herself free.

"Look, Tiger, either you want help or you don't! Now which is it?"

"I'm not leaving London," she replied obstinately.

I was annoyed, but quietly I replied, "Okay then, I have a friend who'll take you in. But if you muck him about, I'll never lift a finger to help you again. He's got some of your mates already."

"Is he one of them Christians?" she sneered.

"As a matter of fact he is. But don't worry; he won't preach to you." We had reached the car, and once again she hesitated. I bundled her in before she could run off down the road, and we began to drive towards Crystal Palace. I kept up a fruitless chatter all the way, hoping to relax her, but she sat there with her hands clenched and trembling. With the headlights of oncoming cars, I was having to concentrate fairly hard on my driving, and as I always imagine I'm on a racing track, I was speeding at over fifty miles an hour. I did not hear the click as she opened the door to throw herself out, but I felt the sudden rush of air. Her head and shoulders were out as I made a desperate grab for her. I felt the car heave on to the pavement and I heard the brakes squeal as I jammed them on. In an instant I had to decide whether to keep my hands on the wheel or hold Tiger down, for she was now hanging half in and half out. I must have put my faith in God, for I found myself hauling her back on the seat. I hit the windscreen as we jerked to a halt in fourth gear, and Tiger was thrown on to the floor. Shakily I got out of the car. It was facing in the opposite direction, its nose not two inches away from someone's front room window. Two children clung to each other a few yards away.

"You all right?" I asked with a trembling voice. They were too frightened to speak, and tears poured down their white faces. I saw a figure go into a telephone booth on the other side of the road and it pulled me together. I could not afford to get involved with the police with Tiger in my car. I jumped in, slamming and locking Tiger's door, and with one movement reversed on to the road and was away before any onlooker could have got through to the police. I just prayed that no one had had the sense to take my number. Tiger was whimpering on the seat beside me as I drove towards Crystal Palace. My fear had turned to anger and I became quite voluble: "Tiger, if you try that again when you're in my car, I'll do it for you, you bloody idiot. Go ahead and kill yourself—I'll give you a helping hand—but don't you dare involve other people. You nearly killed three people with you then." She was crying openly now. "If you feel the same now, I'll take you somewhere where there are no spectators and you can do it very quietly and quickly without anyone seeing, and I'll just drive on as if nothing has happened. You won't be missed."

I pulled into the side of the road and waited for her to stop crying; my anger had subsided but it made me no less harsh. "Now, I want a decision from you. Either you want to see tomorrow, and then I'll take you to my friend, or I will accommodate you by taking you on to Wimbledon Common where all the best people commit suicide. And I promise I won't tell a soul." She looked up to see if I was smiling. It was the last thing I was doing. "Come on. Stop snivelling. What do you want me to do? It makes no difference either way to me. Wimbledon Common or Crystal Palace?"

She sniffed, and wiped her nose on her sleeve. "Crystal Palace," I was relieved to hear her say. So with one eye on the road and with the other on Tiger, I took her to my friend. He agreed to take her in on condition I looked for a bed-sitter meanwhile.

Next morning before work I was scanning the advertisements in the papers for accommodation; I must have rung a least a dozen agents, but none of them were suitable. Either they were too expensive for my weekly wage, or they wanted to see her personally which would have been fatal. During my lunch hour I walked round the newsagents looking in their windows, but with no luck. For three days I continued searching, but on the fourth my friend reported that he had been forced to throw her back on the road because she was a trouble-maker and a bad influence. My first reaction on hearing this was to rage round the office like an angry bear. Friends, they call themselves, I screamed to myself. But as the day passed and it became less important, I began to recognise this as the reaction of any normal person. Millions in his place had thrown out, expelled, got rid of bad influences; one automatically did not want to become involved with 'bad' people, the responsibility was too much, so they were removed. My friend's reaction to Tiger was absolutely normal. Did this make me abnormal? Quite suddenly I was worried. Had I lost perspective? Had my love for these people unwittingly become their downfall? Was I acting like an over-doting mum, spoiling and coddling them? It was my turn to be frightened and lonely. I needed advice quickly; unprejudiced advice.

That night I wrote to Lady Henriques, who during the war had founded the Bernhard Baron St George's Jewish Settlement with her husband. I had heard her broadcasting the week before, telling the listeners of her memories of London's East End during the bombing raids. I had been fascinated by her reminiscences then, and now I felt that she was the best person to help me. I wrote with little faith, for she was not only a very busy woman but a very important one, and I presumed such letters as mine would be passed on to a secretary and would be accordingly answered. I was shattered when two days later I received a handwritten reply inviting me to tea. Since I was working till six this was eventually changed, and it was decided that dinner would give us more time to talk.

It was a very shy and unsure person who arrived at the Settlement that night to dine with the very wise and grand old lady to whom so many owe so much. I was greeted by Lady Henriques herself, muffled up in an apron and waving a wooden spoon at me, dripping mushroom soup over the parquet flooring. "You're early, child. Never mind, go and give yourself a sherry and sit yourself down."

I was ushered into an office which was cluttered with ancestral antiques and fading photographs and dowdy filing cabinets. Scattered around were green plants, some just sprouting from their pots, others bending rather dubiously in the middle as they jammed against the ceiling. They brought life into the brown room. Beautifully leather-bound books filled the bookcases, intermingled with drab ancient paperbacks. Lady Henriques appeared. She had changed for dinner. "I'm afraid I've had a disaster with the fishes. I've burnt their bottoms." I chuckled with delight. We ate a simple dinner, without the fishes' bottoms, and only when we were at the coffee stage did I reveal the cause of my letter.

"Well, I'm thrilled you wrote to me," she said. "Please excuse the salt spoons in the coffee saucers, but most of my silver's gone. My husband had your habit of mixing with down-and-outs, and he always brought them back here; and every time they came, more of my silver went." She smiled good-humouredly. "Now tell me how you first started in this work." I told her everything, ending up with my concern about the young drug addicts. She listened quietly, occasionally interrupting to ask a question. Her face was grave throughout, her eyes piercing mine. When I had finished we sat in silence for a time. She seemed to have gone into another world, completely unaware that I was no longer talking.

"Well my dear," she suddenly said, "the Lord has used you for this very special work. He has given you the vision and you must not let Him down. Obviously you have the vocation and the

104

resilience that is so necessary, for this work is very demanding as you have discovered. At your age you shouldn't have those mauve lines under your eyes; you must learn to look after yourself as well as others. Taking care of oneself is a much more difficult task you know." I acknowledged her wisdom. "My child," she continued, "you have succeeded with stage one: identifying yourself with them so that they now respect and trust you; at the same time you have gained the knowledge and understanding that you need. This is excellent, but now you must prepare yourself for stage two instead of jumping into stage three as you are proposing to do." I frowned with confusion.

"You don't understand, do you?"

"Not really," I admitted.

"Child, you are intelligent enough to realise that this problem is far too big and far too advanced for you to handle single-handed. Yet you are now trying to open a flat for them and support them. This is not helping them, this is condoning them. The first step you must take is to help them regain their self-respect; you won't be doing this if you leave them to lounge around at home whilst you go out and slave yourself in order to keep them alive. They must pull their weight too. Now if they go out to work and pay their whack of the rent and food, then it is an excellent idea and I'll take off my hat to you and in time, so will they. By all means get them a flat and live with them then."

"Lady Henriques, they won't work. I'm flogging a dead horse."

"Then dear, refuse to find them somewhere to live; what is it you want to do for them — get them off the road? Or get at the root of their trouble, which is fixing?" How sensible she was.

"What role do I play now, then? Just play for time?" I asked.

"No dear, you must move on to stage two — recruitment."

"Recruitment?"

"Stage three is when you have enough money or enough backing to open a house for them. But when that time comes you must have enough young dedicated people like yourself to run the establishment. You see, the burdens and responsibilities and emotional strains are so vast that they cannot be put on to one pair of shoulders. You must, during the next year, find people with your drive and dedication to help you in this work, so that when stage three is possible, nine or ten people, sharing the same vision, will be able to mobilise a pilot scheme together, and then you won't be worn out by the age of twenty-four. During this coming year, continue mixing with them so that they can go on trusting and believing in you, and of course it is important you don't lose contact with them. At the same time interest your young friends, recruit doctors, lawyers and people who could help you in the future. Spread the word that when you have saved enough money you will know that you have the best, and only the best people behind you." How wise she was; how foolish I had been. "Of course, you will find this year frustrating; you will feel that you're not doing anything practical, but remember child, don't rush God. In His own time He will let you have the money you require and not before. Work hard, save as much as you can, keep with them so that you can continue learning, but recruit as fast as you can. God is with you, and well ahead of you too!" She smiled sweetly and put a hand on my shoulder, "And my child, don't try and force your way ahead of Him."

The message transmitted to me was as clear as the six o'clock news headlines. I left Lady Henriques without ever showing my immense gratitude to her. Her words were ringing in my ears as I passed the ramp that night, and the little prayer book she had given me was grasped with pride. In time to come I was to read an extract from it every night, and if I was in a derry with the lads, they would listen respectfully and repeat the words after me. Lady Henriques' prayer book became our evening meal!

Five days later, I was with Keith and the boys at Duke's.

"Found a place yet, Christian?" someone asked.

"No," I replied and continued firmly, "I've decided that I really can't afford to get a flat. My money just wouldn't keep you all."

"Don't worry about that, Christian, we'll help you out there."
I knew what he was implying.

"No go, buddy. Before I fork out, I want to see you working."
The shattered expressions on their faces made me want to laugh.
Keith forced a grin.

"You're joking, work? I've never done a stroke of work in all
my life. And anyway I can't, I'm registered," he excused himself.

"No, Keith, I wasn't joking. I meant that. We're all equals.
I'm no better than you; if I can work, you can work."

"Man, I'm sick. Don't talk daft, Sal."

"Yeah, yer gone mad or somethin'?" Jimmy butted in.

"Nope; I'm as sane as the next man. I agree, Keith, you can't
work at present, but you can go into hospital and get yourself
well and fit for work, can't you? Anyway that's my final decision
– no work, no flat." I walked away, their glazed eyes following
me out of the pub. I wondered where I went from here. Should
the next move be theirs? It was like a game of chess, but there
was more at stake for me.

The following night we were all in Duke's; nothing was said,
nothing was mentioned. We all went on to the Alphabet and
then to Coco's. At about three in the morning I discreetly left
by the back door and wandered down to the Embankment. I
loved the winding Thames at night, the street lights reflecting
over its massive waters, the rolling shadows of towering, over-
powering office blocks. There was a great stillness in the air. I
tried to pray.

" 'Ello, Sal, wot yer doin' with yerself 'ere, lookin' like Cleo-
patra's Needle?" Dirty, fat and flea-ridden, with his stringy beard
and horse-like hair, Kelly stood before me.

"My old pal, my old beauty," I exclaimed and hugged him.

He squashed me so tight that I thought he was going to break
one of my ribs. " 'Ow are yer, darlin'?" Kelly was passionate in
every way!

"Fine, love; where have you been these last few months?"

"Over new ground; did a bit of 'bird' up in Nottingham, but

they released me a month ago and I've been wandering down here since."

"You old fraud; and you never let me know. Come and have a cuppa at Joe's; we haven't been there together for about a year."

"Orrite. Won't be amiss if I do – I pay, of course."

"Of course," I agreed. "In kind or kisses?"

"Darlin' wot d'yer take me for, a millionaire? Kisses of course."

"You wild sexy Irishman – always penniless." I pretended to grumble.

We reached Joe's stall and I bought him a tea; we stood over the brazier toasting our hands. He produced a dog-end and offered it to me. "Keep it, Kelly, I've kicked the habit." He lifted his eyes to heaven.

"An' wot other foolish things 'ave yer been up to whilst I've been away? Ye'll be sayin' in a minute yer don't like the old tipple."

"You know I don't drink, you old rogue." I gave him a dig in the ribs.

"Yer know, Sal, I do all the things yer don't want me to do and yer never tell me off. Is it because yer a Christian and that's yer philosophy?"

"It's not a philosophy, Kelly; it's more simple than that. Christianity is the fellowship of love and you can't truly love without forgiving."

"Yer barmy, but yer great with it, kiddo; 'ere take these and give 'em to someone who don't mind smoking with yer Lord." He pressed his packet of cigarettes into the palm of my hand. "Ta very much for the cuppa, Sal. Perhaps I'll meet this 'ere Lord of yers one day and 'e'll do to me wot 'e's done to yer. But 'e won't want the likes of me." He picked up his bundle of rags and sadly slouched away.

I called after him: "Kelly, He wants the likes of you more than anyone else." The words drifted into the night as Kelly had done. I hoped he had heard them. Poor Kelly, poor, poor Kelly.

I made my way back to Soho. I was ambling towards the Alphabet, engrossed in my thoughts, when I saw Tubby running down the road. For Tubby to run I realised that something was seriously amiss. I shouted at him to attract his attention. He waved frantically. I quickened my pace. Tubby was blowing hard, his face was red with exertion.

"What's up?" I asked, as I drew up beside him.

"It's Reg and Ponce, they're fighting."

"That's not unusual," I commented. This did not unduly worry me.

"They've drawn knives," Tubby squeaked.

"Knives?" I responded sharply.

"Yea, and they mean business, Sal. Stop 'em, they won't listen to us."

"Lead on, Macduff." We ran some hundred yards up an alleyway to a basement flat. As we descended the steps, female screams could be heard, and abusive language cut the brief silences. I entered the semi-dark room. Several of the junkies were standing round while Reg and Ponce faced each other, their knives poised, the long evil blades flashing. Someone shouted, "Ponce, lay off him. Come away!" It went unheard. Reg, with a ripped coat, suddenly charged. The knife flashed towards the other's chest. Ponce seemed to leap to the side, and with a jeer brought his own knife down towards Reg's neck. People screamed with terror. Someone knocked the knife from Ponce's hand. The two fighters were sprawled in the centre of the floor with one knife. A friend of Reg's neatly stepped forward and clouted Ponce across the head. Shouts of indignation from Ponce's supporters, who fell upon the victim and it became a free for all. I stood watching completely baffled until someone punched me in the groin. I doubled up with pain and anger but it produced the best result in the end. Furious, I grabbed a chair from nearby and bore down on the room swivelling it from side to side. I scattered groups of fighters. With a blood-curdling yell, I hurled it against the wall where it crashed explosively into smithereens. I looked around for another, and there was the faithful Tubby with another one. I yelled at the top of my voice, "Coppers" and crashed the second one against the opposite wall.

It had a startling effect. Everyone became quiet. I stood trying to look composed and said in a breathless voice, "If you don't belt up, you'll have the coppers down here." I heard a gasp behind me and turned to find Reg creeping towards me. "Yer f... well stop interfering, yer bitch." I saw the knife when he was almost on me. I was just too frightened to defend myself, let alone run. I felt the blade hit me as Ponce leaped at him. The knife fell to the ground. Someone was pulling me to one side and telling me to lie down. I felt ice-cold with fear. Some of the junkies were holding Reg down. Tubby was picking up the two weapons. Ponce was kneeling on Reg's arms, sitting across his chest: his hands were wrapped round Reg's neck. "No, no!" I stuttered and crawled across to him. "Leave him, Ponce, he didn't mean it."

Ponce looked at me. His face was a mask of hatred. "Sal, 'e would 'ave killed yer, and 'e ain't gettin' away with that." His fingers tightened their grasp. He was probably right, but it had been a moment of impulse and not a meditated act of violence. I struggled to my feet, and with all my strength grasped Ponce by the neck. He went red in the face as he tried in vain to breathe.

"Ponce, this is what it's like to be strangled alive." I gripped harder. "And this is no impulse so you couldn't get away with manslaughter. It would be a murder charge." I let go and he began to breathe heavily. His hands round Reg relaxed. The terrified faces around relaxed also. Reg, though his eyes were closed, was breathing again.

"Right, the party's over. Let's get out of here before we're shopped," I suggested. Some of the boys lifted Reg to his feet and helped him into the fresh air. Ponce glumly hauled himself upright and without another glance took his leave.

Tubby was fingering my sheepskin jacket. "Yer were lucky," he said, pointing to a tear where the knife had caught me. "Bloody lucky, in fact," he mused.

"The Lord was with me, thank God," was all I could reply.

CHAPTER NINE

IT was Good Friday. A day of prayer and fasting, a day for spiritual recollection. I sat alone, lonely, watching coaches draw up on Westminster Bridge and excited foreigners filing out with their cameras to photograph Big Ben and the Houses of Parliament. It was the beginning of their Easter holidays, as it was for the millions of others I had watched driving bumper to bumper in slow procession out of London. The occasional doddery couple, too old and forgotten to join the vacational drift to the country, passed me on their way to church. I followed their example.

The last month had been hell. I had been feeling a little fragile for some time and had had a very bad cough since Christmas. Determined at the time that it was a mild dose of flu that I could walk off, I continued my gallivantings down to the ramp and Soho. The beats began to comment on my facial appearance; I began to look pale and drawn, and my cough became deep and husky. As the spring came on I became optimistic; with the warmer nights I would start to feel more myself. Alas! I was under a misapprehension. I forced myself to continue my East End visits and to help the beats whenever I could, but now it was a burden. I became bad-tempered and only had to climb a flight of stairs to find myself utterly exhausted and breathless. One Sunday night I was with the beats at the Orange Street Mission when the Youth Leader, an evangelical pastor, approached me. He took me aside, thinking I was a drug addict.

"I've been watching you for some time," he told me, "and somehow you seem different from the type of beatniks that come down here. How come you're in this mess?"

"I'm in no mess," I assured him emphatically.

"Are you a Christian?" he demanded.

"Yes, as a matter of fact I am. I was brought up a Roman Catholic."

"You come from a good home, don't you? Do you keep in touch with home? Where do your family live?"

"Around and about," I replied airily.

"Why are you on the road then?"

"What's wrong with being on the road?" I demanded defensively.

"When you're mixing with people like this, there's plenty wrong, girl."

Still I offered him no information, but I could not hide a fleeting smile.

"You look sick, are you on the needle?"

"Nope."

"Where are you sleeping?"

"Around." He must have realised then that he was wasting his time pumping me, so he brought the rather one-sided conversation to an end with, "Come and see me next Wednesday at my home, here's the address."

I did turn up when the time came, though I had had second thoughts. His home was in Norwood, where his wife ran a guest house. I spent the evening with them, telling them of some of my real work; intermittently I shoved in the odd lie as a protective barrier. I hoped that in the end he would not know what was truth and what was fantasy. I wanted to remain an unknown quantity until I knew more about him. In the past it had always paid me to be one step ahead of the enemy, and the pastor before me was no exception. During the evening it transpired that he was a devout evangelist and that his life's dedication was to save souls. Brother Vic was a little man with a pale fox-like face and he preached the word of God with fiery passion. His direct manner was frank and forthright. He withheld nothing and yielded everything. His methods to help the drug addicts were contentious, I thought, but he was sincere and he believed that what he was doing was right. I respected him for this.

The next time I saw him was at one of his meetings in Victoria where he talked about the sins of drug addiction and homosexuality. He told me nothing I did not know. The meeting ended about ten-thirty at night, and only a few remained behind chattering. I wandered out into the street feeling very weak and sick. I had walked a hundred yards towards my car when I had a very bad coughing fit. To regain my breath I sat down on the kerb. I was still sitting there an hour later when two coppers came by. "Hey-ho, and what have we got here—Little Girl Lost? What's your name, Dearie?" I did not answer.

"Where are you going? You can't stay here."

"Nowhere."

"Where have you come from?" the other asked.

"Nowhere."

"What are you doing here then?"

"Nothing."

"How old are you?"

"Over eighteen," I assured him.

"Where are your parents?"

"Somewhere I guess," I said unhelpfully.

They looked at my torn jacket and my soleless shoes. "I think you'd better come along to the station."

"On what charge?" I asked.

"Well, if you don't come of your own free will, loitering with intent."

"Loitering with intent," I laughed. "There's no man in sight except you. I have no intent, nor am I loitering. I was feeling sick so I sat down for a rest."

"When did you last sleep?" One of them lifted my chin and saw the dark shadows under my eyes. "Come on, up you get." I was lifted to my feet.

"Hold your horses." I had an idea. "If you go down to the hall down there, someone will vouch for me." I hoped Brother Vic was still there.

The hall was closed, but one of Brother Vic's evangelistic followers was just getting into his car when he saw me. He came over.

"Do you know this young lady?"

"Yes, sort of."

"What's her name?"

"I don't know," he admitted.

"We're old friends," I butted in, "I see them every Sunday night down at Orange Street Mission."

"What's his name then?" the policeman asked me.

"I dunno." I confessed.

"You're old friends and you meet every Sunday, and neither of you knows the other's name. Who's trying to pull the wool over my eyes?" the policeman said good-naturedly. "Come on, dear, we'll take you to the station and perhaps we can sort out who you are there." As I was led away between the two policemen, the evangelist shouted after me, "Don't worry, I'll ring Vic."

"Tell him I've been loitering with intent," I shouted back jocularly.

At the station I was put in a little room and told to empty my pockets. I did with the exception of my driving licence which I had managed to slip into my bra when supposedly scratching a flea under my arm! The station superintendent was brought in to view me and give me the heavy father act. "Now my dear, a few details. You don't want to have to stay in a cell for the night, do you?"

"Not really," I agreed.

"Well then, I want your full name and age and where your parents live. Have you run away from home?"

"No. Actually I'm quite innocent." He was gazing at my eyes. "And I'm not taking drugs either," I confirmed for him.

"How long have you been on the road? Some time, by the look of you," he concluded. "Come on, what's your name?" His tone had changed from a friendly note to a brisk business one. Gone were the kind, understanding eyes. "Your name, I said," he repeated. I realised that if I lied I would be in deep water, yet if I did not lie I would be in twice as deep where my own family was concerned. If only Vic would ring, he could stand surety for me. The superintendent turned to the constable. "You'd better call Sergeant Rastle, she's in the canteen."

"Yes, sir." The constable disappeared. Trouble was brewing up.

"Sally Dobbie's the name," I said unhesitatingly. "My parents are abroad, so I live with my uncle in Wanstead. He's Colonel Dobbie, headmaster of a grammar school. You can ring him, he's on the phone." I gave the colonel's number and prayed that he would play the game. Sergeant Rastle appeared and sat with me whilst the superintendent made the phone call. Through the half open door, I heard, "I have your niece here." I felt myself blush, and simultaneously I crossed my fingers. "I hear she lives with you since her parents are abroad," the voice continued. I put my hands over my ears so that I did not have to listen to any more. The superintendent came in smiling. I wondered what the colonel had said to him to put him in such a good humour. "Colonel Dobbie doesn't exactly verify your story, but he says have you got your car here? If you haven't he'll come and get you?"

"I have, thanks. Can I go now?"

"Yes," he waved his hand and added, "What sort of car have you? A Bentley?" I was relieved to leave the station on such good terms. Trumps up, for Colonel Dobbie I thought.

Even after this episode, I avoided facing the fact that I was sick. When I had a pain in the chest I put it down to being unfit, but I never sat down on the kerbside until I felt better. Some nights I could not breathe, and the pain was so fierce that I did not know where to put myself. I refused to give in, thinking foolishly that to be sick was a weakness, and what-ever the cost I must remain on my feet. The cost nearly became irreparable.

I had arranged to meet Brother Vic and his assistant, Brother Eric, at eleven-thirty one Saturday night to take him to the ramp and round the 'Skipper' sights of London. He had said he wanted to see the dossers and the meths drinkers because he realised that these people were what the beatniks of today would become. So

I showed him. Six men and one woman were lying in the ash of the dead ramp fire amongst the bottles and rats. Nine men were lying in the cold smelly debris of the bomb-site caves, and eighty-nine lay prostrate, staggered, or sat hunched in Waterloo Station. When I dropped Vic and Eric that early morning we prayed for them and that our young beats should never have to follow in their footsteps. I completed the prayer with one of my coughing fits and sat doubled up over the wheel of my car fighting for breath. I then heard Vic and Eric praying for me.

I slept in the van that night, but sleep came fitfully. At one part of the night I felt as if I were fighting for my life and the next minute I lay back numb and as weak as a baby. I wondered whether I would see the morning and then I found myself laughing, crying, convincing myself that I was being ridiculously dramatic and that my sickness was psychological. Again I found myself doubled up with pain, coughing and vomiting, and the fear of death crept in. I wondered whether to crawl out on to the road, but I knew this would mean hospital, being disciplined to a bed possibly for some time. What would happen then to my dossers and my prayer meetings with the beats? I had got so far, I could not stop now. So I lay there, shivering with cold, and perspiring with heat, one minute determined that I would be fine in the morning, and the next terrified of dying. Even prayer seemed little comfort. I tried to visualise the pain our Lord suffered at His crucifixion, and comforted myself that He at one point thought His Father had forsaken Him.

Morning did eventually arrive, and needless to say I was there to see it! The light of day took away the fear of death and I was able to doze fairly peacefully. In the afternoon I went to a meeting, but I was making so much noise coughing that I had to come out in the middle. Once again in the van I doubled up, fighting to breathe. I began to drive round hoping this would take my mind off my sickness. I found myself in Brixton. Half-way to Vic's house, I thought. It was a miracle that I reached his house without crashing the van, for on my arrival my knees were buckling under me and my head was whirling. I staggered groggily in. I saw the figure of Vic's wife. "Could I borrow a bed for a few hours?"

"Of course. Somehow I thought you'd be here today. Vic was very worried about you last night." Thank God she was expecting me, I thought. I was bundled into a bed and told to stay there. Before Vic left for the Orange Street Mission that evening he came into my room.

"How are you feeling?"

"Much better, thanks." I tried to give a vivacious grin, without success.

"You'll stay here till I see you in the morning. All right?"

"Sorry, not a hope. I've got to meet someone tonight." I could not let the lads on the ramp down. I had always brought them food on Sunday night. "And anyway I'm meeting a bloke out of Pentonville in the morning."

"Can't someone do it for you?"

"Nope, he wouldn't let anyone help him except me."

"Okay. You know you're very sick at the moment?"

"Not really; I've got a bit of a cough that's all — nothing serious."

"Come on, girl, who's kidding who? You're very sick." I said nothing. "Will you promise me one thing, that you'll come back here tomorrow?"

I hated committing myself, but underneath I knew it was the most sensible commitment I could possibly have made. At about nine-thirty that evening I crept out and made a very laborious way to the ramp where I spent the night watching over the lads to see that they didn't fall into the fire. I was outside Pentonville Prison first thing in the morning to meet Big Jo.

"Hello, Sal, thought yer wouldn't let me down." Silently I thanked the Lord that he had given me the strength not to stay at Vic's house last night. "Got me fixed up any place?" he continued.

"I'm sorry, Big Jo, I've been so busy I haven't. But if you

come with me, I thought we'd go to St Luke's and see the warden together."

"The alcoholic place?"

"Yes, they're awfully nice there and the warden's a first-class chap." He began to hang back. "Oh please Jo, don't give me any trouble. I just couldn't take it today." I was not sure whether it was the distressed tone of my voice or the dried haggard expression on my face that caused him to say roughly, "Yer okay, kiddo? Yer look as if yer overdoing it. 'Ere 'ang on to me." He gave me his arm.

St Luke's accepted him, and at last I was in the position of keeping my promise to Vic and had a clear two days ahead of me in which I had nothing specific to do. On the coming Thursday I was a witness in St Marylebone court, so if Vic would have me I had the rest of that day, Tuesday and Wednesday to get myself on my feet again. I dug into my pocket to see how much money I had for bus fare – I had returned the van to its rightful owner last night. Of course I was penniless, having bought Big Jo some breakfast. I glanced at my watch. It read nine-thirty.

I had a long walk to West Norwood, too long for my sick body. Within half an hour I was vomiting, and my legs were like jelly. Beads of perspiration were falling like tears down my cheeks. My haversack, which I had picked up from Charing Cross left luggage department earlier that morning, weighed heavier and heavier. I was gasping for breath, my chest was one searing pain. Sheer force of habit made me go on. Blurred faces seemed to bear down on me, noises bored through my head. The pavement was moving like an escalator, and the buildings around seemed to be crashing down on top of me. On and on I drove myself until all pain had gone. I was completely numb. My legs weren't holding me any longer. Someone was tearing out of her house towards me. I had a great sense of being closed in. The pavement hit me, the clouds descended and the woman was standing over me. I was walking again, the woman's voice was piercing me to consciousness. I was lying on a bed. A woman was pouring water down me. How I wished it was brandy! She was wiping the perspiration from my face. I opened my eyes and tried to focus them on my surroundings; it was all hazy. Her voice was coming at me again. "Shall I call an ambulance, or have you any family near here that I can ring?"

The word ambulance brought me out of my state of mental obscurity.

"No, Vic, I must get to Vic. Must keep my promise."

"Yes dear, is he on the telephone so that you can ring him?"

"Yes, I'll telephone him." What a brilliant suggestion, I thought. The telephone was right beside the bed, but for the life of me I couldn't find the finger holes with the letters and numbers.

"What's the number, dear, and I'll dial it for you." What a kind woman she was, full of magnificent suggestions and so sweet with them.

"Hello is that you, Vic? Sally here. I'm afraid I can't make it, I'm sick."

"Where are you?"

"I don't know, hold on." Turning to the woman I asked, "Where am I?"

"153 Trinity Rise, Tulse Hill." I repeated it over the phone to Vic.

"I'm coming right over." The phone went dead.

"He's coming to pick me up," I told her, and fell back unconscious.

The next forty-eight hours I drifted between consciousness and unconsciousness. When Vic got me back to his house he had to get Jean, a nurse who gave up her career to join the evangelists, to help carry me in. Vaguely I remember Jean propping me up as I coughed uncontrollably; other faces were also there, faces that I had seen down at the Orange Street Mission, but then they faded into the wall and I was asleep again. Someone was feeding me. Darkness. Was I dreaming, or could I hear breathing? I groaned.

My mouth was so dry from coughing. The nurse was there, she was giving me something sweet and moist; it was delicious. The ceiling was coming towards me again. It was light, someone was wiping the perspiration from my head with a damp towel. There were other people in the room. I began to cough, and my chest burnt as if on fire. Then all was darkness again. Singer and Betty were there on the ramp but somehow I could not get there. Every step I took towards them took me a step further away.

"I'll get to them," I shouted. My arms were caught tight and I began to fight myself free. The harder I fought, the firmer the grip became.

"You're not going any place today," a man's voice came through. I opened my eyes. I was in bed and a man was holding my arms, Jean was beside me and behind her was Vic. "Okay, Sally?" he asked.

I nodded.

"Then relax, so Eric doesn't have to hold you down."

The man let me go and began a prayer of thanks. I shut my eyes and fell into a deep peaceful sleep. I awoke next morning to find Jean had brought me a large cooked breakfast. "I want everything eaten up, you haven't had anything solid in you since you arrived," she instructed.

"You bet," I replied. "I'm famished." The door opened and Eric came in.

"That's a good sign," he approved. "So the patient's on the mend?"

"Yes, the fever's left her," Jean answered.

"The Lord is the greatest healer," he said, disappearing.

"How long have I been here?" I asked Jean.

"This is your third day, and we've had quite a time keeping you here. You've kept trying to get back to the ramp. We've had to have someone with you every minute, after catching you sneaking out the first evening you were here."

"Truly? I can't remember a thing."

"No, you wouldn't. You were delirious. Now that you're conscious, you won't do a bolt for it, will you? You won't get very far if you try, because you're very weak."

"No, I won't."

"Make a promise of it, then I know I can trust you."

"I never make promises if I don't think I can keep them and I don't want to risk this one," I replied honestly.

"That's what I was frightened of."

"How long will I have to stay here?"

"Another week and then a week's convalescence." I gasped.

"You've got a hope!"

"We'll see what Vic says," and the conversation halted there.

As the days passed, I grew stronger. I was still coughing, but the pain had eased up and I felt much more ready to cope with life. The rest had obviously done me good. The more revived I felt, the more unsettled I became with my own inactivity. I had a great sense of urgency to return to the ramp. Vic must have realised this because repeatedly he told me that Colonel Dobbie was keeping his eye on the boys there. But still this did not put my mind at ease. In my bones I felt there was something wrong. "Give it to the Lord," the evangelists kept saying. I did, and then took it back! Giving it to the Lord, telling Him all about it did not seem good enough. It did not seem practical just to tell Him and leave it in His hands. The more I prayed, the more perturbed I became. Vic had stayed pretty silent, he was watching this spiritual battle but to date had not felt it was necessary to interfere.

The time came when I packed my haversack and got dressed – I was going to the ramp. Vic entered my room. "Going somewhere?"

"Yes, to the ramp. Sorry, Vic, but I've got to."

"Sally, stop doing what your will wants and instead follow God's will."

"I do; you don't think I've spent the past four years existing from one day to the next for my own sake?"

"No, you're quite right there; I believe you've been working for God."

"I'm quite sure that I wouldn't be alive to tell the tale now, had it not been the Lord's work," I replied confidently.

"Yes, Sally, but there's a difference between working for God and working with Him — you have yet to learn to work with Him." I was dumbfounded. I had no answer. "Let's pray, shall we?" Vic said.

We got on to our knees and we prayed. My heart was burdened when Vic left me. I took a walk and paid a visit to church before returning to Vic's. This evangelical pastor had hit the nail fair and square on the head. I saw Vic as I walked in. "Is there a prayer meeting tonight anywhere?" I asked.

"As a matter of fact there's one at Denison House. I'll be going, do you want to come?"

"Yes please," and as I accepted my heart became light like the sun shining. I knew I was half-way to the answer.

The prayer meeting was very evangelical, but no less inspiring. Denomination be blowed, it was the ultimate aim of finding a closer union with God that interested me, and here I found it. The words "When I am weak, then am I strong," pounded through my head. The realisation that until self-reliance is shattered to bits, until we despair of ourselves, we go around trusting and believing in our own powers and in consequence do not employ the power of God. My own failures were not due to my weaknesses but to my neglect to employ God's strength. I came away knowing the answer to my mental and spiritual sickness; it was not to be found in bemoaning my shortcomings, but in striving to place my trust in His hands. If I clung to God without fail, I would advance without failure.

I stayed with Vic and his family for about a month until I moved into a flat with Jean, and then she decided to go abroad and thus gave the flat up. Once again I was on the road, but in a much better physical and spiritual condition. I passed my nights either on the ramp or down in some grotty club in Soho; now that the summer was here, I joined the beats in St James's Park where we slept all day in the sun. If it rained, we moved into the tube stations or back to our familiar resting haunt, the National Gallery.

It was on such a wet May day that, in my jeans and leather jerkin, I lounged into the art gallery for a quiet kip. I hailed some familiar bearded faces and moved on to a less conspicuous seat where two youngsters sat. People were milling to and fro, gaping at the pictures or frowning with disapproval at us. I was just about to close my eyes when two ordinary men in sports jackets and neatly cropped hair caught my attention. They were facing one of Turner's sea pictures, but were hard in quiet conversation. There's a saying amongst us beats, that we can smell a copper anywhere; and I didn't have to smell these two – they stuck out a mile. I was about to get up and casually walk away when they came over to my seat and began talking to the two scruffy kids next to me. Now, did I risk getting up and walking out and by so doing drawing attention to myself, or did I sit tight and hope they would pass me by? Quite suddenly I engrossed myself in the picture before me; I leaned forward with a 'cultured' expression on my face and verbally 'ahed!' my appreciation of the great hanging masterpiece. My view was suddenly hampered as a man in a sports jacket stepped in front of me. Under my nose he shoved his dirty little card that gave him all the power he wanted. In a big strong voice he said, "C.I.D."

"So what?" I replied in an equally big, strong voice, and hung my head to one side so that I could continue studying the picture. But I knew I had burnt my boats for getting away. I felt his hand clutch my jerkin, and he roughly pulled me to my feet. "George, we have a funny girl here," he remarked, and addressing me he said, "You'll be laughing on the other side of your face back at the station."

"You threatening me?" I answered viciously.

123

"No, just making a statement. Come on." He pushed me ahead of him.

"What's the charge?" I demanded.

"No charge at the moment, but we'll accommodate you with one."

"Get lost." I shrugged my shoulder free from his hand. It came back with a grip that was twice as firm. "Okay, mate, I'm not a jail bird yet," I said, freeing my shoulder again. He took the hint, but kept within a hand's grasp of me. I noticed George was bringing the two youngsters along behind me. People watched us curiously as we were paraded from the highly respectable National Gallery in the direction of Charing Cross Station. I waved across at Big Bill and Gipsy Jason who were astride the fountain wall.

"Keep moving!" My jailer shoved me forward as I tried to stop to say a few words to Brazil Nut and Judy, who were passing.

We reached the railway station. George had now taken the lead with his two frightened catches. We halted in front of a green door. George knocked on it, and I heard the heavy, unmistakable steps of a policeman as he approached the door and unlocked it. "In you go." I was pushed into a bare room with three desks and a few tinny lockers. George, the older and more humane of the two, took up his official position behind the desk, whilst my jailer kept a firm hand on me. He was determined I wasn't going to escape despite the room having no windows and the door having been locked behind us.

"Full names, please, and your addresses," George ordered his now thoroughly dejected captives. They mumbled something, and George produced a little black book. "Well, you're not on my list of London layabouts, so you'd better have a good reason for being in the Gallery," he said, after fingering through the C's and S's. C. mumbled something further and S. agreed whole-heartedly with the excuse. George lit a cigarette and sat back, staring thoughtfully at the two petrified boys. Gently he warned,

124

"If you're on the run, save me the trouble of checking up, will you?"

The boys shuffled uncomfortably. No word passed their quivering lips. My jailer beside me broke into a satisfied smile. Livid at his sadistic streak, I broke out, "That's made your day, hasn't it?"

"Not yet — not until we've booked you," he replied cuttingly.

"That's enough of that, David," George interrupted sharply. "Now lads, who should I ring up to say you're safe?"

"B—— Remand Home," came the sullen reply. Ten minutes later they were put in a black maria and driven away.

"Now, ma'am," he turned to me. "First, you can give me your name."

"Sally Trench." George reached for his black book of London layabouts. "Oh I don't think I'll be in that." I tried not to sound too indignant.

He checked. "No, you're not. So you're new to the Square as well?"

"Not really. I drift from district to district actually."

"Have you an address?"

"No. N.F.A."

"Where are your parents?"

"I don't know," I lied.

"What were you doing in the Gallery?"

"I was about to have a kip, actually."

"Didn't you sleep last night?"

"No."

"Where did you spend last night?"

"The Spit and Fizz." His eyebrows shot up.

"Not a very suitable place for any young lady, especially you."

"Why especially me?" I knew my accent had startled him.

"Well, you're obviously from a fairly good family."

"What in your terms makes 'a fairly good family'?" He ignored me.

"You know that place is full of prostitutes and queers?"

125

"Well, the queers wouldn't look at me, would they? Yes, as a matter of fact I did know – and drug addicts and lesbians," I added.

"What were you doing there, then?" my jailer suddenly shouted.

"I didn't think you'd keep quiet for much longer," I taunted.

"Watch your tongue!" George addressed me sternly.

"I often go there," I replied.

"What for?"

"To get out of the rain."

"Not to pick up drugs, of course!" Sweet sarcasm from my jailer.

"Want to search me?" I challenged.

"You know we can't do that, Miss Trench." George's temper was fraying. "I think you'd better come with us, all the same."

I was ushered out and into a parked Wolseley opposite the station. We drove in silence to K—— Street police station, my jailer sitting next to me in the back seat. The sergeant on duty put me in a little room on my arrival; it was small, and had no window for escape. There was no fireplace, and the only pieces of furniture were a table and two drab chairs. I tiptoed to the door and peered through the keyhole, sure enough they had placed a constable on duty outside. It was all so dramatic that I had to laugh. I slumped into one of the chairs and went through my pockets; the only form of identification on me was my driving licence which I shoved under the heel flap in my shoe. I was only just in time, for a policewoman entered. Her uniform covered a portly figure, one that I would not like to get on the wrong side of! Her eyes were mistrusting and well shaded by her long lashes; a thick braid of black hair coiled twice round her head was held together by pins and kirby grips. Her voice was pleasant, but had a hard ring of authority about it.

"I'd like you to answer some questions, please." She sat herself in the opposite chair and began writing on her charge sheet.

The routine questions that I had been asked at Charing Cross

Station were repeated, and so were the answers; the interview was icily polite on both sides. In the middle we were interrupted by a woman police constable entering; she was gaunt and had a tawny tint to her skin. I was politely introduced.

"Now, Miss Trench, would you kindly undress?"

"What the devil for?" I rudely demanded.

"We want to search your clothes," was the cold reply.

"What if I refuse?"

"I shouldn't if I were you; we don't want to have to use force."

One by one my garments came off until I was standing in my underwear, feeling most embarrassed, especially since I hadn't washed it lately in the Charing Cross toilets! In fact I was so aware that they were not Daz white, but dirty grey, that I apologised for them: "Sorry about that, I wasn't expecting visitors." Their faces remained masks of unemotion.

"Take it off," the younger one ordered.

"What! My underwear too?" This was going a bit too far.

"All of it."

"But I'll get cold standing here naked," I feebly pointed out.

"Go and get Miss Trench a blanket, Constable."

Wrapped in a grey blanket I sat on the chair whilst they searched my clothes; they knew their job and were thorough, very thorough. Every hem, every cuff, every lining was expertly fingered as they sought for some kind of concrete evidence with which they could charge me. My driving licence was found. "This yours?" I was asked.

"Of course, it's got my name on it, hasn't it?"

"That doesn't mean it's your real name."

"For crying out loud, do you believe anything anyone says?"

"Miss Trench, we're only doing our duty," I was stiffly told. "You may get dressed now. When you are ready the constable will take you downstairs. I'll be along to see you later."

"Look, what's the trouble now? You've searched me, and I'm as clean as a whistle. Can't you let me go?"

"I'm sorry. I'm not satisfied yet." She left.

127

"Satisfied with what?" I repeated the question to the constable.

"I suppose she's not sure whether you're telling the truth," she said.

"So she's gone to check up?"

"Yes, I should think so. Are you ready?"

"Sure, I'm ready for anything now."

I followed her out of the room and down the dimly lit corridor. The occasional uniformed policeman passed us, but paid us no attention. She opened a cell door. Three solid brick walls faced me. On the left was a bunk with a straw mattress, on which lay two grey blankets neatly folded. The cell was tiny, neat and clinically clean.

"Would you like a cup of tea?" the constable was asking.

"On the house, I presume?" I sneered. I had hated tea ever since my boarding-school days. "Okay, I'll have a cup — without sugar." The door slammed behind her. I took off my shoes and paced the uncarpeted floor. I sat on my bunk and studied the spotless walls. I stretched myself out and put a blanket over me. Underneath it I felt protected. All was quiet. There seemed a hopeless finality in the silence of the tiny enclosed room. It was an unnatural silence — not the usual comforting absence of noise. I turned over. I felt frightened. "Don't be an idiot, you've done nothing wrong; they're only frightening you, they've got nothing on you." Listening to my own voice comforted me. "You're innocent. They've only taken you in on sus." I convinced myself. The silence seemed to swallow up my voice. I wanted to scream and tear it apart, but instead I lay quiet and allowed it to persist. There was no sound beyond the rock-like door. There was no movement. It was as if the building had frozen. "Oh, God!" I cried aloud, but it was stifled in the silent solidity. "God, let me out of here," I cried again. I shut my eyes to hide from the reality of my surroundings. I thought about the words, "When I am weak, then am I strong." I tore the blanket aside, and fell to my knees and prayed.

The melancholy rattle of a key turning brought me to my feet.

It was the young policewoman with my cup of tea. "I brought some biscuits down, too; I wasn't sure when you last ate."

"Thanks," I replied gratefully. "How long do you think I'll have to stay here?"

"As soon as they've cleared you, you'll be free to go. If you want anything, just bang on the door." She departed once again into the dimly lit corridor and again I was left alone in the tiny locked cell. I sipped the warm tea and enjoyed it. Funny, I thought, I hate tea. I chewed the biscuits. They were sweet and flavoured with lemon cream. They were delicious. I sat on the bunk warming my hands on the cup. Fear had left me. It had smothered the thin voice of reason, but now I was thinking logically. "Thank God!" I said aloud, and suddenly the full meaning of those words flowed through me. I realised once again that until we despair of ourselves and throw our trust into God's hands, we cannot escape these tortures and infirmities. If we neglect to employ God's strength instead of our own, we will forever fail. The words from the Scripture, "Without me you can do nothing," and, "I can do all things in him who strengthens me," shot into my memory. The cell door was opening.

"Miss Trench, I'm sorry to have kept you. You're free to go. Here's your driving licence." She was smiling at me. The door was wide open. The dim light in the corridor was friendly. "I'm sorry, I do hope we haven't inconvenienced you too much," she was saying, but I was not really listening. I climbed the stairs away from the cells. I passed the affable duty sergeant who cheered me goodbye. I pushed open the swing doors, and then I was in the open, breathing in the vegetable smells of Covent Garden. I had been locked away for nearly two hours; it had felt like two years. I walked down the street smiling at every passer-by. I hailed every lorry driver with a hearty "Good afternoon". I patted every lorry with affection as I passed. I was free.

CHAPTER TEN

I SPENT that night on the ramp; it was like any other night, but I enjoyed it more than the others. Probably because I had triumphed in that cell. My self-reliance had been shattered and I had confided in God and He had brought me through. Singer brought me back from my reminiscences with a loud moan. From the iron milk crate on which I was perched, I could see him lying next to Betty in the ash of the dead fire. Kelly groaned himself awake and groggily blinked at me. He scrabbled around in the dirt and found what he was looking for. He took a swig and it dribbled down his chin. "Want a drink?" He passed me the bottle.

"No thanks, Kelly, and I don't think you need any more." I broke it behind my milk crate. Singer moaned again.

" 'E's sick, Sal. 'E's real sick. Can't yer 'elp 'im?" I had never heard Kelly talk with such sincere concern before. I moved over to Singer, stepping over the prostrate bodies of Paddy and Mac. His face was turned to the ground, whilst his frozen body lay with doll-like stiffness. I rolled him on to his back. His mouth was wide open and spittle ran thinly from the sides of his lips. His matted hair was glued with charcoal and nits. The distant draw to death was drumming slowly, the pulse was weak. He lay unconscious, with his meths-ridden girl-friend sharing the same oblivion beside him.

I dispatched the drunken Kelly to fetch some wood to make a fire. He returned after a while with some long planks of wood. Wondering which building site he had swiped them from, I added them to the blaze I had got going with some cellophane and bits of rubbish. Clearly Singer ought to be got into hospital, but I knew of no hospital which would take him in that loused-up condition. I had tried before on other occasions.

"Yer can't do much for 'im, Sal; 'e's a goner," commented Kelly. "Listen, luv, you couldn't fix me up with a pair of shoes?

Size eight." How could he think of a new pair of shoes while his friend was dying? "I'll see what I can do," I promised, and he flopped down and instantly fell asleep.

A feeling of helplessness came over me. I began to pray. Singer did see the night through, and when dawn broke, and the light brought life, he stirred.

At five I nipped down to the market and scrounged around for some bruised potatoes and cabbage leaves: on my way back to the ramp I begged some bread off a baker and some water from a garage. I fed Singer the soup from a bottle top. This warm nourishment brought new strength, and as he drifted into a peaceful sleep the bells chimed the hour and the Sunday church-goers crept into their pews to take their communion. I spent the day with Singer, but as the evening came and it began to rain I began to worry — he would not survive another night out.

At about six I left him, and walked across London to fetch a car; on the way back I picked up a friend, Sue. We were back with Singer an hour later, and half carried him and half dragged him across the ramp to the car. We had difficulty getting him all in, and when we did he overlapped on to the driving seat. Sue meanwhile went back for his girl-friend, who, inseparable from her meths bottle, was staggering towards us clutching it. We somehow managed to push her into the back of the mini, and Sue very gamely climbed in after her. I slithered behind the driving wheel, propping up Singer against my shoulder. Within seconds of the doors being shut, the stench of meths and stale urine stung our nostrils. Furiously we opened all the windows, but even this provided little relief. I drove as fast as I dared to-wards Cable Street. I jumped the lights and accelerated. Singer was becoming heavy, and his dribble was oozing down my left hand as I kept hold of the gear lever. Betty was having hallucina-tions in the back and Sue was trying to pacify her.

At last I drew up opposite a derelict building. We waited for some cars to pass, and when the road was clear we grabbed the unconscious Singer and heaved and shoved him towards the empty building. I put my shoulder to the door and it swung open. "Dump him here and let's get Betty in before some curious passer-by decides to nose around." Sue brought her in while I cased the joint. The front room on the second floor was the warmest, with half a pane of glass still in the window. It also had a fireplace. I found some under-felt on the floor above and brought it down for the two to lie on. In another room I tore down some tattered curtains for them to use as blankets. When I had made it as comfortable as possible, I descended the stairs to collect Singer and Betty, who were both lying on the stone floor in utter oblivion. We bedded them down. Singer was ice-cold, and I could hardly feel his pulse.

"What about lighting a fire?" Sue suggested.

"Not yet. I'm going to leave them for an hour; with their clothes drenched in meths they'll go up in a blaze of flame if a spark comes in contact with them."

I had decided to go to Orange Street to see if anyone there could help. We climbed into the car and left the doors open for the night air to clear away the smells our passengers had left behind.

"They ought to be in hospital." Sue was echoing my thoughts. "Sally, I'm no nurse, but that man's dying."

"The hospitals won't take him in that state."

"Then what about the police? He'd be better off in prison."

"Yes, but he'd suffer all the agonies of going dry and being shut away. Sure it would help him temporarily, but in the long run it's a hindrance rather than a help."

"Maybe, but at least it would give him the medical treatment he needs at the moment."

Sue was right, and I knew it, although it went against my principles. I drove to the nearest police station where I recognised the duty sergeant from my earlier days in Cable Street.

"I thought you'd better know that there are two vagrants in a derry down the road."

"You wouldn't know their names by any chance?" I wondered if he was being sarcastic.

"As a matter of fact, I do. One's Patrick O'Leary . . ."

". . . and his girl-friend, Elizabeth Duncan. Meths drinkers. I know. Thanks for telling us, I'll send a constable down to throw them out."

"Throw them out?" I was horrified. "Aren't you going to take them in?"

"Them! Not likely! Heavens above, we have enough problems here without them coming in and lousing up the place and stinking us out."

I turned away, disgusted. His was a typical reaction, and one I would never understand. He was ready to throw them back on to the street and hasten their degradation, rather than make an effort to find a solution to their problems.

Sue and I pushed on to Orange Street. Vic Ramsey was in full swing administering the Word of God, and the beats were in full swing grabbing at the food that was being given out by his helpers. I was greeted with the usual enthusiasm, and asked if I had any spare 'bread' on me. I saw Flo Dobbie ladling out soup in the far corner, and edged my way towards her. She greeted me with a dazzling smile that always made one feel good. "How are you, Sal? We thought you might be down here tonight."

"Is the Colonel around?"

"He's sitting over there with two German friends who are staying with us. You must meet them, Sal; I've told them all about you. They're fascinated by your work, especially André, who's qualifying as a doctor."

"A doctor?" I could have howled with joy.

I found the Colonel with André and his fiancée, and explained the situation. They wanted to leave there and then but I was delayed by Paul, who asked me if I could find him somewhere to sleep. Having at last got him fixed up in a pad with another beat, Sue and I led the Dobbies and their German friends to Singer's derry.

The police had not called. The black mass that was Singer was in exactly the same position next to Betty as when Sue and I had left him. I bent over him and felt his weak pulse, and put my hand on his chest to feel his heart. It was dangerously slow. André examined him and confirmed that he was very seriously ill. We discussed the problem.

"There's only one way of getting him accepted into a hospital," I concluded, "and that's to dry him out, clean him up and take him there sober and not leave until the authorities have agreed to take him. He'll be sober in the morning, and probably desperately hungry. If you could bring some breakfast and some soap and water we can clean him up. I've got some clothes in the boot of my car that we can put him into and make him look a little more respectable."

I declined the offer of a bed for the night. I drove Sue back to her flat in Baker Street, and eventually bedded down at 2 a.m. next to Singer and Betty, on some old newspapers I had scavenged from Fleet Street on my way back.

I was awakened two hours later by an unusual noise. There were footsteps on the landing below. Police? No, the steps were slow and shuffling. The door swung open and I saw that it was Danny, extremely drunk. To my relief he turned away and continued upstairs.

Singer didn't stir. I was freezing cold, having given him my jacket as an extra covering. I tolerated it for another hour and then got up. Singer and Betty were still sound asleep and looked as if they would remain so for some time. I got in my car for warmth and drove around for some hours, ending up at the Dobbies' for breakfast.

Over large plates of bacon and eggs we discussed the problem of Singer.

"I think our best hope is to get him back into the hospital where he was before, for another alcoholic cure," I said. "At least they know exactly what they're up against with him."

"Will they have him back, do you think? I gather he discharged himself last time half-way through the course."

"I think that's up to us. We'll have to talk them down. But first we've got to talk to Singer himself. There's no point in doing

134

this against his will. He's got to be agreeable to going back into hospital. If he doesn't stay — well, we will have done our best."

Flo was preparing hard boiled eggs, cheese sandwiches and hot tea, and collecting flannel, soap and a towel.

"What are we going to do with Betty?" she asked. This was indeed a big problem that I had purposely forgotten about.

"You might well ask. She'll be furious with us for taking Singer off. But if she wants a fight, there's four of us."

It took us some time to reach our destination because of the rush-hour traffic, but when we arrived, armed with cigarettes and food, Singer was awake. He acknowledged me in a feeble voice, "Hello, Sal!"

"Where's Betty?"

"She's gone to the ramp to get my crutches. Hello, Mrs Dobbie."

"Hello, Singer, I've brought some German friends to see you."

Singer shook hands with them and broke into fluent German. When Betty returned with the crutches, which I had left behind on purpose the previous night knowing he could not wander far without them, we sat round a fire drinking hot tea. Singer was still expounding in German and enjoying every minute of it. I felt the time had come to get down to brass tacks:

"Well my old beauty, what are we going to do with you?"

His answer came somewhat as a surprise. "Oh, Sal, get me away!"

"But where to? No hostel will have you." I hoped he would make the suggestion I had been plugging towards, but Betty interrupted.

"Can you no' get us a flat, Sal?"

"Where are we going to get the money to pay for it?"

"We'll get a job, won't we, Singer?"

"Do you honestly think either of you could hold down a job?" I answered them frankly. "The first thing you must do, buddy, is to get yourself well. You need decent food and good sleep and proper looking after for a week or so."

135

There was a silence. Each one of us knew what I was insinuating. Singer sadly replied, "I'll go back into hospital if you want and finish that cure."

"Ye don't want to go back into hospital, Singer, you're all right." Betty had begun. For a while they argued between themselves, both tempers rising until I interrupted.

"Look, Betty, you love Singer?" She nodded her agreement. "Well, you know he's a very sick man – don't you want him better?" She looked sulky.

"Look, Betty, luv, I'll come back as soon as I'm out," Singer explained.

"You're not goin' in any bloody hospital." She was really roused now. Turning to me with her fist raised she shouted, "You're not takin' him. You lay a finger on 'im and I'll do yer."

"Betty, don't talk daft," Singer said. "She's only trying to help us."

"By sending yer to 'ospital?" She spat at my feet so that I should realise how disgusted she was with me.

"Singer, the decision's yours." I threw the ball back into his court.

"Well, Sal, I'd go but they won't take me like this."

"That's no problem; a bit of soap and water, which we have, a few clean clothes from the back of the car – they'll have you." I said it with the confidence I lacked. So we set about washing the man down whilst Betty watched scowling from her corner. We washed his nit-infested head, his neck and face. We discarded his shirt and vest and put them on the fire and then washed his almost black chest. We went to the nearest chemist and bought a razor. Whilst André was shaving him, I washed his stinking foot and put a clean sock on it. I scrummaged through the second-hand clothing in the boot of the car and came back with a white nylon shirt, a clean brown V-neck sweater and a sports jacket. As we carried him from the derry, no onlooker would have recognised him as the filthy dosser we had brought in the night before. Betty followed us out screaming curses and insults. As

136

I drove away, I called out to her, "Be on the ramp in the morning tomorrow, and I'll come and pick you up and take you across to see Singer — that is if you're dry."

At the hospital I left Singer in the car with the Germans whilst Mrs Dobbie joined me to add strength to my attack. The duty doctor was a middle-aged man with a rugged face that was pale and drawn, yet despite his obvious weariness his eyes were alert and sympathetic.

"Well, Doctor," I told him, "I won't beat about the bush. I have an ex-patient of yours of the name of Patrick O'Leary; he was admitted about three months ago for an alcoholic cure but he discharged himself a few weeks later; since then he has recognised his folly and would like to return to complete the cure." The doctor said nothing but turned to his filing cabinet and drew out a large foolscap sheet. He studied it for a few minutes before replying. "Where's he been these past few months? On a bomb-site?"

"Yes, we took him off it last night. He's dried out," I added.

"Where's his girl-friend?" How I would have loved to read that record sheet!

"She's in the East End at the moment; at least that's where we left her."

"Last time he was here, she was bringing in meths to him, and finally we had to stop his visitors; how prepared is he to toe the line this time?"

"Why don't you ask him? He's outside sitting in the car." Singer put on a very good show of sincerity. That he was a desperately sick man in both mind and body, I would not have disputed, nor that he really wanted to go through with this treat-ment at present. But whether after a week of good food and plenty of sleep and no crude spirits he would be feeling so much better in himself — then the test would come, and in my heart, much as I believed that Singer really meant what he said, I knew that it was hoping for too much. "Right, we'll have him in; he's really going to make an effort this time," the doctor was saying

137

to Mrs Dobbie. I wondered how many times relations had said it to pessimistic doctors.

From the car I extracted some pyjamas and gave them to Singer. "Yer will bring Betty to see me, Sal?" he was demanding.

It was against my wishes, but I had to stick by my promise. "Sure, I'll bring her across tomorrow."

With that, Singer was wheeled away in a chair and we sighed with relief. "I must dash," I apologised, "I was meant to be in court for one of my lads at eleven this morning; I'll see you, thanks awfully for your help and support."

As I had promised Betty, I turned up at the ramp in the morning. During the night I had found a fifteen-year-old girl on the run from a mental hospital, who had become involved with my beat friends and had taken some drugs and now the boys were ready to take advantage of her. I managed to extract her before they raped her. It then took me six hours of patient waiting before she recovered enough to talk to me. She had run away five days ago and hitched to London where she spent the night in one of the insalubrious dives of Soho until some boy befriended her and took her back to his room. Here he ordered her to undress and she refused. A scuffle followed and she managed to escape; disillusioned, she walked the streets and came upon the wandering beats who shared their bread with her. She followed them to their derries at night and watched them indulge themselves in drug-taking sessions. On the fourth night, depressed and tired with nothing better to do, she joined them and took her first 'smoke'. I found her being undressed by the lads that evening. By the time she had finished telling me her story, she was weeping. I did not sympathise or reprimand her, but let her stew in her misery whilst we drove to the ramp.

Betty was sitting alone on an upturned petrol-can smoking a cigarette. From the empty bottles beside her, I gathered she was far from sober. As I walked across the dump heap, she turned her back on me. I paid no attention but went and sat next to her.

"Morning, Betty!" She made no reply. I sat for five minutes staring at the rubble, and then quietly began to hum the tune, "My bonnie lies over the ocean"; half-way through the third time of singing it Betty swung round to face me and addressed me: "Where's my Singer?"

"In hospital. I'll take you to him in the car." Silence. I changed from humming to whistling.

"I ain't cleaned up and I ain't sober," she replied gruffly.

"Both of which can be rectified," I answered. After another minute she swayed to her feet and tottered towards my stationary car.

"Hop into the back, Betty, next to the girl," I said thoughtfully. I noticed the girl's look of horror as the stinking filthy woman clambered in beside her. I smiled to myself, as I put the car into first gear and drove away. "Betty, I'm going to drop you at the Dobbies' where you can have a bath and wash your hair and sober up, whilst I drive this kid back from whence she came."

"I don't want to go no place, I just want to see Singer."

"Which you shall do, but not until you've cleaned up." I changed into fourth gear, and through my rear-mirror watched her fiddle with the side windows; "Let me out of 'ere, I'm not goin' no place." I accelerated. "Let me out!" Betty screamed at me.

"I can't, Betty, there are no back doors to this car." I drove faster.

"Stop the car!" she ordered. "Stop it, I say!" Resolutely I drove on. Suddenly I felt her hands round my neck. With my elbow, I hit her arm away. "Don't be a fool, Betty, do you want to kill all of us and then there'll be no one to help Singer." She sat back in her seat and went into a sulk.

Needless to say, Mrs Dobbie was wonderful. She welcomed Betty as a long-lost daughter, and found her bath salts and all sorts of luxuries to help pacify her. I drove on to Chelmsford with the girl.

"Where's the hospital?"

"I'm not going back there," she replied defiantly.

"Oh! Where do your parents live then?"

"Don't want to see them." I drove on. In Chelmsford, I drew up outside the police station. "Get out," I said, opening the passenger seat door for her, "We're going over there."

"The police station!"

"Well, you don't leave me any alternative, do you?" I replied. She sat there sullenly chewing over the situation. Innocently, she looked up. "Okay, I'll play fair," she offered. "You can take me home, but you'd better ring them first. There's a telephone box over there." She pointed to one on the corner.

"I wasn't born yesterday." She dropped her eyes and actually blushed. I had been caught before with this one; whilst I'm phoning for them, they run.

"Take your choice now. This is your last chance." Once again she burst into tears.

I let her cry herself out, and then gently said: "Look, kid, you've had a hell of an unpleasant week. Whatever you've got to face now, won't be as bad as what you've just been through, believe me, so take a bit of courage and let's go home." I smiled at her and added, "Anyway there's two of us facing it this time." For the first time she smiled, and I suddenly realised what a very attractive girl she was.

We went to her home and I returned her to two desperately anxious parents. They gave me lunch and told me all about their difficulties with their daughter: how for no reason at all she had refused to eat and become desperately ill, and eventually how after two years the child welfare authorities had stepped in and put her under child care because they said the parents were unable to look after her properly. When she still refused to eat and became ill and difficult, the authorities had put her in a mental hospital. Her father concluded, "You'll never know the anguish it caused us when we were told that we did not adequately give our child the parental care she needed. You have no idea what we've tried to do for her; my wife has spent three hours at a time feeding her because she just refused to eat. After all, the child-care people have done no better than us."

I left a very disturbed family, yet knowing I was helpless to do any more than I had done. I commenced my drive back to London to pick up Betty. She was sitting there – spotless! Her fair hair sparkled with cleanliness; she had washed, cut and groomed it. Her usually rough face was smooth and powdered, and a slight touch of lipstick matched the delicate rosiness of her cheeks. She had dispensed with her filthy clothes, and now sat immaculately dressed in an outfit of Mrs Dobbie's. She grinned self-consciously as I entered.

"Woo-ah! Singer won't recognise you," I remarked with delight. "Are you ready to go then?"

"Och, woman, I've been ready to go for hours." I gave Mrs Dobbie a wink and opened the door for my elegant passenger. Betty talked non-stop all the way to the hospital, telling me all about her youth forty years ago, and how in her day she had been quite a 'peach'. Her mind was quite clear without the drink to befuddle it, and it boosted my ego no end to see her so animated and happy. On our arrival I tactfully let her go up to the ward by herself and said I would follow in about half-an-hour. She tripped up the stairs like an excited teenager going to her first date!

Whilst Betty was occupied with Singer, I made my way to another ward to see Keith who was in for a drug cure. I rang the bell outside the two massive doors of the ward. I heard steps approach, followed by the grating of the key in the lock. It reminded me of the mental hospital I had been in.

I walked past the communal bathroom into the ward. It was all in dull yellow, even the bed heads, except those that were chipped; the mustard coloured lino added to the general yellowness. It was more like a mortuary than a hospital.

"Hiya, Sal!" Keith had recognised me. He was sitting amidst the yellow in yellow striped pyjamas, his long fair hair draped over his shoulders. I began to wonder if I was going colour blind when I saw that his eyes were yellow to match the rest of his surroundings.

"What's the matter, Sal?"

"Nothing, I'm going mad that's all; everything seems yellow, even you."

Keith burst out laughing. "I've just had jaundice."

He had put on some weight and was not looking so gaunt, yet his eyes seemed very glazed for a person off drugs. "How's it going? Get a lot of pain or aren't you going 'cold turkey'?" Once again he burst into laughter.

"Come off it, Sal, you know the signs after all this time." I saw his hand quiver slightly as he put a cigarette in his mouth.

"You're not getting the stuff in here?" I asked amazed.

" 'Course I am; pay them enough and they'll bring anything in."

"Pay who?"

"The male nurses, or the guys that are allowed out, though you have to be careful there, because recently they've been searching them as they come in. Man, you can get anything you want in here, from purple hearts, black bombers, to meths and heroin."

"Where do you hide the stuff when you've got it?"

"In the locker – they never go through our lockers. Here, come and have a peek, I've got the whole 'jacks' here." I peered into the top drawer of his locker and saw his 'works'. I was dumbfounded. "But don't the doctors notice you're high?"

"Well, I'm careful when I take a dosage; I mean I wouldn't be so daft as to take one just before he comes to see me," he explained unashamedly.

"Where do you get the money from?"

"Anyone. Everyone nicks from everyone in here; the other night when I was asleep, some geezer nicked my N.A.B. money from my locker, so the next night I went and nicked it back and took his whilst I was about it."

"But, Keith, what's the point of coming in here for a cure if you're going to make no effort to give the stuff up?"

"Be reasonable, Christian. It ain't fair on a man to just cut him off his only salvation; they've got no idea of moderation. When they eventually cut me right off the stuff, I thought I wouldn't live. Man, the agony of it; as it was I nearly went berserk and tried to kill a bloke, and three of them had to hold me down. You wouldn't understand, you've never taken the stuff," he said, shrugging his shoulders.

"I'm trying to understand, Keith, believe me, I'm trying to understand."

"Sorry, Sal, it's just I've got to have it. Since I've been in here, I have been cutting it down." For me this was no compensation. Still, I could not see how the doctors did not recognise the symptoms; they must have known he was fixing on the quiet.

I felt utterly discouraged as I climbed the steps to Singer's ward; it was all so futile and pointless. Unless Keith was prepared to help himself first, no doctor, no psychologist, no parson could minister successfully to him.

Once again I rang a bell and the ward doors were unlocked. Singer was at the far end, with Betty sitting beside him. He was fairly doped, but already looked more like himself.

"Oh, Sal, it's great to be in a bed; I was at my last tether."

"I know, buddy, you don't have to tell me that; what do you think of your sparkling girl-friend?" Betty blushed.

"She's a chick," Singer replied admiringly. "A real chick." They sat holding each other's hands like a couple of newly-weds; it was incredible how far away we were from that infernal ramp, and to think in half-an-hour I would be returning Betty there – my heart ached at the thought. Yet I knew if I suggested putting her in a hostel she would automatically rear up in opposition; unless she was prepared to help herself, I was wasting my time and fighting a losing battle. If only I could put the idea into her mind!

I looked at my watch. "Well, Singer, I'm afraid I must take your girl-friend from you."

143

"Where are you taking her?" Singer had given me the opportunity.

"There's only one place where she belongs," I replied harshly. It had the effect I hoped it would. Betty flushed with anger, and Singer rushed to her defence: "Hey, Sal, watch what you say; she's as good as any woman. She's the finest woman here." I looked unconvinced. "Look how smart she can look and, see, she can leave the drink."

"Sure she can, for six hours at a time," I replied provokingly.

Betty was fuming. "Sal, can't you try and fix her up somewhere?" asked Singer.

"Sure if she agrees, but she won't agree, we both know Betty." Betty was nearly falling off her seat with irritation.

" 'Course I will," she replied hotly.

"There you are, she will," Singer repeated.

"You mean that, Betty? Truly? Where I can get you fixed up for the night you'll willingly go?"

For an instant she hesitated, and then said: "On condition it ain't going to be too far away from Singer."

What a sauce, I thought, but I was not going to query it, having reached this far with her. "Fine, right, that's fixed then," I concluded.

"Can you bring her tomorrow, Sal?" Singer asked.

"Yes, I should think so. Come on, Betty, it's getting late. See you, Singer, behave yourself now." I rose and walked away so they could have a few minutes by themselves. Meanwhile, I was racking my brains for ideas; though Betty had accepted the challenge in front of Singer, I realised that within a very short time she would want to back out. I had to act fast and firmly. I knew of no place near Singer that would take her in; all my friends who had flats lived right the other side of London. I knew she would not go into the Salvation Army or Church Army hostels.

Betty was at my side and talking to me.

"Don't 'e look better?"

"Much better. I only hope he'll stick the cure out, then he'll be really on his feet." As I said this, a vague idea passed through my mind. It was a brilliant idea if I could work it right. We got into the car as if to drive away, when I turned to Betty: "Singer was thrilled to see you looking so smart!" She giggled with pleasure. "Won't it be marvellous, if he can leave that hospital a cured man?"

"Och, Sal, it would be terrific," Betty mused thoughtfully.

"He'd be able to get a job, and have some money for some digs, and you'd both be able to go out to parties together."

"And it would all be thanks to you," she complimented.

"No, Betty, there's only one person who can help Singer back on to his feet, and that's the person he really loves and respects." Our eyes met.

"Do you mean me?" She looked surprised.

"Mmm, I do, only you. You could be setting the example after all," I explained.

"How do you mean, Sally?" She was interested.

"Well, to begin with you could also have a cure." I dropped the bombshell as calmly as I could. Her face was a mask of control as she sat there silently chewing it over.

"Where would I have to go?" She was nibbling at the bait.

I played my trump card, "Why not here, so you can be near Singer?" Her face relaxed into a triumphant grin.

"Okay, I'll have a try. When can I come in?" she enquired eagerly.

"There's no better time than now; come on, let's go and see the duty doctor." Silently I sent up a thank-you prayer to the good Lord, and together Betty and I made for the main hall. The porter put us in the waiting room, and we settled down to reading some crumby magazines. Half-an-hour passed before the porter popped his head round the door to say there was some trouble and the doctor would be a bit of time; another half-an-hour passed, and Betty was becoming fidgety and nervous.

"Och, Sal, let's go, I need a drink!"

"Wait a few more minutes, I'll go and see what's keeping him." Once again I approached the porter who said he was very sorry but the doctor was still being delayed. I returned to Betty, who was now striding up and down impatiently. "He's just coming," I lied, closing the door firmly behind me. In another fifteen minutes Betty had returned to her usual self, swearing and cursing, demanding that we left that instant, threatening to kill me unless I let her out. I tried pacifying her, but it was getting beyond my control as she began to crave for her bottle of meths. Suddenly she threw up her arms to punch me in the face because I was standing between her and the door; I managed to see it coming and ducked in time but still held my position; she swung round and swiftly made for the window. I did a splendid tackle, and brought her down. She was a heavy woman and a dirty fighter, but I was taller, much fitter and perhaps even a dirtier fighter! I managed to sit astride her stomach with my elbows resting on her arms; she lay there squawking with fury but totally unable to budge me from my tight hold. Suddenly the door opened and a wiry, fresh-faced young doctor entered: "Eh — which is the patient?" he asked as I helped the livid Betty to her feet and brushed her down.

"Perhaps you'd like to come into my office. I'm sorry for having kept you so long." Betty, sulking, followed him, and I came up behind her, just in case she was thinking of making another bolt. I explained the position once we were seated, and assured him Betty really wanted to take this cure; I only prayed he was not going to ask why I had been sitting on her.

"Well, obviously, we don't like turning willing patients away," he was saying, "doubly so if it may help another patient."

"Most certainly it will put Mr O'Leary's mind at rest," I assured him.

"Yes, very well then, I'll make arrangements for her to go to A1 ward." He went out to call a nurse, and I turned to Betty. "Well, Singer's less than three hundred yards away. I can't do any better than that for you; the rest is up to you." A nurse came in smiling cheerfully and led Betty away. Without a word to me, she went. Poor Betty!

It was dark outside, and I looked at my watch; it was nine p.m. and time I started my round on Waterloo Station.

The days seemed to fly, I had so much to cram in, yet not once did I miss my daily visit to the hospital. It gave me great joy to see both Singer and Betty so contented and well as they went from strength to strength. Meanwhile my visits to Keith had to cease when a male nurse told me that drugs were being smuggled in to him and that he was forbidden visitors except his immediate family. With a bottle of orange juice in my hand I tiptoed round to the side, to the window opposite his bed. Gently, I lifted it a few inches and peered in. I could see him in the far bed reading a book; a male nurse passed in front of me and I ducked, hoping he would not notice the window ajar. I hissed Keith's name and the chap in the bed nearest the window turned and stared at me, "What do you want?" he asked.

"The bloke in the far bed over there, please."

"Keith," he shouted, "there's a friend to see you — she's at the window." I could have throttled him for letting the world know, but no irate nurse came running. Feeling like a criminal, I knelt on the window-ledge. Keith got out of bed and came across. "Hi, Sal!" he greeted me. "Won't they let you in either? They found out I was still getting the stuff."

"That doesn't surprise me. Anyway, here's the orange you asked for." I passed it under the window.

"Thanks, Sal, you're a poppet."

"How are things going? You look much better. All the yellow's gone."

"I'm fine now; I'm going to discharge myself tomorrow. I'm fed up with this blasted place; you haven't got a 'pad' have you?"

"You're joking, boy! Even if I had, I wouldn't have you back there, you're much better off in hospital. Why the hell don't you have a real bash at this cure and stop mucking about? You're not being fair on yourself or your doctors, and more important, you're taking up a bed which could be being used for someone who's really prepared to buckle under. I know it's not easy, Keith, but nothing in life is given to us on a plate. We've all got to work at it, that's what life is all about. Why not just give it a try?" I pleaded.

He shrugged his shoulders amiably and replied, "Not me, Sal, I'm hooked good and proper; there's no cure for me, I know that. I'd better get back to bed. Thanks for bringing the orange." Bare-footed he made towards his bed, and as he did so he turned round and quietly said, "God bless you, Sally." I pulled the window down so that he might not see the tears in my eyes. I had never thought I would hear those words from Keith.

Next day he did discharge himself, and the rumour went round that he had gone home to Bristol, which gave me hope; but before the week was out I saw him coming out of one of the Trafalgar Square toilets, his eyes as glazed as ever.

Every afternoon I spent an hour with Betty and Singer; and Betty would never allow me to come empty-handed. "Sally, I need a brown handbag." "Sally, Singer needs another shirt now that he gets up every day." I lost many a friend taking their clothes from them, in order to provide for my two demanding friends. But it was worth it, just to watch them taking an interest in their clothes. My hour's visit was a jocular one; Singer never tired of telling me his Irish jokes — they were never-ending! I was glad that he could keep us amused and off the subject of the ramp. My hours with Betty and Singer during this period were some of the happiest I have ever spent, yet I did not deceive myself. I waited and prepared myself for the ending.

The first signs of discontent came from Betty three weeks later; she began talking about the ramp and the lads. Singer and I jollied her along, but our efforts were fruitless. The next day Singer was in a filthy temper and I was forced to make the conversation and tell my only two jokes! The day after, I arrived at the hospital to see a nurse approaching me: "Miss Trench, the matron would like to see you." Before I entered her office, I knew the gist of the story. Betty had got out and gone down to town and bought a bottle. She had returned with it to Singer's ward and between them they had consumed it and now, with Betty urging Singer on, they surged down the ward in full flight, cracking one man over the head with the bottle as he tried to stop them, and out they went never to be seen again.

I did not bother to query the small details: how were they able to consume a bottle without anyone noticing, and how did they get hold of the keys to unlock the ward doors? I did not really care – the point was, they had gone. Though I had been preparing myself for this, it choked me. Perhaps, it injured my pride more than anything and left me deflated. I wanted to blame God and say, "Why did you allow this to happen after all I had done?" And then I realised this was far more of a disappointment to Him than me, for it had not been through my strength that I managed to help Betty and Singer, but through His strength. I was just His instrument and had no right to have any pride. This knowledge helped me, but did not repress the pain of failure.

CHAPTER ELEVEN

Singer and Betty were back on the ramp again, and there I left them; from previous experience I had learnt that only when meths drinkers had reached the end of their tether and were close to death, did they turn to someone for help; I gave my friends a month of the ramp and then they would be begging for my assistance again. In fact, I was wrong, because a few weeks later they were picked up for stealing milk and brawling and were each given a month. I was glad of the rest!

With five of my meths drinkers now 'inside' I did not visit the ramp so often, but spent more of my nights in Soho; I visited most of the dives and memorised the faces belonging to them. It was interesting to see the same faces night after night at the same dive but as I frequented them more often, I realised that each club specialised in a particular type. One of the most popular drew the homosexuals. It was situated in a dark alley opposite numerous other obscene clubs. It was in the basement and cost five shillings; as I entered, I noted the little fat man, smoking a cigar nearly as big as his head, who gave me my ticket and locked the doors behind me. In fact the doors remained permanently locked unless the little fat man opened them.

I crept down the stairs, feeling rather conspicuous all by myself and entered a dark room, barely lit by the illuminated red bar at the end. Soft seats were round the room and people were dancing in the middle; the continuous loud pop music drummed through one's ears at first, though by six in the morning one hardly noticed it! I parked myself in the corner nearest the exit and just studied the youngsters dancing. Despite my mixing with young long-haired beatniks day-in, day-out, for the life of me, I could not differentiate between girl and boy. They all had long hair, effeminate faces and wore rings. They all wore bell-bottom trousers and long polo-neck sweaters which gave them no shape. The couples all danced very closely, some tickling their partners' necks or scraping their long, painted nails through their lanky hair. Some were embracing and kissing, whilst others were fondling each other and swapping love-bites. Suddenly the horror of it all dawned upon me — that they were all young men except for the odd one who had a woman. Watching them making love to each other made me want to vomit. I was still fixed with horror when a young man came and sat next to me. He was completely out of character with his short-cropped hair and tapered grey flannel trousers and sports jacket. He obviously thought the same of me as he looked me up and down.

"Would you like a cigarette?" he offered in a soft Irish voice.

"No thanks, I don't smoke."

"Where do you come from; you're new down here?"

"This is my first visit. Tell me, am I right, are all these people men?" I asked incredulously.

"Most of them — they're all homos." He laughed, "You look shocked."

"Do I? It's funny, I've seen a lot of iniquity, filth and sickness, but it's never made me feel quite so repulsed as this."

"Are you new to London then?"

"No, not at all; I mean I've seen and known many homos but just sitting here watching them make love to each other — ugh!" I couldn't go on.

"Well, what are you doing here anyway?" he asked curiously.

"It's somewhere to sit the night out," I replied.

"Haven't you got a pad? Are you on the run or something?"

"No — just N.F.A."

"You don't add up — a girl of your education roaming like this."

He was referring to my accent. "Well, if it comes to that nor do you? How come you're down here? Don't tell me you're a homo too?" I said.

151

"No, I've come down to get some smoke; I come every night for it."

"The peddlers are down here then?"

"Sure, most of the guys here are on horse, or pills."

"Don't the police raid it ever?"

"Occasionally, but no one ever keeps the stuff on them."

"Where do they hide it then?"

"In the Gents – here, I'll go and get you some," and he disappeared into the toilet, only to reappear a few minutes later with some hash. "This was hidden on top of the cistern," he explained, "but they hide it anywhere, sometimes in the centre hole of the toilet roll."

"Do you work?" I asked him.

"You joking? Of course not."

"How do you get the money to pay for it then, and keep well dressed?"

"If you come with me, I'll show you."

I followed him up the steps and out into the alleyway. It was a warm, mild night, and it was a relief to be able to breathe in the pure night air. We walked into Wardour Street and moved past the striptease clubs. We came to an open doorway and stopped. "Stand behind the door out of sight and watch through the crack," he ordered. He leaned himself up against the door post and watched the passers-by. He must have stood there about fifteen minutes before he nodded at a middle-aged man walking along the opposite side of the street; he was dressed in an immaculate dark suit and wore well-polished shoes; underneath his suit he was clad in a dazzling white shirt and a dark red bow tie. Not a hair was out of place as he crossed the road towards John with a spring of confidence in his stride. At first I thought John knew him, but as I listened to the conversation I realised how wrong I was.

"Good evening, sir," John politely addressed the stranger. "Were you wanting to see a show?"

The man hesitated.

152

"Your choice, sir, ordinary dull striptease for five guineas or two homosexuals performing, ten guineas, sir; or the best, sir, two lesbians — that of course is fifteen."

"Make it twelve pounds," the stranger bartered.

"For you, sir, I'll make it twelve." John handed him a ticket as he gathered up the notes. "Top floor, sir, door nine."

The man brushed past him and hurried up the stairs. He must have reached the first landing when John grabbed me by the hand and whispered, "Run." We sprinted down Wardour Street and turned into a side road where John halted, breathless with laughter.

"Couldn't be easier, could it?" he laughed.

"Do you mean there are no such shows on there?"

"Of course not, at least not in that flat. Sometimes I just give them an address and put them in a taxi and they go off to it all excited, only to find I've sent them to a warehouse or something." He burst into more laughter. "It's just too easy for words, because when they get there and find nothing, they can't do anything about it or go to the police, and I'm usually miles away by the time they come back to look for me."

"How much do you make a week doing this?"

"Average is about fifty pounds, sometimes less, sometimes more; depends if I can catch the right kind of guy. Usually the best type is the well-to-do frustrated married businessman who's told his wife he's got a board meeting and then comes into the West End for a bit of excitement. There are hundreds of suckers around."

"One day you'll be the sucker when you do it to a copper."

"Maybe. Meanwhile, I've plenty of money and live well — like to come to my pad for the night? We can have a smoke back there."

"No thanks, I'm not that sort."

"What are you going to do then?"

"Probably go and spend the rest of the night in the Spit and Fizz," I answered.

"I tell you, you're safer in my pad than there."

"That's a risk I'd prefer to take. Anyway it's been nice to meet you – in fact quite a revelation."

The Spit and Fizz was reputed to be inundated with young people on the run; I think the main reason was that it was the only club one could go and sit in without having to pay an entry fee nor buy a drink. It was grotty like the people who ran it, but it had a roof and was a place to sit out of the rain throughout the night. The only rule they had was that no one could sleep there, and periodically a big brawny fellow would come round the benches and kick those who had drifted into sleep awake. Prostitutes wandered in and picked up young kids who did not know what it was all about. Every other night it was raided by the police and they never went away empty-handed. Homos wandered in to try their hand with some new kid. It was the same every night as I watched the child's eyes brighten as the homo stuffed a five pound note in his pocket and then together they moved off. I stayed here till the dawn broke and then took a walk down to deserted Piccadilly Circus. I had just reached Shaftesbury Avenue when a flashy American car drew up beside me; a man in a dinner jacket was at the wheel and his girl-friend, sparkling in diamonds and mink, was in the passenger seat.

"What's matter luv, looking for a girl-friend?"

You dirty-minded beast, I thought, but calmly replied, "No, just a sugar-daddy, I gave her the boot the other day for kissing me on my big toe." They roared with laughter which surprised me.

"That's great – can we give you a lift somewhere, honey?"

"No thanks, I'd prefer to walk."

"Isn't it dangerous for a lone girl, walking the streets at night?"

"It's safer walking the streets than getting into cars with strange men," I replied curtly, thinking this would close the conversation. Instead he laughed again and turning to his girl-friend he remarked,

"Isn't she cute – give her a dollar for her breakfast tomorrow."

154

I stood there stunned for a minute, wondering if I had heard right. The girl-friend drew a pound note from her purse and gave it to the man. "Here," he said, "I like a girl with spirit. Take this."

I hesitated. "Go on, take it, kid, there are plenty more where I come from," he drawled. I took it.

It was Sunday. Late Night Special was over and the beats were drifting away into the night. I was with Kinky Cowboy and Little Jack who were discussing where they were going to spend the night; Skinny Jinx joined us. We decided to sleep in the York Terrace derry. This large house, behind Madame Tussaud's wax-works, was at the rear of some of the most expensive property in London, fronting Regent's Park. Although it was Crown property, the interior was a complete wreck and had been used as a pad by destitute beatniks for over a year. There was only one snag and that was getting in, for the doors and windows were bolted; if you did not mind heights it was a piece of cake, but if you suffered from vertigo, as I did, it was purgatory. I had done it before, shinning up the long drain-pipe of the house next door, clambering across the flat roof and down into the pad. On this night, though I accompanied the lads there, I was not prepared to do the climb, so I left them as Kinky Cowboy began his ascent.

It was over twenty-four hours later that I saw them again, at three in the morning in Covent Garden.

Cowboy's voice boomed out aggressively, "Why didn't you come into the pad with us last night? Did you know?"

"Know what?" I had not an inkling what he was talking about.

"You bitch, you did know, didn't you?" his eyes were full of suspicion.

"Jack, what's he talking about?" Little Jack was white and drawn, and was twisting his fingers with nervousness.

"The body!" Jack spat out.

"The body?" I repeated. "What body?"

"I found a body." Cowboy's voice had a note of pride in it.

"A dead one," Skinny Jinx added.

"Anyone we know?" was all I could think of saying.

"Yes, but I'm not going to tell you, because you already know." He really believed that I had not followed him into the pad because I knew that there was a dead body to be found there.

It was Skinny Jinx who explained what had happened. "Cowboy climbed over the roof, as you know, and he was going to try and let us in so that we didn't have to shin up the drain-pipe. When he was creeping down the stairs to the cellar he fell over something, but being so dark he couldn't see anything, so didn't think twice about it. At least not until the morning when we noticed he was covered in blood; so we went down to investigate. The body had been hidden under cardboard boxes and whisky bottles, and we could just see this leg hanging out. We would have left there and then and said nothing, but Cowboy's fingerprints were all over the joint where he had fallen. It was a right mess; his head was battered in and the maniac who did it had bound and gagged him; there was blood everywhere."

"Who was the guy?"

"We all knew him as Dave — he used to visit the Duke a lot." I knew many Daves at the Duke. "What did he look like?"

"His face was so battered, we couldn't see."

Cowboy, less furious now, interrupted, "The police kept us for hours. I bet they think we did it."

"Oh! I don't expect they think you did it, Cowboy; after all you did report it. They probably kept you to help with their enquiries."

"It weren't too bad, really; they treated us quite well," Skinny Jinx mused.

"Let's get hold of a paper and see if our names are in it; hey, we could make our fortune out of this. Let's go and offer an exclusive story to one of the papers for a price," said the unperturbed Cowboy.

"F... off," replied Jack, "I don't want any more to do with it."

"Well I'm going down Fleet Street, this'll make us famous," Cowboy shouted as he moved away. "After all I know who the murderer is." Jack and Skinny Jinx followed him.

It was in all the national papers next morning, though no names were mentioned. By midday the police had identified the body, and his name appeared under the small passport photograph in the *Evening Standard*. I recognised it instantly as a drug addict whom I knew fairly well. I read the brief paragraph over again:

> "Scotland Yard are appealing to beatniks and drug addicts for information about the associates of David G——. He was found dead on Monday morning in the basement of a derelict building."

I sat motionless, remembering an incident in Lyons about a week ago. I had been alone drinking a coffee when a tall youth with a college scarf approached me; all I knew about him was his name was Sid. "Sal," he had said to me, "You wouldn't know where that bastard, G—— is? He's done me, he was meant to be getting me some pills and he's got my money."

"No," I had replied, "he'll probably be at the Duke tonight, though," and Sid left. Later that evening, the rumour was that he had been going round asking everyone if they knew where he could get a revolver from.

That night I wandered the streets, my conscience tearing me apart. I knew it was my civil duty to go and give this information to the police, but I also had a moral obligation to the youngsters who trusted me and gave me their confidence. If I should 'rat' on him and the other beats should find out, my relationship with them would be a closed book. No one had liked the dead man. As one of the lads had remarked in the Duke, he deserved what he got; Sid had not been the first he had double-crossed. By morning, I had decided to give the information anonymously over the telephone. But I was to make a very foolish mistake. Not sure where the murder enquiries were being held, I asked a policeman; instantly, he was on me. "So you've got information, have you? You'd better come with me." He dragged me off to his police box where he rang St John's Wood police station. My heart sank; of all the places in London, it had to be my own local police station, where most of the policemen knew me. The policeman was thrusting the receiver into my hand, "Here, you'd better speak to the detective sergeant yourself."

"I have some information that might help you with your enquiries, but I have a few complications with it," I explained incoherently, wondering how I was going to explain myself.

"We'll send a car round for you right away," the voice came back.

"Oh, no, please not, that would be disastrous." I could imagine the lads' faces if they saw me being driven away in a police car.

"Well, can you come direct to the station here?"

"Not exactly." It was just too risky if my parents were about. "Would it be possible to meet you somewhere else completely? I'm sorry for all this secrecy but I can explain it when I see you." So it was agreed that we should meet outside a tube station in an hour's time. The green Wolseley was there as I came out of the station; a pleasant-looking middle-aged man, whom I presumed was the detective sergeant, was behind the wheel, and beside him sat a young well-built man. As I approached them, the young one got out and opened the back door for me. I climbed in.

The older man addressed me: "I understand you have some information for us regarding the body found in York Terrace last Monday."

"That's right."

He suddenly produced a photograph before I could continue, and said: "Who's this – do you recognise him?" It was a very youthful picture of Dave. I identified him at once.

"Did you know him well?"

"Not exactly; he wasn't a personal friend, but I knew him to talk to."

"When did you last see him?"

"About ten days ago, at the Duke of York."

"When did you last go to York Terrace?" I was slightly taken aback.

"I walked along the road last Sunday with Kinky Cowboy, but I haven't slept there going on three months now. Look, can I explain my position before we go any further?"

"Certainly, go ahead."

I told them everything, emphasising that I would be very grateful if they could keep my visit to them quiet. They were very co-operative and kind, and having written out my statement covering over two pages, they let me go. They asked me to keep my ears open, and stay in touch with them, and then suggested that if I could visit the Soho dives that Sid frequented and let them know if I met up with him, it could be of great help. I made no promises, the last thing I wanted to become was a policeman's stooge.

I was relieved to leave them and return to Trafalgar Square, yet glad I had done the right thing; later that afternoon I bought an *Evening News* and under the caption *Interpol Join Hunt for Beatnik Killer,* I read:

"This afternoon five men and a girl were being interviewed at St John's Wood police station, after the girl had dialled 999 in the West End and said she had vital information about the murder."

I wondered if that girl was me?

One afternoon in the Square I met Rex mooching around with a little girl; she was dressed as if to look in her late teens, but her refreshingly youthful face gave her away. "Hi, Christian, come and have a coffee?" Rex offered.

"You're feeling in a very generous mood," I commented, for it was the first time Rex had ever offered to buy me anything. We went into a café nearby and Rex told me how he was about to have his first record made. He was very full of himself, and I was forced to let him rattle on for a good fifteen minutes before I could get my say in. "Where's the girl from?"

He turned and looked at the silent youngster on his left. "Dunno — where are you from?" he demanded.

The child blushed and said nothing. "Nowhere," said Rex, "apparently."

"Where did you come across her?"

"Don't rightly know; one minute she wasn't there, the next minute she was, since when she's never left my side."

"You don't want her as a millstone round your neck, do you?" I asked.

"Not really," he agreed.

"I'll take her from you if you want," I suggested casually.

"You're welcome; if you don't, I'll only sell her for a dollar to a Pakistani."

I was glad he was agreeable. When he had finished his coffee, he departed leaving me with the youngster. She had long well-groomed hair and a fair, spotless complexion; her clothes were clean and of good quality.

"What's your name? I'm Sally."

"I thought he called you Christian," she answered in a soft, well-spoken voice. I wondered if I had mistaken her age.

"Christian's a nickname; I prefer to be called Sally."

"I'm Amanda."

"When did you arrive in the Square?"

"What Square?"

"Trafalgar Square. You're obviously a new girl around here." She did not answer, but blushed again; I tried another line.

"How long have you been in with Rex?"

"About an hour."

"Where did he pick you up?" I knew Rex well.

"In Dean Street, in Soho."

"Lost your way or something?" She nodded the lie.

"Well I guess you're better off with me than a Pakistani."

She looked at me in horror. "Wasn't he joking when he said that?"

I pretended to look surprised, "No, of course not, don't be so naive." I had plenty of experience when it came to lying.

"What would happen if he had?" she questioned fearfully.

"Oh, he'd do what they all do — tear off your clothes and get at your body." Tears began to stream down her cheeks in disillusionment.

"But he seemed so nice and kind," she pleaded.

"So what! He's still penniless without a girl like you to support him, isn't he?"

"You mean — " When the word came out it was almost swallowed up in shame and distress, "prostitution?"

"Well, of course, what else do you expect? Of course they all end up having abortions, but that wouldn't worry you!" She swallowed and went as white as a sheet as she listened to me rambling on. "Well, what else are little girls made for, especially ones so young and pretty as you; you're what's called a sitting target." By the time I had finished with her, she was a very frightened child indeed.

"Where do you live?" I asked her gently.

"Portland Terrace, opposite Hyde Park."

"Would you like another coffee? When did you last eat?"

"This morning; can I have another coffee please?"

We both had second cups before I said: "Right, let's go."

She shied away from me her eyes popping out of her head with fear. "To my car." I took her by the arm and pushed her ahead of me. Once in the car, I locked the door.

"Are you a policewoman?"

I laughed. "No, you'd be in a mess if I was."

"Where are you taking me?"

"Wait and see; tell me, how old are you?"

"Fourteen."

"Still at school?"

"Yes."

I took a guess. "Convent school?" She blushed again.

"How did you know?"

"I didn't; it was just a guess. What did you come up here for?"

She had lost her fear and was talking quite freely. "I don't really know; kicks I suppose. I've often seen the people in Trafalgar Square, and think I would like to be like them, free and independent."

"You call it freedom and independence?" I queried. "Where's the independence when you have to rely on other people for your food and money? Where's the freedom when you're being moved on all the time by the police? Where's the freedom in having to con and beg? Where's the freedom when you're caught in a network of destruction and become a slave to drugs or alcohol?" Her eyes were filled with fear again as she wept. She cried: "I didn't realise it was like that, I had no idea . . ."

I interrupted her sternly. "No, and you didn't reckon that I'd find you before you got yourself into serious trouble either. You'd better thank the Lord your luck was in."

We had reached Portland Terrace.

"You're not going to tell my parents?"

"Not this time—but if I ever catch you down there by yourself again, I'll not only inform your parents but also your headmistress at school, and this is no idle threat," I warned her.

She climbed out of the car. "Thanks for bringing me back."

"You're welcome, just don't let me have to do it again," and with that I drove off. But she left me thinking, for this was how so many like her came to be on the road in London. Many from perfectly secure and happy homes saw my young wandering beats demonstrating their so-called emancipation, with no ties or responsibilities, and fell under the deception that this was freedom; and by the time the initial glamour of it had worn off and it had become a drudge it was too late to go home, for the parents had by then severed the relationship. I had caught Amanda in time.

Now that I had been on the road for a year with the beats, I could divide them into three classes; the permanent beat, who never wanders further than the Square or the Duke of York; the homing beat who wanders off for the season or a weekend but always returns to the Square; and the wandering beat who can never stay in the same place for more than twenty-four hours.

The permanent beat was the most obnoxious; he went around owning the whole of London, expecting everyone else to comply with his wishes and know his face. Being in one area they usually slept in pads, having found and worked on a sugar-daddy from the first day of their arrival. All strangers were brusquely brushed aside and taken advantage of without exception.

The homing beats were loyal and patriotic members of the Square, and sucked up to the permanent beats who shared their pads with them if they felt it would be worth-while. Otherwise they skippered in derries, always returning to the Square in day-light. They usually went about in groups, having met up with other kids from their own town.

The wandering beats were the lone wolves. They were the most tough and most grotty, sleeping anywhere and everywhere; far more self-reliant and having more initiative, they kept on the move; an acquaintance of all and sundry, a friend to none. But whatever classification they fell under, not one had any respect for the opposite sex, and only the very occasional one had any manners. They all blasphemed in every sentence without fail and their minds were pathetically imprisoned with sex or drugs.

When a new face came on the scene, one ignored it until it approached you. That was how Jess first introduced himself to me. He was a tall, skinny fellow, and reminded me of a runner-bean. He had honest eyes and a large generous smile. I was sitting on the steps of Trafalgar Square as the rain poured down. It was evening, and most of the kids had moved off to the Duke of York. Jess slouched over to me and without invitation parked himself beside me.

"Where do you come from?" I began the conversation.
"Channel Isles."

"Arrive today?"

"No, some days ago I got in; been skippering since; what about yourself?"

"Been here a year; come from nowhere and going nowhere," I replied.

"Sounds enterprising!" he commented, and I laughed dryly.

"Come and have some chips, I've just about enough for six-pennyworth."

And that was my introduction to this intelligent and sensitive boy. He attached himself to me without any encouragement on my part; from our first meeting I felt he was an unusual beat, and he became the first and only beat I knew who had any kind of manners. I was also to notice, as time went on, that these began to slip. Within three months of mixing with the kids in the Square he was swearing like a trooper and had his arm round anything in a skirt. It had not taken long to change him into a completely different boy. I was to discover that Jess had gone to a public school, and was the son of a literary scholar. Unfortunately I never discovered what made him hit the road, but from my knowledge of him it could have been social rebellion.

Another, similar to Jess, was Tony the alcoholic, a tiny unassuming Irishman who, though full of Irish blarney and charm, never managed to con himself some digs. He was young and clean and stood by his principles; he had a derry in New Compton Street, and it was like an obstacle course getting to it! But once there, it was a good hide-out with an old Victorian bed to sink into. Tony was an acute alcoholic; if he was unable to get any conventional form of drink he would not think twice about consuming surgical spirits or eau-de-cologne. Yet when he was sober, one could not be introduced to a more pleasant boy. The times I've picked him up off his face and supported him to some cover and stayed with him for fear of the police picking him up! Sticking like a leech, I've followed him, waiting for the moment when he reached beyond his own strength, and would be forced to call out for my help. Then came the process of drying him out, a process that made him sick for some days, getting him on his feet and finally back to work. I usually had a couple of months' rest before we repeated the same procedure. Tony's drinking problems went back six years when his junkie girl-friend committed suicide and her body was hauled out of the Thames. To hide himself from the horror of realisation that he could have foreseen this tragedy, or perhaps even stopped it, he turned to drink and was soon drinking to vile excess.

Tony's story is like a hundred others and his ruination is like a hundred others. None of them were sick in body, but all of them were sick in mind with a harmful addiction; together I watched them rot, helpless. All I could do was pray that God would keep His guiding hand on them.

CHAPTER TWELVE

"Everybody has a right to be loved." The words were mine, the voice was mine. "We were made by love for love." The kids puffed at their dog-ends, but they were listening; the stench of sweet wine wafted through the darkness as the bottle changed hands.

"Why don't my Mum want me then?" a young voice challenged.

With all my heart I wanted to give Dustie a satisfactory answer but as so many other times before, I had none. "Well then, Sal?" he persisted, leaning over his girl-friend's legs and grabbing at my jerkin, pulling me within inches of his shaking body. In the semi-darkness I could see his puppy-like face was contorted with rage and bewilderment. "Love!" he bleated, "F . . . love. Tell us, Sal, what is love?"

Someone cuffed him. "Lay off, Dustie, leave 'er alone." He released his grip and sat back discontentedly. I watched him draw a syringe from his pocket before he added, "Ain't got an answer 'ave yer, Sal?" He wiped the needle on his shirt cuff. I groped for words.

"Dustie, the meaning of the word love to me is to give. When you stop giving you stop loving. When you stop loving you stop growing." He began to take off his belt and wrapped it tightly round his arm which was scarred with burnt-out veins.

"Love is your passport to life, Dustie." I threw it out in desperation as he plunged the needle in.

"Save it, Sal." Someone was trying to spare me. "We know what yer tryin' to get at and we love yer for it — 'ere puss, pass us a fag — but yer wastin' yer time on us, Sal."

"We're done for — there ain't no hope for us," another voice said.

"Ay! Speak for yerself," another piped up from the far corner.

"Who's sittin' on the bloody vino then?" a sleepy voice floated through.

"Can yer no' sleep for . . ." Scottie was interrupted as the door downstairs was smashed open and the heavy steps echoed in the room beneath us. "Fuzz," someone hissed, and without a sound we emerged from our corners and crept towards the back window. In an orderly fashion, we filed out on to the window-ledge and one by one shinned down the drain-pipe of the derelict building which had been our haven for the past week. Without a word or a glance we separated and drifted off into the night, probably never to meet again. Some would go underground, some I would possibly meet tomorrow night, and others would spend it in a cell. They came and they went, young and vulnerable; they passed on hurt and bitter. The night swallowed them up. I pushed my hands into my jeans pockets and deliberately quickened my pace for warmth. I heard footsteps following me and a lanky, sparsely clothed youth drew up beside me.

"Where yer off to, luv?"

"Just walking, cooling my heels you might say."

"Come an' 'ave a coffee wiv me?"

"No thanks mate, don't drink coffee," I cheerfully replied.

"Tea then?" he persisted.

"No mate, don't like tea – nor milk," I added quickly.

"Wot do yer drink then?"

"I don't. What goes in, has got to come out!"

He guffawed. "Yer jokin'."

"No, I'm quite serious, put it this way, it's just more convenient if I don't drink; still, I'll take a hot dog off you," I offered. We wandered through Soho, past the shuttered cinemas and empty theatres.

"On the road?" he enquired.

"Yes and you?"

"Came down from Manchester yesterday, with an empty pocket. Suppose yer dunno any mates who're flushed, like?"

"You're joking!" I replied in return.

167

"Forget it. I'll see yer around then," and he left me.

Cad, I thought, trying to con another down and out! And I never even got the hot dog! I turned down Greek Street, where the odd man lounged optimistically out of the shadows as I passed. I peered at my watch under the lamplight. It was three-thirty. It would soon be dawn, and with it came the security of daylight.

"Hey, Sal." It was Sheila. She was panting heavily, and her long tangled hair fell in rats' tails over her face. "Quick, help Jinnie." I could see she was very frightened. "She's gone and done herself."

"How do you mean?"

"I was going to my room and I saw her lying there . . ."

"Take me to her," I ordered sharply. We turned back down Greek Street and ran up to Shaftesbury Avenue. "Come on, stop lagging," I urged my friend as she struggled to keep up with me. "Anyone else seen her?"

"No," was all she could gulp as she tried to draw breath. We tore towards the coloured lights of the striptease clubs.

"How long ago did she do it?"

"Dunno, I only just found her a minute ago." She pointed to a doorway and we began to ascend the stone stairs. Sheila had taken the lead, and on reaching the second landing flung the door open. I pushed by her and nearly fell over Jinnie's body. I crouched beside the nearly naked figure and felt for her pulse. She was lying on her back, clad only in her underclothes, on the bare floorboards. Only then did I realise I was squatting in a mass of blood. She looked dead, but I had caught a very weak pulse beat, her body was still warm . . . "Call an ambulance," I shouted to the stricken Sheila, standing like a statue in the doorway. "There's a call box on the corner, dial 999 — for God's sake, woman, pull yourself together! Hurry!" The door swung shut, and I heard her descending. I took off my jerkin and covered Jinnie and then I saw the long thin blood-stained knitting needle. I stared at it in horror. I thought I was going to faint. I fought down the nausea and, steadying my hand, I carefully withdrew it. The blood poured out. I crossed her legs, hoping to somehow control the haemorrhage, but it just seemed to pour out all the more. I tore her vest from her back and made it into an absorbent pad. Then I just prayed.

I heard the flurry of steps as Sheila started up the stairs, so I shouted to her, "Stay downstairs and wait for the ambulance so that you can show them up." Thankfully I heard her go down again. Jinnie lay motionless, her thin cadaverous face expressionless. She hardly looked her seventeen years. "Where's that ruddy ambulance?" I cursed under my breath. I found myself fingering the knitting needle and needlessly wiping the blood from it. Of course the police would have to be informed, and so would her parents. They would certainly not want her home now. Perhaps she might not live? It would be the best thing for everyone if she did . . . Oh, God, what was I saying? But what would become of her.

"They're here, Sal." Sheila's voice forced me back to reality. I strode to the door and blocked Sheila's view. I was not sure how much she had seen previously. From behind her appeared the ambulance men with their stretcher. They lifted the limp body on to it. "You'd better come with us, Miss," one of them said, as his eyes fell upon the knitting needle I was still holding. "The law will have to be informed, you know."

"I quite understand. You won't need my friend, though?"

"Who found the body?" He talked about Jinnie as if she were already dead.

"I'll come, Sal, she is my friend you know. I don't mind." So together we climbed into the ambulance. The siren squealed and the brakes were released.

"Nasty bit of work that," the ambulance man commented. "Don't understand what makes a kid do a silly thing like that — what drives them to it?" I could have told him, but I didn't.

"Do you know her?" he was addressing me again.

"Yes, quite well; she's been in London a year."

"Was she . . . er . . . well . . . you know?" It was funny how he was frightened to use the word.

"A prostitute, you mean?" I said helpfully, "Yes, she was."

"They all come to a bad end." I nearly throttled him.

"Is she going to live?" Sheila asked, as he took her pulse for the third time. The sirens stopped as the vehicle halted; the back doors swung open and Jinnie was lifted out.

For two hours Sheila and I waited in Casualty; occasionally we picked up a magazine, but though our eyes read the words, our minds were far away. We paced the corridor, looked up expectantly each time a nurse passed us, and then threw ourselves wearily back into our seats. At last the sister appeared and briskly asked us for details about Jinnie. We gave what information we could.

"Did you know she was pregnant?" she asked.

I heard Sheila gasp with surprise.

"No," I replied. "Jinnie never talked much, and certainly never about her personal life."

"Did she have a steady boy-friend?"

"I couldn't honestly tell you; she had a lot of friends," I hedged. "How is she — is she going to live?"

"She's lost a lot of blood — we're giving her a transfusion now." She rose as if to go but I grabbed her arm.

"That doesn't exactly answer my question," I pointed out boldly.

"Dear, I can't, only the doctor can answer that question," she gently replied and took her leave.

The hours passed slowly. When it was daylight, a policeman arrived. We went through the same rigmarole of questions. Sheila was exhausted and fell into a fitful sleep. I took a short walk in the cold nippy morning before joining her. Just before midday a nurse shook me out of my drowsiness. I wondered what the outpatients sitting opposite me thought. "Miss Trench, Doctor Sage thought you might like to know that your friend is going to be all right." Sheila, who had been aroused by her voice, burst into tears of relief. If she hadn't I probably would have done.

"When she wakes up, will you tell her we were here and we'll come and see her tonight," I asked.

"Yes dear, now why don't you both go home and get some sleep?"

"Yes we will," I lied, and firmly taking Sheila by the arm went out into the sunlight. If only that nurse knew the impossibility behind her utterly reasonable suggestion!

That was the first of seven abortions I had to deal with over the next six months. Some, like Jinnie, survived them; some did not; and those who had, wished they had not. What happened to them afterwards? The hardened ones returned to their old life in Soho and would chalk up a few more; the very sensitive ones suffered the loss of their self-respect, and having only rejected society before, now rejected themselves. If they did not successfully commit suicide, they were placed in mental homes; some were sent to centres administered by the Home Office; the rare case went home.

Sometimes the kids asked me to visit their homes to plead for them with their parents; I always found this disheartening, for I felt that if one had to persuade the parent to have her child back, the child was possibly better off without the parent. Often I found the parent was obviously in a more neurotic state than the kid, and sheer fear of any more problems forced them not to take on this further responsibility. The more I went to their homes, the more apparent the reason became why the kids could not, or would not get on with their families. More often than not, the obstacle in the relationship was not total lack of love, but total lack of trust. It was not helped by neither side acknowledging the others' limitations, or always undermining the other's accomplishments. Every human being is looking for self-perfection and subsequently self-fulfilment, therefore, instead of maturing a relationship by assisting one another, petty jealousies and pride took predominance and the relationship suffered. The more I visited these families, the more aware I became of the

171

frightening responsibility of parenthood. As time went on, I found myself sympathising more and more with the parents, and less and less with the kids. Not being a parent myself I could not fully understand, but I felt the burning desire of a distraught mother to help her sixteen-year-old daughter who had started taking her first doses of heroin and cocaine. Again, I felt the tears of hopelessness of a father weeping for his son as he was led away to start a Borstal sentence. The cruelty of youth, I discovered upon reflection, was that we expected adults to resolve every problem, overcome every difficulty and make every decision correctly because of their status as parents, and it never occurred to us that they were no more equipped for life than we were. For me it was a shattering discovery.

We were all outside the Duke; it had closed early after trouble had broken out between two junkies, and the police had to be called. I was sitting on my bed-roll, with my back against the wall, dozing. I had not been to sleep for two nights, having spent them on the ramp with Steela Horse, who had burnt off three of his toes earlier that week. I had no idea where I was going to spend tonight. Tiny Geordie, his arm round a girl, came and sat beside me.

"I've got a message from Freddy."

"Freddy? Which Freddy?"

"Freddy the queer. He's going up to Newcastle tomorrow, and should you hitch up there, you'll be able to find him in the Forth Café where they all hang out."

"Thanks. I can't somehow see myself going up there for some time." I yawned, and stretched my legs out across the pavement.

"Where are you kipping?" Geordie asked.

"Haven't really organised myself yet; thought I might go to that derry in Camden Town; I looked in on the one in South Kensington the other night and it was full of Germans and froggies."

"That's miles away; if you'd like to come with Annie and me, you're welcome; it's a lovely derry and not very far from here."

"I'm ready when you are."

"Okay. Annie, shall we go there now?" She grunted something inaudible and snuggled into Geordie's chest. "Wait five minutes, she's a bit tired. She came in from St Albans today." We continued sitting there.

Jess came along and fell over my feet. "Stick 'em in," he shouted as he went on his way; to which some youth replied, "Don't be so vulgar!" and silence once more reigned.

"Come on, Sal, we're off." Geordie was hauling me to my feet and lifting my bed-roll on to my back. On the way Annie managed to con half-a-dollar off an American and we bought a packet of cigarettes from a slot machine.

It was only eleven o'clock when we reached the derelict. It was in splendid condition. Every window had glass in, the door was all in one piece, and some of the rooms even had curtains. "There's only one snag, and that's getting in," Geordie explained. "I'll do the climbing if you stand in the doorway." With the agility of a cat he climbed over the spiky railings and for a second balanced there as he judged his jump over the gap with a twenty feet fall; he landed perfectly on the window-sill and clambered through the top window. The next minute, he had opened the front door for us. "Top floor," he ordered as he placed a row of milk bottles across the doorway.

We climbed the carpeted stairs and I heard Geordie locking the door behind us. It was a small room on the fourth landing. "Cosy, ain't it?" Annie commented with pride. It was bare except for an under-felt on the floor and curtains over the window. In a corner, stacked neatly, were a couple of bed-rolls and blankets. "Who do they belong to?" I asked.

"The other kids who come here." Geordie had joined us and was spreading his bed-roll out, so I followed suit in the opposite corner. "I shouldn't sleep there, Sal, that's where Ralph pisses when he comes in drunk. Jenny was lying there last night and he pissed all over her." I quickly moved myself to another corner.

173

"Actually, we have all mod cons here. There's a lavatory next door, though no flushing water, I'm afraid."

"Why the devil doesn't Ralph use it then?"

"He's so drunk he doesn't know what he's doing; do you know, the other night he must have climbed over the railings to get in and missed his jump on to the window-sill, for we found him unconscious at the bottom of the basement. I thought he was probably dead. Anyway, Annie and I lifted him up and put him in the room nearest the door. When he woke up next morning he didn't remember anything about it. Ralph's as tough as nails – he's a dirty-minded bastard, but you can't help liking him, can you?" Geordie summed him up in a nutshell. "Hey, wanna fag?"

"No thanks, I don't smoke."

"You a Christian and all that?" Annie asked.

"Yes – and all that!"

"Oh, God!" she groaned, and Geordie butted in:

"She's not like the others, Annie; Sally won't preach, she's not a religious fanatic – just a working Christian." I snuggled into my sleeping-bag. It was extraordinary, these kids all reacted the same if they discovered someone was a Christian. To them, a Christian was a religious fanatic who only had one topic of conversation – God – and someone who never smoked, drank or allowed his hair to grow. This was the idea which was put into their minds by naive evangelists who worked amongst the beats to spread the Gospel; to these narrow-minded preachers, Christianity meant one couldn't go to a cinema or a dance, and they told the beats that juke boxes were part of the devil's work! These well-meaning people were doing more harm than good towards the daily practice of Christianity.

"She looks after the meths drinkers in the East End," Geordie was explaining to Annie. "I must come over and see them some time, Sal; perhaps I could help by conning food for you."

"Great!" I commented, as I took off my leather jerkin and made it into a pillow for my head. I was beautifully warm. The half moon was shining through the window, and outside the

174

night was so clear I could see all the stars. Geordie and Annie lay enveloped in each other's arms in one sleeping-bag. I could see the burning tips of their cigarettes resting on the carpet. "Don't burn us to death," I whispered, and saw Geordie untwine his arm from Annie and put them out. I must have dropped off when I heard footsteps coming up the stairs; the door swung open and a voice said, "We're the police." Someone behind the figure that loomed in the doorway, giggled. "I arrest you in the name of the law," the voice came again.

Annie stirred. "I didn't know we had the London Palladium with us."

Three grotty bodies entered; in the dark with their long flowing hair, they all looked like girls.

"Who's here?" one asked.

I heard Geordie mumble, "F. . . off, we're trying to sleep."

"F. . . off yourself, you c. . ."

"Don't make so much bloody noise."

"Anyone got a fag?"

"Put the sleeping-bag down, Selby."

"Get off my back, man, I want a fag first."

"Shut up, you two, or I'll kick you in the . . ."

"I'm going to have a piss." He turned towards the corner.

"There's a lavatory next door," I suggested.

"You dirty pig, Les, do as the girl says."

"Who are you, anyway?" One of them was addressing me.

"I'm Sally," I answered.

"You're the Christian I met earlier this evening."

"Am I?" I had not a clue to whom I was talking, and was too tired to really care. I wished they would all shut up so that I could go back to sleep.

"Selby, give us a draw?" The cigarette passed between them.

"God Almighty, I wish I were back in Chicago."

"Button up, man. This is one of the best derries in London."

"Man, I think it's crumby."

"Keep your bloody opinions to yourself, mate." It was Geordie.

175

"I wasn't talking to you."

"I was talking to you, though."

"Belt up all of you!" I raised my voice so as to be heard.

"F. . . off." One of them kicked me. I paid no heed.

"What's the bloody time?"

"One-thirty."

"Why can't you come in at a decent hour?" Geordie was talking.

"Because this c. . . here took us walking round looking for the bloody place; we started off in a derry with some froggies, but they expected us to lie in their shit, f. . . froggies."

"Do pipe down!" I urged, and curled myself into a smaller target for Selby's boot; he caught me on the ankle, and I pulled my sleeping-bag over my head so that I did not have to listen to their language. Again, I dropped off and must have been asleep for some minutes when a beam of light fell on me. I froze still. The beam slid from my sleeping-bag over to the huddled forms of Annie and Geordie. Everyone else was still sleeping. I suddenly realised that the torch beam was coming through the window; this meant that someone must be on the roof of the building opposite. In the silence I heard quiet voices and then a shout, "There he goes!" I jumped out of my sleeping-bag and crawled over to the window and edged myself up. Geordie was quick to join me, and Selby was on my other side. "Is it the fuzz?" he whispered.

"Must be, they've just shone a light in here."

"Look!" Geordie exclaimed. "It's Jock!" A crouching figure was scurrying over the roof; in the moonlight we could see the frightened face of the young beat. As he mounted a drain-pipe, three figures appeared on the roof in pursuit. They must have seen Jock, because they ran across the roof like lightning. "Go on, Jock, hurry!" I heard Geordie whisper. "He'll never make it," Selby was saying. Jock was parallel with the second floor windows, skimming with experience down the pipe when the policemen reached the top of it; but from our position I could see a police car making towards us from down the end of the road.

"If he keeps his head and doubles back and goes down the drain-pipe at the back, he could lose them."

"Not a hope, them fuzz know all the tricks."

Jock had decided his best way was to get to the ground and run for it. He must have seen the approaching police car, because he was literally falling down that pipe, trying to make up time; and then it happened. He had outspeeded his own capabilities, and instead of stopping and losing seconds to regain his balance, he lost his nerve. He seemed just to let go. As he fell, he let out a blood-curdling scream. He lay absolutely still in the road, the three policemen above stood motionless, and we crouched painfully with every muscle taut, terrified for Jock. The police car skidded to a halt and two plain clothes men stepped out and bent over Jock's body. "Do you think he's dead?" I gulped. "God, what a fall! Did you hear the crunch as he hit the road?"

"He must be dead," Selby said.

"Please, God, no." And I began to pray. At the end of it I heard everyone awake say, "amen". From the Middlesex Hospital we heard the ambulance siren, and then it appeared streaking towards Jock's prostrate body. It was amazing that no one else in the street had heard the rumpus, for it was a residential area. Jock's body was placed on a stretcher, and with three policemen to accompany him, he was driven away.

"Phew! Poor bloody Jock."

"What the devil was he up to there anyway?"

"Casing the joint, probably."

"Could be another derry, and when he heard voices he lost his nerve and ran for it."

"Jock's too experienced to do that, surely?" I argued.

"Och! You can never tell with these Scotsmen."

"Watch it! Keep down; there are some policemen on the roof still." We ducked and crawled back to our sleeping-bags. "Pass us the fags, Les," Selby whispered. The beam of the torch shone through our window. We flattened ourselves against the wall. "Keep as still as you can," Geordie ordered. "Put that bloody fag out." We all sat motionless, hardly daring to breathe. "Did you lot shut the front door when you got in?"

"Yeah, but I heard some guys come up after us," Les replied.

"Well, if they didn't shut it, the fuzz'll be in here soon enough."

The flashing torches continued to throw a strong beam into our room, but the six of us had by now crawled under the window and the beam could only flash on to the opposite wall. We sat in a close bunch for half-an-hour in complete silence. I think we were all wondering how Jock was. Eventually it was Annie who broke it. "Can I have a fag, Geordie? It's all quiet now, they ain't around. If I don't have one soon, my nerves are going to bust."

"Wait and I'll have a look." Geordie knelt under the window-sill and cautiously raised his head and studied the road below, and the building across the way. He watched for five whole minutes before he gave the all-clear. "Okay, let's have the fags."

"That was a close shave; I feel sorry for Jock when he comes round."

"If he comes round," someone dismally replied.

We all sat there musing; I shut my eyes, which were watering with the cigarette smoke. And then we heard it. An almighty crash. Silence. And then the heavy steps of boots climbed the stairs.

"Cigarettes out," someone hissed. We followed the loud steps into every room. And then the boots were on the landing beneath us. He threw every door open wide with a crash, and seemed to tour every room until he was satisfied that no one was hiding in any corner, nook or cranny. The boots were climbing the last few steps. They clumped to a halt outside our door. We waited. With a forcible crack the boot landed on the door and it smashed open. I saw a pair of eyes searching the room. This is it, I thought, I'm going to be nicked; and for the first time in my life I had no excuse. The boots entered, and smashed against poor Les. I heard him swear under his breath.

"Well?" the voice belonging to the boots bellowed out. I could not think of anything to say. My first thoughts were that they would need more than one black maria to take us all away. "Well?" came the voice again, "What's the matter with you all?" I recognised that northern accent instantly.

"You fraud, Ralph," I broke out, relieved, and everyone simultaneously burst into hysterical giggles. "Those wretched hob-nail boots of yours sound just like those the police wear."

"I didn't think it could be Ralph, 'cause his step was so firm."

"I'm dead sober tonight, if that's what you mean," Ralph protested.

"Why did you have to look into every room before you got here?"

"I was looking for Jenny, she ain't been around since I gave her those love bites and socked her one last night."

Everyone re-lit their cigarettes and settled back to relax. Ralph began to clump around. "Where's my blanket?" he demanded. "Hey, you bastard, you're lying on it." He thumped Selby.

"So what, mate, I got here first."

"F . . . off!" Ralph let rip with both feet. Selby's shadow buckled up and he began to whimper. Les rose to his feet, his fists clenched, and a fight was about to start. "For crying out loud, all of you, we've had the police here once tonight. You're asking for trouble if we have a free-for-all here," I pointed out in desperation. "Ralph, you can borrow my blanket if you like." Anything to avoid trouble.

"Come on, let's get some sleep around here," a voice said.

"Here you are, Ralph." I produced the blanket.

"What's the time?" another voice asked.

"Four o'clock," someone replied. Ralph spread the blanket over himself, having taken off his boots; the smell was atrocious. I laughed to myself as I remembered the first time I had slept in a derry, wondering whether I was safer keeping my boots on or taking them off! It was fantastic that a year had passed since those hard and lonely days. A whole year since I left the Simon Community! I saw it in my mind as clearly as yesterday. Yet so much had happened, and I had learned so much since then, that I would have thought the memory of it would be distant. Not in the least.

At last I fell asleep. I awoke when the sun was pouring through the window. I looked at my neighbours, huddled together for warmth; I counted nine heaps which I presumed were bodies lying under coats, blankets and dust sheets. I glanced at my watch; it read six-fifteen. It was time I departed, for I had promised to meet someone at seven. As quietly as I could, I rose and rolled up my sleeping-bag, leaving my blanket over Ralph. I picked my way between the bodies and through the front door. Crash! Milk bottles went flying and splintered all over the pavement. I cursed volubly and scuttled out of sight, quite certain I must have woken the entire district.

As I passed the Middlesex Hospital I popped into Casualty to enquire about Jock. The nurse was very informative, and told me that he was suffering from shock and had broken both ankles and injured his head.

I was glad he was alive.

CHAPTER THIRTEEN

I FELT no pain, no sickness, no fear, just numb. Quietly and deliberately I counted the minutes. Without panic, or wasting what.little strength I had left, I waited for them to turn to seconds. Time was running out. Now people were rushing madly round me; an ambulance had been called – but it would arrive too late. Pleasant, almost Utopian recollections flooded in a mass of confusion before me. I think I laughed, but no one heard it. Blurred, frightened faces, outstretched arms, sweet comforting voices slowly dissolved as I felt myself being dragged down, away into the vacant distances. So this was death? A soundless voice emerged from the vacuum: "Of course, delinquency starts at home, not in the schools." I gave a mental reply: "True! but you must remember that in this affluent society, adolescents tend to have much weaker family ties, and consequently they should be compensated by a stronger sense of guidance and security in their school life. Let's face it, this recent rise in delinquency seems to have occurred in conditions of an equally rising materialistic welfare." The seconds were passing, and I was dying, and delinquency was rising. Oh hell! what does it all matter? I am no longer a part of it any more, I'm dead. I had made a final comforting recession.

I lay between the crisp white sheets, gazing at the bare clinical walls. "You awake, dear? Can you turn over on your side so I can give you this injection?" I heard the words but they had no meaning. "Nurse Gallay, will you help me turn this patient on her side?" I wanted to struggle, but the effort was too great. I felt the pin-prick, and as a wave of nausea swept over me, I suddenly realised I had been given a fix. Struck with panic, I fought to keep my eyes open and my faculties functioning. What bastard had hooked me? So I was a junkie now. What did it matter? I slept. Now someone was leaning over me. My eyes were sore and burning and my head ached. I focused on the white coat, and then on the tourniquet round my arm. The doctor was taking my blood pressure.

"How are you feeling now?" he asked, on seeing I was awake.

"Peculiar," I grunted.

"Not to worry; that's the adrenalin we've pumped into you. It'll wear off soon. You gave us quite a fright."

"Sorry," I muttered dispassionately.

"Another few minutes and you would have been dead," he added for good measure. "You mean to say you've never had a reaction to penicillin before?"

"No, never."

"Well, don't you ever look at it again; you're highly allergic to it, and the next time you won't last long enough for anyone to call an ambulance. We'll give you a disc when you leave here, and make sure you keep it on you." He turned away to tell the nurse to continue to take my blood pressure every hour. I felt utterly stupid and deflated. After all I had survived these past few years, what an undramatic way to die! Not stabbed, not raped, not struck down with some terrible disease I had picked up in the grotty haunts I frequented! Just allergic to a penicillin tablet which the doctor had prescribed for blood poisoning in my jaw. I felt a buffoon.

Like everything that had ever happened to me this enforced rest was not without a purpose. It gave me the time which at one stage or another every one needs — to review the past and plan out the future. I wondered how long I could remain morally and mentally unharmed if I stayed on the road. I endeavoured to analyse my motives for returning to this arduous existence. Putting these factors aside meanwhile, I had to consider the inevitable that had happened. I was in love and due to be married in the following month. Our intentions were to emigrate to Australia. As exciting as it was, it became a painful decision to carry out. He would have to leave his family to whom he was very close, and I would have to leave my work. Like most engaged couples, we had our doubts; we would have been adventuring forth in the true pioneering spirit, penniless, homeless and jobless. But all that was important was that we had each other. Yet God had different plans for us both. Fourteen days before the wedding my fiancé called it off. I was left stranded, bitterly hurt, yet I understood his reasons perfectly. My first reaction was to return to the road directly and lose myself in other people's problems, but instead I sat on my emotions and allowed my judgement to rule me. What future had I continuing work at that level? Eventually I would weaken and be dragged down. One can stand alone for so long, but the break would come! I kept telling myself that God had made a community, to live as a community, to be community builders, not to be alone. I suddenly realised I had yet to learn to work compatibly with other people, and that as long as I failed to communicate or blend in with ordinary normal people I would never mature. The axle of existence amongst my beatniks was my daily communion with them; why should it be any different for others?

I ditched my dosser clothes and went home. My days were spent ringing up the employment bureaux, or visiting the local welfare departments in search of work. I wrote up to various social organisations offering my services. I had interview after interview. No one wanted me. What use was I to them unqualified? They were not interested in my practical experience: they really could not care a damn for what I had achieved over the last four years, because it was not down in black and white on paper. I would be a menace rather than a help, because I would act on instinct and not knowledge, they politely explained. Angry and disillusioned, I walked about London convincing myself that someone, somewhere was waiting for a person with my experience – somewhere there must be a niche which I could fit into. Deflated by continuous rejections, I began to seek employment in other fields apart from social work. I tried the BBC, the newspapers; I answered box numbers in the personal column of *The Times*, but it was as if I was doomed not to land a job.

The tables were reversed – I had come from a field of work where I was important and needed to a level where I was a nobody and utterly unwanted. At this juncture it would have been easier to turn my back on society and return to where I knew I was welcomed and accepted. At the same time I knew that if I took that course, there would be no reprieve. In my heart, I was fully aware that my work at that level had come to an end, yet the forces of progress niggled me and I searched for a way to continue this vocational work. I had experienced youthful lawlessness and a deliberate cult of amorality; now had come the time to use this knowledge to the best advantage. Yet how could I, when no one wanted to listen? It was like reaching a crossroads, and each lead I took ended in a cul-de-sac. Coming face to face with my inadequacies, and frustrated by other people's intolerance, I began to yearn for my old life on the road. At least I was doing something constructive there, even if it was a poor second best because I was unqualified!

It was in desperation that one morning I contacted a professional social worker about the possibilities of working in a youth club. Her reaction was similar to everyone else – undisciplined and untrained, I could be more trouble than good. My heart sank.

"Of course, your answer is to get yourself qualified," she said.

"Me?" I replied in horror. "No one will have me with only three 'O' levels."

"You're young and intelligent enough to acquire some more."

"But I haven't studied for six years."

"So what? Believe me if you want to continue doing social work, you have no alternative; anyone else will tell you the same."

"They have," I moaned. "My brain's too rusty to start getting exams."

"Nonsense! Just a bit of will-power and determination, and of course self-discipline which you won't like." I left her office knowing well that what she said was true – I had no alternative, but whether I had the self-discipline to settle down to a routine day of swotting at books was another question altogether.

I worked out a time-table, decided to take two 'O' levels and two 'A' levels, and then viewed the possible courses I could take if I passed them in six months' time. I discovered exactly what I wanted in a college at Birmingham, a two-year course on youth and adolescent work. This became my goal.

I went down to Soho and explained my plan to the kids; it was greeted with the same scorn and disbelief as I had received from my family. "Gi' over, Sal, yer no' cut out to be a book worm," Creeping Jesus had said. "Wot's goin' to happen to us while yer gettin' all that crap into yer head?" "So you're swapping sides and becoming one of them." This summed up their attitude. I had become a traitor. I wondered if I should ever come back as a professional social worker; whether I would have to earn their acceptance or whether because of my newly enrolled status, I would always be unacceptable. I said a sad farewell and returned to my books.

The first few weeks were unbearable. Sightless, my eyes read the words of the history book in front of me; diagrams on the opposite pages miraculously transformed into pictures of the ramp. At night my dreams were of the derries I used to sleep in. It was like an addiction – I lived, smelt, breathed, 'the road'. I was drugged with it, I thought of nothing else, it was like being hooked; but unlike drugs my craving was purely a mental state and not a physical compulsion, so it was just a question of mind over matter. Hating every minute of it, I forced myself to the library every day where I sat and swotted. I had little encouragement; understandably my friends and family were sceptical. This made me all the more determined to prove them wrong. I kept to this routine during the day, but most nights I managed to visit the ramp and see the lads. I received a tremendous welcome every time, intermingled with just a few curses because I had not been bringing them breakfast recently. Of course I was always forgiven, and affectionately they pulled my leg about becoming a student. They were far more sympathetic to my plans than the young beats. In fact, they were pleased. "Good on yer, Sal," they repeated numerous times. "Don't forget us, though," they always added. How could I?

I had managed to get myself accepted for college and was due to go up in the autumn. I had four months to kill, so I combined visiting the ramp with studying in order to try and get my brain functioning full-time, rather than at brief moments when I had nothing else to think about. One of my visits was to Kelly, who was now living in a cellar down on a Stepney bomb-site. Just like the old days; it was night, and my pockets were crammed with cigarettes and candles for them. I jumped the low brick wall and diligently side-stepped the fallen chunks of masonry. Once in the dip, out of sight, I turned on my torch and entered the jet black caves. Some of the lads were already asleep, curled up under newspapers. In the far cave I found Kelly and Pat sharing a cigarette. Pat jumped to his feet and offered me his milk crate. I declined, and instead squatted next to the horizontal body of Kelly.

"How are the legs?" I asked him, lighting a candle so as not to waste the battery in my torch.

"Shockin', Sal; 'aven't been able to leave 'ere all day to go conning, they're so painful."

"Those heavy boots don't help," I pointed out. "Anyway, let's have a look at them. I've got some first-aid kit on me." I rolled up his trouser legs and tried to pull off his soleless riding boot. It was not only stiff with mud but far too tight round his calf.

"When did you last take these off?"

"When you last dressed my ulcers; some weeks ago, ain't it?"

"Wriggle your foot, here it comes." The boot slid over his heel, revealing a pussy blood-soaked bandage. The smell was over-powering.

"Coo! don't 'alf stink!" Pat had never known what the word tact meant! I unwound the filthy dressing in order to see the ulcerated leg. From his kneecap down to his ankle the flesh had

186

been eaten away as if some animal had been feeding on it for the past few weeks. Horrified, I dressed it and calmly said, "Leave the boot off tonight and I'll take you to the hospital tomorrow. I think you ought to have it looked at."

"Yer not takin' me no place, Sal. I ain't goin' there. They don't take to me and I don't take to 'em."

"But it needs attention; can't you forget your differences this once?"

"Nope; yer go on dressing it for me and it'll turn." I wished I had his confidence. I left them the food and moved out into the night air. I shuddered to reflect how I used to pass nights in that squalid depraved cellar. Briskly I walked across a few acres of derelict land, thankful to be out in the open. I bounded across another wall and on to the road. Under some arches and into a narrow unlit side street with boarded-up warehouses on either side. Half-way down this street, wedged together for support, were two crumbling houses. I tried to kick the door open but it would not budge, so carefully I slipped through the smashed window. I took three steps to the right, five forward, and three back to the left – one night some dosser would break his leg falling down that hole! I heard no noise and wondered if they were here. I climbed the disintegrating staircase and as I did so the sweet sickly smell of meths hit me like a whirlwind. They were here! I edged the door open and saw six bodies saturated in methylated spirits strewn out like flattened sacking. None of them would be wanting to tell me their problems tonight! I found a space littered with rags and bottles which I shoved to one side and promptly laid myself out. I was very tired, having not been out on an all-night stint for some months; it was strange how quickly I had adjusted back to a relatively normal pattern of existence. Sleeping normal hours, eating proper meals, digesting normal conversation; it had been my world once, and I had rejected it for this. Had it been worthwhile? Oh yes, a hundred thousand times yes. Every second, every minute had been worthwhile. I had not just been part of a social revolution, but had been grounded in a social culture that society, rather than trying to understand, had deliberately rejected. No, there was nothing to regret, and the more I thought about my future, the more certain I became that to return to society and work from that level was the right move. Very content with life, now at home in either environment, I drifted into sleep.

I was wide awake and it was still dark. The lads were snoring away. What had alerted me so suddenly? Perhaps the pungent smell of the wood fire? I lay back, ill at ease. No one stirred. I closed my eyes and took a deep breath. That's strange, I thought, there was no fire when I came in earlier. I opened my eyes wide and momentarily froze with fear. "God Almighty!" I screamed, jumping to my feet and in one leap reached the door. As I opened it, my worst fears were proved; flames were leaping up the stairs. I rushed back inside and leaned out of the window; it was a thirty foot drop and no drain-pipe. "Get up you lazy bastards," I screamed, simultaneously kicking them to consciousness. I knew this would anger them and consequently wake them up. "Come on you drunken swine!"

Neil was the first to gather his inebriated wits together.

"And wot in the neem of the devil's the matter wi' ye?"

"Fire! Take a man with you and get down those stairs before I throw you down!" I lifted him to his feet and dragged another muttering man up and shoved him into Neil's arms. "Get out!" I yelled, thrusting them on to the outside landing. I grabbed at the insalubrious bundle of humanity nearest the door and hoisted it towards the stairs. Neil and his bundle had disappeared through the flames, which were beginning to creep towards us. The heat was scorching, and the noise of the devouring flames fantastic. The bundle in my arms collapsed in a heap on the landing, so, hoping that God was on his side, I rolled him down the stairs and, grasping another staggering body, followed suit. Like a pair of bullets we exploded through the fire head over heels. Now the flames were behind us and we were sprawled across the poor unfortunate bundle I had sent down ahead. He was still oblivious

188

to his surroundings. Coughing and spluttering, inhaling smoke, we pushed and pulled the bundle into the street.

"Och, Sal! Is anyone else in there?" Neil was asking.

I gulped before replying. "Yes. Get these lads away further down the street in case the building collapses and then find a telephone and ring the fire brigade. Hurry now!" I exhorted. "Hey, lend me that overcoat!" I grabbed it from him and ran a hundred yards down the road to where I could see a puddle. As I laid the coat in it and soaked it thoroughly, I remember thanking God for having let it rain. Then throwing it over my head, I galloped like a charging blinkered horse into the burning house.

To this day I do not know how I ascended those stairs of charcoal surrounded by walls alight with flames. It was a miracle. The heat and smoke choked me, and my hands burned agonisingly as I groped for support. I flung myself from the blazing landing into the room. The wizened face of Joe, emaciated, smiling drunkenly at me, appeared through the smoke. Lying beside him was the comparatively virile baby-faced Sandy. "Up!" was all I could wheeze. Joe shook his head sadly and pointed to the crabbed body beside him. "Come on," I choked, as I hauled Sandy across my shoulders. Again he shook his head and gesticulated that we should get a move on. What the hell was the matter with him? If he could get on his feet he could totter to the landing — if there was any landing now? Sandy was becoming heavy. I turned to see if Joe was coming. I made one last desperate appeal, "Please, Joe!" and as I leapt into the flames I heard a surprisingly sober voice cry out: "Sal, bury me in my boots will you?" The intense heat was like a red-hot iron branding its stamp on shrivelling flesh. Leeched to Sandy, I floundered forward. We somersaulted through the air, then quite suddenly re-established contact with the ground. It was black and smouldering, and as I crawled to my knees it was as if I had landed on the spine of a hedgehog. Someone was lifting me up. I wondered whether Sandy had landed in one piece. And what of Joe? What had he asked me to do about his boots?

189

"Hey, put me down, I'm okay!" I ordered. "Joe's still in there."

"No kid, not any more." We watched the roof crinkle slowly and finally melt into the roaring flames. Joe was in there somewhere.

It was not till the next day, when I was narrating this story in full detail to the police, telling them how I had managed to re-enter the burning building in a sodden overcoat, that I was corrected. "You must be a bit confused. It hasn't rained for five days." I sat dumbfounded.

"You're sure it was a puddle?"

"Absolutely certain. I couldn't have gone back in there for Sandy otherwise," I explained.

"That's the young meths drinker isn't it?"

"Yes," and as an afterthought, "I left the old one in there to make his own way down, but he wouldn't come."

"That was Joe Sayers wasn't it? Oh well, I can probably tell you the answer to that. We found him at the bottom of the gents' toilets the other night, stone drunk. Well, we didn't want to nick him, and since he obviously had a broken ankle, we dropped him off at the hospital, and quite by chance the following morning one of the constables was doing some routine checking round there and the night sister coming off duty told him that Joe had hobbled off with one of his meth-drinking mates before they had a chance to attend to him. Suppose he knew he hadn't an earthly chance last night. He's no real loss, he never did anyone any good while he was alive."

I was weeping. "What's the matter with you, you got the rest of them out alive!"

"It's not that. You got Joe all wrong." There was no point explaining to this police officer the epitome of my cause; the Joes who demanded nothing, the Joes who never advertised their plight, were the people the world rejected, judged and con-demned. To me Joe Sayers is a hero, but to the world he was a dirty foul meths drinker, and my one regret which will be for ever with me is that I was never able to carry out that last request.

190

Whether I become a detached professional social worker or remain an immature do-gooder, too involved for my own good, only time will tell, but I thank God He has shown me the potency of love and tolerance.

And that puddle with no rain? Only God can explain.

ST JOHN OF THE CROSS

ST JOHN OF THE CROSS

His Life and Poetry

GERALD BRENAN

WITH A TRANSLATION OF HIS POETRY BY
LYNDA NICHOLSON

CAMBRIDGE
AT THE UNIVERSITY PRESS
1973

Published by the Syndics of the Cambridge University Press
Bentley House, 200 Euston Road, London NW1 2DB
American Branch: 32 East 57th Street, New York, N.Y.10022

Library of Congress Catalogue Card Number: 72-83577

ISBN: 0 521 20006 7

Printed in Great Britain
at the University Printing House, Cambridge
(Brooke Crutchley, University Printer)

TO CYRIL CONNOLLY

Contents

CONTENTS

Illustrations

Preface

St John of the Cross is the first Spanish poet I read when I went to live in Spain. He did not at that time seem to be much known or appreciated except as a writer on mysticism for I could find no separate edition of his verse and had to read it in the big *Autores Españoles* collection of the lyric poets of the century, with its small, almost illegible print and cheap paper. But the impression he made on me was very great. No other poet in any country seemed to me to have reached such heights of lyrical expression and that is an opinion I still hold today.

Later, when I went to live in London, I decided for my first apprenticeship in writing to try my hand at a biography. I chose as my subject Saint Teresa, more because the material for her life was abundant and the psychological interest considerable than from any special interest I took in the mystics, though on starting to explore the ground I was delighted to discover what a large part St John of the Cross had played in her affairs and how vivid and dramatic his story was. In this way I spent more than two years on research in the British Museum till, finding the subject too remote from my other interests, I dropped it and left my book unfinished. However, thinking that some day I might take it up again, I continued to read any new books that came out on the religious life of the period and in 1934 I visited all the places that were especially connected either with St Teresa or with St John of the Cross.

Then in 1947, at the request of Cyril Connolly, I wrote two longish articles on St John of the Cross's life and poetry for a series entitled *Studies in Genius* that was coming out in *Horizon*. They were well received and I thought that some day I would republish them in a small volume together with his poetry. But when in 1969 I felt myself free to do this, I saw on reading through my articles that they were full of inaccuracies, partly because I had written them too rapidly, but also because new material on him had come to light and been published by Father Crisógono de Jesús and others. I therefore decided to write an entirely new and much fuller life, making use of the recent research that had been done on St John and his age and also revising and expanding what I had said about his poetry. This is how the present book came to be written.

A few words are needed to explain the principles adopted by Lynda Nicholson in her translation of the poems. St John of the Cross is notoriously difficult to render in English verse. One of the reasons for this lies in the luminous purity and simplicity of his language. It is very precise and economical and completely lacking in rhetorical constructions and in amplifying nouns and adjectives. In his best lyrics every word tells. This offers a strong temptation to his translator to fill out and pad and, if he decides to adhere to his rhyming pattern, to twist and distort the content in his search for a rhyme.

Seeing this, what ought the translator to do? He has three methods open to him. He can either offer a prose crib which accurately conveys the sense, but kills everything else. Or he can employ a fully developed verse form, complete with rhymes. This will have the poetic quality and consistency of an original poem, but it will necessarily be in the poet-translator's own style and manner and so be far removed in both its tone and its content from the original. It will be a parallel version rather than a true translation.

Then there is a third approach which attempts to steer a course between these two methods by following the text as closely as possible, yet at the same time conveying some of the qualities of its poetic form. In order to be free to do this it will abandon the attempt to keep to a fixed rhyming pattern, but will suggest one by means of assonances whenever it is feasible. That is the method offered here. It implies that these translations do not stand as perfected verse forms in their own right, but serve as mediators to the originals. Thus while no rendering can do justice to St John of the Cross's poems, these not only give the reader something very near their prose sense, but catch in many places their rhythm and intonation. Then across the page stands the Spanish text. Anyone who has spent a few weeks in Spain and has a feeling for poetry should find this accessible to him with the help of these translations.

Malaga   G.B.
November 1972

PART ONE

THE LIFE

Silencio fue su lenguaje
Y los yermos su poblado;
Estregaba en los zarzales
Su cuerpo muy delicado
Por tener dentro de la carne
Espíritu libertado.

Fray Ambrosio Montesino

1

Childhood and Youth

St John of the Cross owes his fame to being one of the greatest and most uncompromising of the Catholic mystics. It is less known that he is one of the supreme lyric poets of any age or country. It is in that capacity that I am writing about him here. But no poet's work can be properly understood without some reference to his life and this is especially true of St John of the Cross whose best poems are autobiographical, though in rather a peculiar sense. That is why some preliminary account of it seems to be called for.

As it happens, it was a very extraordinary life. Merely as a story it is full of dramatic interest. It takes us into a strange world of ascetics who spent long hours in prayer, fasting and penance in their search for Christian perfection, yet who often turned out to have much the same passions and vices as the world outside. It shows us faked elections and unjust purges as well as a daring escape from prison, while within the microcosm of a struggle between friars we get a very real political issue. How many people, I wonder, know that St John of the Cross owed his final disgrace to having resisted despotism and made himself the champion of the vote by secret ballot? Yet he was not a man who enjoyed struggle. His tragedy was that while his only ambition was to spend his days and nights in prayer and mortification, his fate was to be involved during most of his adult life in a fierce conflict with his brother friars, which ended in his disgrace and death.

Juan de Yepes y Álvarez – this was St John of the Cross's original name – was born in 1542 at Fontiveros or Hontiveros, a small *villa* or town of some five thousand inhabitants which lies half way between Avila and Salamanca in that district of Old Castile that is known as La Moraña. His father, Gonzalo de Yepes, was a man of good family who, after losing both his parents in childhood, had been brought up by his uncles, prosperous silk merchants at Toledo, and placed in their business. Others of his uncles and near relatives were eminent ecclesiastics, four of them being canons of Toledo

3   I-2

Cathedral, another the Archdeacon of the collegiate church of Torrijos and a sixth an inquisitor. The least successful was a doctor. Such a family tree raises the question whether, like Santa Teresa of Avila, he may not have been of Jewish descent because so many of the canons of Toledo Cathedral were New Christians, while the silk trade had for a century and longer been almost entirely in their hands. This has more than a pedantic interest because in those days the misfortune of having Jewish blood in one's veins was apt to impart a sense of guilt which could deepen the religious consciousness by giving it, as it were, a double dose of original sin. But up to now no proof of the Jewish origins of the Yepes family has come to light.*

The young man seemed to have a prosperous career in front of him when, stopping at Fontiveros on his way to the fair at Medina del Campo, he fell in love with a poor girl, an orphan of the name of Catalina Álvarez who earned her living as a silk weaver in the small *telar* or workshop where he lodged. He married her and on this his uncles, proud of their family tree, cut him off and refused to have anything more to do with him. Left to his own resources, he settled at Fontiveros, where he sank to his wife's humble level and became a weaver himself. Here he remained for some twelve years until, a few months after Juan's birth, he died of a lingering illness, leaving his widow and three sons in great poverty.

Finding herself unable to support her children by her own labour, Catalina set out to seek help from her husband's relatives, carrying the infant Juan in her arms while her other two children walked by her side. In this way, begging her food in the villages, she travelled some two hundred miles through New Castile, but came back as poor as when she had left. The only assistance she obtained came from one of her husband's uncles, a doctor at Gálvez, who, being childless, offered to adopt her eldest son, Francisco, who was at that time a boy of twelve. But this arrangement did not last long because the boy, who was mentally retarded, did not get on with the doctor's wife, so that Catalina was obliged to fetch him home again.

Fontiveros is today a small pueblo of sun-dried mud and stone standing on a wide plain sown with wheat. It has no stream to water it and few trees. In the distance rises a long wall of mountains, the Sierra de Gredos, covered during the winter with snow. Here Juan spent the first years of his childhood, while his mother worked to

* See appendix 1 on page 91.

support her family at the loom. But the harvest had been poor for several years in succession: the import of American silver was producing a steady inflation and the wages she earned were insufficient to keep them in health. Thus, like the bulk of the Spanish labouring classes at this time, they suffered great privations. Their only food was barley bread and lentils: through the icy winters, when snow often lay on the ground, they had no means of warming themselves and their clothes were thin because they could only afford the poorest materials. This was no doubt a good training for Juan's future life of ascetism, but only a robust nature could stand it and before long his second brother Luis fell sick and died. After this, Juan being now six, his mother moved to the neighbouring town of Arévalo and later, in 1551, to Medina del Campo.

Medina was not then the dusty, decayed place it is today. Its new brick palaces, faced with armorial bearings, its churches and convents and hospitals and above all its great square marked the site of one of the largest fairs in Europe. Here, during three months of each year, the streets were thronged with merchants from every part of the world who came to exchange the goods of France and Flanders and Portugal for those of Spain. Nowhere else in this country of priests and friars and peasants, except Seville, could such movement and animation be seen. But none of the wealth that changed hands so readily in the booths of the square found its way into the pockets of Catalina Álvarez. The only trade she knew – that of weaving *burato*, which was a fine silk and cotton material – was badly paid, so, to save on her rent, she took a house with her eldest son, Francisco, who was now twenty-one, and his young wife, both of them weavers too, and pooled her resources with theirs. But she could not afford to keep Juan. Instead, she boarded him out at an orphanage, the Colegio de la Doctrina, where he was fed and clothed as well as taught to read and write. The boys wore a uniform, attended funerals as mutes and collected alms for the institution. But their future was also considered and, to fit them for a trade, they were sent out for part of each day to workshops of various kinds. Thus Juan was apprenticed in turn to a carpenter, a wood sculptor and a printer, but such was his incapacity for manual work that he was soon returned as useless by all of them. Instead he found some employment in the sacristy of a convent, where his quiet and devout ways pleased the nuns.

There was in Medina a hospital for the poor known as *el hospital*

5

de las bubas, or tumours, where advanced cases of syphilis were treated free of charge. It was administered by a youngish man of good family called Antonio Álvarez de Toledo who had dedicated his life to this service, for if in the Spain of Philip II there were a vast number of the poor, there were also many charitable institutions run by private people for succouring them. No doubt it was on the recommendation of the nuns that Juan was now taken on at this place. He slept in the building and worked both in the wards among the horrible cases which the later stages of syphilis provide and at collecting alms in the town. But his quickness at his books was soon noticed by the administrator, who arranged that he should be enrolled in the *colegio*, or grammar school, which the Jesuits, those great promoters of education, had recently founded. He was just seventeen at the time and the course lasted for four years. There were three masters, none of them older than twenty-one, and forty pupils. The subjects taught were Latin grammar, history and literature with a special emphasis on Virgil, Horace, Seneca, Cicero and Livy and, since the head master, Juan Bonifacio, was an enthusiastic Latinist as well as a man with a real vocation for teaching, we may suppose that Juan got a good grounding in the humanities. Although his duties at the hospital obliged him to miss many classes, he made up for this by assiduous homework. One night, his brother tells us, their mother found him sitting up in a room stacked with firewood, studying by the light of a *candil*, or primitive oil lamp. In this he was very different from Francisco, a man of simple mind who never learned to read and remained all his life a poor weaver.

The profession of priest was the obvious one for a young man of poor family but studious disposition to adopt and Álvarez de Toledo offered him a chaplaincy at the hospital if he did so. But Juan, though strongly pressed, was unwilling to accept. His heart was already set on leaving the world, so, stealing out of the hospital one night, *a oscuras y en celada*, in order to avoid the administrator's opposition, he knocked on the door of the Carmelite priory of Santa Ana and took the habit. He was just twenty-one. In his delight at being received into the Order of the Blessed Virgin he wrote a poem in heroic verse and in a pastoral style which has not been preserved. A year later he made his profession under the name of Fray Juan de San Matías.

His education however was not complete if he wished to be

ordained so in the same year, 1564, he was admitted, thanks to his proficiency in Latin, to the university of Salamanca and took up his residence there in the Carmelite college of San Andrés next to the river. It was a small college, containing only nine students, for the Carmelites were not given to learning. Here he remained until 1567, following the usual triennial course of arts, but returning to Medina for the vacations.

Salamanca at this time was at the height of its fame with seven thousand students and some of the most eminent professors in Europe to teach them. It was a city of churches, colleges, *mesones* or inns and lodging houses, but it lacked any life but the scholastic one, since it had neither industry nor agriculture. In the general decay of the country the fine clay loam of its fields had gone out of cultivation, so that, in spite of its imposing buildings, the visitor was struck by a depressing air of poverty and wretchedness. Most of the students went about hungry and badly dressed and, though the discipline was severe, there was a good deal of rowdiness. What gave the place its vitality were the furious disputes between the professors in which the students took sides and the intrigues and backbiting, sometimes accompanied by accusations of heresy which could lead to the intervention of the Inquisition.

We know little of Juan's life during his stay here. Did he attend the lectures of the great humanist and poet, Fray Luis de León? One would expect him to have felt drawn to the personality of that vivid and outspoken man, only some twelve years older than himself, who was a little later to spend five years in the dungeons of the Holy Office on the charge of having translated the *Song of Songs* into Spanish. Yet we know that he never came into personal contact with him. Then what were his theological studies? The teaching of philosophy in Salamanca at this time followed strictly scholastic lines – Aristotle and Aquinas with a certain leaning to Plato and St Augustine. Little attention was paid to St Bonaventura, whom Juan would have found to his taste, and Occam and his successors were neglected, though at the college of San Andrés lectures were given on John Baconthorpe, the fourteenth-century Averroist, because, though of doubtful orthodoxy, he had been a provincial of the Carmelites.

But no doubt the precise tenor of Juan's theological studies hardly mattered. The young friar had not got a speculative mind: all he required of theology was a conventional system which he could use

7

as a frame for his inner experience. This took the form of mental prayer – what we today call mysticism – yet, as it happened, anything of that kind was regarded with suspicion. The whole spirit of the university authorities was against it and it was largely through the influence of its professors that a number of Spanish and Flemish works on the subject, including most of those from which Santa Teresa had learned her trade, had been placed on the Index. We know however that he had read and absorbed that source book of mystical theology that goes under the name of Dionysius the Areopagite, as well as Boethius' *Consolation of Philosophy* and a treatise on the *Song of Songs* attributed to St Gregory. He must too have read other more recent books on these subjects for during his last year at Salamanca he wrote a dissertation that has not been preserved in which he distinguished between certain new, apparently illuminist methods of prayer that were being talked of and which he found reprehensible, and the tradition of ascetic and mystical practices which had come down from the Early Fathers. But we can see the mark left on him by the official courses of the university more clearly in another field. The teaching of the great Salamancan humanist, Francisco de Vitoria, still held a large place in the curriculum and he had attached the greatest importance to the study of the Bible and of the Early Fathers. This teaching bore fruit in Fray Juan's mind for the Bible was to be his constant companion through his life. No Protestant divine ever quoted Scripture more often.

Some of Juan's fellow students have left an account of what he was like at this time. When not attending lectures he would sit at his desk in his dark, bare cell poring over his books, while he spent a large part of every night in prayer. He fasted assiduously, whipped his shoulders till he drew blood and refused to join his companions in their light conversations. He was especially severe about any breach of the rule and when he caught one of his fellow Carmelites, even a much older friar, acting in this way, he would reprimand him with all the ardour and lack of tact of the neophyte. No wonder that, though admired, he was not liked, for no one could feel free in his presence. 'Let's be off – that devil is coming,' his brother friars would say when they saw him approaching. It is hardly surprising therefore that he made only one friend at Salamanca, Fray Pedro de Orozco, who had gone up with him from Medina, and it was many years before he made another.

The turning point of Juan's career came in September 1567 when he had just been ordained priest and had gone home, as the custom was, to say his first mass in the presence of his mother. Teresa de Jesús, now a woman of past fifty, had arrived at Medina to found a convent of reformed Carmelites – that is, of nuns who wished to return to the primitive rule. It was her second foundation, the first having been that of San José at Avila. She was also anxious to spread her reform to the friars of the order so that her nuns should have confessors trained in their way of prayer and, as luck would have it, she found that the prior of the Carmelite house at Medina, whom she had previously known at Avila, was ready to lead the way. This worthy man, Antonio de Heredia, was approaching sixty, of cheerful nature but dignified and fond of his comforts – hardly the sort of person one would expect to join an ascetic reform. But he had curried favour with the king by, it was said, acting as a spy for him, and on this leaking out in his priory he had become unpopular. Vain and greedy for pre-eminence, he had seen that he could reassert his importance by becoming the first prior of a new movement. Teresa had doubts of his suitability, but he won her over by promising to persuade a young friar, of whose devout and ascetic life Pedro de Orozco had spoken with enthusiasm, to join him. This was Fray Juan de San Matías who, dissatisfied with the laxity of his own order and intensely given to solitude and contemplation, had been considering joining the Carthusians. Teresa saw him and approved of him. She was not a person whose solicitations it was easy to resist and she had a good argument – ought he to desert the Order of the Blessed Virgin, as the Carmelites called themselves, for a community that had a different spirit? Juan yielded and agreed to do as she wished 'provided' – here one sees the young man's impatience – 'he did not have to wait too long'. After that he went back to Salamanca to take a year's course in theology while she committed herself to making the necessary arrangements for the foundation of a priory in which the life of the friars would be based on the primitive rule.

2

The Carmelite Reform

The Order of Carmel, whose reformed rule Fray Juan de San Matías was now preparing to adopt, could show a long and illustrious history, of which the early stages were wrapped in legend. Founded, so its members claimed, by Enoch, the father of Methusaleh, on Mount Carmel in Palestine, it had been renewed by the prophet Elijah, who had recognized as a prefiguration of the Virgin Mary that 'small cloud like a man's hand' which, according to the Book of Kings, had risen out of the sea over its summit. From that time on she had floated in the form of a mist over the solitaries who had settled there, among whom were later to be counted the Prophets, the Essenes and the Apostles.

From a more reliable source we learn that Mount Carmel – the name in Hebrew means 'garden' – had from early times been regarded as a sanctuary. Iamblicus speaks of it as sacred above all mountains and its access forbidden to the public, affirming that Pythagoras once spent a night on it in silent prayer. Tacitus reports that it had an altar without a temple or image, and Suetonius that Vespasian consulted its oracle before making war on the Jews. Then at some undetermined date a band of Christian monks or anchorites settled there, but our first positive information about its religious occupants comes from a Greek monk called Phocas who visited it in 1185 and found a community of hermits established on its summit.

They told him that some thirty years before this a white-haired Crusader from Calabria, by name Berthold, had come here on the strength of a vision of the prophet Elijah, had built a tower, a rampart and an oratory out of the ruins of a previous monastery and assembled ten brothers round him.

Phocas found them living in little cells scattered among the rocks, 'like bees making their honey', coming together only for liturgical services and leading lives of great seclusion and austerity as they worked to support themselves. A few years later this community of anchorites was given a rule that comprised sixteen articles by the

Latin Patriarch of Jerusalem, St Albert, and from this moment the Order of Carmel dates its official existence.

But although they grew in numbers the Saracens were steadily closing in on them, so in 1238, six years before the fall of Jerusalem, they began to emigrate in small parties to Cyprus, Sicily, France and England. The few who remained were massacred. The country in which they took root most strongly was England. A Kentish hermit, Simon Stock, who like one of the figures in Edward Lear's Book of Limericks, had lived for twenty years in great piety in a hollow oak, joined them and became their general. Under his leadership the first chapter of the order was held in 1247 at Aylesford on the Medway and at this they adopted a somewhat milder rule that was better suited to Western conditions and for which they claimed the authority of Pope Innocent IV. They now ceased to be anchorites and became one of the four orders of mendicant friars, with special duties of prayer and mortification, but relieved of the obligation to work. In England they were known as the White Friars because of the white cloaks they wore over their brown habits.

The Carmelites had come to Europe at a time when the Franciscans and Dominicans were spreading rapidly, and they had to face their competition. The more religious orders there were, the less alms there would be to go round. The popes too, dismayed by the number of mendicant friars who were wandering across Europe, hesitated to recognize them fully, so that for fifty years they lived on sufferance. They were therefore led to compensate for their doubtful status and for their lack of an eminent founder who would lend them the prestige of his name by the extravagance of their claims, tracing their origins back into the mists of time and boasting of being under the special protection of the Blessed Virgin. As an instance of this they alleged that she had appeared to St Simon Stock and handed him a scapular (a sort of apron worn by various religious orders) with the promise that all who died in it should escape hell fire. These scapulars, which they distributed to their lay patrons, became much coveted and in the course of time further privileges were added to them, such as that the Virgin would descend every Saturday to purgatory and carry up to heaven everyone who wore it.

With this romantic history to point to and these tempting inducements to offer, the Carmelites expanded rapidly, but in doing so they

11

fell from their original austerity. Their rule was too severe for an age of increasing laxity, so in 1432 Pope Eugenius IV gave them a milder one, which was that which prevailed in Spain till 1562, when Teresa of Avila founded the reform.

The constitutions she drew up for her converts were based on the rule of 1247, which was usually spoken of as the rule of St Albert, and laid a special emphasis on poverty, strict enclosure, fasting and prayer. By prayer was meant chiefly mental prayer – that is, meditation and recollection – the practice of which had led Teresa by way of visions, locutions, trances and raptures to the 'state of union' in which the will is united to the will of God. But since these 'supernatural' states were not granted to everyone, she was satisfied if her daughters made progress in moral perfection and especially in love for God. A higher level however was to be expected of men than of simple women so that the friars' rule was to be more severe. They were to have certain duties of preaching in churches, but the greater part of their time was to be spent in chapel and in solitary devotions. Prolonged fasting, reduced hours of sleep, weekly penances were required of them, though practices of extreme asceticism were not permitted. In the letter patent which the Carmelite general, Rubeo, issued when he authorized their foundations, he made it clear that they were to be above everything contemplative.

'Our desire is [he wrote] that they should be like mirrors, like shining lamps, glowing torches, brilliant stars, enlightening and guiding the wanderers in this dark world, . . . raised above themselves by raptures both ineffable and indescribable, . . . their senses transformed and more exalted than they generally are in this dark life: their eyes filled with tears and their hearts with a sweet dew productive of abundant fruit.'

Yet for Teresa at least the aim was not simply, as it had been in the days of the hermits, to further their own spiritual state. Prayer was also a weapon. She was deeply conscious of the civil wars and heresies that were tearing Europe to pieces and hoped by these acts of contrition to mitigate them.

Perhaps we can see these Carmelites best in their historical perspective if we regard them as a new sort of *Conquistadors*. The age of geographic explorations and conquests had been followed by an age of interior ones that plumbed the individual self. Montaigne in France and more indirectly Shakespeare and Donne in England provide examples of this. Yet it was not an intellectual enterprise that these friars and nuns were engaged on, but an active and spiritual one: they believed, and in this the authority of the church supported them, that, if grace were given to them, they could carry the whole mind with its will and affections to union with the source of that mind, which is God. Since love was the motive, Eros the engine in the hull, this course took the form and is explained in the language of a love affair.* It was the extreme of sublimation, the final point, if one likes, of that historic movement of love for the absent, *amor de lonh*, which had inspired the Provençal poets and through them Dante and Petrarch. Such was the venture, *la dichosa ventura*, to which Fray Juan was now committed.

In the summer of 1568, Juan left Salamanca for the last time, with his course of theology completed, for the Carmelite priory of Medina to keep his appointment with Teresa. He found her already awaiting him and set off at once with her and her nuns for Valladolid, where she was to found a convent. Here he spent some weeks in her company, while the workmen were repairing the building and she was out of enclosure, in order to learn the way of life of her communities. One of her letters, dated in September, to her old friend Francisco de Salcedo of Avila, gives her impressions of him:

'I beg you to have a talk with this Father and help him in his undertaking for, though he is small of stature, I believe he is great in the eyes of God. We are certainly going to miss him greatly for he is sensible and well fitted for our way of life, so that I believe our Lord has called him for this work. There is not a friar but speaks well of him for he leads a life of great penitence, though he entered upon it so recently. But the Lord seems to be leading him by the hand for, although we have had a few disagreements here over business matters, of which I have been the cause, and I have sometimes been vexed with him, we have never seen the least imperfection in him. He has courage: but, as he is quite alone, he needs all that the Lord gives him.'

In her *Book of the Foundations*, written eight years later, she again describes her impressions of Fray Juan de San Matías, as he

---

* *Aunque es verdad que la gloria consiste en el entendimiento, el fin del alma es amar.* Note in San Juan de la Cruz's handwriting on the margin of the *Cántico espiritual*, Stanza 37, *Allí me mostrarías.*

13

was at that time. After saying that she had given him an exact account of the way of life followed in her convents –

> 'both the mortifications practised, the form of sisterly affection and the recreations, which are all followed with such moderation that they help to bring out the faults of the sisters and give them some relief from the severity of the rule'

– she went on in her usual tone of ironical humility:

> 'He was so good a man that I, at least, could have learned more from him than he from me. I did not do so however, but merely showed him the way in which the sisters live.'

From Valladolid Juan went to Avila and from there set out with a mason for the lonely and half-ruined bailiff's cottage which Teresa, after a brief visit of inspection a couple of months before, had chosen to be the first priory of the reform. As soon as it had been made habitable, Antonio de Heredia and another prior arrived with the provincial of the order and the three of them made their vows to live according to the primitive rule established in 1247 by Innocent IV. This was in November 1568 and Fray Juan de San Matías, who was now twenty-six, put on the rough habit that Teresa had sewn for him with her own hands and changed his name to Fray Juan de la Cruz.

There is a charm about the small beginnings of heroic enterprises. The foundation of the first reformed Carmelite priory recalls in its great hopes and tiny resources that of the first hermitage of the ruined chapel of the Portiuncula by St Francis of Assisi. The site that had been chosen for it stood in a hamlet called Duruelo that lay only a few miles from Fontiveros, Juan's birthplace. Today Duruelo is a farmhouse standing in a shallow valley. A little stream, the Rio del Mar, runs past between green fields and thistles; a few willows line it; there are a few evergreen oaks. Beyond the rim of the valley lies the snow-covered Sierra de Gredos, some thirty miles off. It was here among tumbled-down buildings and barns that the three friars founded their new house.

Teresa, who on first seeing it had doubted the habitability of the place, which had for long been used only for storing wheat, visited it again in the spring. In her *Book of the Foundations* she has left an enthusiastic account of her impressions. Fray Antonio, clad in his white serge cape and coarse brown habit, with a look of gaiety on his face, was sweeping the porch when she came up. 'How is this, Father?' she said to him. 'What has become of your dignity?' and he replied, smiling, 'I curse the day I ever had any.'

The entrance hall had been converted into a chapel. It was full of crosses and skulls. The attic above formed the choir. At one end of it, close under the eaves, were two little cells or hermitages, giving a view of the attic and so low that one could only enter them on one's hands and knees. Here, with stones for pillows, their feet wrapped in hay, among more crosses and skulls, the friars remained praying from midnight to daybreak while the snow drifted onto their clothes through the tiles. They ate from broken crockery and drank from gourds; their only other possessions were a few books, some scourges and bells and five hour-glasses, which the meticulous Fray Antonio had to Teresa's amusement insisted on bringing with him. Delighted by their enthusiasm, she told them that they must all the same moderate their penances. For example, they must not go about barefoot in winter.

The foundation of a convent belonging to one of the stricter orders set up an excitement in the sixteenth century that we find hard to understand today. Four or five nuns, whose faces no one would ever see and whose voices few would hear, had only to barricade themselves in a ruined house for the whole town to be in commotion. The same can be said to a somewhat lesser extent of the priories. For the men of that age believed that spiritual things were not only more important than material ones, but that in a direct and immediate way they controlled them. A convent or priory, therefore, whose inmates spent their lives in fasting and prayer, was looked on as a sort of power-house that radiated benefits upon the whole neighbourhood. Quarrels and dissensions would decrease, the interest on loans would fall, alms-giving would be more abundant, above all purgatory would be shortened. Thus it was that the little community of Duruelo, as soon as the rumour of its austerities got around, caused a stir in the whole district. Many people came to visit it, including Fray Juan's mother, brother and sister-in-law, who, proud of his new fame, camped down in his shadow, cooking, washing and sweeping for him and his fellow friars. Although he was much attached to his simple-minded brother, who later followed him to Granada, he shrank from any dealings with strangers and an anecdote tells us how, when preaching in the neighbouring villages, he would refuse the meal offered him by the parish priest and retire to the edge of a field, by the bank of a stream, to eat his bread and cheese alone. So the community, though founded on such exiguous means, flourished and grew till at the end of eighteen months it was found necessary to move to a larger and more convenient building in the neighbouring village of Mancera. Duruelo was then abandoned.

The reformed Carmelites spread rapidly during the next few years. Many new convents and priories were founded. The first of these priories was at Pastrana, forty miles to the east of Madrid, a town of silk weavers and New Christians (that is, people of Jewish descent) which had not long before been a great centre for *Alumbrados*.* Ruy Gómez, the Prince of Éboli, a personal friend and adviser of Philip II, provided a hermitage on a rocky hillside just outside the town and three friars took the habit in it. One of these was an elderly and impetuous Neapolitan engineer called Ambrosio Mariano who with his inseparable peasant-friend Juan de la Miseria had till then been living as a hermit on the Sierra Morena. Only a few weeks before their arrival Teresa had founded a convent of nuns in the town under the patronage of the Prince's wife, so that her ideal of having friars of the reform living within reach of her nuns was fulfilled.

Pastrana was not far from Alcalá de Henares with its famous Renaissance university, which meant that the new priory was well placed for drawing the attention of students to the methods of interior prayer that were practised in it. It thus grew rapidly and within a few months of its foundation could claim to have fourteen novices and friars. Some of these novices were men of good education who would soon become leading members in the reform and Fray Juan de la Cruz came over from Mancera and spent a few weeks in organizing their training.

But almost at once things began to go wrong. An extraordinary female hermit called Doña Catalina de Cardona appeared on the scene and with her visions and miracles and, not least, her ferocious penances began to turn the heads of the friars. Her history was a strange one. Born in 1519, the illegitimate daughter of a Spanish duke, she had been brought up in a convent at Naples, had then married and been widowed, after which she had become a lady in waiting to an impoverished Italian princess and come with her to Spain. On the death of her employer she had been taken over by

* For an explanation of this word, see appendix II on page 96.

the Princess of Éboli, but, driven by her craving for extravagant penances, she had fled from the Éboli palace at Pastrana and settled in a cave in a lonely wilderness near La Roda. Here she had lived on roots and herbs, whipped herself till the blood clotted her hair shirt, wrapped herself in heavy chains and worn a man's dress. For a time she was much troubled by evil spirits who, taking the form of huge mastiffs, would leap onto her shoulders, but to make up for this the rabbits and partridges came in flocks to pay court to her and gambolled at her feet. These were followed by pious admirers from the villages and finally by ladies in carriages. After she had spent eight years in this way her growing fame excited the curiosity of the Princess of Éboli, who invited her to Pastrana. She arrived in May 1571. She had already been informed in a vision of the existence of the reformed Carmelites, though no one had spoken to her about them, and now she met them and decided to take their habit. But she would not become a nun because, she said, she could not endure the insipid conversation in convents: she had to be a friar, and such was the impression made by her tiny, hunched form, her perpetually smiling, leather-coloured face, her stained and ragged tunic and her bloody penances – the sound of her lashings went on every night for hours – that she was solemnly received into the order on her own terms in the presence of the Prince and Princess of Éboli. She was now, as a female friar, the nine days' wonder of Castile. Paraded round Madrid in an open carriage, she blessed the crowds who had assembled to scoff or kiss her dress and even obtained an audience with the king. Then, having collected a considerable sum of money, she returned with her accompaniment of friars to La Roda where with great expense and labour Ambrosio Mariano built her a priory, she herself taking up her quarters in an artificial cave close by. Her example had been infectious and the friars of Pastrana went on to found other priories in Andalusia, among them one at Granada.

In spite of the enthusiasm aroused in those who met her, Doña Catalina's impact on the reformed Carmelites had a deeply unsettling effect. Teresa, who knew her only by report, could not help admiring her courage and her fierce penances, which called up in her mind what she had read of the hermits of the Thebaid. That a woman all by herself could do such things! Yet she also felt an uneasiness that she concealed when she drew her portrait in the *Book of the Foundations.* For one thing she found her penances too

17

severe. She wanted men of talent to enter the reform and they would be put off by the wave of extremism, almost of hysteria, that was sweeping through the friars of Pastrana. Just now the young novice-master had introduced a regime of extravagant and humiliating mortifications which were giving the priory a bad name. Promising novices, who had not bargained for such treatment, were considering leaving the order. Teresa saw that this would have to stop, so she arranged for Fray Juan de la Cruz to be sent there to restore things to their proper state. But the novice-master proved obstinate and the prior was absent in the train of Doña Catalina. Unable to interfere directly she consulted Fray Domingo Báñez, the famous Dominican theologian, who had once been her confessor, and he sent back a reasoned statement that supported Fray Juan's opinion that severe or exaggerated penances were forbidden by the rule. The novice-master was suspended and by the end of a month or so things had returned to their normal channels. Yet Doña Catalina's influence lived on, especially in Andalusia, and kept up a ferment there because it appealed to those elements in the reform who admired the fierce and independent ways of anchorites and hermits. Thirty years later there were still friars who held her in greater esteem than they did Santa Teresa.*

In the meantime the Prince of Éboli, whose health was failing, had offered to found a Discalced Carmelite college at the university of Alcalá. This held out great opportunities to the reform as it would bring in novices of the right sort from among the students and in April 1571 Juan de la Cruz was appointed its rector. But the college did not prosper. Although Juan's quiet, modest bearing created a favourable impression, he lacked the dynamism and the gift for making friends that were required for such an undertaking. His whole bent was towards interior prayers and contemplation and although he could be firm and clear-sighted where questions of principle or discipline were involved, he was so averse to all practical affairs that he shrank even from the office of prior. It seems clear that, in spite of the valuable support he had given at Pastrana, he was something of a disappointment to Teresa. She needed a really able and active man to steer the priories through the troubles that had been created by Doña Catalina, and for a moment she regretted having spread the reform to the friars. But just as

* For this new view of Doña Catalina de Cardona's life and influence I have drawn on P. Efrén's *Tiempo y Vida de Santa Teresa*, 1968.

she was thinking this the person whom she was looking for turned up. This was Jerónimo Gracián, a young doctor of theology at Alcalá University who in April 1572 joined the reform at Pastrana under the name of Jerónimo de la Madre de Dios.

Gracián, as he was usually called, was the son of a secretary of the Emperor Charles V and of the daughter of the Polish ambassador. After marrying when she was only twelve, his mother had had thirteen children of whom Jerónimo was the third. Brought up in a cultured and literary environment, he had had a brilliant career at the university, which his father hoped would be the prelude to his entering the king's service. But instead of this he took orders with the intention of joining the Jesuits, where his talents would have been put to good use. Then at the last moment he changed his mind. A chance meeting with a friend, a conversation with the prioress of a reformed convent, brought back to him the romantic devotion to the Virgin which he had had as a youth, when he used to offer flowers to her statue and call her *mi enamorada*, so that, in spite of the strong opposition of his parents, he took the habit of her order.

This new adherent to the reform was a man who was gifted with exceptional powers of fascination. Handsome, blue-eyed, with great charm and sweetness of manner, an eloquent preacher and talker yet tactful and conciliatory, he quickly became the favourite of the sisters. He was not by nature an ascetic, for his delicate health forbade severe austerities, but he had a decided leaning to mysticism, while a certain softness in his disposition led him to lay more stress on the spirit of the rule than on its letter. This made him a poor disciplinarian. Nor was he better as a fighter, for when he met with opposition his self-confidence failed him and he gave way to his opponents. That however lay in the future. Just now his charm, his candour and his enthusiasm made him friends everywhere, so that he rose rapidly in an order that was deficient in men of judgement and ability.

But it was his meeting with Teresa that was to prove decisive. It took place in May 1575 at Beas de Segura, a small town on the eastern borders of Andalusia where she had gone to found a convent. She was then sixty, exactly twice his age, and the result was startling. There can be no other word for it – she fell in love with him.

'Oh, Mother,' she wrote to her cousin, the Prioress of Medina, 'how I wish you could have been with me these last few days!

Without exaggeration, they have been the best days of my life. For more than three weeks we have had the Father, Master Gracián, here with us and, much though I have seen of him, I have not yet fathomed his worth. In my eyes he is perfect and better for our needs than anyone we could have asked God to send us. . . . Such perfection joined with such gentleness I never saw before.'

Gracián was strongly affected too. At their first meeting he confided to her things about himself that he had not told to anyone, while she, authorized by a vision in which Jesus Christ took her hand and placed it in Gracián's, telling her to accept him in His place for the rest of her life, made a vow to obey him in everything. He became from that moment her closest friend and confidant, to whom she wrote every few days, filling her letters with expressions of admiration and affection. She could even be jealous of him. On one occasion she asked him whether he loved her or his mother best, saying, 'Your mother has a husband and children to love her, but poor Laurencia [one of her code names for herself] has no one in the world but you.' If she wrote to him so often, she said, it was because she needed to do so, for 'O Jesus, how wonderful it is when two souls understand one another! They are never at a loss for anything to say and never grow tired of saying it.' And in another of her letters she spoke of Christ as having been the matchmaker (*casamentero*) who had tied the knot so tight between them that even death would not break it. Towards the end of her life she complained many times of the loneliness she felt when he did not write to her, though she could only, she declared, be truly happy in his company.

Such was the feeling that bound these two together. The touching devotion of the elderly nun to the young friar who was to become the head of the order never faltered. Although she came in time to see his weaknesses and did her best to save him from their consequences, she kept her deep affection for him and it was this affection that, more than anything else, gave rise to the jealousies that in the end led to his disgrace and fall.

To return now to 1571, while Gracián was still hesitating whether or not to take the Discalced* habit, the fame and success of Teresa's reform had raised against her a host of enemies of whom the most bitter belonged to the unreformed body of her own order. To these

* Various terms were used for the two branches of the Carmelite order. The reformed were usually known as the Discalced, because they went about either

20

lax, easy-living friars the austerity of her convents and priories
was felt to be a constant reproach. But there were doubts and sus-
picions in some of the higher circles of the church as well. The
conservatives – and since the rise of Luther Spain was every day
becoming a more conservative country – looked askance at this
'gad-about nun' who travelled all over the place founding convents
for contemplatives and having visions and raptures. One of the
leading theologians of the time, the Dominican Melchor Cano,
held like his still more eminent uncle of the same name that
the chief heresy of the day was the tendency to interior prayer,
of which Luther, he thought, provided an example. He was therefore bitterly opposed to all mystics from Eckhart and Tauler on,
declaring that they were *Alumbrados* or *Illuminati*,* who, unless
they were suppressed, would complete the ruin that the Gnostics
had begun. The Inquisition, doubtless aware that Teresa was of
Jewish descent and therefore in their view especially prone to
heresy, would soon possess a copy of her autobiography. Only the
charm of her personality and her skill in using it to win over her
enemies had allowed her to initiate her reform. Her great humility
too, her continual doubts about herself and the genuineness of her
visions together with the total assent she gave to the teachings of
the church and to the theologians who defined it worked in her
favour. That is, she showed the proper submissiveness that women
were expected to show in a man-made world. Yet there were some
who, while admiring her reforming zeal, thought it should be
turned from the channel it had taken and given the task of disciplining the lax and unreformed Carmelites whom she had left. She was
to be made, not to form a small élite of spiritual persons, but to
raise the general level of the conventual proletariat. The apostolic
visitor, who represented the authority of the nuncio and of the king,
was one of those people who thought this and in October 1571 he
nominated her prioress for three years of the large, unreformed
convent of the Encarnación in Avila. So Teresa returned to the
rambling building in which she had spent more than twenty years

barefoot or in rope-soled shoes or sandals, while the unreformed were known
either as the Calced, because they wore leather shoes, or as the 'friars of the
Observance' or the 'Mitigated', because in 1432 the pope had mitigated
the primitive rule and given them a milder one. Teresa usually called them
los del paño because their habits were of fine cloth, whereas the reformed
dressed in coarse, undyed serge.
* See appendix II on page 96.

21

of her life and where the majority of the nuns – a hundred and thirty of them, half starved and rebellious – were hostile to her. To assist her in her task she arranged for Fray Juan de la Cruz and another Discalced prior to be appointed confessors and spiritual directors to the convent. This was in September 1572.

Let us pause for a moment to see if we can form any impression of Fray Juan's character at this time. I think we can best do this if we try to see him through Madre Teresa's eyes. From her first meeting with him she had been a little ironical about this shy, reserved, but self-assured young man – 'my little Seneca', she called him – who was less than five feet tall and half her age. 'Thanks be to God, daughters,' she exclaimed to her nuns when she first recruited him and Antonio de Heredia, 'I have found a friar and a half to start the Reform with.' Later, when she mentioned him in her letters, it was to say that he was perfect – but she did not mention him often. The fact is that the men who attracted her most were those who had mingled with the world and had a flair for dealing with it. Provided that they were truly devout, she did not mind if they had failings, but they had to be cheerful and conversable and have a certain talent for practical affairs. Now Juan's whole nature was so strongly inclined to contemplation that until he was past forty he was of little use for anything else. 'We friars do not travel to see, but in order not to see,' he once said to a monk who had asked him to admire certain buildings. In other words he was the perfect Carmelite – the type of man Teresa was trying to produce – but her nature was curiously divided between action and contemplation, and it was on the active side that she now needed collaborators.

We detect therefore a certain tension between Madre Teresa and her young neophyte during the early years of their acquaintance. We noted it first at Valladolid while she was instructing him in the ways of her convents and it led her to speak in a letter I have already quoted as 'having been at various times vexed with him'. For not only was Fray Juan a man who was sure of himself to the point of obstinacy, but it would seem that, though he and Teresa agreed on fundamentals, there was something in her strong yet insidious personality that brought out in him a secret opposition. Thus we hear of him mortifying her by handing her an unusually small host at communion when he knew that she liked large ones, giving his reason for this that she was too fond of *gustos* or spiritual consolations.* He could also be sharp with her. One day he said to her in front of the other nuns, 'When you are confessing, Mother, you excuse yourself beautifully.' Intended probably in a playful way, his remark was taken by the nuns as a reproof. Then there is the story of his setting out from Baeza with a bag of her letters on his shoulder and scattering them on the road because, as he remarked to his companion, 'a friar should not be encumbered with unnecessary possessions'. This was no doubt a very proper sentiment for a Discalced Carmelite to hold, yet to anyone else in Teresa's entourage it would have seemed a sacrilege.

On her side too there was a cause for some irritation in his refusal to attach importance to anything but the higher forms of contemplation. In one of those literary games that were played in her convents she set various friars and pious men among her friends the task of commenting on the words 'Seek thyself in Me'. She then criticized their comments in, as the spirit of the game required, a playful and ironic tone. In her criticism of Juan de la Cruz's reply she wrote, 'It would be a bad business for us if we could not seek God till we were dead to the world. Neither the Magdalene nor the woman of Samaria were dead to the world when they found Him.' And she ended: 'God deliver us from people who are so spiritual that they want to turn everything into perfect contemplation.' On another occasion she remarked: 'If one tries to talk to Padre Fray Juan de la Cruz of God, he falls into a trance and you along with him.'

But under the reservation she felt about his narrowness, there came to be a deep admiration. He was her confessor so long as she remained at Avila and she never had a better one. This comes out in a letter she wrote some years later to Ana de Jesús, the prioress of Beas, in which she warmly praised the delicacy of his spiritual direction – that is, his perfect understanding of the various states that are brought about by mental prayer. As his prose works show, he was a man of great psychological penetration as well as of wide experience in these matters. And as the troubles in the order mounted she came to admire his courage and fixity of purpose.

* She got her own back on him however. Immediately after her communion she heard a voice saying, 'Have no fear, my daughter, that anyone will be able to separate you from Me.' Thereupon Christ appeared to her in a vision and offered her a nail from his Cross as a sign that from that day on she was his bride. This, the Spiritual Espousal, as it is called, was the culmination of her religious life. See her *Relation* xxxv.

Towards the end of her life we find her twice begging Gracián – in vain, for he was jealous – to send Fray Juan back to her in Castille.

Juan de la Cruz spent the next five years as confessor to the Calced nuns of the Encarnación at Avila. We may regard this as a period of growth and preparation. He had had no contacts with women up to this time – now he was surrounded by them. As the last twelve years of his life were to show, he felt a sympathy for them that he did not so easily feel for men, unless they were much younger than himself. Most of those he now saw in the confession box would have been very ordinary girls, given to dreaming about young men, to receiving their friends in the parlour and gossiping with their fellow nuns, while others would have had a genuine bent for the religious life. He seems to have treated the first gently, making allowances for their limitations,* yet leading them gradually towards more serious views by stimulating their desire to be better, while the latter he directed along the thorny road of mental prayer. Another of his gifts was for casting out devils, by which was meant treating cases of possession and hysteria. One of the strangest of these cases was that of an Augustinian nun who, without having been taught, showed an astonishing proficiency in quoting and commenting on the Scriptures. When Juan examined her she confessed that at the age of six she had sold her soul to the devil, who for his own mysterious purposes had taught her this skill. Things had now gone on for so long that she was possessed by as many as seven legions of demons. On being exorcised she went into convulsions and used terrible language, but after several months of Juan's treatment the demons left her and she was cured. Presumably she now lost her previous familiarity with the Holy Scriptures. His success in this and in other cases of possession gave him a great reputation in the city, while the nuns of the Encarnación, who were witnesses of his austerity, regarded him as a saint.

More important to his inner life must have been the society of Teresa. Until, eight months after his arrival, she ceased to be prioress of the convent, he was having conversations with her every week in the parlour and hearing her confession. She had just at this time reached the apex of her spiritual life and was engaged in put-

* Juan de la Cruz's observation on this was: 'The holier a man is, the gentler he is and the less scandalized by the faults of others, because he knows the weak condition of man.'

ting down her thoughts upon certain words in the *Song of Songs*. Some three years later she was to begin writing her greatest work on interior prayer, *Las Moradas* or *The Interior Castle*. Although Juan could never be described as her pupil, for he followed a harsher and more austere road of his own, his close intercourse with her at this time must have been a stimulus to him. We may suppose too that she lent him some of the works on mystical theology that had most influenced her, such as those by Francisco de Osuna, Bernadino de Laredo and García de Cisneros. They had recently been put on the Index, like nearly all works that taught interior prayer, so that he may not till now have had access to them, but as they were still in Teresa's possession she must have had permission to continue reading them. We may thus take it that although Juan's initiation into the higher states of prayer had certainly already begun, this long spell of quiet in the society of Teresa allowed him to make great progress in them.

He had at first taken up his quarters at the Calced Carmelite priory within the walls of the city. By mingling the friars of the reform with those of the observance the apostolic visitor was endeavouring to raise the tone of the latter. However this seems to have led to friction for after a little he went to live with another friar in a small house adjoining the garden of the Encarnación. This house stood on the site of the old Jewish cemetery where in 1305 Moses de León, the author of the *Zohar*, the most famous of the Cabbalistic works, had been buried. But Fray Juan de la Cruz can never have heard of his eminent predecessor.

3

Prison

While Juan de la Cruz was living quietly at Avila as confessor to the nuns of Teresa's old convent, a violent storm had been brewing in the affairs of the Carmelite order. The friars of the observance were becoming increasingly jealous of the reform and afraid it would end by supplanting them. In their endeavour to check it they were supported by the Carmelite general in Italy, Father Rubeo, while the reform found an ally in the papal nuncio, Ormaneto, who had the king's backing. This ambiguous situation had come about through the imprudent zeal of Teresa and her friends. When ten years before Rubeo had visited Spain, he had been greatly impressed by her first reformed convent at Avila and had given her permission to make any new foundations she pleased in Castile, including two for friars, while expressly forbidding her to undertake any in Andalusia, where he had been deeply shocked by the relaxed condition of the religious houses. But the friars of the reform were determined to spread their influence southwards, so, to get round the general's prohibition, they appealed to the nuncio, who gave them permission to found wherever they pleased and further appointed two visitors to supervise all the Carmelite priories and convents in the country. One of these visitors was Jerónimo Gracián, who, though he had only just made his profession, was put in charge both of the Discalced and of the Calced houses in Andalusia. The friars of these last, seeing their easy way of life interrupted, appealed to the general who, being a very impulsive man, forgot his previous indignation with them and turned his rage upon the Discalced, who, in spite of the encouragement he had given to their foundress, had wilfully disobeyed his orders. At the chapter-general which was held that month at Piacenza he denounced the nuns and friars of the reform as rebellious and contumacious, placed their houses under the direction of the Calced and ordered that those which they had founded in Andalusia should be dissolved. To ensure this was done he despatched a certain Fray Jerónimo Tostado to Spain as his vicar-general, giving him full authority over all the Carmelites there.

But the friars of the reform could not be crushed so easily. After all they had the nuncio on their side. He, supported by a bull from the pope, directed Gracián to carry on as before with his visitations of the Andalusian houses, while the king, or rather his council, refused to allow Tostado to execute his commission. This gave new hope to the Discalced, yet, as the outcome was still undecided, the tension remained great. Gracián, fearful of being poisoned when he visited the Calced priories, took the precaution of eating nothing there but boiled eggs, while Teresa wrote in a state of intense anxiety to her prioress at Seville, directing her, in spite of a rule to the contrary, to give him his meals in the convent parlour and sending her the money for this with the injunction that she must not mind how much she spent on him. They had some reason for their fears, since a few months before this Fray Juan de la Cruz and his companion had been kidnapped by the Calced and taken to Medina del Campo where they had been imprisoned until, after a few days, an order of the nuncio released them.

Still these things, disagreeable though they were, seemed but the last flickers of rage from the friars of the observance. The reform, backed by both the nuncio and the king, was clearly winning when suddenly the worst happened. The nuncio Ormaneto died and his successor Sega arrived in Spain with a strong prejudice against the reform and gave his support to the general's emissary, Tostado. It looked as if the whole of Teresa's work was to be undone.

The effects of this change were soon felt. The friars of the Discalced were ordered to resign their offices and hand them over to the Calced. None of them obeyed. Then Tostado ordered Fray Juan de la Cruz and his companion to move out of the Encarnación and return at once to their own houses. They expressed their inability to do this for the reason that they had been appointed as confessors to that convent by the apostolic visitor, who still held his commission, and so could not leave without his authority. The refusal of the two friars to relinquish their post must have been particularly irritating to the Calced because of an election that was about to take place there. Teresa's term as prioress had lapsed, her successor had come and gone and now a third choice had to be made. There were two parties among the nuns – the strict party who wanted Teresa back and the lax party who wanted someone else. Tostado sent down the provincial to superintend the affair with instructions to make sure that the Calced candidate was elected, and he, thinking he could best secure this by frightening the nuns, threatened to excommunicate any of them who should vote for Teresa. But in spite of this, fifty-five of them, encouraged by Fray Juan de la Cruz's exhortations, declared their intention to vote for her, and they formed a majority. The scene that followed has been described by Teresa in one of the more vivid of her letters. The provincial took his stand by the grille, abusing and excommunicating those nuns who voted contrary to his wishes and striking, crumpling and burning their voting papers. But even this did not produce the effect that he wanted. He therefore gave orders that none of the recalcitrant nuns should attend mass or enter the chapel or see either their confessors or their parents until they had voted as he desired. When they once again refused to do this he declared the election null and void, excommunicated them a second time and appointed the nun who had obtained the lesser number of votes as prioress.

This election took place in October 1577 and the two friars who had encouraged the uncomplying nuns did not have to wait long before feeling the effect of the Calced's anger. On 2 or 3 December a posse of armed men led by an *alguacil* or constable broke into the house where Fray Juan de la Cruz and his companion Fray Germán de San Matías were living and carried them away as prisoners. Juan was able to escape an hour or two later and destroy his papers, but was followed and re-apprehended. Then he and his companion vanished.*

Teresa was in Avila at the time at her reformed convent of San José, and at once learned of the two friars' sequestration. On the very next day she wrote to King Philip to tell him what had happened, extolling Fray Juan for the immense good he had worked among the nuns of the Encarnación and declaring that in the city he was regarded as a saint, which in her opinion he was and had been all his life. But now, she went on, the Calced friars, who seemed to have no respect either for justice or for God, had made off with him. For her part she would rather see him in the hands of the Moors than in those of the observance, 'for they would have more pity'. And she begged Philip to order his release. A few weeks later she

---

* According to a MSS account, these were not his personal papers, but a correspondence on the affairs of the reform between Teresa, Gracián and himself. Some people suppose that his destruction of his papers had occurred a year and a half before, when he was carried off to Medina, but this is quite uncertain.

wrote again, this time to the archbishop of Évora, a man of much influence, repeating what she had said to the king about Fray Juan and adding, 'He is a tower of strength.' Then in March she was writing to Gracián: 'I am deeply distressed about Fray Juan and afraid they may bring some further accusation against him. God's treatment of his friends is terrible, though really they have nothing to complain of since he did the same to his own Son.' In every letter that she wrote her anxiety about him comes out and her suspicion that the leading friars of the reform, among them Gracián, were not doing all they could to secure his release. 'I don't know how it is,' she wrote to him in August, 'that that saint is so unfortunate that no one remembers him.' Indeed he could not have vanished more completely if he had been in the dungeons of the Inquisition.

But where had Fray Juan been taken? His first place of detention was in the Calced priory at Avila, where, as a sample of what was coming to him, he was twice flogged. Then, as a rescue was feared, he was transferred in great secrecy, by unfrequented roads, to Toledo. Led into the city by night and with his eyes blindfolded so that he should not know where he was, he was locked up in the prison cell of the Carmelite priory. Here he was brought before a tribunal composed of the vicar-general, Tostado, the prior, Maldonado, and several other friars. They began by reading him the acts drawn up by the general chapter of the order at Piacenza by which the Discalced were to abandon their name and their distinction in dress, to cease to take in novices or to form a separate body. They then reminded him of the personal order he had received from the vicar-general to return at once to the Calced priory of Medina. By refusing to comply with this, they said, he had been guilty of gross disobedience to a superior, which was the worst crime that a friar could be guilty of. However, if he submitted now, his offence would be overlooked and he would be given a high office in the order with a good cell and a library and even, one of the tribunal added, a gold crucifix. But Juan de la Cruz was hardly the man to be tempted by the offer of promotion or comforts. In his reply he said that, although he venerated the acts of the chapter and the orders of the vicar-general, he was not obliged nor even permitted to obey them because he had received an express order from the apostolic visitor, who was his immediate superior, not to do so. Further he said that he had made a sacred vow to follow the primitive rule and was not free to break it. As for the punishment they threatened him with, he welcomed it, while it was precisely to avoid comforts and honours that he had joined the Discalced. Tostado now pronounced sentence. Fray Juan was found guilty of rebellion and contumacy and as such was condemned to be imprisoned during the general's good pleasure.

During the first two months of his confinement he was lodged in the ordinary prison cell of the priory, but on the news that his companion at the Encarnación, Fray Germán de San Matías, had effected his escape from the house in which he had been confined, he was moved to a place of greater safety. This was a closet six feet by ten which served as a privy to the adjoining guest chamber. It was lit by a loop-hole three fingers wide and set high in the wall so that to read the offices he had to stand on a bench and hold up his book to the light, and even then he could only make out the print at midday. Through this opening he would hear the Tagus running in its deep trench immediately below. His bed was a board laid on the floor and covered with two old rugs so that, as the temperature of Toledo sinks to below freezing point in winter and a damp chill struck through the stone walls, he suffered greatly from the cold. Later when the summer came round he suffered equally in his stifling closet from the heat. Since he was given no change of clothes during the nine months that he was in prison, he was devoured by lice. His food consisted of scraps of bread and a few sardines – sometimes only half a sardine. These gave him dysentery so that, like Abelard, he wondered whether the monks were not trying to poison him. As a change from this there were the fast days – at first on three days in the week, later only on Fridays. On these occasions he was taken out to the refectory where the friars sat at table, and, kneeling in the centre of the room, given his dry bread and water like a dog. After this the prior would upbraid him:

'So you had to be the first to dishonour the Order of the Virgin with the folly of renouncing your shoes and inventing a new habit, sowing discord among friars and scandalizing laymen. This was your way of putting your name in their mouths and making yourself out to be more reformed than the others. If you wished to be good, what hindered you from remaining in an order that has produced so many friars who have been and holy? Who forbade you to mortify yourself? To rise to the heights of contemplation or be a pattern of virtue? But you, hypocrite, were not aiming at being a saint, but only at being thought one: not at the edification of the people but at the satisfaction of your own self-esteem. Look at him, brothers, this miserable, wretched little friar, scarcely good enough to be a convent porter! He seeks to reform others when what he needs is to reform himself. Now bare your shoulders: it is on them that we will write the rules of the new reform.'*

Upon this he would be given the circular discipline on his bare shoulders, each of the friars striking him in turn with a cane while the *Miserere* was recited. This was the penalty laid down in the constitutions for the contumacious and it was the severest as well as the most degrading punishment that could be given to a friar. Juan bore these scourgings in silence. The young friars pitied him, exclaiming, 'Say what they like, he is a saint,' but the older ones grew more angry than ever at his submissiveness, calling him a sly boots and a snake in the grass. He bore the marks of these scourgings to the end of his life.

From his cell, Juan could hear the friars talking in the guest room next door, no doubt with the intention of being overheard by him. They spoke of the suppression of the Discalced houses by order of the nuncio and of the imminent destruction of the whole reform. Some said that both Teresa and Gracián were in prison – were they not worse heretics than Luther? Then he heard one friar say, 'What are we keeping this man for? Let's throw him into a well and finish with him.' Other voices declared he would never leave the prison except to be buried. This seemed only too likely, for he was feeling weaker every day. His dysentery was becoming worse and the suspicion kept returning that they might be slowly poisoning him. He felt a great dread that he might die there alone, in secret, his fate unknown to anyone. Even now the foundress, Madre Teresa, might be imagining that he had given way and deserted to the other side. But his worst torment, he afterwards declared, was his fear that he might after all have sinned through disobedience to his

---

* This speech of the prior's is taken from Jerónimo de San José's biography of Juan de la Cruz which was published in 1641, but on information collected more than twenty years before from people who had known him. In imitation of the Latin historians he made up into a formal speech the various accounts Fray Juan had given of the accusations which the prior had levelled against him. In its essence therefore Maldonado's speech is true, as is shown by the various depositions of witnesses which have come down to us.

superiors. Could not the prior be right? By what authority was he
defying the general of his order? The constant recriminations he had
to listen to began, against his better judgement, to undermine his
belief that he was acting rightly and he even began to wonder
whether his adoption of the primitive rule had not been an act of
presumption and folly. This doubt made him fear all the more to die
because, if he did so while he was in mortal sin, he would die
eternally, cast off by God. These scruples and temptations were the
worst part of his sufferings in prison – far more severe than the
merely physical ones – and one finds them recapitulated in his prose
works, *The Ascent of Mount Carmel* and *The Dark Night of the Soul*.

All this time he had no communication with anyone. His jailor
was forbidden to speak to him. Instead he looked at him with
hatred, opening the door of his cell only to throw his food on the
floor and leaving his bucket for days without emptying it so that the
stench that came from it made him vomit. Juan even came to look
forward to his scourgings in the refectory because on these occasions the prior spoke to him, though always in an angry and contemptuous manner. Then, as the warm weather drew on, he began
to suffer in other ways. His tunic, which was clotted with blood
from his scourgings, stuck to his back and putrified. Worms bred
in it so that his whole body became intolerable to him. He lost both
sleep and appetite and felt that he had only death to look forward to.

After he had been in prison for about six months a new jailor was
appointed. This was a young man from another priory and he took
pity on him and gave him a clean tunic. He also gave him a pen and
ink so that he could 'compose from time to time a few things
profitable to devotion' and, as we shall see later he used them to
write down certain poems. A story, recorded by his first biographer,
Jerónimo de San José, throws light on how he came to compose
them. One evening, when he was in very low spirits, he heard a
young man's voice singing a *villancico* or love song in the street
outside. The words were:

> Muérome de amores,
> Carillo. ¿Qué haré?
> – Que te mueras, alahé.

'I am dying of love, dearest. What shall I do? – Die.'
And at once he was carried away in an ecstasy. When, some years
later, he was asked by a nun, Ana de San Alberto, if any consola-

tions had been given him in prison, he replied, 'My daughter Ana, one single grace of those that God gave me there could not be paid for by many years of prison.' The phrase is underlined in the account she dictated to her confessor ten or more years after his death. To María de Jesús, a nun who saw him at Toledo just after his escape, he said that the Lord had shown him many favours. But some of the best authenticated statements give a different picture. To another María de Jesús, whose confessor he became at Beas early in the following year, he said that he received few consolations – 'and I even think that he said none, but that every part of him suffered both body and soul' – while to Inocencio de San Andrés, who became his penitent at El Calvario at the same time, he said that he had suffered 'great interior afflictions and dryness'. Yet although we must suppose that he had had some moments of 'consolation', since he composed a part of his poem, the *Cántico espiritual* in prison, his experiences were, like Dostoevsky's in Siberia, traumatic, so that he not only owed to them his outburst of poetry, but also those forbidding accounts of the suffering the soul undergoes in its quest for perfection which he gives in his prose works, *The Ascent of Mount Carmel* and *The Dark Night*.

August came and the heat in his airless cell grew stifling. He felt that if he remained in it much longer he would reach a point of no-recovery. One night, if his first biographer is to be believed, the Virgin appeared to him in a vision, filling the cell with her beauty and brilliance, and announced to him that his trials would soon be over and that he would leave the prison. This dream drew on an early memory. Once as a little boy at Fontiveros he had fallen into a pond. As he struggled in the mud and water he had seen a well-dressed lady on the bank whom he had taken to be the Virgin. He had stretched out his arms to her, but with the fists closed because his hands were too dirty to take hers. Then someone else had pulled him out. Later at Medina, when he was about twelve, he had fallen into a deep well and, invoking her, had, after sinking several times, found a piece of wood on which he had supported himself until he was rescued. He now felt assured that, in spite of his weakness, he would be able with her help to escape from his prison and so he set about considering how he could do so.*

* Juan himself never spoke of this vision: that was not his way. He merely told the nuns at Toledo of the 'help, consolation and interior impulses' which Christ and the Virgin had given him when he had prayed to them for aid in his escape, and later he said the same thing to two of his friars. We do not

The new jailor, to allow his prisoner to get a little air, had taken to leaving the door of his cell open while the friars were taking their siesta, and he accepted his offer to let him empty his bucket. This gave Juan an opportunity for exploring the part of the building in which he was confined. The Carmelite priory was a huge block of reddish masonry that rose some ninety feet above the rocky bed of the Tagus not far downstream from the Puente de Alcántara. Although it was destroyed during the Peninsular War one could still in 1933 see its broken walls jutting out of the slope of rubble that lies between the Gobierno Militar and the river. On the eastern side, opening off the great room, there was a broad gallery that served as a cloister and whose arched windows looked down onto a small *corral* or yard that abutted the city wall, beyond which ran the river. The jailor had given Juan a needle and thread and a pair of scissors to mend his habit. Attaching the thread to a small stone Juan let it down from the window that lay immediately above the city wall at the point where it joined the high wall of the priory. From this he was able to calculate that if he cut up his two rugs into strips and tied them together they would reach within ten feet of the top of the battlements. But he must also find a way of opening the door of his cell. It was fastened by a padlock and two eyed-staples that screwed into the wood. Every afternoon when his cell door was left open he worked at loosening them so that, if it was given a strong push, they would fall out. Finally he begged an iron *candil*, or oil lamp, from his jailor on the pretext of reading his offices by it.

On 14 August, on the eve of the Assumption, the prior, Fray Maldonado, came into his cell. Juan was on his knees with his head bent to the ground and too absorbed in his prayer to notice his entry. The prior, angry at such a lack of respect, gave him a kick with his foot and asked why he did not stand up to receive him. Juan excused himself and rose to his feet with an effort. 'What were you thinking of that you were so absorbed?' asked Maldonado. 'I was thinking that tomorrow will be the feast of the Blessed Virgin and that I should be very happy if I could say mass.' 'That will not be in my time,' replied the other and went out.

in fact know whether he ever had a vision in his life and he deprecated any importance being attached to such things in other people. The childhood stories of his falling into water are true as they were reported by his brother and if I have mentioned this vision it is because it or something like it seems to be probable.

Juan was now ready to make his bid for liberty. First, to show his gratitude to his jailor, he presented him with a crucifix of fine wood with a bronze Christ on it that had been given him by Teresa and which he always wore round his neck. Some people have seen in this an indication that the jailor was conniving in his escape, but when in 1616, during the process of Juan's beatification, the man was questioned, he refused to admit this, although it would have stood to his credit had he done so. He merely praised Juan's gentleness and the gratitude and affection he showed for any favours done to him.

The night that would decide everything now arrived. While the jailor, who was bringing him his supper, went back to fetch a jug of water, Juan once more loosened the screws of the staple on which his padlock fastened. He had now only to cut his two rugs into strips and tie them together by the light of the lamp to be completely ready. As it happened, the provincial and a party of friars had arrived that evening and two of these friars were lodged in the guest room off his cell. This seemed at first to ruin everything, but at least they left open the door leading to the gallery so as to get more air. After going to bed they continued talking for a long time, but when two o'clock struck Juan judged they were asleep. A voice in his head said 'Be quick, be quick', and he took the lamp and the rope of blanket strips in his hand and gave a push to the door. The screws came out and the padlock fell with a crash to the ground, waking the friars. '*Deo gratias*, what is that?' said one of them, but Juan did not move and they fell asleep again. Then, passing between their beds, he stole out into the gallery.

A full moon was shining, lighting up the steep slope beyond the river with its rocks and gnarled olive trees and throwing the yard below into deep shadow. The window that Juan had chosen for his descent gave onto a small balcony or *miradorcillo* that was enclosed by a thin brick wall, covered by a wooden rail to prevent the friars from soiling their clothes when they leaned on it. In one place there was a slight gap between the wood and the bricks and in this he wedged the iron lamp and slipped the blanket rope which he had attached to it over the edge. Then, taking off his habit and throwing it down in front of him, he seized the rope in his hands and, gripping it between his knees, slid to the end of it and let himself fall. He landed on a heap of loose stones that littered the coping of the city wall within a couple of feet of the sheer drop to the rocks of the

Tagus. He could hear the noise of the river as it ran rapidly, insistently, through its narrow gorge below. After putting on his habit, he scrambled along the top of the wall till he came to a place where a heap of rubble enabled him to descend to the ground. He now found himself in a large enclosure bounded on one side by the wall of the city and on another by the great pile of the Carmelite priory, while in front of him there were various lower walls and buildings. From what the jailor had told him he realized that he was in the courtyard belonging to the Franciscan nuns of the Conception. He walked all round it, but, except for a door which was bolted, could find no way out.

Despair came over him. Had he done all this only to find himself trapped? When morning came he would be discovered within the precincts of an enclosed convent, a cause of scandal to the entire city. He thought of calling out to the friars of the Carmelite priory, asleep in their cells above, and giving himself up. They would take him back to his prison cell and he would submit to whatever punishment they might choose to give him. But then, fighting off his despair, he decided to make a last effort. According to one account he saw a dog nosing among the offal that had been thrown out of the refectory window. To see how it had got in, he threatened it and (the details are a little confused) it ran off and leapt over a low wall. Juan tried to follow it, but found the wall too high for him to climb in his enfeebled state. Calling on the Virgin for help, he found himself all at once, he did not know how, in the street on the far side. Another account, that of Fray Juan de Santa Ana, who a short time later was to become one of the closest of his disciples, describes him as groping about for some time and then finding a place at the junction of two walls where the plaster had come out and left footholes. He managed, he did not know how, to climb it 'feeling as though an angel had guided him' and dropped down on the other side. While we can discount miracles, we must bear in mind that in Juan's enfeebled state, neither his descent by the rope nor his climbing of the wall would have been possible if he had not been sustained by his faith that Christ and the Virgin were helping him.

Juan was now free in a city he did not know and at an hour when the life of all cities is mysterious and strange. Almost at once he saw a tavern that was still open. The man who kept it, thinking that he had been locked out of his priory, invited him to come in and wait there till its doors were unfastened, but Juan hurried by without a word. The lane he was following led him to the Plaza de Zocodover, where he saw the lights of the stalls and the market women busy arranging their wares: as he passed they jeered and shouted out dirty words. Then he met a woman leaving her house to go to her stall and asked her the way to the Discalced Carmelite convent. She told him, but since it would be shut till daybreak, offered to let him remain in her house till then. He refused. A little further on he came to the door of a *caballero's* mansion which stood open. The *caballero*, with a naked sword in his hand, was searching the *zaguán* or entrance hall, whilst a servant held a torch to light him. Juan asked his permission to sit in his hall till daylight. The *caballero* consented, the door was shut and the household went to bed.

At daybreak Juan wished to leave but the street door was still closed. In a state of great anxiety lest he should be recaptured, he hammered loudly and at length a servant came down the stairs and unlocked it. As he left the house it was close on eight. He had no cape and his black habit, given him by the Observant friars, was torn and dirty and his feet bare, so that he looked like a student returning from a revel. The passers-by called out after him. But, as he hurried along, in all the churches and convents of the city the angelus was ringing. On reaching the Carmelite house he found the nuns just out of chapel. The extern sister, Leonor de Jesús, came to the grille. *Hija*, he said, *Fray Juan de la Cruz soy, que me he salido esta noche de la prisión. Dígaselo a la Madre Priora.* The prioress, Ana de los Ángeles, was called, and, summoning the two other nuns who held the keys, opened in their presence the three locks that fastened the door of the enclosure and let him in. A sick nun who needed confession was the excuse for this grave breach of the rules.

The sisters, heavily veiled in black muslin over their long white robes, gathered round. Some light refreshment – pears stewed in cinnamon, which was all he could digest – was set before him and, as he ate, he told his exciting story. His thin beard had grown, his habit was ragged and dirty, he had no white cape or hood. He spoke in a whisper and was so weak he could hardly stand. So thin and disfigured was he from hunger that, as one of them later said, he looked like an image of death. But meanwhile his escape had been discovered and the Carmelites of the Observance were looking for him. Two friars arrived with *alguaciles* or constables and searched the outer premises, but did not dare to violate the enclosure. As soon as they had gone Fray Juan was let into the chapel. Here he dictated some verses that he had composed in prison, the nuns sitting in their long black veils in their choir while he stood against the iron grille that divided it from the nave. These verses comprised three *romances* or ballads* on the Trinity, beginning, *En el principio moraba*, which are not among his best productions. But according to Magdalena del Espíritu Santo, a nun who later came to know him well and was employed to make copies of his verses, he had brought out of prison a notebook in which he had written down both these and other more important poems. These are the stanzas of the *Cántico espiritual* as far as the verse that begins, *Oh, ninfas de Judea*, the poem that begins *Que bien sé yo la fonte que mana y corre* and a rhymed version of the psalm *Super flumina Babylonis*. There are other witnesses to the fact that he had written these poems down in prison and it would seem that he also recited them to the nuns in the choir though they did not take copies of them. This haste to read them aloud to the sisters when he was almost too exhausted to speak or to stand is a proof of the great importance he attached to them.

The prioress was unwilling that he should spend the night in the chapel, where he was not in safety since it lay outside the enclosure. She therefore sent a message to a canon of the Cathedral, Don Pedro González de Mendoza, who belonged to the great Mendoza family and was a friend of the reform. He came to see her and that night took Fray Juan de la Cruz away in his coach, disguised in a priest's cassock, to the Hospital de la Cruz, of which he was the administrator. Here, though scarcely more than a hundred yards from the Carmelite priory he had just escaped from, Juan was safe.

* A *romance* is a poem composed in octosyllabic lines with an identical vowel assonance on every even one. Originally the form used for ballads, it came to be employed by poets in a rather more general way, though Juan's choice of it for a theological exposition was exceptional.

4

El Calvario and Baeza

While Juan de la Cruz was languishing in prison things had been going badly for the reform. Tostado, it is true, had left Spain because the royal council had prevented him from acting, but the nuncio Sega was still there and as hostile as ever. After annulling the visitor's patents that had been issued by his predecessor, he placed the Discalced immediately under the authority of the Calced and forbade them to receive any novices. Although the king and the royal council remained friendly, they had no power to intervene. In this emergency some of the leading friars of the reform proposed to call a chapter which would be asked to set up a separate province for the Discalced. This was flying in the face of all authority, for only the pope and the general had the power to act in that way. Both Teresa and Gracián were half-hearted about it, but in spite of their doubts the chapter met at Almodóvar del Río on 9 October 1578. Fray Juan de la Cruz, who had spent the last six weeks in Don Pedro de Mendoza's house at Toledo, slowly recovering his strength, was invited to attend it and accepted.

Almodóvar lies some hundred miles to the south of Toledo on the western border of La Mancha. Juan travelled there on a donkey, escorted by two of Don Pedro's servants who were sent to take care of him. Teresa had been deeply distressed to hear that he was to make the journey in his sick and enfeebled state and wrote to Gracián from Avila asking him as a favour to her to see that he was well looked after. 'Don't neglect this,' she urged. 'I assure your Paternity that if he dies you will be left with few who are like him.' As it happened, Gracián, taking fright at the last moment, did not attend the meeting, but the friars who did, shocked by Fray Juan's emaciated appearance, appointed a young novice to wait on him.

The chapter, which was composed of seven of the leading friars of the reform, at once proceeded to set up a separate province for the Discalced and to elect a provincial. The man chosen was Antonio de Jesús, or Heredia, who had been the co-founder with

Juan de la Cruz of the first Discalced house at Duruelo. He was now in his late sixties, a large, imposing, smiling man of dignified presence, a generation older than his brother friars and, though austere in his habits, touchy and unreliable. He professed to have a low opinion of women and in the past had been fond of teasing Juan for having had his habit made by one of them – that is, by Teresa. Yet he was intensely jealous of her esteem for her former pupil and confessor and still more of her deep regard for Gracián, for he thought that he deserved to occupy the first place both in her thoughts and in the reform. Now as provincial he had reached the summit of his ambitions.

The election had of course been totally illegal and Juan had refused to vote in it. The proper course, he declared, was to petition the king and the pope to create a separate province for the Discalced and not to set up one themselves. However his advice was not taken and, as was to be expected, the consequences of this rash act were immediately felt. Sega excommunicated all the friars who had voted in it and imprisoned others, including the absent Gracián, in Calced priories. But before this happened Juan de la Cruz had been appointed temporary prior of the priory-hermitage of El Calvario, far down on the eastern border of Andalusia on the upper waters of the Guadalquivir. In such a remote place it was felt that he would be safe from the clutches of his enemies. The distance from Almodóvar was a hundred and thirty miles and as before Mendoza sent his servants to escort him.

A few miles short of his destination Juan stopped to rest for a few days at the convent of Beas de Segura, which had been founded by Teresa three and a half years before. It was a place that called up the happiest memories for her as it was there that she had first met Gracián. The little town lies in a valley under the Sierra de Segura among poplars, olive trees and running streams. The soil is red, the houses white, the fields green – a great contrast to the austere landscapes of Castile and La Mancha. Ana de Jesús, the most outstanding of Teresa's nuns though by no means the one she liked best, was the prioress. Juan knew her already, for he had met her eight years before at Mancera when she had been a beautiful and intelligent novice of twenty-five – so beautiful indeed that in her home town of Medina del Campo she had been known as La Reina. Now she was maturing into the capable, strong willed yet spiritually minded woman who would later resist the tyranny of the Superiors who were undermining the liberty of the nuns and carry the reform to France and the Low Countries. Like the other sisters of her convent she was struck by Fray Juan's worn and emaciated appearance – 'he was like a dead man, with nothing but skin on his bones, so drained and exhausted he could hardly speak.' A story illustrates this. One day when he was in the parlour conversing with the sisters, as they sat during their hour of recreation behind the double grille, the prioress told a young nun to sing some verses. She began:

> Quien no sabe de penas
> en este valle de dolores,
> no sabe cosas buenas
> ni ha gustado de amores,
> pues penas son el traje de amadores.

> He who knows nothing of pains
> in this valley of sorrows
> nothing knows of good things
> nor has tasted of love,
> since pains are the garment of lovers.

Juan in his weakness and exhaustion was so overcome with emotion on hearing this song that the tears poured down his cheeks and he gripped the bars of the grille with both hands. Making a sign for the singer to cease, he remained in that position unable to move or speak for an hour. When he had recovered he began to tell them how the Lord had made him understand the value of suffering, yet how little of it he had been able to offer to Him. This, after what he had gone through, amazed them. But although Ana de Jesús felt sorry for him, she did not warm to him. Small – he measured under five feet, as a post mortem examination of his bones showed – muddy-complexioned and silent, he was not made to please women at first sight.

The priory-hermitage that Juan was bound for lay two hours ride away across rough hills covered with rocks, pines and aromatic shrubs. It comprised a whitewashed farm house, a small oratory and several acres of orchard and farming land which had been bought from the parish priest of Villanueva two years before. A spring shaded by trees stood in a courtyard outside and all around there were olives, pines and ilexes. The original name of the place had been Corenzuela, but the friars had changed it to El Calvario when they put up a rustic *via crucis*.

El Calvario is reached today by a road that branches off the main Jaén–Albacete highway and drops into the gorge of the Guadalquivir on its way to an artificial lake and electric power station. The deep green water flows between red rocks: tamarisks and oleanders lean over it, while on the opposite bank the mountain rises up, spur above spur, like a crumpled, greyish curtain. To reach the hermitage one must take a steep path up the hill to the left. The path zigzags through broom and lavender and cistus among which, if it is spring, one will find small irises, jonquils and bee orchids. Then one comes to a piece of flatter ground. There is a barking of dogs, the bushes give way and one sees before one a couple of whitewashed buildings, some elm trees shading a well, a tiny domed chapel and a few ancient olives. All around, pine trees and aromatic shrubs.

The eight months that Juan de la Cruz spent in this house were among the happiest in his life. He was thirty-six. He had emerged from the darkness of his prison – 'that whale', as he called it after the Book of Jonah – into the beauty of an Andalusian spring and the sort of wild landscape – *montes, valles, riberas* – that he preferred. Here he wrote, it would seem, the poem beginning *En una noche oscura* and all but six of the remaining stanzas of the *Cántico espiritual*, which he had commenced in prison. When he left El Calvario his career as a poet was almost finished. But his happiness was not only due to solitude and scenery. There were some thirty friars in the little farmhouse on the hillside and some of them were old hermits from the Sierra Morena who had joined the reform a few years previously. (The Carmelite order had, as we have seen, a tradition of descent from anchorites which made it easier for them to assimilate these eccentrics.) Among them we read of Brother Hilarión, an old man of seventy with flowing white beard and hair, who recalled the Early Fathers of the Desert, and Brother Alonso, the cook, who picked for salad any herb that his mule stopped to eat. The simplicity of these men must have delighted Juan, whose lighter reading since boyhood had been the legends of the primitive monks and anchorites contained in the *Flos Sanctorum*. Indeed it still remained his favourite book after the Bible. But he had also, as once before at Pastrana, to restrain some of his friars from excesses that would injure their health. It would seem that he was thinking of them when he wrote of 'those beginners, who, seeking after spiritual sweetness for its own sake, a demon of gluttony takes possession of them and they kill themselves by fasting and penance' (*Dark Night* 1: 6,1). This was an aftermath of the impact of Doña Catalina de Cardona and it had to be combated.

The diet however was austere. The friars lived almost entirely on bread, vegetables and salads, and sometimes the bread ran out. Fish, though permitted, was rarely obtainable and on feast days they ate *migas*, a porridge made of bread crumbs and olive oil, seasoned with garlic and pepper. They were not allowed to sample the plums, cherries and oranges that grew in their orchard unless, as rarely happened, they were served to them in the refectory. One day, while picking cherries, a young friar put one of them in his mouth. Overcome by guilt he stood up that evening at supper and confessed his fault. The prior took it seriously. Though gentle in his mode of speech, he was very strict about breaches of the rule and punished them severely, often with the discipline. After that the matter was forgotten.

Yet it must not be thought that such an abstemious life led to melancholy. These friars could be gay. Fasts and penances were to them what throwing over ballast is to a balloonist. The less they were chained to their bodies, the more their spirits rose, the lighter they became, the freer to give all their faculties to the love that had brought them there. Juan too employed special methods for raising their minds to contemplation. He would take them out under the trees and, instead of giving them a passage from the Bible to meditate on, would speak to them of the beauties of the Creation, of the birds and flowers, trees and streams, sky and sun, which were a reflection of the Divine Beauty. Then he would send them off to meditate alone, under a rock or a tree or beside a running brook, scattered about on the hillside. Thus, like true hermits, they were much of the time in the open air, for they had also to work on their patch of land and bring in the crops. Only if it rained did they stay indoors and then in the recreation hour Juan would occupy himself with weaving willow baskets or carving small wooden images with a knife. He sometimes drew too and at the convent of the Encarnación at Avila there is preserved a remarkable drawing by him of Christ on the Cross, seen obliquely from above (see plate 3).

He had besides another occupation which took up much of his time. When he left Beas for El Calvario the prioress Ana de Jesús had been offended by his speaking of the venerable foundress, Madre Teresa, as his 'special daughter'. Coming from a young man this seemed to border on the impertinent and she mentioned the bad impression she had received in a letter she wrote to Teresa to tell her that she was in a great fix because she could not find a suitable confessor for her nuns. The answer came back at once:

'It has really amused me, daughter, to see you complaining with so little reason when you have with you my Father Fray Juan de la Cruz, that divine and heavenly man. I assure you, my daughter, that since he left these parts I have not found another like him in the whole of Castile, nor one who inspires souls with such fervour on their journey to Heaven. Only consider what a great treasure you have in that saint and let all the sisters in your house talk with him and confide in him about their souls. They will then see how much good it does them and advance rapidly in spirituality and perfection, for Our Lord has given him in this a special grace. . . .

'I give you my word that I should be only too glad to have my Father Fray Juan de la Cruz here with me, for he is indeed the Father of my soul and one of those with whom it does me most good to converse. Treat him, daughters, with complete frankness, for I assure you that you can be as open with him as you would be with me and he will satisfy all your needs since he is very spiritual and has great experience and learning. He is badly missed here by those who were brought up on his teaching. So give thanks to God for having ordained that you have him so near you. I am writing to tell him to attend to your wants and I know he is so kind that he will do so whenever the need presents itself.'

Teresa's letter bore immediate fruit. Ana de Jesús asked him to be the confessor of her convent. Every Saturday after that Juan would set out on foot for Beas, dressed in his old torn habit of coarse serge. The distance was rather over two leagues. After climbing a little, he kept along the summit of the ridge with views of great mountains whenever the pine woods opened out and then descended by a twisting path into the valley. He would start confessing the nuns on the same day, and continue on Sunday, sitting in a high chair which is still preserved while they knelt at his feet. As the rule prescribed, both his companion and another sister stood nearby though out of earshot and the sisters were of course heavily veiled so that he could not see their faces. He gave each one a considerable time, for he regarded himself more as a spiritual director than as a confessor and he spoke gently though, when the occasion required, he could be severe. He treated every sister in precisely the same way, showing no favouritism and refusing the little presents which it was the custom to offer confessors. Afterwards, seated in the parlour, he would read to them from the Gospels, making comments that filled them with enthusiasm for though, since he disliked rhetoric, he was not an eloquent preacher, he talked with great lucidity and conviction.

Various anecdotes about his conversation have been preserved. One of the nuns, a simple girl called Catalina who acted as cook, asked him why, when she went past the tank in the garden, the frogs that had been sitting on the edge jumped into the water and hid themselves. Fray Juan replied that this was the place where they felt most secure. Only there could they defend and preserve themselves. So it ought to be, he went on, with her. She should flee from the creatures and hide herself in the depths, which was God. Many years later, in a letter to the prioress, he sent her a message: 'Remember me to our sister Catalina and tell her to hide herself and seek the depths.'

In the course of his spiritual directions he gave each sister a sheet of paper with a drawing of Mount Carmel on it symbolizing his doctrine of mortification and detachment from all earthly things and with it a *sentencia* or maxim designed to suit her special needs and circumstances. Some of these maxims were worked into his long prose work, *The Ascent of Mount Carmel*, which he began to write at this time in the form of a commentary on his poem *En una noche oscura*, and finished four or five years later. He also lent them a notebook containing his poems which one of them, Magdalena del Espíritu Santo, made copies of. The nuns were deeply affected by the *Cántico espiritual* and asked him to explain it for them and this is the origin of his prose commentary on it, which he began to put down in short paragraphs at the same time that he was writing *The Ascent*.

These visits to the nuns of Beas made a profound impact on Juan de la Cruz's life and work. After his harsh sequestration in prison the tender and delicate intimacy that grew up between him and these sisters of his order supplied something that he was badly in need of, while their questions and demands gave him the stimulus to write his prose works in the form of explanations of his poems. He could only give himself to those who were travelling on the same road as himself, and more easily to nuns and young friars than to his contemporaries in the order, who had already formed their own ideas on the course to be followed and who would have resented his guidance. This association was to be a lasting one for, as we shall see, he continued to write to and visit these nuns of Beas for many years after he had left their neighbourhood.

Juan de la Cruz's residence at El Calvario ended in June 1579 when he was appointed rector of the new Carmelite college at Baeza, some thirty-six miles further down the Guadalquivir. His nomination to this post came as one of the consequences of a sudden change in the affairs of the Discalced. Only the previous winter the nuncio Sega had appeared to be on the point of destroying Teresa's reform by placing them under the authority of the Calced. But she had powerful friends in Spain, among whom was the king, and Sega, feeling the atmosphere at court becoming more and more hostile to him, was obliged at the last minute to draw back. On Philip's suggestion four assessors were appointed to examine the issue between the Observance and the Reform and they decided that the two branches must be separated and made into separate provinces. Sega yielded and appointed Ángel de Salazar, a Calced Carmelite who was moderately favourable to the reform, to be vicar-general to the Discalced, while the king sent to Rome to request the pope to set up a separate province for them. While the pope's reply was awaited, Salazar directed Fray Juan to found the new college.

Baeza is a small but ancient city built on a long spur of high land: all around it are rolling hollows of chalk down, green with corn in spring and in summer red with poppies. In the distance a vast circuit of mountains. Today it is a stagnant, decaying place, a museum of fine Renaissance buildings, but in Fray Juan's time it was very prosperous, with a population of more than 50,000 and a flourishing wool and silk industry. Its university, founded in 1540 by Juan de Ávila, the 'Apostle of Andalusia', had a high reputation and some of its professors, admirers of that great preacher of poverty, were anxious to have among them a Discalced Carmelite college which would give instruction in the higher forms of prayer. There were also many well-to-do families in the city who could be counted on to provide a sufficient income. So Fray Juan purchased a house and moved into it with three friars, to be joined later by four student novices. He at once found himself caught up in a life of great bustle and activity. Besides teaching and receiving visits, he was much sought after by devout persons of both sexes who were anxious to have him as their spiritual director. He found some relief from the business of the college in visiting the hospitals. The year 1580 saw an epidemic of *catarro universal* or influenza which killed his mother and left Teresa in a state of prostration from which she never fully recovered. Juan waived all his ascetic principles when he nursed the sick, begging money from his rich patrons to provide the meat and wine which he considered they needed. He found time also to continue his prose works.

But the two years and more that he spent at Baeza were not happy ones. As he wrote to Teresa, he could not endure the Andalusians, and since that was her feeling too after the twelve months she had spent in the noise and chatter of Seville, she sympathized with him about it. But besides his antipathy for the facile Andalusian temperament, Juan had other reasons for feeling caged and exiled. As he wrote in the *Spiritual Canticle* (*Annotation for Stanza* 29; see Peers's translation of the *Canticle*, p. 345):

'until the soul has reached the state of union, it finds it useful to exercise love in the active life as well as in the contemplative, but, after it has attained it, exterior works and actions become an impediment to its progress. The reason for this is that a little of that pure and solitary love, although it appears to effect nothing, is more precious to God and to the soul, as well as of more profit to the Church, than all actions together can be. That is why Mary Magdalene, although by her preaching she could have done a great deal of good, hid in the desert for thirty years to give herself wholly to this love.'

Although Teresa with her divided nature thought differently, for she had found the state of union to be the prelude to a life of intense activity, it is clear that Juan felt at this time a deep need to resume the long hours of prayer and mortification and communion with nature that he had enjoyed at El Calvario. We are told for example that his propensity for falling into ecstatic states and raptures had increased. To say mass had become an extreme joy to him, but also a torment because he was afraid of being transported while he was saying it. Once this actually happened and the congregation saw him stand motionless with the chalice in his hand for a good while and then walk off to the sacristy as though the mass had been completed. One can understand therefore how the business he had to transact at Baeza and the society of uncongenial and worldly people must have been a great hindrance to his inner life.

But there were always the nuns at Beas. Every few weeks he set out on foot to visit them, a broad-brimmed hat on his head, a long staff in his hand and with a friar as companion. As he went he would either intone psalms or sing songs of his own composition and when he arrived he would remain for several days. Sometimes he stopped to spend the night at a Trinitarian monastery close to the village of Iznatoraf where the monks had caught the new vogue for mental prayer. I visited this place in 1933 and was told an anecdote that has never, I believe, been published. The prior said that a story had been handed down in the community that San Juan, when he stayed with them, used to disappear from sight into a little room in the belfry and remain there for several hours, looking through a small aperture. However, as no such room existed, he had always supposed that it must be a legend. Then, a year or two before my visit, some repairs had been done to the tower and they had come across this room. He took me to see it. It was a tiny cavity, little more than a cupboard, a couple of yards square, but through a loop-hole in the wall one had a view of hills and green fields.

There are other examples in the life of Juan de la Cruz of his predilection for retiring to some dark and confined place that opened onto a wide view. At Pastrana there had been a small cave that he used to crouch in and look out over a great expanse of country. At Segovia, as we shall see later, there was a grotto. But he also liked to sit or walk in the open, under a tree or rock or by a stream. While he was at Baeza a priest presented the Carmelite college with a small farm, the Granja de Santa Ana, which stood a mile or two to the south of Sorihuela, overlooking the Rio Guadalimar in the parish of Castellar de Santisteban, some thirty miles to the north-east. It was a place that had enchanted Teresa with its flowers and birds when some years before she had stopped there for a siesta on her way from Beas to Seville. Now Juan would come here with a brother friar and spend several days. He would pace along with his companion over the *montes y riberas*, the hills and the riverbanks, often singing as he went, happy to be in the peace and solitude of these hillsides with their aromatic smell of gum cistus

1 A drawing from a contemporary engraving of the Alcázar of Toledo, showing in the foreground the Calced Carmelite priory in which St John was imprisoned. The window from which he escaped is shown on the extreme right of the building (see pp. 29ff.)

2 St John in prayer before the picture of Christ which had spoken
to him in the priory of Segovia (see pp. 66, 76)

3 St John's drawing of 'Christ, Crucified', preserved in the convent
of the Encarnación at Avila (see p. 43)

4 A sketch of Mount Carmel as drawn by St John showing the road
to perfection, and engraved for the 1619 edition of his works
(see pp. 45, 133ff.)

and lavender. Not content with this he would sit in the meadow beside a small stream till far on into the night, talking to his companion upon the beauty of the sky and of the stars. Such a strong impressionability to nature was rare in the city-dwelling Spaniards of that age and among their poets I can only think of Góngora and Pedro Espinosa who possessed it to that degree.

It is to this period that we must assign two visits made by Juan de la Cruz to the Discalced convent of Caravaca, 170 miles by wild mountain tracks over the Sierra de Segura in the direction of Murcia. Ana de San Alberto was the prioress and Teresa, in reply to a request for a good confessor to her nuns, had arranged that he should visit them. 'Treat him,' she wrote, 'as though he were myself.' Juan seems to have gone there early in 1580, but he paid a second visit in June 1581 to supervise the election of a prioress, which resulted in Ana de San Alberto being chosen again. He was clearly concerned by the isolation of this convent, for in December 1586 he founded a priory of friars there so that the nuns should have confessors of their own order close at hand. Several of his letters to Ana de San Alberto have come down to us. Unlike most of the Discalced nuns, who were continually being moved about to provide for new foundations, she spent the rest of her life, forty-eight years, in this little convent by the stream, most of the time as prioress. She died there in 1624.

It was either during his rectorship at Baeza or, more probably at Granada two years later, that he completed his great poem, the *Cántico espiritual*, which he had begun in prison, by writing the last five stanzas of it. It happened in this way. On one of his regular visits to Beas, he asked one of the sisters, Francisca de la Madre de Dios, what prayer meant to her. 'It means contemplating the beauty of God,' she replied, 'and rejoicing that I am able to do so.' Juan was so delighted with this answer that for several days after he kept saying *cosas muy levantadas*, very sublime things, on His beauty and it was soon after this that he composed the last five stanzas of the *Cántico* which begin *Gocémonos, Amado,/y vámonos a ver en tu hermosura.*

The pope having now authorized the Discalced Carmelites to form a separate province, they held a chapter, known as the Chapter of the Separation, at Alcalá de Henares to celebrate this. It met in March 1581. It was their moment of triumph, for their seven years' struggle with the Calced Carmelites and with the general of their order was now at length settled to the satisfaction of all and they were free to develop in their own way. Their first act was to choose a provincial, and Jerónimo Gracián was elected, though only by eleven votes to nine. His rival, Antonio de Heredia, got seven and it shows how unpopular Gracián had become with many of the priors that such an unstable and mediocre man as his rival could do so well. But Heredia, besides being well liked, had stood up to Sega and the general at the illegal chapter at Almodóvar, whereas Gracián had shilly-shallied and finally not gone to it at all.

Fray Juan de la Cruz naturally travelled up to attend the chapter. His term as rector of the college at Baeza was almost up and he was very concerned lest he should be re-elected. He therefore wrote to Teresa to ask her to use her influence to have him sent back to Castile, if possible as a simple friar. She passed this request on to Gracián, begging him as a special favour to her that if this happened he would not confirm the election, 'for it would be only right to give him this comfort since he has had his fill of suffering'. But the new provincial did not comply with her request, whether out of jealousy or because he felt that Juan was more needed in Andalusia, but appointed him third definitor and prior of Los Mártires at Granada, though with the proviso that he should remain on as rector of the college at Baeza for the time being. Juan's disappointment breaks out in a letter he wrote in July to Catalina de Jesús, a nun at Palencia:

'Jesus be with your soul, my daughter. Although I do not know where you are, I want to write you these lines, feeling sure that our Mother will send them on to you if you are not with her; should that be the case, console yourself by thinking that I am more of an exile than you are and more alone. Since that whale swallowed me and vomited me up in this foreign port, I have not been found worthy to see her again nor the saints of those parts. God has done well, though, since in the long run affliction is a file and by suffering darkness we come to a great light. Please God we don't have to remain in it. Oh what things I should like to tell you! Only I write in the dark as I cannot be sure you will get my letter and so I break off without finishing. Recommend me to God. I don't wish to speak any more of the things here because I have not the heart for it.*

* San Juan de la Cruz was not the only great poet to have lived in Baeza and disliked it. In 1912 Antonio Machado, a man almost as shabbily dressed,

Meanwhile it had been decided to found a convent of nuns at Granada with Ana de Jesús as prioress and it was hoped that Madre Teresa would come down and give the occasion the prestige of her presence. Juan de la Cruz set off in November to fetch her and spent a few days at Avila in her company. They had not met since his imprisonment and he was never to see her again as she died within a year. A touching meeting, one would have thought, of the two greatest religious figures of their age, old associates and companions, but all we know of what passed between them is that she wrote a duty letter to a priest who had preached a sermon to her nuns that she felt tired 'after spending an evening with a Father of the Order'. Had that father been Gracián, how differently she would have expressed herself! Then, as it turned out, she was unable to make the journey to Granada, because, since promising to do so, she had arranged to go to Burgos with Gracián himself and found a convent there. Fray Juan therefore set off on the following morning with two of her nuns for Beas, where he picked up Ana de Jesús and five more nuns and escorted them to Granada. The little party arrived in the first days of 1582 after a terrible journey through torrents of rain and flashes of lightning, one of which struck the archbishop's palace and destroyed his library. Finding the building they had counted on buying to be unavailable, they set up a convent temporarily in a house which was lent them by a rich and devout lady, Doña Ana de Peñalosa. The archbishop, who had till now been hesitating whether or not to give them a licence, was so frightened by the thunderbolt that he gave way and did so. A few weeks later an election at Los Mártires confirmed Fray Juan's nomination to be prior and he took up his residence there. It was to be his home continuously for the next three years and intermittently for another three years after that.

solitary and inward-turned as Juan, came here from Soria and remained for seven years, which he regarded as years of loneliness and exile. To both of them the Andalusians seemed a frivolous people. Yet Baeza is one of the most Castilian-seeming towns in the south of Spain, standing as it does on a bare, treeless down with a great view of distant mountains, and its inhabitants are more serious and reserved in their manner than are most Andalusians.

5

Granada

The priory of Los Mártires (or The Martyrs) had been founded nine years before by the prior of Pastrana on a spur of the Alhambra hill just below the present Hotel Washington Irving. Its name was derived from the underground dungeons in which the Moors had kept their Christian prisoners. It was pulled down in the last century, but its foundations could still be seen in 1930 in the garden of a private house. Today they have been removed and the site converted into a public park. In Juan's time the elm woods that gave such beauty to the Alhambra park had not yet been planted and the summit of the hill was stark and bare, but the windows of the priory looked out over the flat green *vega*, dotted with white farms and grey, well-branched olive trees and bounded on the left by the snow-covered Sierra Nevada. Here, with one of the most beautiful views in the world before him, Juan de la Cruz wrote the greater part of his prose works in the form of commentaries on three of his poems. If it was Beas and El Calvario that had put the pen in the hand, it was at Granada that he worked out what he had begun there.

His character seems to have matured and expanded with the responsibilities of office. During his first year he had a dozen friars and four novices under his jurisdiction and more came in later. To meet their needs he set out to extend the priory by putting up first a substantial cloister and then an aqueduct to bring water from the Generalife. At the same time, in a strengthening of family feeling caused by his mother's death, he brought his brother, Francisco de Yepes, down from Medina and installed him as a mason and gardener. Francisco, like many weavers, was much given to singing. We are told that he always had a popular song, which would of course be a love song, on his lips. Juan, who took them in a religious sense, had a strong feeling for them too and no doubt it was from his early contacts with his brother that he had acquired this.

In his dealings with his friars he was gentle and full of considera-

tion except when he had to reprove one of them for a breach of the
rules. He could then be severe. He believed in personal contacts
rather than in general homilies and arranged every night to have a
private talk with one of them, questioning him about his spiritual
state, the progress he was making in interior prayer and his particular temptations. He gave advice rather than instructions for he
held that all forcing or constraint was wrong since everyone had
his own way of making progress; yet the letters he wrote to his
spiritual daughters invariably stress the same points – the need for
silence, mortification, patience in suffering and the complete emptying of the mind of everything that is not love for God. Aridity was to
be regarded as a test to be endured gladly and there must be no
hankering after those *gustos* or favours which the contemplative
expects to receive as a reward for his persistence. For that is spiritual
gluttony, the fault he had once reproved in Teresa. The young friars
whom he directed in this manner seemed to have valued his
teaching and to have become much attached to him, whereas to
his contemporaries in the order he appeared negative and un-
impressive because he displayed none of those active qualities which
the rapid expansion of the Discalced seemed to require. Unobtrusive,
silent, with downcast eyes that hid the inner fire, he looked as if
he had no other wish than to pass unnoticed and unconsidered
through the world.

But to the friars who were under his direction he showed something of his true self. Now, as before at El Calvario, he would take
them out for long rambles in the country. When asked why he did
this he would answer dryly that it was because, if they were left too
long within the walls of the priory, they would want to leave it.
But that was not the only reason. He believed in teaching them to
pray in two different manners, now fixing their minds on God to
the exclusion of everything else and now calling on the sky and
hills, the trees and plants (*toda la hermosura de las cosas* – all the
beauty of created things), to praise Him. So he would take them
out for the whole day over the red, stony hills, scattered with ilexes
and patches of scrub oak, where the humming of an occasional bee
or the chirping of a cricket were the only sounds that broke the
silence. A few miles away, cutting the blue sky, lay the long line of
snowy mountains. Then, when he had reached a suitable spot, he
would stop and send each of them off by himself to spend an hour
or two in prayer and praising God. He would withdraw too and

when he did not return the others would go to look for him and perhaps find him lost in a trance with his elbow propped on a bush of thyme or lavender. At other times he would take them to an orchard on the banks of the Genil or Darro and, while they talked and amused themselves, would sit absorbed on the edge watching the fish swimming in the water. 'Look, brothers,' he would call out, 'how these creatures of God are busy praising Him.' He would sometimes be so wrapped up in his thoughts that to attract his attention they would have to tug at his habit.

However all was not prayer, uplifting of the mind and contemplation. On feast days he would take his little party out and, sitting with them in a circle on the ground as they ate their meal, which on such an occasion might include an orange or an apple, he would tell them *cuentos graciosos*, that is, amusing stories which made them laugh. He believed, for them at least, in relaxation, but it is not easy to imagine what these stories were like for, we are told, they were all on the subject of God, since he could not turn his thoughts for more than a few moments onto anything else. However we are told that his conversation at such times was delightful.

The world of the Discalced Carmelite friars of that century is not one which it is easy to enter into today. Since faith was unquestioned, there was no false shame about speaking of religious matters. Devout people turned up their eyes to heaven when praying, as they do in Baroque paintings, crossed their hands on their chest and prostrated themselves on the ground, as Muslims still do at prayer. And their penances and austerities were often severe. Juan de la Cruz, writing to a man who wished to join the order, warned him what to expect – 'a great harshness of life, poverty and deprivation, much mortification and self-denial and a negation of all the creatures'. The man who sought God must empty his mind of all thoughts and feelings, however good they might be in themselves, so that He could fill it. Only solitude and *desnudez* or nakedness of mind, inflamed by love, could draw down that immense benefit. Such was the life, and though Juan softened it a little for his novices because they were beginners, and would not allow them to carry their austerities so far as to undermine their health, he never spared himself. Whereas the food served in the refectory except on fast days consisted of bread, herbs, a little fish and chick peas, with rice on holidays, he commonly refused everything but dry bread and herbs which, as a penance, he would often eat kneeling on the floor in the middle of the room. Nor was his hospitality lavish. When he invited his rich penitents from the city to a meal, the menu would consist of dry bread with chick peas and boiled nettles. Only the sick were cosseted.

Humility too was important because the leading vice of ascetics is apt to be pride. Juan took for himself the smallest cell in the building, though it is true that it had a window looking out over the *vega* in front of which he used to kneel when he prayed. Its only contents were a rough cross, a print of the Virgin, a straw pallet and three books, a Bible, the *Flos Sanctorum* and a breviary, though sometimes there was also a copy of St Augustine's *Contra Haereses*. When it came to taking a share in the household chores, he chose the most demeaning ones, such as cleaning out the latrines. But Friday was the day on which he castigated his pride most severely. He would then kiss the unwashed feet of his brothers before eating and after the meal was over stand in the doorway without his white cloak so that as they left the room they were obliged, as the rule laid down for the chastisement of such faults, to strike him in the face. It is recorded that once, after he had rebuked a friar for a breach of discipline and the young man had answered him back in anger, Juan had prostrated himself on the ground till he had finished speaking. Whether Madre Teresa would have approved of such extreme examples of self-abasement may be questioned. 'Tell Sister Jerónima, who signed herself Dunghill,' she once wrote, 'that I hope her humility is not merely a matter of words.' But no one could question Juan's sincerity or his belief that all pride must be destroyed.

It seems clear that he was happier at Los Mártires than he had been at Baeza, if one may apply the term happy to the states of mind that he desired. Yet Granada was far from being an attractive place of residence. The Morisco population had been expelled a dozen years previously after the failure of their two years' rebellion in the Alpujarras and now a new and uprooted class with the vices and pretensions of colonials had moved in from the North. Sullen-looking slaves filled the streets and, while the newcomers quarrelled over points of honour and precedence, the fertile countryside was going to ruin. The triumph of the Cross had turned this once prosperous city into a camp and brothel. But Juan lived outside the walls and mixed little with the inhabitants. So averse was he to having any dealings with the principal families, much less touting from them for alms, that he brought down on himself a censure from the vicar-provincial. Out of obedience to him he payed a formal call on the municipal authorities, only to be told that they were too busy to receive unnecessary visits. After that he did not repeat the attempt.

But he had in the society of his friars a compensation for being obliged to live in this foreign land which was so different in temper from Castile. The extreme introversion and love of being alone which had characterized his youth had been succeeded by a stage in which he liked to be surrounded by those who were committed to the same road as himself. These young men were his disciples whom he enjoyed encouraging and teaching, so, as was natural, he became much attached to some of them and in particular to two – Juan de Santa Ana, who had followed him from El Calvario, and Juan Evangelista, who first came to him as a novice at Granada, aged only nineteen. This last became his secretary and companion, travelling everywhere with him and not leaving him until a few months before his death. He survived him by thirty-seven years, dying at Los Mártires in 1638, and provided, as did Juan de Santa Ana, some of the most reliable information we have about their Master's habits and character.

However Juan was not dependent only on his friars for close human contacts. He was able to resume with Ana de Jesús and her nuns the same tender and intimate relations that he had formed with them at Beas. They occupied at first a house in the Calle de Elvira,* and after that they acquired the Casa del Gran Capitán, in which the great general of the Catholic kings had died, that stood only five minutes walk below Los Mártires. Every few days he went to confess them and sat talking to them afterwards in the parlour while they squatted on the floor, as Spanish women always did in those days, busy at their needlework behind the double grille. One Christmas, while visiting the enclosed part of the convent to confess

---

* As a point of curiosity it may be observed that there lived at that time at the Puerta de Elvira, only a few yards from the Carmelite convent, an old Muslim *beata* or holy woman, a follower of the great Sufi mystic Al-Gazzali, who practised much the same sort of imageless prayer or contemplation that Juan de la Cruz did. Only Juan is not likely, given his general lack of curiosity, to have known her. The idea, sometimes given credence today, that a Spaniard of those times could have seen any merit in the religion of Islam or in its methods of mental prayer seems to me entirely unacceptable. Nor had any of their books been translated into Spanish,

the prioress, Ana de Jesús, who had fallen seriously ill, he noticed an image of the infant Jesus laid as though asleep against a skull. Taking it up and, according to one account, making a few dance steps, he sang the first lines of a love song that was then popular, addressing them to the infant:

> Mi dulce y tierno Jesús,
> Si amores me han de matar,
> Agora tienen lugar.

'Sweet and tender Jesus, if love has to kill me, now it has its chance.'*

The sisters, starved of their natural love for men, worshipped him. When on one of his yearly visitations he was admitted to the enclosure, they would fall on their knees and kiss his hands or his feet. Sometimes he took his midday meal there, and then after he had gone they would finish up the scraps of bread he had left on his platter and drink the water that remained in his mug. In return for their hospitality he would send them presents of fish and vegetables from his priory. Nor were these the only nuns whom he directed. His office of definitor required him to visit those of Beas in spite of their being several days' journey away, and towards the end of his first term of prior at Los Mártires he presided over the foundation of a convent at Málaga, composed of nuns drawn from Granada, Beas and Caravaca. Nearly all these sisters were Castilians, speaking with the clear accent of Old Castile, which no doubt gave him an extra bond of sympathy with them.

As we have said, these three years that he spent at Granada were years of great literary activity. He continued and completed *The Ascent of Mount Carmel*, which he had begun at El Calvario, and wrote the companion work to it, *The Dark Night of the Soul*, both of them being prose commentaries, or *declaraciones*, as he called them, on the poem that begins *En una noche oscura*. He also continued and completed the first version of his prose commentary on

---

* Jerónimo de San José, the first biographer of Fray Juan, placed this episode in the college of Baeza and some recent writers have followed him. Father Crisógono, however, by quoting from the declaration of a nun who was present, has shown that it occurred in the Discalced convent at Granada in December 1582. At Los Mártires on the hill above Christmas was celebrated with processions and with the singing of *villancicos*, so that Juan's action was in no way exceptional. As regards Ana de Jesús, who was often ill, Juan used to say, 'She is sick of love.' In fact she lived to be 76, dying at Brussels in 1621.

the *Cántico espiritual,* which he had begun at El Calvario, and dedicated it to Ana de Jesús, Finally he wrote the last of his great poems, *Llama de amor viva,* and a little later his prose commentary on it at the request of Doña Ana de Peñalosa, that rich and devout widow whose spiritual director he was. According to his secretary, Fray Juan Evangelista, he wrote his commentary on this in fifteen days sometime between August 1585 and April 1587 when, though still prior of Los Mártires, he was also vicar-provincial of Andalusia and therefore spent little time at Granada.

The same witness tells us how Juan's first three prose works were written. He had begun by putting down at El Calvario short passages which he later incorporated without alteration into the *Ascent* and the *Spiritual Canticle.* He did not write every day, but in short snatches with breaks between them and so built up the books gradually. The same process of composition is true of his long poem, the *Cántico espiritual,* which he began in prison and continued at El Calvario and later. Then some time before August 1586, he rearranged the order of its stanzas and wrote a new recension of his prose commentary on them. As we are told by two good witnesses, he wrote the whole of this long prose work on his knees out of reverence for the subject. As soon as he had finished anything he got one of the nuns or else Juan Evangelista to make a fair copy of it and then took his own rough copy back and apparently destroyed it. That seems to be why only one autograph manuscript of his has survived. He was so unwilling to part with the originals except to friars or nuns who were in his confidence that Ana de Peñalosa had to send her servant to Los Mártires to copy the *Living Flame of Love* under his eyes. Many copies were made, both of his poems and of his prose works, because he wished his friars and nuns to read them. After all they had been written to help them.

Juan de la Cruz also wrote, either at Granada or later, a prose work entitled *Propriedades del pájaro solitario* or *Properties of the Solitary Bird,* which has not come down to us. Another late work on the distinction between true and false states of mind and true and false miracles has also been lost. Finally there are some short pieces, *Cautelas* or *Cautions,* and *Dichos de luz y amor, Sayings of light and love,* which consist of aphorisms written down for the nuns of Beas.*

---

* I have given the titles of Juan de la Cruz's poems in Spanish and the titles of his prose works in English to make the distinction clearer.

6

Segovia

A new figure was now coming to the front in the ranks of the discalced Carmelites. This was a Genoese financier called Nicolás Doria. Born in 1539 of a famous banking family he had first arrived in Spain in 1570. Within a year or two he had succeeded in earning the goodwill of Philip II by arranging a loan for him and that of the archbishop of Seville by putting his tangled finances in order. Then suddenly, in one of those revulsions of feeling that were so common in that age, he had renounced the world, gone to study with the Dominicans, been ordained priest and in 1578 taken the Discalced Carmelite habit under the name of Fray Nicolás de Jesús Maria. Teresa, with whom he spent three days at Avila, formed a high opinion of him in spite of his lack of charm or amenity and wrote to her dear Paul, as she called Gracián, that she was sure he would be of the greatest comfort and assistance to him in helping him to bear his responsibilities. She was right in thinking that Doria was an able man as well as an austere one, but if her intuitions had been a little more acute she would have seen that what he enjoyed above everything was the exercise of power and that he was almost totally lacking in the inward-looking spirit of the contemplative.

He was in fact a disciplinarian and a man of action. The bright, extroverted eyes, hooked nose and receding forehead shown by his portrait confirm what we know from other sources of his character. Inflexible, calculating, despotic, with great business capacity and drive, he had his own ideas on how the Discalced should be governed and wished to be free to carry them out. In doing so he would show no respect for persons. So at the chapter which met at Almodóvar in May 1583 – that is, only a few months after Teresa's death – he came out in strong opposition to the provincial Gracián, whose gentle, idealistic nature, so attractive to women because it conveyed a chivalrous regard for them, was the opposite to his. From this moment the reform, which had been held together by the tact and authority of its foundress, became split into two hostile factions.

The first matter to be discussed at Almodóvar was whether

priors should be elected by their communities or appointed by a chapter-general. Juan de la Cruz held strong views on this. He maintained that they should be elected, but that no prior should be returned to office after his two years' term had come to an end. The reason he gave for this was that their desire to retain their posts led them to curry favour both with their superiors and with the friars under them and thus a system of patronage grew up by which certain men became almost permanent office-holders. In this way, he said, the appetite for command and office was sapping the morale of the order. On the objection being made that priors would then be elected who had little experience of affairs, he replied that no religious order had ever become relaxed on that account and that in any case the electors did not always choose the most worthy, but those who agreed best with themselves. In other words, those who had favoured their interests. However he spoke in vain, for none of the other members of the chapter agreed with him.

The next matters to be discussed were whether missions should be sent to pagan Africa and whether there should be more preaching in churches. Juan was opposed to missions being sent to savage countries, where the people were not prepared for this mode of life, as well as to any extension of preaching, maintaining that the principal rôle of the Discalced lay in prayer and contemplation. 'Let those,' he wrote at this time, 'who are great actives, who think to girdle the world with their outward works and their preachings, take note that they would bring far more profit to the Church and be far more pleasing to God . . . if they spent half as much time in abiding with Him in prayer.'* In this he came up against Gracián, who not only favoured more missionary work but also, being eloquent in the pulpit himself, more preaching in city churches. 'With the whole world ablaze,' he declared, 'the chief task of the Order must lie not in remaining in one's cell or missing a moment of choir . . . nor in multiplying the number of priories and convents in tiny villages . . . but in saving souls.'† Juan spoke with such fervour against these views that, dropping his usual reticence, he moved forward a few steps from his place. Doria supported him on the question of missions and of preaching, though he urged that the reform should be spread to civilized countries such as Italy, but at the last session of the chapter, which was devoted to the correc-

* See *Spiritual Canticle*, Second Redaction: *Annotation for Stanza 28*.
† See Jerónimo Gracián, *Peregrinación de Anastasio*, p. 98.

tion of faults, he made a violent personal attack on Gracián for his allegedly bad government and excessive love of preaching, which he said 'had ruined the Order'. After that he left for Genoa to found a priory there, while Gracián set about organizing a mission to the Congo.

In the spring of 1585 – that is, two years later – a chapter was held at Lisbon and Fray Juan, as prior of Los Mártires, attended it. Gracián's four years' term as provincial had now expired and he presented his report of it. This showed that though in certain respects his rule might have been lax, great progress had been made in extending the order. Unfortunately he thought fit in the course of his speech to find fault with 'certain most weighty persons' who had caused unrest in the reform. By these persons he meant Doria and his friends and for this the Italian never forgave him. However, sensing the wishes of the other friars and not being a combative man, he proposed that his rival, who was still in Italy, should succeed him, and this motion was carried by 26 votes out of 28. Juan de la Cruz, who liked Gracián personally, is said to have remarked to him, 'Your Reverence has made Provincial the man who will strip you of your habit'.

At this chapter Juan again proposed that priors should not be eligible for immediate reappointment to office. His views upon the bad effects produced by the habitual exercise of power were growing stronger, but he could get no one to agree with him. The belief that certain people were more fitted to govern than others prevailed over his opinion that authority should lie rather with the rule than with the superior, while his allegation that ambition for office inevitably led to an undue subservience to the higher authorities in the order was not discussed. As an ironic comment on his proposal the chapter reappointed him for the third time to be prior of Los Mártires and also made him second definitor – the definitors; of whom there were at that time four, being the chief persons of authority under the provincial. Although he begged not to be given another office, as this was contrary both to his wishes and to his principles, he was compelled out of obedience to submit.

During his stay in Lisbon a certain nun, Sor María de la Visitación, was making herself much talked of. A beautiful girl who impressed everyone by her sweetness and sincerity, she was, it seemed, gifted with miraculous powers. During her raptures she was lifted into the air and surrounded by lights, she healed the sick and finally she developed the wounds of the stigmata. The most eminent ecclesiastics, after examining her minutely, testified to her genuineness while her confessor, Luis de Granada, proclaimed her to be a saint. Such was her fame that when, three years later, the Great Armada set out on its voyage, it sailed in line past her convent so that she could bless it. Since no pious person went to Lisbon without visiting her, the priors of the Discalced all did so and came back with pieces of cloth stained with her blood as relics. Only Juan de la Cruz refused to go, saying sharply that he had no need to see anyone's wounds. With his distaste for all outward manifestations of saintliness, he believed her to be a fraud.

A few years later he was proved to be right. Sor María made the mistake of taking up the national cause against Philip II (the five wounds of Christ were on the Portuguese arms) and the Inquisition was instructed to open an investigation. It questioned a nun who, looking through the keyhole, had seen her painting her wounds and proved the truth of this evidence by washing them. Juan de la Cruz's opinion was vindicated.

The new provincial, Doria, returned from Italy that summer and called a chapter – or rather an extension of the previous chapter – at Pastrana in October. Here he made another speech attacking Gracián for his laxity. 'Let us pluck up the barren fig tree,' he said, 'and cut off the rotten limb and the body will recover its strength.' In future, he announced, he would insist on a strict conformity to the rule. 'rigorous observance, my brothers,' he declared, 'rigorous observance. I trust to God that after my death my bones, knocking one on the other in their coffin, will cry out, "Rigorous observance, rigorous observance".' Gracián was not however shelved, for he had many supporters, but was made vicar-provincial of Portugal and prior of the Discalced house there, while Juan de la Cruz, without relinquishing his posts as second definitor and prior of Los Mártires, became vicar-provincial of Andalusia. His appointment, we are told, was received with general applause among the friars and nuns of that province, but it meant that he would have to do more travelling than ever.

He now had nine priories to visit regularly, to which were soon added three more, the most notable being that of Córdoba, which he founded in great state, the Cathedral clergy turning out to receive him. Besides these he had some half a dozen convents of nuns to keep an eye on. His journeys included several to Madrid and on one of these he founded the house which Teresa had always dreamed of setting up, with Ana de Jesús as its prioress. A rough calculation shows that in the course of these two years he must have travelled over six thousand miles – that is, the distance from Granada to Calcutta. Except when his journey was short, he went on horseback. As he rode he either read the Bible or else sang hymns or verses from the *Song of Songs*. But he also prayed, sometimes becoming so rapt in his prayer that he fell off his horse. One can picture him, this tiny, absent-minded man with his grave expression, dressed in an old dark habit of the coarsest serge which was too short and tight for him and over which he wore the white Carmelite cloak fastened at the neck; his feet shod in sandals and in summer a white, broad-brimmed felt hat on his head. In cooler weather he wore a *calotte*, or skull cap, of grey felt. In the *ventas* or wayside inns where he put up he slept wrapped in a rug on the cobbled floor, undisturbed by the noise and bustle of the muleteers or by their drinking and swearing. To mortify himself he wore drawers of rough esparto next to his skin and once, when he fell seriously ill of pleurisy at Guadalcázar close to Seville, he was found to be wearing a chain with points that cut into his flesh, which in places had grown over it.

In April 1587 the biennial chapter was held at Valladolid. Juan de la Cruz ceased to be definitor and vicar-provincial, but was reappointed for the fourth time prior of Los Mártires. He is said to have fallen on his knees and wept when he heard of this, begging not to be continued in office, but at least he was now relieved of travelling. A couple of months later the pope's brief, setting up the Discalced as a separate congregation, arrived from Rome. With it came the text of a new constitution. According to this the congregation would be governed, under the nominal authority of the general of the order, by a vicar-general who would be elected every six years, and to assist him there would be a body known as the *consulta*, composed of six elected councillors or *consiliarios*, which would be in permanent session. The authority that had hitherto been held by the priors in chapter would henceforth be exercised by the *consulta* and the vicar-provincials (now to be called provincials) would lose most of their influence, and have merely executive functions. Such was the system of government which Doria had himself designed and drawn up and for which he had enlisted the king's support in Rome. It had been modelled partly on the Jesuit constitution and it gave the vicar-general great powers. With it came a bull which had been issued by the pope only after considerable pressure, authorizing the vicar-general to expel any contumacious friar he pleased from the order. This was a power that did not exist in any of the other orders of friars and in pressing for it Doria had clearly had in mind the case of Jerónimo Gracián.

The moment for using it had not however come. Doria's first plan for dealing with his rival was to send him out of the country. A Discalced priory had recently been founded in Mexico so he had him elected vicar-provincial of that country, hoping in this way to see the last of him. But, as it happened, the sailings that year were cancelled on account of Drake's activities, so Gracián was not able to leave. Instead he went as a simple friar to Lisbon where he was protected by the archbishop of Évora and the cardinal, Prince Alberto. Meanwhile he had published a book on foreign missions which contained some indirect criticisms of his opponents that angered Doria. His reply was to send a friar to examine him on certain charges that had been made against him, such as accepting meals in convents, giving permission to eat meat and sleeping between sheets. Gracián defended himself in a long written statement accompanied by confirmatory documents, but the definitors found him guilty in his absence and deprived him of his vote in the next two chapters. Although the intention of this manoeuvre was obvious and the sentence unjust, Gracián made an abject submission, admitting that he had erred, 'though from oversights caused by the frankness of my nature and not from malice'. And he asked to be exempted from office altogether and allowed to spend the rest of his life in prayer and contemplation.

In June 1588, just as the Great Armada was preparing to set sail for the English Channel, the first chapter-general of the new Discalced congregation met at Madrid. Doria was elected vicar-general, but only by 32 votes out of 50. The 18 who voted against him belonged to the party of Gracián, which could have gained more votes had its leader been prepared to rally his supporters. But, unwilling to widen the breach, he had refused to attend the chapter. Juan de la Cruz became first in rank of the four definitors and one of the six councillors on the *consulta*. Since it had been decided that the seat of this body should be at Segovia, he was also appointed prior of the Discalced house there so that he could act as deputy vicar-general in Doria's absence. It was his opposition to

Gracián's proposals at the chapter of Lisbon as well as his great prestige in Andalusia that had given him this position of second in command, yet he was not Doria's man. If the vicar-general thought that he was, he was greatly mistaken.

Juan was now back in Castile after eight years' absence. His priory stood a little to the north of the city, facing the great pile of the Alcázar, but looking eastwards over the poplar-fringed river and the city ramparts beyond. In a sense he had been its founder, for two years before this his penitent, Ana de Peñalosa, who had done so much for the nuns at Granada, had on his advice bought the building, which had till then been a Trinitarian monastery, and given it to the Carmelite reform. But now that the *consulta* was to have its headquarters here, it would have to be enlarged. More land was therefore bought – an orchard running up to the fringe of low cliffs that formed the rim of the valley – and masons were engaged. The seven friars lent a hand and Juan, who had a taste for building, was tireless in supervising the work. When Fray Juan Evangelista, his close companion during these years, exclaimed at his love of handling rocks and stones, he replied: 'Don't be surprised, son, for when I am dealing with them I have fewer sins to confess than when I am dealing with men.'

The three years that Juan de la Cruz spent at Segovia seem to have brought him to some new peak of his spiritual ascension. He would sit for hours at the windows of his tiny cell, looking out over the trees by the river. Then on the face of the cliff that overhung the orchard there was a shallow grotto, half blocked by bushes and brambles, and so low that it could only be entered on hands and knees. Jackdaws nested in the crevices around and filled the air with their 'chack-chacks', while from it one had a wide view over the city and distant mountains, which were covered during a large part of the year with snow. Here Juan would spend hours sunk in contemplation. There was a hermitage too in the garden where he liked to pray, while on summer nights he would lie with his arms stretched out in a cross under the trees, listening to the murmur of the river close by and to the warbling of the nightingales. He would sometimes remain here till dawn without sleeping and come in so stiff in body and so absorbed in spirit that it was some hours before he could return to himself. The effects of this trance would last all day. He now shrank more than ever from business. When fetched down from his grotto to see someone, he would say, 'For the love

of God, let me be, for I am not in a fit state to deal with people.'
And when he finally came he would still be so absorbed in his prayer
that often he would not understand what was said to him. To bring
himself back to earth he would knock with his knuckles against the
wall till it hurt him.

Yet he had a great deal of business to transact. As prior he had to
direct his friars and as deputy for Doria he had a large correspondence to handle. Then he was confessor to various devout
people in the city as well as to the nuns in the nearby convent that
had been founded fifteen years before by Teresa in his own presence.
We hear of his great reluctance to speak of worldly or practical
matters and of how he would cut any conversation on them short
with the words, 'Let us now leave these trivialities and come back
to God.' On this subject he spoke with great eloquence. A nun who
was at the convent at this time declared that 'he could speak of
nothing else and that his words were so apt that they remained in
the soul of the hearer and enkindled in it the fire of the love of
God. It always seemed that his soul was at prayer.' Yet at this time,
we are told, he was sleeping only two hours each night.

His brother Francisco had come over from Medina to visit him
and they spent a few days together. Though simple, he was a deeply
religious man and Juan liked talking to him. Just before he left
Juan led him out into the orchard and confided to him something
extraordinary that had recently happened to him. One evening, he
told him, as he was praying in front of a picture of Christ bearing
his Cross, the figure had spoken to him and said: 'Fray Juan, ask
what favour you will of me and I will grant it in return for the
services you have done me.' He had replied: 'Lord, make me to
suffer and be despised for Thy sake.' (See plate 2.) He was now
about to receive what he had asked for.*

While Juan was settling into his duties of prior, Doria had
been making a tour of the priories and convents of the reform to
explain to their occupants the new method of government. His
attempts to do so were far from successful. He was not gifted, as
Gracián was, with tact and it would have required a great deal of

---

* Juan visited Madrid in June 1590, for a chapter-general extraordinary. It is
an amusing reflection that he might have passed in the street a young English
Catholic, still in his teens, who took an interest in Spanish poetry and bought
several volumes of it. This was John Donne, who is thought to have come to
Madrid from Naples at around this time. See *John Donne, A Life*, by R. C.
Bald (London 1970).

this to persuade the friars and nuns, accustomed as they were to a flexible personal rule which took account of their special needs and problems, to accept this rigid, authoritarian system. Many of the friars and all of the nuns distrusted him and his visits merely succeeded in increasing their misgivings.

Their opposition to his innovations soon began to gather force. Nothing but complaints and murmurings were to be heard in the convents. One nun wrote of 'the machine of the *consulta*' and there was a general belief that the new organization reflected Doria's Italian mentality and so was unsuited to Spaniards. The friars too complained bitterly at their loss of influence. Seeing this, Gracián who, though reluctant to defend his personal conduct, felt his responsibilities for safeguarding Teresa's reform and wrote to the king to protest against this perversion of it and to point out the unrest it was causing. Doria, on learning of this, wrote to defend it and used his personal influence with the royal council to secure its support. Since the members of the council were people who believed in firm, autocratic rule, this was not difficult, and the king once more expressed his approval of the new constitution.

But the nuns continued to be deeply disturbed. Instead of being under the authority of the vicar-provincial, who visited them regularly, they would from now on be subject to a body of six men, the *consulta*, who lived far from them and could not understand their problems. All their small female concerns would be submitted to these friars' scrutiny. If, as they had reason to fear, the constitution which they had been granted in 1581 at the chapter of Alcalá, should be revoked, they would lose many of their liberties, such as the right to choose their own confessors (if they wished, from outside the order), to elect their own prioresses and to refuse to be transferred against their will from one convent to another. These constitutions had been drawn up after much thought by Teresa herself and embodied her desire to give as much autonomy as possible to each of her convents and to protect them against undue interference from the friars. Their revocation would undermine the whole spirit of the reform and the nuns therefore decided to seek assurances from the papal nuncio that they would not be altered. The nuncio agreed to satisfy their request and gave them a written guarantee of their 'perpetual stability'.

However Ana de Jesús, the prioress at Madrid, who was regarded by most of the nuns as Teresa's successor, was not satisfied. She felt a deep distrust of Doria's intentions. So after consulting Fray Luis de León, that famous champion of justice and fair dealing who was now editing Teresa's *Works*, and the Dominican, Fray Domingo Báñez, the eminent theologian who had been the foundress's close friend and supporter, and obtaining, as she was bound to do, Doria's verbal consent, she appealed to the pope not only to confirm the nuns' constitutions, but to appoint Fray Juan de la Cruz as their superior instead of the *consulta*. Sixtus V acceded to her request and issued a brief that both confirmed the constitutions and authorized the creation of a commissary-general for the nuns, the holder to be elected triennially by the chapter and to rank immediately below the vicar-general. None of the members of the *consulta* were to have any jurisdiction over them because 'it was not right that the nuns should be diversely governed by many superiors'. Luis de León and the archbishop of Évora, an old friend of Teresa's, were appointed to execute the brief.

Doria was very angry when he heard of this. He had expected Mother Ana to make her appeal to the pope through her superiors in the order, whereas she, distrusting him and his associates, had done so independently through an outsider. It infuriated him to think that, with all his experience of affairs, he had been outwitted by a nun. When therefore he was urged by Luis de León to call a special chapter-general to implement the brief, he emphatically refused. Rather than do this, he said, he would disown the nuns altogether and leave them to manage their own affairs. This threat had the effect of frightening many of them into submission because they needed the friars' co-operation and support. So the matter stood when, in August 1590, Pope Sixtus died. This event confirmed Doria in his resolve not to accept the brief and, though Domingo Báñez told him that his proposal to disown the nuns was infamous and without a parallel in the annals of the church, he persisted in his intention of going through with it. However there was also the possibility that with the king's help the obnoxious document could be annulled. He therefore approached the new pope, Gregory XIV, with the request that he would issue another brief, cancelling the previous one and placing the nuns firmly under the authority of the *consulta*. The pope, pressed by the Spanish ambassador, showed himself willing and a second brief was promulgated that spring. At first sight it appeared to be a compromise because it placed the nuns under the provincials, but since by the new constitution these had been deprived of their authority and made directly subject to the *consulta*, it gave Doria most of what he wanted.

Juan de la Cruz's position during these last two years had been growing more and more difficult. He disapproved of almost everything that was being done by Doria and the *consulta*. In his view the sole cause of the revolutionary changes that were convulsing the order lay in the ambition and craving for power of the vicar-general and of the young friars who supported him because they wished for preferment. He had watched this ambition growing over the years and in successive chapters had warned his fellow priors against it. Speaking to Eliseo de los Mártires, who had been one of his friars at Granada, he had said: 'The vice of ambition among the Reformed is incurable because it is so insidious. It colours and taints the Order with an appearance of virtue and perfection so that it seems wrong to combat it and the evil remains.'* Now its consequences were plain for all to see, and he, as first definitor and *consiliario*, found himself trapped in a situation in which he was responsible for acts to which he was strongly opposed. He especially disapproved of the persecution that was being mounted against Gracián and had more than once protested against it to Doria and to the other members of the *consulta*. If courtesy, he said to Fray Eliseo, were lost in an order and instead there should enter cruelty and ferocity, then the order would be ruined. One day, after his companion Fray Juan Evangelista had found him absorbed in a deep trance in his cell, he described to him a vision he had just had.

> 'I saw our Father the Vicar-General and the Definitors wading into the sea and I called to them that if they did not draw back they would be drowned. I saw the water rising to their ankles and to their knees and then to their waists and I continued to call out that they should not go any further. But they paid no attention and went on till they were all drowned.'

This vision took place at the time when Gracián's total disgrace was being planned and the warnings that Juan called out stood for the letters that he was writing to Doria and the *consulta*, whose

* This is taken from a document written by Fray Eliseo de los Mártires which lists seventeen of Juan de la Cruz's sayings. It was first published by P. Gerardo in his complete edition of San Juan's works (1912–14) and is included with some small alterations in Allison Peers's translation under the title of *Spiritual Sayings*.

meetings he had ceased to attend since they now took place in Madrid.

Then, though he had taken no part in the nuns' appeal to Rome, he shared their concern for the integrity of their constitution and did not approve of their being governed by a composite body such as the *consulta*. He had made his opinion on this, as well as on the affair of Gracián, clear to Doria, expressing himself so strongly in one letter that Juan Evangelista advised him to tone it down before sending it. But Juan refused to alter a word, saying that one should not hesitate to speak strongly whenever questions of justice or charity were involved. He might long to bury himself in a remote priory, given up to prayer and meditation, but while he held an office in the government of the order he must discharge his duty and oppose what he believed to be wrong.

This outspokenness on the part of Juan de la Cruz had the result that one would expect. He began to take the place of the discredited Gracián as the principal obstacle to the accomplishment of the vicar-general's plans. Carrying as he did great prestige among the Discalced, both as their first member and as the author of ascetic and mystical works that were arousing a deep admiration in the priories and convents, it would not be enough only to push him aside. Doria saw that he must either destroy his reputation or exile him from Spain.

7

Disgrace and Death

In June 1591, a chapter-general was held, as the constitution required, at Madrid, and Juan as first definitor and member of the *consulta* prepared to attend it. Before leaving Segovia he went to see the prioress of the convent there. 'Who knows, Father,' she exclaimed in the course of their conversation, 'but that Your Reverence will come back as our Superior.' 'No, no, daughter,' he replied, 'that will not happen. It has been revealed to me that I shall be taken and thrown into a corner like an old kitchen cloth.'

His prophecy was soon fulfilled. He ceased to be a definitor or a member of the *consulta* and was not reappointed prior nor elected to any other office. Of the six new definitors and *consiliarios* four were men of straw who would do as they were told while two were filled with a strong animosity against Juan. One of these seems to have been Ambrosio Mariano, the one-time admirer of Doña Catalina de Cardona, who had always disliked him, while the other and much the more virulent was a young friar called Diego Evangelista. Some years before, while Juan was acting as vicar-provincial of Andalusia, he had had occasion to reprove him for giving too much time to preaching and on that excuse absenting himself for days on end from his priory. This man had then been a follower of Gracián, but he had since like so many other able and ambitious friars gone over to Doria, and now that he was in a position to do so he was determined to revenge himself. Juan's warnings about the danger that lay in the appetite for command and office had been fully justified for, thanks to it, the vicar-general had been able to fill all the chief posts in the order with his satellites and so take the first steps towards the crushing of his opponents. Perhaps it is not going too far to see in the contrast between his system of government and that advocated by Juan the same antithesis as that which existed during the Spanish Civil War between the Communists and the Anarchists. The former desired power above everything and overreached themselves in their endeavour to obtain it, whereas the latter wished to destroy power and substitute for it a set of moral values or principles.

Since Gregory's brief had still not been published in Spain the chief matters to be discussed at the chapter were the further measures to be taken against Gracián and the vicar-general's proposal to disassociate the nuns entirely from the friars and place them directly under the pope. Juan de la Cruz, we are told, began his address as follows:

> 'If at Chapters, assemblies and meetings men no longer have the courage to say what the laws of justice and charity oblige them to say, out of weakness, pusillanimity or fear of annoying their superior and consequently not obtaining office, the Order is utterly lost and ruined.'*

And he asked for the voting to be by secret ballot. No one supported him in this. His fears were borne out, for when in the course of the debate he spoke up strongly on the question both of the nuns and of Gracián, none of those present, though some of them privately agreed with him, had the courage to oppose the vicar-general. He also complained of the number of new laws and regulations that were being made – three hundred since Doria had come into office. It must have been clear to everyone that he was defending the tradition established by Teresa, who was now regarded by everyone as a saint, whereas the vicar-general was perverting it. But the reform had expanded so fast that it contained few genuine contemplatives and what most of the more able friars wanted was promotion and the comparatively active life that office provided. To obtain that they must vote as the vicar-general wished.

Since Juan's name had been put forward as a possible superior for the nuns, Doria saw that it was necessary to get him out of the way as quickly as possible and he therefore proposed sending him to Mexico, where the recently founded priory was asking for more friars. This was the same plan as had been adopted in the case of Gracián and then dropped for lack of a ship to take him. On being approached, Juan said that he was ready to go. But a week or two later Gregory's brief arrived and, as there was no longer any question of Juan's being made superior of the nuns, his removal from Spain became less pressing. Since Juan was not a man whom it was wise to disgrace suddenly, Doria offered to reinstate him as

---

* See P. Bruno, *Saint Jean de la Croix* (1929), quoted from Fray Eliseo de los Mártires. Although Fray Eliseo does not say that San Juan used these words at the chapter, we know that he spoke in this sense.

prior at Segovia. But Juan begged not to be sent back there, no doubt feeling that, if that happened, he would once again be involved in controversies. It was therefore decided that he was to proceed to Andalusia where he would recruit twelve friars for the voyage to Mexico and accompany them there as visitor. In the meantime, while the necessary arrangements were being made, he was to go as a simple friar to La Peñuela, a lonely priory in the heart of the Sierra Morena, not far from Baeza. Antonio de Heredia, his old companion at Duruelo, who was now the provincial of that province, would decide whether he was to remain there or be sent elsewhere.

While Juan's destination was being settled he remained in the Discalced priory at Madrid. Here he had to put up with the insults of Diego Evangelista, who now occupied his old place on the *consulta*, where he acted as Doria's right-hand man. Not content with seeing his enemy disgraced and without office, this friar took every opportunity he could of reprimanding him in public. Juan bore his insults in silence. Everyone knew that he was in some way under suspicion, for the prior, Ambrosio Mariano, who was a strong supporter of Doria, had told one of his friars to accompany him everywhere and report on what he did and said. We can see his reaction to these events in a letter he wrote at this time to Ana de Jesús, the prioress at Madrid, in reply to one of hers. After urging submission to the will of God, who had ordered these matters for the best, he went on:

'Things that do not please us, however good and fitting they may be, seem to us bad and harmful, but you should see that in this case they are not so, either for myself or for anyone else: indeed to me they are welcome, since now that I am free and no longer have charge of souls I can, if I so wish, enjoy peace, solitude and the delectable fruit of forgetfulness of self and of all things; while for others it is well that I should be out of the way, for then they will be free of the faults which they would have had to commit through my unworthiness.

'What I would beg you, daughter, is that you ask the Lord to let this mercy of his go through, because I still fear that they may make me go to Segovia and not leave me wholly free, though I shall do whatever I can to prevent that from happening. But if it cannot be, Mother Ana de Jesús must not think that she has escaped from my hands or that she will die with the regret that, as she supposes, she has lost the opportunity to be very holy. For whether going or staying, wherever or however I may be, I shall not forget her because I truly desire her lasting good.'

In another letter, written on the same day, to the prioress of Segovia, he said that one must not blame men for these things since it was not they who caused them, but God, who knew what was best for us. And he added the memorable phrase, *Adonde no hay amor, ponga amor y sacará amor*, 'Where there is no love, put love and you will get back love.'

Before leaving Madrid he went to say what he knew would be a last farewell to Ana de Peñalosa, to the family of Gracián, who had just been thrown into prison, and to Ana de Jesús and her nuns. To one of these, who had condoled with him for having been sent to such a remote spot, he replied, 'Daughter, I shall be better off among stones than among men.' Such a horror of men's malignancy, by which he no doubt meant that of some of his brother friars, seems to have possessed him at this time that when walking near Madrid with a young friar and coming to an unused sidetrack he said, 'Let us take this one for no one who has offended God has passed along it.' Finally he revisited Segovia. The prioress of the convent there was shocked by his haggard appearance, but he refused to speak of his disgrace or to criticize the new order of things.

The priory of La Peñuela was an old hermitage that had been taken over eighteen years before, together with its hermits, by the Discalced Carmelites of Pastrana during the time of their enthusiasm for Doña Catalina de Cardona. As the place had proved to be unhealthy it had been abandoned a few years later for El Calvario. Now it had been resettled. It stood on a small plain surrounded by evergreen oaks and cistus heath on the lower slopes of the Sierra Morena, at the foot of the famous pass of Despeñaperros. Today the site is occupied by the town of La Carolina, which was built in the eighteenth century as part of a colonization scheme and populated with Germans. But in Juan's time it was the loneliest and most isolated of all the Discalced houses.

The prior, Diego de la Concepción, had been one of Juan's novices at Los Mártires and regarded him with respect and affection. He appointed him to be the spiritual director of the community but otherwise assigned him no duties except that of obeying the rule. For this reason Juan seems to have been happier here than he had been for many years. In a letter he wrote a few days after his arrival to Ana de Peñalosa he said that he felt very well and that the vastness of the heath (*la anchura del desierto*) greatly helped both body and soul. 'This morning,' he went on, 'we have been picking our chick peas and will be picking them all this week. Then we shall shell them. It is pleasant to handle these inanimate creatures – far pleasanter than being ourselves handled by living ones.'

His custom was to rise before dawn and kneel in prayer under some willow trees by a running stream, where he would remain until the heat of the day drove him in. The priory was surrounded by an orchard, an olive plantation of three thousand trees, a vine-yard and a hundred and fifty acres of arable land on which the friars grew their corn. It was thus really a farm or *cortijo*. But sometimes he would ask permission to go beyond its limits – as far as the wild scrub of cistus, terebinth, arbutus and giant heather that covered the surrounding hills. Then once a week he would set off for Linares to preach in the church there and confess penitents, making the journey of fifteen miles each way while fasting or, if he was feeling unwell, stopping to eat some bread and watercress by a stream. At night he slept on a mat woven of rosemary and broom, but most of the time that was allotted for sleep he devoted to prayer. As usual he spent much of his free time in writing. While at Segovia he had written the poem that begins *Entréme donde no supe* on coming out of an ecstasy. Here, it seems, he was engaged on a second version of his prose work, *The Living Flame of Love*.

The last years of Juan de la Cruz's life were seen by those who were close to him through a haze of miracles. At Segovia bright lights were observed coming out of his cell, aromatic odours hung about his confession box. While praying in the garden he would be lifted a few inches into the air. Since he impressed everyone about him as a saint, miraculous happenings had to cling to him. One of the powers with which he was credited was that of driving away storms. He would go out bareheaded and make four crosses in the air and the storm would change its direction. What the friars who recorded this omit to tell us is that it was one of the ordinary duties of priests, kept up until quite recent times, to conjure storms in this way. Then we are told that at La Peñuela he stopped a field fire that was on the point of burning down the priory by kneeling in front of it. The church was filled with smoke and on the doors being opened a hare ran out and twice in succession hid itself in his robes. This we can credit for it is well attested and has a natural explanation. The only supernatural event that Juan ever admitted to in connection with himself took place at Segovia when, as we have said, the figure of Christ in a painting addressed him as he was praying in front of it. The real miracle, if one likes to call it that, lies in his life of constant absorption in God to the exclusion of everything else. One is reminded of Schubert's total absorption in music.

While Juan de la Cruz was living quietly at La Peñuela, Doria was acting in a very strange manner. He sent Fray Diego Evangelista, the first definitor and a member of the *consulta*, that man who hated Juan so much, down to Andalusia to visit convents and priories and collect evidence of Juan's scandalous conduct. We know how Diego set about his task from the sworn depositions that were later made by the nuns and friars who had been interrogated by him. He would question them minutely for hours on end and if he could not get what he wanted by threats would misconstrue and falsify what they had said and then, without giving them what he had written to read through, order them to sign. Some of his questions to the nuns passed the bounds of decency and a nun at Málaga was made to declare that Fray Juan had kissed her through the grille. As Teresa had remarked eleven years before, at a time when the Calced were stirring up trouble in the convent of Seville, if a friar questioned a not very intelligent nun for several hours on end he could make her say anything he wanted because nuns were easily frightened and accustomed to obeying their superiors.* All the same many of the sisters protested vigorously and a friar, shocked by these proceedings, wrote to Juan about them, telling him that Diego Evangelista made no secret of his intention to get him stripped of his habit. Juan's letter of reply has come down to us: 'Son, don't trouble yourself about this, for they cannot take away my habit except for incorrigibility or disobedience and I am entirely ready to amend in anything in which I have erred and to accept any penance they may give me.' Advised by his prior to protest to Doria, he refused to do so or to defend himself in any way. No doubt he thought it would be useless, seeing that Diego Evangelista could only be acting on his superior's instructions.

* See Teresa's *Letters*, 263 and 264.

We may recall here the calumnies that the Calced had spread about Teresa at the time of Juan de la Cruz's imprisonment at Toledo. In Rome there were cardinals who had been persuaded to believe that, when she was supposed to be founding new convents, she was in reality taking young women from town to town to prostitute them. Her closed waggon, it was said, had once come to pieces in the square at Medina and a large number of people had seen her engaged in 'offending God' with a certain friar. In secular life, though there were jealousies enough among the members of the royal councils, one does not hear of slanders of this sort being spread. Only friars, dedicated to the service of God, seem to have been capable of such monstrous and deliberate perversions of the truth.

A panic now began to spread among the nuns and friars who had been directed by Fray Juan de la Cruz. A nun at Granada, Agustina de San José, deposed later that she had been made the custodian of a bag of his letters, which the sisters regarded 'as though they were the epistles of Saint Paul', as well as of notebooks containing 'the most sublime spiritual writings', but as the persecution increased she had been told to burn them so that they should not fall into the hands of his enemy. It is for this reason no doubt that so few of his letters have come down to us, though he had a large correspondence and every letter he wrote to his penitents would have been treasured. The books that he was engaged on towards the end of his life have also vanished while his prose works, *The Ascent of Mount Carmel* and *The Dark Night of the Soul*, break off abruptly. Either he did not finish them or the last sections, which would have described the state of union, have been destroyed. This is a matter I shall go into later when I come to discuss the poetry.

The panic of the nuns, the unfinished manuscripts, have suggested to many people that his case was being examined by the Inquisition and even that he was on the point of being arrested by it. The first historian of that institution, Juan Antonio Llorente, who had himself been an Inquisitor before he went over to the ideas of the Enlightenment and whose book, *Historia crítica de la Inquisición en España*, came out in 1818, states definitely that Juan was delated to the Inquisitions of Seville, Toledo and Valladolid at the same time as Gracián and other Carmelites who followed a similar method of mental prayer, on the charge of practising the *alumbrado* or illuminist heresy.* Juan's imprisonment by the friars of the Calced, declares

Llorente, saved him from arrest in 1577 by the Holy Office, but as they did not find sufficient evidence for a prosecution the Inquisitors held back and continued to watch him in the hopes of obtaining one. Now Llorente was an inaccurate and prejudiced historian, but he had access to files of the Inquisition which have since disappeared. A little later the great Catholic critic and literary historian, Menéndez y Pelayo, the most erudite man of his day, declared without naming his source that Juan de la Cruz had been four times delated to them. This is the only evidence that we have on this matter since the records seen by Llorente have vanished, but Juan's recent biographer, Father Gerardo, considers these statements to be in all probability true.

The Inquisition however received many delations which it did not act on. At the time of Juan's imprisonment at Toledo they could have had little that was positive to bring against him, but now the manuscripts of his books, of which many copies were in circulation, would provide ample evidence on which to prosecute him, if not to convict him, so fine was the dividing line in those days between heresy and orthodoxy. All we can say is that they did not do so, though the destruction of his letters and papers strongly suggests that he had again been delated, no doubt by one of his brother friars, and that the danger of arrest and conveyance to the secret cells hung over him and that this was known to the Discalced nuns and friars.

Juan's stay at La Peñuela was a brief one. He had been there only six weeks when in September 1591 he was struck down with a fever which came from an inflammation on his right foot. Another friar had fallen ill at the same time and the prior arranged that they should travel together to Baeza, some thirty miles away, where there would be doctors. But Juan asked to be allowed to go instead to Úbeda, five miles further on, where a priory of the reform had recently been founded. At Baeza he was well known and liked: at Úbeda he hoped to find neglect and oblivion.

The prior of Úbeda, Fray Francisco Crisóstomo, was a harsh and rigid man who felt a special antipathy for those who were regarded by others as saints.† He also bore a grudge against Juan who, when vicar-provincial of Andalusia, had had occasion to

---

* See appendix ii on page 96.

† Father Francisco Crisóstomo cannot have been the worst of these Discalced friars, for, if we read the remarks of Juan de la Cruz that were taken down by

correct him, together with his companion Fray Diego Evangelista, for too much preaching in churches and absenting himself for long periods from his priory. He therefore gave him the smallest and poorest cell in the building and one day, when Juan felt too sick to drag himself to the refectory, he sent for him and reprimanded him harshly in front of the other friars. In the meantime Juan's fever and inflammation were growing worse. A surgeon opened his foot with a knife and a large quantity of pus came out. Soon after this the whole of his leg, which was very swollen, broke out into ulcers. The surgeon cut, probed and cauterized, causing the sick man intense pain which he bore with such patience and gentleness that the doctor who was attending him became convinced that he was a saint and preserved as relics the swabs that had been used on his sores and which he had noticed smelt sweet and fragrant. The women who washed his bandages, struck by the odour of musk they gave off, did the same and a belief in his saintliness began to spread among the other friars and through the town. Only the prior remained hostile. Irritated by the attention that was paid to the sick man, he complained that the house could not afford the food that the doctors prescribed although most of what he ate was sent in by friends. He would go to see him every day and stand by his bedside, scolding him for his faults and taunting him for the reprimand which Juan had given him six years before. At the same time he forbade the other friars in the priory to visit him without his express permission and, as a last straw, deprived him of the attendant who looked after him. The friars were so shocked by the inhumanity of his conduct that one of them wrote to the provincial, Antonio de Heredia, to tell him what was happening.

Fray Antonio had often in the past shown his jealousy of Juan de la Cruz because he resented the high opinion that Teresa had of him, and he had recently been heard talking of him in a derogatory

Eliseo de los Mártires, we find that he inveighs against certain priors who treated the friars under them with 'irrational severity, so that they became pusillanimous in undertaking things of great merit, as if they had been brought up among wild beasts. . . . For who has ever seen men persuaded to love God by harshness and with blows?' It seems likely that some of these friars had been influenced by the extraordinary penances imposed on herself by Doña Catalina de Cardona, though it is clear that others were just petty tyrants who took it out of the young friars who were subject to them. See Allison Peers's translation, *The Works of San Juan de la Cruz*, vol. iii, *Spiritual Sayings*.

way. Ana de Peñalosa had been so painfully impressed by this that she had written to warn Juan against him. But when he heard that his old companion was sick and harshly treated, he hurried over from Granada in spite of his eighty-one years and the wintry weather, reprimanded the prior for his cruelty and spent several days there to make sure that he was well looked after. But the company of this garrulous old man does not seem to have been agreeable to Juan. He was too fond of reminiscing about the past. 'Tomorrow, Father,' he observed to him, 'will be the 28 of November – that is, just twenty years since we started the Reform.' And to the visible embarrassment and impatience of his former companion he began discoursing to the eagerly listening friars about the privations they had then suffered.

The sick man continued to grow worse. Tumours broke out all over his body, the largest and most painful being on his shoulder. Since he could not bear to be touched, a rope was hung from the ceiling by which he could lift himself. As his suffering increased, he would mutter, 'More patience, more love and more pain.' Very soon it became clear that he was dying. On being told this he asked that a wallet containing the letters that had been written to him about the defamatory depositions which Diego Evangelista was collecting against him should be burned in his presence so as not to incriminate their writers. After this he asked to see the prior and begged his forgiveness for all the trouble he had given him. The man, struck by shame and remorse, apologized for not having attended to him better, making the face-saving excuse that the priory was very poor. 'Father,' replied Juan, 'I have been treated far better than I deserve. But do not let yourself be distressed by the poverty of the house for if you have faith in the Lord it will soon be relieved.' The prior left the cell weeping.

The sick man was given extreme unction, after which he lay still all day in great pain, unable to speak. Then at 11.30 he sat up in bed, his face flushed with happiness, and said, 'How well I feel!' He asked the time and on being told it, said, 'The hour is approaching. Call the Fathers.' The fourteen or so friars who were staying in the priory, among them Antonio de Heredia, trooped into his cell, each of them carrying a small *candil* or oil lamp which they hung on the wall. Standing at the foot of his bed in that tiny room they recited the *De profundis* and the *Miserere*. Then the dying man asked one of them to read aloud some verses from the

Song of Songs. Oh, qué preciosas margaritas! he murmured. 'What exquisite pearls!' The friars trooped out. The church clock struck midnight – the hour for matins. 'Tonight I shall sing matins in Heaven,' said Juan and, folding his hands in front of him, ceased to breathe. It was 14 December 1591.

8

The Sequel

Juan de la Cruz's death was followed by some extraordinary scenes which his recent biographers have preferred to pass over in silence. Hardly had his breath ceased than, though it was an hour past midnight, cold and raining hard, crowds assembled in the street and poured into the priory. Pressing into the room where he lay, they knelt to kiss his feet and hands. They cut off pieces from his clothes and bandages and pulled out the swabs soaked in pus that had been placed on his sores. One of them bit off his toe, others took snippings from his hair or tore off his nails and would have cut pieces from his flesh had they not been prevented. At his funeral next day these scenes were repeated. Forcing their way past the friars who guarded his body, the mob tore off his habits and scapular, in which he had asked to be buried, and even took parts of his ulcered flesh.

A contest then began for his body. The patrons of the priory of Segovia, Ana de Peñalosa and her brother, were determined to acquire it for their city. After securing a royal warrant and the permission of Doria, they had it dug up by night in great secrecy. Although nine months had passed since Juan's death, it was found not to have decayed and to give out an aromatic smell. They placed it in a trunk and set off by a roundabout route for Castile.

Here a curious piece of folklore is reported by Juan's first biographer. The guardian angel of Úbeda wished to defend the body and prevent it from being removed to Segovia. After failing to rouse the friars of the priory in time, he appeared by night on a hilltop outside Martos and called in a loud voice to the bearers to take the body of the saint back to Úbeda. Their hair stood on end. But the *alguacil* replied that he was acting on the king's orders and the mysterious apparition then allowed them to pass. We are reminded of the contest between Saguntum and Saragossa in Prudentius' poem on the martyrdom of St Vincent.

San Juan's body, less an arm and a foot and several fingers left at Úbeda, finally reached Segovia. Dressed and covered with laurel leaves and flowers, it was shown to the city through a *reja* or iron grille. Although the lime packed in the place of the entrails had dried up the body, the face was still recognizable. Other vicissitudes followed, for after an appeal to Rome, the remaining limbs were cut off and, except for an arm given to Medina del Campo and a finger or two bestowed elsewhere, were restored to Úbeda. Segovia kept only the head and trunk. But these, to our modern taste, somewhat ghoulish episodes, have an important bearing on the story. Juan de la Cruz, to us who read his writings, was a poet and a mystic. But to his contemporaries he was a saint, with a sanctity doubly proclaimed by the austerity of his life and by the fragrant odour given off by his corpse. The people, with their medieval instinct for such things, recognized this and canonized him in their own way. And it was precisely this overwhelming movement of popular veneration, issuing from the streets as well as from the convents and priories and confirmed by the miraculous cures his relics began to effect, that silenced his enemies and led to the first steps for his beatification being taken twenty years later. It is very possible that we owe to it the preservation of his poems and prose works, for if he had not died when he did he would almost certainly have ended his life in disgrace and never been heard of, except as a contumacious or heretical friar who had once been a companion of Santa Teresa.

In appearance Juan de la Cruz was a very small man with dark hair and complexion, a face round rather than long and a slightly aquiline nose. His glance, we are told, was gentle. He grew a slight beard and went bald early. But of his character it is more difficult to speak. Unlike Teresa, he was singularly devoid of all those vivid and arresting features that one calls personality. We see an inward looking, silent man with downcast eyes, hurrying off to hide himself in his cell and so absent-minded that he often did not take in what was said to him. We note the immense tenacity of purpose that underlay his somewhat feminine sensibility, his strictness in matters of discipline and his entire and whole-hearted devotion to the contemplative life. Perhaps no one ever had a vocation that drew him so irresistibly. He had also, as Teresa observed, plenty of common sense and an insight into character and events that prevented him from being taken in and often allowed him to foretell the future. It is harder to speak of his relations with other people since he took great care to treat all his friars and nuns in the same way and to show no favouritism. 'Do not love one person more than another,' he wrote, 'but keep for everyone the same love and the same forgetfulness.' Such an attitude suggests an inhuman detachment from his fellows yet, as Friedrich von Hügel has pointed out,* this was a mystic's counsel of perfection rather than a rule of daily conduct and Juan's deep and tender affection for some of his penitents, especially for Ana de Jesús and Doña Ana de Peñalosa, comes out very clearly in his letters, in spite of the reserve he put upon himself. It seems scarcely necessary to say that he showed no animosity towards his enemies, making excuses for the Calced superiors who had treated him so barbarously in prison and refusing to allow anyone to speak disparagingly of other people, even of Diego Evangelista, in his presence. For after all they were merely acting as the agents of God.

This was not, we may note, the way of Teresa, who displayed a far more human attitude, liking some people and disliking others and not feeling ashamed of having favourites. But then she was outgoing and positive both in her life and in her opinions, whereas what strikes us most about Juan de la Cruz is his willed and deliberate negativity. All his contemporaries agree on his reluctance to speak about himself and his dislike of unnecessary conversation. His voice was never raised, his features never lost their habitual calm. No one ever saw him lose his composure or show annoyance. Perhaps it was for this reason that his brother friars, those who were most active in the order, thought little of him. And through his poems and prose works there runs like a refrain the words 'secret', 'hidden', 'forgotten', 'in disguise', 'silence', 'emptiness', 'night'. We are left, as he would have wished, with the necessity of describing the image he presented to the world by negatives, and leaving it to his poetry to display the richness and exuberance of his inner life.

For it is there, of course, in his inner life, that the spring and motive-force of Juan's nature is to be found. To compress its content into a few words, the central impulse of his system was love. That is, love for God and through him for other men and for the whole of creation. Just as a beam of light, when concentrated to form a laser, acquires an extraordinary power of penetration, so the mind is able to attain a preternatural intensity of vision when con-

* See *The Mystical Element in Religion* (1908), vol. I, pp. 67–8.

centrated on one object, God, though, being incomprehensible, He can only be approached by what Juan calls 'the dark and loving knowledge of faith'. It is this need for concentration that explains his insistence on poverty, emptiness, deprivation, freedom from earthly desires. Both the thoughts and the sense perceptions must be stilled to receive the impression of the divine. Then there is the emphasis he lays on the value of suffering, which in time became almost an obsession with him. 'The purest suffering,' he said, 'bears and carries in its train the purest understanding.' This view is to be explained partly by his desire to share in the sufferings of Christ on the Cross, but more, I think, to his discovery in the prison of Toledo that suffering purges the mind of its natural desires and so helps it to fix itself on the one object that is fitted for its love. He carried his ascetic practices to such lengths that it is difficult for a person of our times to read his prose works without a feeling of claustrophobia. When one becomes too conscious of that one must turn to his poems to see the delicacy and profusion that lay within.

We cannot close this account of Juan de la Cruz's life and character without saying something of what happened to the Carmelite reform after his death, if only to show by how narrow a margin he escaped his enemies. The persecution of Doria's opponents continued. Ana de Jesús and María de San José, the prioress at Seville who had been Teresa's best loved associate, were degraded and placed in close confinement to pay them out for having attempted to retain her constitutions for the nuns. But the worst punishment was meted out to Jerónimo Gracián. A few months before Diego Evangelista's visit to Andalusia to fabricate evidence against Juan de la Cruz, an enquiry was opened into the late provincial's conduct in Lisbon. The things brought forward against him did not amount to more than indiscretions – breaches of the letter of the rule made under special circumstances – though some of them could be twisted to give them a worse meaning. Had he stood up boldly to his accusers and refused to leave Lisbon, where his popularity with both high and low was great, nothing could have been done against him. But he was a man who was subject to attacks of weakness and self-distrust – 'now up in the air,' as Teresa had said of him, 'now in the depths of the sea' – so that, against the advice of Luis de León, he wrote a letter of total submission and left for Madrid. Here, in

July 1591, he was arrested by the *consulta* and, while the accusations against him were being prepared, kept in solitary confinement. Diego Evangelista, who had once been his friend and disciple, was then sent to interview him. With his now wheedling, now threatening ways he promised him forgiveness if he made a full confession and finally, at the end of several days, squeezed out of him an admission to one of the most serious faults he was charged with – too close an intimacy with a certain nun, though not of a kind that amounted to immorality. He was immediately brought before a tribunal of Doria's puppets. But he had now recovered his nerve and denied the truth of what he had been made to say. Nothing could shake him, yet in spite of this he was condemned to close and solitary imprisonment for three years in a priory, to severe fasts and to a circular whipping administered daily by the community. It was the same punishment that the Calced had meted out to Juan de la Cruz at Toledo. After five months of this treatment, his judges sent for him again. His spirit was now completely broken and he was ready to confess to anything. To understand such weakness in an otherwise courageous man one must remember that it was the custom of the Discalced, when accused of offences against the rule, as some of them were every Friday by the zealator, to make no reply however unjust the accusation seemed to them except the words, 'I will amend'. As Gracián himself said, if he defended himself he was called disobedient. Then, aware that he had at least been indiscreet, he was exposed to all the pressure of a conscience which, since it was subject to original sin, could never be entirely free from guilt. Could he be sure that he had not unconsciously desired to commit some of the acts that he was unjustly accused of? At all events his enemies had now got all the evidence they wanted. He was condemned to be stripped ignominiously of his habit and expelled from the Carmelite order. This took place in February 1592, just two months after Juan de la Cruz's death.

Gracián had suffered for having been Teresa's best loved and most trusted associate. This had provoked jealousies among his brother friars which had weakened his position when he made a stand, however feeble, against the sabotage of her principles. Doria's persistence in getting an expulsion clause inserted into the new constitution shows that he had from the first contemplated driving him out of the order. It was an outrageously harsh and unjust action, for had he merely wished to put an end to Gracián's influence, he could have left him, under a cloud as he was, as a simple friar in some remote priory or else sent him to Mexico. But this Italian operator was a man who never forgave anyone who had once opposed his interests. Yet he took care to dissemble his rancour for when in November 1589 he was seeking the king's support, he had written to him: 'I have never felt anything for Father Gracián but deep friendship and there has not once been so much as a hard word between us.' This last phrase was probably true for Doria had learned from the Jesuits the art of mental reserve and never gave away his true feelings or intentions till the moment came for doing so.

Gracián's subsequent history can be briefly told. He went to Rome to seek justice from the pope, only to find that the king, warned by Doria, had instructed his ambassador to see that he was not given an audience. Foiled again at Naples and in Sicily in his attempt to join some other order, he had the bad luck to be captured by Barbary pirates off the coast and taken to Tunis. Here he spent more than two years loaded with chains in an underground dungeon, displaying all the time the greatest courage and devoting himself to the care of his fellow prisoners. Ransomed at last, he returned to Rome where the pope ordered the Discalced to receive him back into their order. But, though Doria was now dead, they refused to do this as their pride would not allow them to admit that they had acted wrongfully. Instead the Calced Carmelites invited him to join them, paying him every honour and consideration and allowing him to follow the rule of the reform. Finally, after revisiting Spain, he went to Brussels where he died in 1614 at the age of 69. Some years previously he had published an account of his life in dialogue form, entitled *Peregrinación de Anastasio*, in which he performed the feat of relating the history of the Carmelite reform without mentioning Fray Juan de la Cruz. Yet with his many faults, of which jealousy was one, he strikes us as having been the most accomplished and likeable of Teresa's friars. That was why she, the most human and balanced of all the Catholic saints, had felt so drawn to him.

We must now, having told the story of Gracián's fall, return to the year 1591. As Juan de la Cruz lay dying at Úbeda, Doria received the depositions that had been submitted to him by Diego Evangelista of Juan's supposedly immoral dealings with the nuns. He already knew a good deal about them because so many complaints had reached him from those who had been interrogated. According to his secretary Gregorio de San Ángelo he threw the papers violently on the floor with the words that such allegations could not be true. But in a man of Doria's stamp we must look at this gesture more carefully. Since Gregorio was an old disciple and admirer of Juan's, it may have been a piece of theatre designed for his benefit. Or else, if he was really taken aback, the reason may have been that he found the depositions too crude, since if, as seems likely – and what other explanation is there? – he was intending to use this evidence to have Juan disgraced and expelled from the order, it would not do for it to be too patently false and out of keeping with his known character. But Juan's death almost at once relieved him of that necessity, while the strong feeling that was growing up of the dead man's sanctity and the many cures his relics were effecting would make any immediate publication of these slanders injudicious. Yet he did not destroy the false depositions, though they reflected on his late friar's honour, but put them away for possible future use in the archives, while at the same time he continued his close intimacy with Diego Evangelista, taking him with him to Italy that spring when he attended the chapter-general of the order at Cremona. Here this man continued to collect evidence against Juan's character and to speak badly of him, which shows that his superior had not found fault with him over his report.

Meanwhile under Doria's energetic leadership the reform was spreading rapidly. Many new priories were founded, among them certain places of retreat, known as *desiertos*, where the friars could live in solitary hermitages outside the central buildings. The first of these was at Bolarque near Pastrana, where some of the friars attained great heights of contemplation and Fray Bartolomé de San Basilio preached to the birds and trees in an ecstasy of love. Then at last the great aim of the Discalced was achieved: the pope made them a separate order under their own general. To implement this a chapter was convened to meet at Madrid in April 1594. No one doubted that Doria would be elected to the supreme post, but on his way to it he fell ill and died at Alcalá de Henares.

The dynamic leader gone, a reaction set in. A modest and unassuming friar, Elías de San Martín, became general and one of his first acts was to destroy the evidence that had been collected against Juan de la Cruz. At the same time Diego Evangelista was punished by being twice given the circular discipline on his shoulders and put on bread and water for two days. This was a mild sentence for a persistent calumniator, but he had already been elected a provincial and had friends in the *consulta*. Yet he got his deserts, for on his way to Granada to take up his new office he died suddenly at Alcalá la Real, aged only 34. The relics of the dead saint were evidently working something more than cures.

Such is the story, so far as we know it, of Juan de la Cruz's second persecution. Yet many things in it are obscure. The reason for this is that as soon as the Carmelites decided to press for his beatification all the papers that bore on Doria's secret intentions towards him were destroyed. Thus the *Libro Negro*, in which were recorded the acts of the chapters and definitories, vanished except for a few extracts which had previously been copied out. Much later, in the nineteenth century, the files of the Inquisition which related to his case were made to disappear. The motive for this can only have been that no imputation should be left either on the character of a canonized saint or on that of Doria, who still continued to be admired as the man who had got the Discalced Carmelites made a separate order. Indeed to this day the Discalced friars in Spain are divided in their sympathies between him and Gracián. Only the nuns are without exception 'Gracianistas'.

The collection of affidavits for the process of Juan de la Cruz's beatification began in 1614 and continued till 1627. Most of the friars and nuns who had known him personally and were still alive were asked to testify, yet according to one of his recent biographers, Father Bruno, many of those approached were afraid of speaking out about his second persecution, presumably because some of the superiors in the order had been adherents of Doria. At the same time his books, with the exception of the *Cántico espiritual* or *Spiritual Canticle*, were published, since his doctrine must be proved sound if the process of beatification was to be successful. For reasons of prudence certain suppressions and additions, which have only recently been rectified, were made by the Carmelite editor, yet in spite of this a strong opposition to his teachings at once broke out both in Spain and Rome. The Spanish Inquisition was at first inclined to condemn his books on the grounds of their containing illuminist and therefore heretical propositions and was only persuaded not to do so by the vigorous defence made by Basilio

Ponce de León, an Augustinian friar who was a professor of theology at Salamanca and a second cousin of Luis de León.

Then in 1675 the church decided. Clement X beatified him and so silenced all opposition. Fifty years later he was canonized by Benedict XIII and in 1926 Pius XI declared him a 'doctor of the universal church'. Since then he has been chosen as the patron saint of Spanish poets. Yet if first he and then Doria had not died when they did it is unlikely that any of these things would have happened. In that case Juan de la Cruz's poetry and prose might well have been lost to us, as would normally happen in the case of any friar who died in disgrace.

The first edition of Juan de la Cruz's works came out at Alcalá de Henares in 1618, but did not include the *Cántico espiritual*. It was reprinted in Barcelona in 1619. The book was delated to the Inquisition, but, as I have just said, successfully defended by an Augustinian friar. A fuller edition containing the *Cántico* (which had previously appeared in French at Paris in 1622 and in Spanish at Brussels in 1627 from a text provided by Ana de Jesús) came out in Madrid in 1630. It too was delated. Other editions appeared in Spain at Barcelona in 1635, at Madrid in 1672 and at Seville in 1703. All of these editions, with other less important ones which I omit, retain the suppressions and additions made by the first editor. The first critical edition to be made came out in 1912–14, and others have followed.

Santa Teresa's Jewish Ancestry

In 1947 an article appeared in the *Boletín de la Real Academia de España* by Narciso Alonso Cortés, which has revolutionized all our ideas on Santa Teresa's Old Christian ancestry. This article contains a summary of the contemporary record of a lawsuit brought in 1519 by the authorities of a small pueblo near Avila against Teresa's father, Alonso Sánchez de Cepeda, for the payment of certain taxes from which he claimed exemption as a *hidalgo*. Evidence was produced to show that his claim was not valid because both he and his father, Juan Sánchez de Cepeda, had been reconciled in 1485 by the Inquisition of Toledo for having relapsed from Christianity into Judaism. By this both he and his descendants had forfeited the rank of *hidalgo* and the privileges that went with it.

The story unfolded is a curious one. Teresa's grandfather, Juan Sánchez de Cepeda, was a prosperous silk and cloth merchant at Toledo who also farmed royal and ecclesiastical taxes and revenues and had financial transactions with several bishops. He was a professing Christian, when all at once he announced his conversion to Judaism and apostatized along with his wife, who was a Cepeda cousin, and his children. Not many years later, in 1485, the tribunal of the Inquisition was set up in Toledo. Street criers announced a free pardon for those who had lapsed into Judaism provided they confessed within forty days. Three hundred people had just been burned by the Inquisition of Seville for failing to do so, so Juan Sánchez de Cepeda had to choose between repenting and being burned at the stake. Not unnaturally he chose the first course and appeared in an *auto-de-fe* with his wife and three sons and seven hundred and fifty other confessed Judaizers. The ceremony was humiliating. Dressed in yellow *sanbenitos* with crosses sewn on them, barefooted, carrying unlighted candles and surrounded by a howling, stone-throwing mob, they were marched to the Cathedral where an Inquisitor read the sentence. This was that they were to be fined one-fifth of their property, forbidden to hold any office or pursue any honourable trade or to wear any but the plainest clothes on pain of being burned if detected. On six successive Fridays they were to walk in public procession to six churches, disciplining themselves on their bare backs with cords. The *sanbenitos* were afterwards to be hung with a suitable inscription in their parish church as a perpetual record of their crime – a mark of infamy which would debar their descendants down to the third, or, as it was later decided, fifth generation from holding any honourable office. Altogether more than 5,000 people in Toledo and the surrounding district, among them canons of the Cathedral, friars and monks, denounced themselves under the pardon offered by the edict of grace, and then there began the burnings of those who had not done so because they regarded themselves as being safe from detection.

Juan Sánchez de Cepeda with his wife and sons, including Teresa's father Alonso who, though only a boy of six, had marched in the procession, now moved to Avila.* Here he opened a branch of his silk trade but later, when purchase taxes were imposed on luxuries, closed down his warehouse to devote himself to the more profitable business of tax farming. The ecclesiastical authorities continued to employ him, for since the New Christians formed what we may call the middle classes of Spain there can have been few men of Old Christian descent to whom financial transactions could be entrusted. In everything he did he prospered and was successful in marrying all his eight sons, except for one who entered the church, to girls with good dowries. But he did not forget the scare he had had, for he brought up his family in true Christian piety and when he died at a ripe age in or around 1507 he left his second son Alonso to succeed him. Teresa was born in 1515 and, as the custom was, took the name of her mother, Beatriz de Ahumada, who may or may not have been of Jewish descent.

According to the statutes of *Limpieza de sangre* or Purity of Blood, freedom from the stain of Judaism or heresy for five generations back was required for anyone to hold the rank of *hidalgo* or to enter the church, university, army or any of the monastic orders. Had this been strictly observed, Teresa's brothers could not have become soldiers nor Teresa a nun. But such a large

* Juan Sánchez's eldest son, Hernando, had escaped this humiliating scene because he was at this time a student at Salamanca. Here he changed his name, married and had children, dying around 1507 unreconciled to the church. To the end of his life he kept up a correspondence with his brothers.

proportion of the educated classes had Jewish blood in their veins, not to speak of those who had secretly or openly relapsed from Christianity and then been reconciled by the Inquisition, that the Cepeda offence was passed over and condoned. Much can be done in Spain by those who have money and friends and the Cepedas of Avila were pious and well liked. Thus it happened that though the whole city must have known of Teresa's Jewish descent and of her father's and grandfather's apostasy, not a word has come down to us about it. It was left to a chance discovery a few years ago to bring out the truth.

Father Efrén de la Madre de Dios, o.c.d., in his recent and definitive biography, *Tiempo y Vida de Santa Teresa* (1968), has accepted this new evidence. But it has been a great shock to public opinion in Spain because it had always been supposed that this most typical and authentic of Spanish saints came of an old Castilian family. Her genealogical tree, which there is no reason for thinking faked, shows that she was descended from a certain Vasco Vázquez de Cepeda who in 1348 was *señor* of the *villa* or township of Cepeda in León. This had been taken to prove that she came of the best Christian blood, but Don Américo Castro, the eminent historian of Medieval Spain, has recently made it clear that in the fourteenth century rich Jews were often given the *señorío* or lordship of a *villa* with a castle to hold and the duty of leading a contingent of their men to the wars. The reaction against this tolerant attitude came later in the century during the civil war between Peter the Cruel and his half-brother Henry of Trastamara. Peter favoured the Jews who collected his taxes and lent him money, whereas Henry, who looked to popular support, was hostile to them. Thus we find that when in 1368 Henry won the war by stabbing his brother on the Campo de Montiel, Vasco Vázquez de Cepeda was deprived of his *señorío*. He settled in Tordesillas, whence some of his grandchildren moved to Toledo and entered the silk trade.

Meanwhile the civil war together with the black death had led to an increasing restlessness among the peasants and city workers which took the form, not as in England of risings against the government, but of attacks on the Jews, who after the nobles and the higher clergy were the wealthiest and most influential people in the country. Thus in 1391 violent pogroms broke out in every town and city of Spain which so frightened the more prosperous among them that large numbers apostatized and were baptised Christians. Many

of these embraced their new faith in sincerity, but others remained
secretly attached to Judaism and taught it to their children, who
continued all through the following century to practise it in their
homes. Among these no doubt were some of the Cepedas of
Toledo, who we know were settled here as silk merchants professing Christianity in the early years of the fifteenth century. It was
to unearth such secret Judaizers that the Inquisition was introduced
by Ferdinand and Isabella in 1480.

But why, it may be asked, did Juan Sánchez de Cepeda suddenly
decide to renounce his evidently nominal Christianity and return
openly to the religion of his ancestors? As it happens, the chronicles
of the time supply a plausible reason for this. Already by the middle
of the century the New Christians were becoming more hated than
the Jews because they were wealthier and more influential. They
controlled the silk and cloth industry, they collected the royal and
ecclesiastical revenues and many of the best offices in the church,
notably the canonries, were filled by them. The judges, lawyers,
doctors and apothecaries came mostly from their ranks and a
contemporary account gives them as numbering one-third of the
population of the larger cities. This hatred for them flared up in
1467 in a terrible riot in Toledo in which the whole of the merchants'
quarter near the Cathedral was sacked and burned down and many
of its inhabitants killed, while the Jewish quarter was left un-
touched. Since the city council had forbidden the New Christians to
carry arms, they were powerless to defend themselves and most of
them fled. A few years later these riots were repeated in Córdoba
and in many towns throughout the country, and the feeble government was unable to prevent them. Under these circumstances it may
well have seemed wiser to that keen man of affairs, Juan Sánchez de
Cepeda, to return to Judaism and move his shop to the comparative
safety of the *aljama* or ghetto. Like so many of the New Christians
of that century, he probably had no personal religion.

I have given this account of Santa Teresa's Jewish ancestry
because to the best of my knowledge it has never before been published in English. On the contrary most of her recent biographers
begin with several pages of genealogy in order to prove her descent
from the early nobility of Spain, and support their claim with much
ingenious erudition upon the quarterings on her coat of arms.
If anyone was ever guaranteed to come of the purest *Cristiano
Viejo*, Old Christian stock, then it was she, who had been chosen

for her typically Castilian and Catholic virtues to share with St James the Moor-slayer the honour of being the patron saint of Spain. Thus W. H. Walsh, the author of the best known biography of her in English, traced her descent from King Sancho of Leon and Castile. His admiration for her came largely from the fact that she represented for him the pure, untainted influence of Old Castile as against that of those eminent Spaniards of Jewish descent who opposed the policies of King Philip II because they were working in the interests of international Jewry. Many of her Spanish admirers have taken the same view and in Father Mir's biography (vol. 1, p. 19, 1912) we read of 14 dukes, 21 marquises, 12 counts, 1 viscount and 64 other illustrious persons who, because of her irreproachable ancestry, have been proud to claim a connection with her through her paternal ancestors. Even the latest biography of her by Marcelle Auclair, though first published in French in 1950, three years after the news of her grandfather's dealings with the Inquisition had come out, does not refer to it.

Yet surely the knowledge of Santa Teresa's Jewish descent adds to the interest of her life and mission. It explains how a deep sense of guilt caused by her consciousness of belonging to the race of deicides, as they were called, helped to drive her against her will along the hard path of the mystic and religious reformer. It also brings out her heroism, for in those days the sort of inner experiences she had – trances, raptures, visions, auditions and so forth – and which she recorded with such detail in her compulsive way were especially suspect to the ecclesiastical authorities when they appeared in persons of Jewish descent.

Indirectly her case throws a certain light upon that of San Juan de la Cruz. His ancestors, like hers, belonged to the corporation of Toledan silk merchants, who appear to have been all New Christians. Only we have no reason for supposing that the Yepes family, who had so many of their members in the church, were anything but sincere Catholics. Indeed Fray Juan may never have known of his Jewish ancestry.

The Alumbrados

The *Alumbrados* or Illuminists, whose name crops up so frequently in the religious history of this century, were not, as is usually supposed, a sect. They consisted of small groups of both clerics and laymen who appeared in New Castile during the first two decades of the sixteenth century and practised an interior Christianity. The movement arose spontaneously, but soon came under the influence of Erasmus, because, like him, they stood for a spiritual Christianity as opposed to a ceremonial one. As he had said, 'It is a new sort of Judaism to be satisfied with exterior and visible works without considering what they mean spiritually.' However they were also affected by the movement towards mental prayer that had recently sprung up among the Franciscans and in particular by the most eminent practitioner of it, Fray Francisco de Osuna, whose *Tercer Abecedario Espiritual*, or *Third Spiritual A.B.C.*, came out in 1537 and was the first work on mysticism to be published in Spanish. Osuna taught what he called *recogimiento* or recollection, which he said required no special aptitude but could be easily practised by anyone. The beginner should withdraw for one or two hours every day and empty his mind of all thought or consideration of earthly things so that it would be free for God to occupy it. If persisted in, this would lead to that outpouring of grace which Santa Teresa called the Prayer of Quiet and then to the brief transport called the Prayer of Union. The adept would continue to progress through various stages, although Osuna does not distinguish between these, but groups all mystical experience in prayer under the name of *recogimiento*. Thus he speaks of it variously as 'a kindling', 'the art of love', 'a spiritual flight towards God' and 'the third heaven to which contemplatives are caught up'. The essential technique lay in emptying the mind of all thought. *Este no pensar nada es pensarlo todo.*

Osuna's six A.B.C.s on the devotional life were immensely popular and went through many editions till in 1559 they were put on the Index. But his third or mystical A.B.C. is chiefly famous as having been read by Santa Teresa when she was a girl of twenty. It made a deep impression on her as she sat looking out on the great ilex trees at her uncle's house of Hortigosa and her copy, which has come down to us, is heavily underlined and scored with crosses, hearts and pointing hands drawn in the margin. It was as a result of reading it that she was launched on her long and adventurous career. But Osuna's book had also, as I have said, a great influence on the *Alumbrados*, who had already discovered the earlier stages of mental prayer by themselves. Indeed he had actually belonged to one of their groups for some years before he published it, so that he might almost be called an *alumbrado* himself.

The peculiarity of Osuna's teaching was that it broke with the Flemish and German school of the contemplatives of the Humanity of Christ which stemmed from the time of Giotto, and went back to the mystical tradition of St Bernard and Richard of St Victor that sought union with the divine element. It was thus in tune with the optimistic spirit of the *Alumbrados*, characteristic of an age of awakening and of the rediscovery of grace. No tears were to be shed over the Passion, for the Resurrection followed it. Beatitude was a sign of faith. One had only to practise *recogimiento* to feel grace rising like a sap within one. These *Alumbrados* were therefore happy and enthusiastic people, confident of their salvation, and it was this that led Melchor Cano to condemn them. According to him, 'the taking away of fear and the giving of reassurance' was a thing that they shared with the Lutherans. The 'good tidings' of divine illumination relieved their souls from its 'little fears'.

There was another form of mental prayer, current among some of the *Alumbrados*. This was *dejamiento*, as opposed to *recogimiento* – 'letting go' instead of 'collecting together' – in which the soul remained passive, without effort or striving, and simply surrendered itself to the love of God. The people who practised this disapproved of ecstasies and unions and sought a continuous operation of God's love on men. *El amor de Dios en el hombre es Dios.* They also held that a person who reached a state of grace could not sin. This was quietism or Molinism and therefore savoured even in the eyes of Rome of heresy.

The Spanish Inquisition, which was stricter than the Roman one, began to persecute the *Alumbrados* in 1524, taking the *dejados* first. Then came the turn of those who practised *recogimiento*. What it objected to in them was not so much their occasional extravagance as the lack of effective control exercised over them by the hierarchy. It was disturbing that they regarded religious services and verbal prayer chiefly as things for beginners: their constant appeals to experience and their claims to be directly illuminated by the spirit were suspect, while it was noted that women played a large and sometimes unseemly rôle among them and that many of them were New Christians. There was an evident danger that if they established themselves too securely they might set up conventicles. For in the background there was always Luther. It was he who had kept the Inquisition in being after the Judaizers had all been picked up. An iron wall must be built to keep his influence from infiltrating across the frontiers.

The persecution of the *Alumbrados* reached its peak in the late 1530s, a few years before that of the Erasmists began, and continued with its usual sentences of abjuration *de vehementi*, long imprisonment and occasional burnings until they had all been extirpated. After that the word became a term of abuse which could be used against anyone who practised mental prayer or who held, even in its orthodox Catholic sense, the doctrine of justification by faith. In 1559, the date of the Council of Trent, the reaction reached its height when almost all mystical works were put on the Index along with translations of the New Testament. After this no one who advocated the practice of mental prayer was safe from arrest by the Inquisition, though a certain latitude was allowed to the religious orders, who were under the close control of the hierarchy, since the old tradition of mystical theology in the church could not be entirely denied. Then the Counter-Reformation, which had its roots in Erasmus, even though his name could not be mentioned, began with the rising to influence of the Jesuits and of the Discalced Carmelites. Yet as late as 1616 a priest, Gerónimo de la Madre de Dios, was tried and sentenced to abjure *de vehementi* on a charge of belonging to the *alumbrado* heresy, because he had written a mystical work that was less extreme in its teaching than those of either Teresa or Juan de la Cruz. Theology is a tricky subject and Inquisitors varied in their opinions, so that it was often a matter of chance whether a writer of a mystical kind was condemned for heresy or not.

PART TWO

THE WORKS

'The qualities of the solitary bird are five: first, that it seeks the heights: second, that it admits of no companionship, not even with its own kind: third, that it stretches out its beak into the air: fourth, that it has no fixed colour: fifth, that it sings sweetly. These are the qualities that the contemplative soul has to possess. . . . It has to sing sweetly for the love of its Spouse.'

Dichos de luz y amor

9

An Examination of the Poetry

The dates

The poems of San Juan de la Cruz that we chiefly want to read take up eighteen pages in the large print of the *Seneca* edition and less than half that in the edition of the *Biblioteca de Autores Cristianos*. Only one of these poems, the *Cántico espiritual*, is of any length. In addition to these he wrote nine *romances* or ballads on the Trinity and Incarnation which have a mainly doctrinal interest.

Most of these poems can be dated with fair accuracy. To start with the first of them, the verses which begin *Vivo sin vivir en mí*, were almost certainly written between 1572 and 1577 at Avila. The reason for thinking this is that Santa Teresa wrote a poem on the same gloss and expressing the same ideas in 1571, not long before San Juan became her confessor. It was not unusual for friars and nuns to write verses on a given theme in competition with one another.

The great burst of San Juan de la Cruz's poetic composition came in 1578 while he was in prison at Toledo and continued with diminishing force for several years after that. It was here, as several witnesses inform us, that he began the *Cántico espiritual*. But this is a long and very great poem and we would like to know how far he got with it before his escape. Our only evidence on this comes from a nun, Magdalena del Espíritu Santo, who said that he reached the stanza that begins *O ninfas de Judea*. She was in a good position to know because, when San Juan was living at El Calvario a few months later, he gave the *cuadernillo* or notebook in which he had written down his verses in prison to the nuns of Beas, and Sister Magdalena made copies of them. She recorded this in a memoir she wrote on San Juan in which she gave examples of his religious teaching that she had taken down from his lips at the time. But unfortunately her statement does not tell us as much as it appears to do because we do not know at what point in the poem the line on the nymphs of Judaea then occurred. In the first version we possess of the *Cántico*, which is preserved in the Carmelite convent at San

Lúcar de Barrameda with annotations in San Juan's own hand, it comes at the beginning of the thirty-first stanza. Since this version contains thirty-nine stanzas, Sister Magdalena's statement would appear to mean that he wrote more than three-quarters of it in prison. In the second arrangement of the *Cántico*, which he made six or seven years later, it comes in the eighteenth stanza, but as this version was made to suit the prose commentary he was then writing and plainly violates the natural flow and impetus of the poem, it cannot have been the one that Sister Magdalena saw in 1579. Yet it is very difficult to believe that San Juan wrote as many as thirty stanzas of this inspired and ecstatic poem, as well as several other poems, in the state of mental abjection and prostration in which he said that he spent almost the whole of his period of incarceration. His general habit was to write in short bursts, composing a few stanzas or prose paragraphs at a time. Since the order of the stanzas is loose and the narrative sequence frequently broken, is it not possible that in his first draft of it the nymphs of Judaea came much earlier?

But there is another and, I think, more plausible explanation of this difficulty. San Juan, we know, continued to add to the *Cántico* after his escape. Let us suppose that when that happened he had written only up to the tenth stanza, where there is an awkward break which he later tried to bridge over by inserting an extra stanza. Then, after recovering his strength, he found himself plunged into the life of a community of friars where everything conspired to make him happy. Spring, the soft Andalusian spring, was coming on and inducing a mood of which the verses that follow the twelfth stanza, with their almost pantheistic celebration of Nature, would have been an appropriate expression. If in fact he wrote them at this time he would presumably have copied them into the notebook in which he had recorded the stanzas he had written in prison, before handing it to the nuns at Beas. By then we may suppose that he had reached the thirty-first stanza in which the nymphs of Judaea occur, so that by a natural misunderstanding Sister Magdalena would have taken it that he had got as far as this point in prison. For, let us note, she does not say that he told her he had done so. All this, of course, is pure guesswork, but it at least offers a more plausible hypothesis than that he wrote the first thirty stanzas of his poem in the darkness and misery of his cell. The fact is that we know nothing for certain.

I have already, in writing of San Juan de la Cruz's life, described how the last five stanzas, beginning *Gocémonos, Amado,* came to be composed. After a nun, Francisca de la Madre de Dios, had said to him that prayer meant for her contemplating the beauty of God and rejoicing that she was able to do so, he became deeply moved and soon afterwards composed these verses. There is some doubt about the date: he either wrote them at Baeza in 1580 or, more probably, at Granada in 1582 after returning from a visit to Beas.

As I have said, San Juan's decision to write a second commentary or *declaración* to accord with his maturer experience of the mystical ascent led to his altering the order of the stanzas. This version of the poem is known as the Jaén version because the best manuscript of it, which derives from Ana de Jesús, to whom the *Cántico* was dedicated, is preserved in the Carmelite convent of that city, whereas the earlier one is known as the Sanlúcar version. The rearrangement took place at some date between 1585 and 1586 when he was prior of Los Mártires in Granada and in the course of making it he added another stanza, number 11, beginning *Descubre tu presencia,* thus bringing the total number up to forty. But in issuing this second version of the *Cántico* he seems to have had no desire to suppress the first one, of which many copies were already in circulation, for written at the top of the Sanlúcar manuscript we find in San Juan's own hand: 'This book is the rough copy (*borrador*) of which a fresh version has been made, Fray Juan de la ✠.' The date of this manuscript is thought to be 1586 or 1587 and the codex in which it is included contains the complete collection of all his poems which are known to be authentic.

Besides the first part of the *Cántico espiritual,* San Juan wrote several other poems while he was in the prison at Toledo. Among these, and probably the first to be written, are the beautiful verses beginning, *Que bien sé yo la fonte que mana y corre.* Then there is his paraphrase to the psalm *Super flumina Babylonis,* and the first three sections in *romance* metre of the long poem which he ended by composing on the mystery of the Trinity and Incarnation. He recited these to the nuns in Toledo immediately after his escape and one of them took them down, but like all his other prison poems they had already been written down in his notebook with the pen and ink which his second jailor had given him.

The most perfect of San Juan's poems, *En una noche oscura,* was almost certainly not written in prison but soon after his escape, either at El Calvario or before he reached it. We can be sure of this terminal date because he began writing his prose commentary on it, the *Ascent of Mount Carmel*, at the request of the nuns at Beas in the early months of 1579.

The *Llama de amor viva* was composed at Granada in 1585 and dedicated with its prose commentary to Doña Ana de Peñalosa. We are told that he wrote the poem *en oración*, that is, in a state of contemplative prayer. It is not known when he wrote the poems beginning *Un pastorcico, solo, está penado* or *Tras de un amoroso lance*, but it was probably about this time. That beginning *Entréme donde no supe* is said to have been composed while he was living at Segovia, but this is not certain as it is included in the Sanlúcar codex, which is thought to have been put together earlier.

Influences

A poet grows up in a certain literary environment and draws his verse forms, diction and so forth from his predecessors. This is what I mean by influences. They are especially important in the case of San Juan de la Cruz because he had read very little poetry. Don Dámaso Alonso, the distinguished Spanish poet and critic, has gone into this question with great thoroughness in his admirable book *La Poesía de San Juan de la Cruz* and in what follows I shall draw heavily on what he has said.

He divides the literary influences into Spanish and biblical. I will take the Spanish first. These are to be found in the popular songs of the time and in one great name, Garcilaso de la Vega. The popular songs are roughly of two kinds – those which were current in San Juan's day and were sung in the streets, and those which had been evolved in a more *cortesano* or cultured atmosphere and were most easily to be found in a song book. Their influence is slight in the *Cántico* and non-existent in the *Noche oscura* and the *Llama*, but it dictates both the form and the style of his other poems. These are what are known as *villancicos*. The peculiarity of the *villancico* is that it begins with an *estribillo* or theme – a verse of two or three lines which is developed or glossed in the succeeding stanzas, while at the end of each stanza the last line of the *estribillo* is repeated. These little verses were sung everywhere as popular *coplas* used to be till the transistor radios drove them out and we know that Juan's brother Francisco often had one on his lips. Their subject was nearly always love, like that of the pop songs of today, but religious writers interpreted them *a lo divino*, that is as expressing love for Christ or the Virgin, and developed them in that sense. It often happened that the theme-verses could give rise to many different developments. The most original and beautiful of San Juan's *villancicos* is that which begins *Que bien sé yo la fonte que mana y corre* with its refrain *Aunque es de noche*. Dámaso Alonso supposes that its theme-verse was taken from a three-lined verselet that is now lost. Yet it was not written in the popular octosyllabic metre that was usual in *villancicos* but in hendecasyllables, a more expressive metre that had recently been introduced from Italy.

Besides *villancicos*, San Juan wrote some *romances*, that is poems in ballad metre. These comprise his long poem on the Trinity and Incarnation and his paraphrase of the psalm 'By the waters of Babylon'. The *romance* was the usual verse form of the time for narrative subjects and its peculiarity is that the same rhyme or assonance runs all through the poem. This is easily achieved in Spanish by ending each alternate line with a verb that is in either the imperfect or the conditional tense.

It is, however, the three major poems – the *Cántico*, *Noche oscura* and *Llama* – that chiefly call for examination because it is on them that his reputation as a supreme lyric poet is founded. They owe their existence to Garcilaso de la Vega, the introducer of the Italian Renaissance style or *arte nuevo* to Spain and the initiator of the great poetry of the Golden Age. Garcilaso was a young Castilian nobleman and soldier at the court of Charles V, who, like Sir Philip Sidney, possessed all those accomplishments of mind and body which Castiglione had declared were proper to a courtier. Influenced by his friend Juan Boscán, he began to write poems in Italian metres with greater smoothness and more musical rhythms than had yet been written in Spanish. This was made possible by his introduction of the hendecasyllable, which had three more syllables than the native Spanish metre. Then in 1536 he was killed with his poems still unpublished. Boscán died in 1542 and it was not until the following year that the work of the two poets was published in one volume by Boscán's widow. The book produced an enormous sensation: edition after edition came out and for a time it was impossible for a young poet to write except in the Italian manner.

The bulk of Garcilaso's work consists of eclogues, *canciones* and sonnets. In its subject matter and style it is Renaissance poetry: the refined sense of beauty, the artificiality of the pastoral themes, the diffused and sublimated sensuality, were all taken from the Italian and introduced for the first time to Spanish readers. But what I think was of more importance than this was the purity and elegance of diction that the new poetry in hendecasyllables brought with it. Up to this time, Castilian had been a strong, rather crude idiom, capable of certain effects in verse but too stiff and limited in scope for others. Garcilaso refined it and made it musical. He did this as much perhaps by the study of Horace and Vergil as by that of Politian and Sannazaro – or rather, let us say, it was these last two who taught him how a rich and sonorous poetry could be written with the aid of an ear trained on the Latins. For Latin poetry taught the importance of quantity. Without attention to the quantity of words, poetry in a stressed language will generally have something thin and monotonous about it. It will flow too quickly and carelessly for the words to produce their full musical effects. Its combinations of vowels and consonants will be elementary. It is only by taking into consideration the length of time that syllables take to be pronounced and the separate quantities of each of them that the speed of the line can be controlled and more intimate rhythms built up within – and even across – the framework of the metrical pattern. And this is Garcilaso's supreme merit. His verse is slow, languorous, melancholy – proper poetry for a young man whose theme is unsuccessful love – but its rhythms charm the ear by their faultlessness like those of *Lycidas*, and every word is made to give out as it passes the full effects that are required of it. It was a poetry suited in every way to express the new, more introverted states of consciousness that were growing up in Spain and it was through Garcilaso's successful acclimatization of the Italian hendeca-syllable that it became possible. This was a thing that only a great poet who knew Italian well could bring off, for it meant digging a new channel through which Spanish poetry could flow and other fine poets such as the Marqués de Santillana had tried without success to accomplish it.

We may suppose that San Juan de la Cruz first read Garcilaso as a young man at Medina del Campo and that he saturated himself in his poetry, for which his ear would already have been prepared by his study of the Latin poets. Indeed we may be sure that this is so for we are told that he wrote some *canciones* or poems 'in heroic verse and in a pastoral style' on making his profession at the Calced Carmelite priory. This can only mean in the style of Garcilaso, which all the young were imitating, but it is highly unlikely that he opened his book again after leaving Salamanca, for when he joined the Carmelite reform he put away everything that did not belong to religion. What then made him think of taking up the writing of poetry again? The idea would seem to have come to him from the reading of a religious poet called Sebastián de Córdoba, an Andalusian from Úbeda. This Córdoba was a third-rate versifier who had brought out a pastiche of Garcilaso in which the love poetry of his eclogues and *canciones* is turned often line by line into a religious allegory of the love of God for the soul. His book was published in 1575, while San Juan was at Avila, and we know that he read it because he quotes from it. The most likely hypothesis is, as Dámaso Alonso suggests, that the reading of Córdoba revived earlier memories of Garcilaso and suggested the possibility of writing poems in Italian metres on a mystical subject. His imprisonment two years later provided the immediate incentive.

But what precisely was Garcilaso's influence on San Juan de la Cruz's poetry? In the first place there is the metre. San Juan's four best poems are all in hendecasyllables. Then his two greatest poems, the *Cántico* and the *Noche oscura*, are written in a verse form known in Spanish as the *lira*, in which Garcilaso had composed a famous *canción*. If one looks at the first two stanzas of *Si de mi baja lira* (sometimes known as the *Flor de Gnido*) and compares them with those of the *Cántico*, one will see the resemblance. The *lira* is a very beautiful form which is capable of great lyric effects. Garcilaso, whose style is a little too quiet for such a measure, took it from Bernardo Tasso, who had invented it to convey in a stressed language the effect of Horace's *Odes*. After this it came to be very generally used in Spain and Fray Luis de León found it suited him so well that he wrote most of his best poems in it. It is possible that San Juan saw some of these in manuscript while he was a student at Salamanca, though his work shows no trace of their influence. The *lira*, it may be said, has scarcely travelled beyond Spain and Italy and the only example I know of its use in English are some rather wooden verses by William Drummond of Hawthornden.

A third poem whose form San Juan borrowed from Garcilaso is the *Llama de amor viva*. In a somewhat confused note which he appended to it he explains that he took the pattern of its stanzas, which he incorrectly called *liras*, from the opening of Garcilaso's *Canción Segunda*, where it figures as a semi-strophe. The fact that the three lines he quotes come from Sebastián de Córdoba's pastiche *a lo divino* shows how much he had forgotten the original.

Another feature that San Juan took from Garcilaso was the pastoral idiom. The *Cántico espiritual* is conceived in the form of a pastoral dialogue in which the Lover and the Beloved converse together and make love among woods and hills. The most rapid reading will show that it teems with the conventional words and images of pastoral poetry, as also, like Milton's early poems, with words and phrases actually used by real shepherds. In this last case San Juan was not following Garcilaso, but acting on his own account. But perhaps the idea of employing such an artificial form as that of the pastoral on a mystical subject will strike us as incongruous: if so, we should remember that the Hebrew *Song of Songs*, which had inspired so much mystical writing in the Middle Ages, had long been regarded as a pastoral poem describing the loves of Christ and the soul. Luis de León, who translated it into Spanish prose, described it as such. However it must be admitted that San Juan's choice of words is not invariably flawless. Thus we are jarred by his using the term 'nymphs of Judaea' for 'daughters of Jerusalem' as well as by an allusion in a passage describing the Beatific Vision to *la dulce Filomena*.

But Garcilaso was not the only influence on San Juan de la Cruz's poetry. An equally important one was the Bible and in particular the *Song of Songs*. This was not of course a prosodic influence, but one of scenes, incidents, images and colour. In the case of the *Cántico* at all events the Latin text of the Vulgate in which he read it provides a secondary layer of imagery and symbolism from which the poem rises and to which in many echoes and allusions it returns. Let me try to show how this happens.

The *Song of Songs* is an anthology of Hebrew folk songs intended for use at marriage festivals and dating in its present state from the third century B.C. The central core of these songs was a ritual drama in which, it would seem, the bridegroom played the part of King Solomon and the various scenes of his courtship and betrothal were acted out during the wedding festivities, with the bridesmaids forming a chorus. The fact that some of the songs contained the name of Solomon led to a belief that it had been written by him and for this reason it was, after much discussion, included in the Jewish canon. From this it was taken over by the Christians who interpreted it allegorically, as they did the other books of the Old

Testament. But the work as we have it is in a very corrupt state. This would seem to be because the Hebrew editors not only included many love songs that do not accord with the main dramatic theme, but jumbled them together so that the book, taken as a whole, is not fully intelligible. This, together with its erotic Oriental imagery, and supposed mystical significance, presented in the superb Latin translation of St Jerome, made it an exciting and stimulating work for poets and mystics to draw on.

By an odd coincidence the first commentary we possess on the *Song of Songs* was written by Gregorius, Bishop of Elvira, as Granada was then called, who died at an advanced age in 392. He took it to be an allegory on the love of Christ for the church, interpreting the cedars of Lebanon as the Patriarchs, the cypresses as the Apostles, the Shulamite's breasts as the two Testaments and the lily of the valley as the Resurrection, while the stag, the wall and the bunch of grapes were all symbols for Christ, and the 'fairest among women' was black because of Eve's sin. Many other commentaries followed, especially during the Early Middle Ages, the most famous being the eighty-six sermons in which St Bernard gives an allegorical exposition of the poem, treating its subject, as all mystics must, as being the love of Christ for the soul. A good deal of Latin poetry too was written on it. Thus St Peter Damian in the eleventh century composed a beautiful poem in which the Bride represented the soul and the Bridegroom Christ. A twelfth-century pastoral composed in dramatic form and beginning *Crebro de mihi basia* gives a different interpretation: here the still unborn Christ acts the part of a knight and the Virgin Mary that of the accosted maiden. These poems, it will be observed, all have a peculiar flavour: they are original poems, but they are built out of the material of another poem, composed in a far-off age and country. To feel them properly one must first have steeped oneself in the biblical poetry that comes through them. Only then will one catch the full richness of the overtones.

Now San Juan de la Cruz's *Cántico espiritual* and *Noche oscura* are to a certain extent poems of this sort. The subject of both is the quest of the soul for God, the mystical union and beatific vision and, since the poet regarded the *Song of Songs* as an allegory written by Solomon upon the same subject, it is natural that he should have drawn for his poem on the same verbal material, allowing Solomon's divinely inspired words to suffuse and saturate his. In fact he lifts whole verses out of the Vulgate. But the fact that he was writing in Spanish – in which no translation of the *Song of Songs* was then available – made for a more complete fusion of the old and new elements than had been possible for those poets who had treated the same theme in Latin verse.

The personal element

It is fairly obvious that most of San Juan de la Cruz's poetry is autobiographical. All his poems and *villancicos* except one are written in the first person singular. The *Cántico*, certainly, is in dialogue, but the character who represents the poet has the principal part. It is true that this *Yo* or *I* stands for the soul and is therefore feminine, but there cannot be any doubt that the poet is describing – or representing rather – his own experiences.

What were these experiences? The first two stanzas of the *Cántico* are clearly a cry of anguish and despair at the abandonment to which he felt himself relegated in prison. In the *Noche oscura* there is an obvious reference to his escape which is brought out more clearly in his commentary (*Ascent of Mount Carmel* I, 15). Yet to stress this would be to misunderstand these poems entirely. San Juan's basic experiences were mystical experiences, which, as he tells us in his prose works, were devoid or almost devoid of sensory or imaginary impressions. They were experiences of which we, his readers, can have scarcely the remotest conception. If poetry is, as some think, a superior form of communication, we shall be at a loss in this case to say what is communicated.

But the question of what he was writing about also troubled the poet. In the Prologue to the *Ascent* he says of his mystical experience: 'Human knowledge is not sufficient to comprehend it nor human experience to describe it, because only he who has passed through it will be able to feel it, but not to tell it.' And he wrote a *villancico* on this subject:

> Entréme donde no supe,
> y quedéme no sabiendo,
> toda sciencia trascendiendo.

'I entered I knew not where and remained not knowing, passing beyond all knowledge.'

Indeed this sense of not understanding his own experience is

110

one of Juan's most recurrent themes. *Era cosa tan secreta/Que me quedé balbuciendo.* Or else: *Y déjame muriendo/Un no sé qué que quedan balbuciendo.* The verb *balbucir,* to stammer (in the sense of people or children stammering when overcome by astonishment), is a word that is frequently met with in San Juan's writings: it belongs to that large family of expressions which we shall presently speak of that are grouped under the general heading of the Dark Night.

But it is not only that the poet cannot understand or explain his own experiences, he cannot fully understand or explain the poems that have come out of those experiences either. 'It would be ignorance,' he wrote in the Prologue to the *Spiritual Canticle,* 'to think that the sayings of love in mystical intelligence, such as are the present verses, can be properly explained in any words whatsoever, because the Spirit of the Lord, aiding our weakness, begs on our behalf for what we ourselves cannot well comprehend or understand, so as to manifest it.' Now although, as we shall see later, San Juan admits to sometimes using the conscious processes of an artist in composing his poems, this is a theory of inspiration in the most literal sense of the word. It implies that, whatever plans he may have made beforehand or corrections afterwards, the actual work of poetry-making was done at the dictation of forces he could not explain. This enables us to understand better the need he felt for drawing so heavily on the *Song of Songs,* for this was a poem whose every word, dark and obscure though its meaning might be, had been inspired by the Holy Spirit.

Fusion of elements

We have now separated out and isolated in San Juan de la Cruz's poems a number of different elements deriving from different sources. There is the popular element of the song books and of rural life; the influence, prosodic and pastoral, of Garcilaso de la Vega and of Renaissance Italy; the erotic and oriental layer of the *Song of Songs* and lastly his personal experiences. We must now ask how these are combined.

I would like at this point to draw attention to one of the most fundamental studies on the genesis of poetry that has ever been written – *The Road to Xanadu* by Professor J. L. Lowes. This book is an examination of two poems by Coleridge – the *Ancient Mariner* and *Kvbla Khan.* The fact that in writing these poems Coleridge's imagination was stimulated mainly by travel books and that his diaries give the titles of those that had most struck him during the preceding years, makes it possible to carry out a detailed study of their sources. And what Professor Lowes has discovered is that the source of nearly every important word, image and episode in these poems lay not in one passage of his reading, but in several. To take a concrete case: Mount Abora in *Kubla Khan* is a composite word, drawn from three or four separate and distinct recollections which have been fused into one another. The water snakes in the *Ancient Mariner* were drawn from seven.

Now this is a process found by psychoanalysts to occur in dream symbolism. They call it condensation. The symbol, as one may term the result, acquires an extra force and potency when it contains a number of different psychic elements fused together within it. Though inexplicable in rational terms, it constitutes a sort of storehouse of unconscious meaning. Now if the case of Coleridge can be taken as a general one, this is one of the principal things that poets do when they write poetry, and it is certainly what San Juan de la Cruz often did with his raw material. It is not possible to demonstrate this in such a complete way as Professor Lowes did in the case of the English poet because San Juan did not draw all his impressions from his reading, but took many from his own experience. However, Dámaso Alonso has been able to show that it is a regular feature of his poetry that elements from different literary sources are found fused together into a single passage or phrase.

Let me give a simple example of this. In Stanza 22 of the *Cántico* that begins *En solo aquel cabello* we are given an image of the Lover caught by the beauty of a single loose hair fluttering on the neck of the Beloved* and then wounded by one of her eyes. Now there is a strong resemblance between this passage and a famous sonnet by Garcilaso that begins *En tanto que de rosa y azucena* and continuing four lines further down:

> Y en tanto que el cabello, que en la vena
> de oro se escogió, con vuelo presto,
> por el hermoso cuello blanco, enhiesto,
> el viento mueve, esparce y desordena.

---

* I have used 'Lover' and 'Beloved' for *Amado* and *Amada* because these are the most appropriate terms to use here, although in the translation of the poems, as in the *Song of Songs*, the word 'Beloved' designates the man.

There can be no doubt that our poet had this passage at the back of his mind – all the more as he draws on the first line of Garcilaso's sonnet in the thirty-second stanza of the *Cántico*, writing *en tanto que en las flores y rosales* – yet there is also a verse of the *Song of Songs* that, in the Vulgate translation, is even closer:

> Thou hast ravished my heart, my sister, my spouse:
> thou hast ravished my heart with one of thine eyes,
> with one hair of thy neck.

And there are further a number of popular *villancicos* of the time which San Juan may well have heard on the same theme. Dámaso Alonso quotes one of these from a manuscript.

There are many other examples to be found in San Juan's poetry of this fusion of passages from Garcilaso and the *Song of Songs*, but if one wants a more complex instance of how he combined materials from different sources I think that the theme of the spring or fount, which plays such a notable part in his writings, will serve.

Let us start with the *villancico* that begins:

> Que bien sé yo la fonte que mana y corre,
> aunque es de noche.

The symbolism of the fountain in this poem (I use the word in its old meaning of spring) derives from two mystical writers, Francisco de Osuna and Bernardino de Laredo, who represented the Trinity under the triple symbol of fountain, river and sea. They were favourite writers of Santa Teresa, and San Juan probably read them while acting as her confessor at Avila. In this poem he associates the fountain with his principal symbolic theme, the Dark Night, which I shall speak of later. But there is a popular element too. The fact that he uses the antique Galician form *fonte* instead of the Castilian *fuente* shows that he had in mind the famous *romance, Fonte frida y con amor*, alluded to in his commentary on the *Cántico* which describes a spring or fountain at which all the birds went to draw consolation. Only the Turtle Dove, that unhappy widow, *que está viuda y con dolor*, did not go there, but practised instead a sort of mourner's mortification. Now the Turtle Dove, *tortolica*, is the name which the Lover gives to his Beloved in a significant passage in the *Cántico*, following the authority of the *Song of Songs* and also, it would seem, of a passage in Garcilaso. One can see why this *romance* struck the poet's imagination and also how complex are the interconnections of meaning binding together the images he used.

But in the *Cántico* there is an even more significant allusion to a fountain. At the end of her fruitless search, worn out by her sufferings, the Beloved comes to a 'crystal spring' and gives vent to her longing that the eyes of her Lover, whom she has not been able to find, should be reflected in its 'silvered faces'. They are, and she is carried away on a *vuelo* or flight, which in the commentary is explained as an *arrobamiento* or brief ecstasy. After this the Lover speaks to her and a new phase of the poem begins.

What is the origin of this image? In Garcilaso's *Second Eclogue* the action takes place around a *fuente* or spring which is something more than the usual spring of pastoral poetry because, as Dámaso Alonso points out, it has an obsessive effect upon the three shepherds who converse by it. The poem begins with an invocation by the love-lorn Albanio to its clear waters, in which he sees, 'as if present, the memory of his beloved and how his joy in her was clouded and darkened when he lost her'. Later he explains this. The shepherdess he was in love with, but to whom he did not dare to declare his passion because she was a nymph of Diana, had asked him why he was always so sad. 'Are you in love?' – 'Yes.' – 'With whom?' 'Look in the water and you will see.' She looked, saw her own reflection and left him. It is this scene that he relives whenever he looks into the clear spring and in the end it drives him mad so that he tries to drown himself. The other shepherds develop the water theme along less painful lines.

The difference between Garcilaso's use of the *fuente* or spring and San Juan de la Cruz's is obvious. Sebastián de Córdoba brings them a little closer by making Albanio see in the depths of the water 'a diverse and varied story which I could not understand'. It is this passage, no doubt, that leads San Juan to interpret his fountain as meaning faith. But behind the spring or fountain symbolism there is also a long history. The magic fountain of Crétien de Troyes and Arthurian legend had led to the *Fontaine d'Amors* of the *Roman de la Rose*, in which the lover saw reflected the flower he wished to pick and, as he stretched out his hand, was shot by the archers. And in Spanish folklore there is a magic fountain (sometimes converted into a mirror) in which the lover whose heart is pure can see the face of his mistress. It is not unreasonable to suppose that San Juan de la Cruz, during his childhood at Fontiveros (he probably took the name to mean 'true fountain' though it really means 'Iberian fountain') had heard such a story and remembered it.

What do we learn from these examples? I would say this. So far as his poetry is concerned San Juan was a man of two books – the *Song of Songs* and Garcilaso. They are combined and woven together in an often astonishing way through his major poems. But he also kept his ears open to the popular love songs of his time and fused them together with his recollections of his book-reading into something that could convey the delights and torments of his mystical journey. It will be remembered that it was a love song, heard through the walls of his prison, that set him off writing poetry.

Finally I would like to draw attention to a rather different kind of evocation – that of the Spanish scene. The *Cántico espiritual* ends with the lines:

> Y el cerco sosegaba,
> y la caballería
> a vista de las aguas descendía.

Here there is no external source. The lines, if we exclude a faint allusion to the *Song of Songs*, are San Juan's own. They mean, we are told, that the passions of the soul have been assuaged and that the senses are descending to be purified in the divine waters. They thus mark the end of the long process of purgation and the reconciliation of the bodily senses with the soul in their union with God. What had been so painfully given up is restored again in a new and dazzling setting. And yet I do not think that in the whole of Spanish poetry there is a passage that calls up so vividly the Castilian–Andalusian scene before the incidence of motor transport: the string of horses or mules descending slowly to the river; the vague suggestion of frontier warfare, now over; that sense of endless repetition, of something that has been done countless times before being done again, which is the gift of Spain to the restless and progressive nations. In these last two wonderful lines, with their gently reassuring fall, the horses descending within sight of the waters are lifted out of time and made the symbol of the peace of this land of eternal recurrence.

Diction

I have separated, as best I can, the different elements that go to make San Juan de la Cruz's poetry and given some indication of how they were combined together. I must now, before going on to discuss the difficult question of the meanings, say something about the style or diction. To avoid prolixity, I shall confine myself to the *Noche oscura* and the *Cántico*.

What is the general impression that these poems make on us when we read them? The *Cántico* starts out with a cry of longing and anguish, but almost at once this changes to an air-borne feeling of lightness, clarity, exhilaration, speed of movement. There is a sense of travel and adventure: mountains, rivers, valleys, dawns, breezes, 'strange islands' come and go; lions, antelopes, birds, flowers are seen and left behind. There are gusts of passion and tenderness and then the clear Castilian air grows heavy for a moment with the scent of cedar wood and lilies, whilst the lovers, in walled gardens or rocky caves or mountain thickets, meet together to perform their mysterious rites. Yet the voluptuousness that blows in from the East is tempered by an astonishing delicacy. This poetry is virginal. And there is at times a penetrating strangeness of tone that recalls, as very little poetry really does, the poignancy of dreams.

There is another feature that one cannot fail to notice – the distinctness and precision of the language. As each verbal note is struck, another follows without blurring or overlap. The words are clear, clean, almost transparent, yet sufficiently full for their purpose: each phrase is perfectly articulated and there is no continuous mood or overtone flowing through the stanzas and blurring their particular effects as in Garcilaso's poetry. What is the mechanism by which these results are obtained? Let us look first at the syntax. Dámaso Alonso has pointed out the great place that the noun occupies in these poems. Although the action is often rapid, verbs are reduced to a minimum and sometimes a whole stanza passes without one. Other stanzas are interjections. In two of them the verbal form *is* is suppressed. Since it is chiefly verbs that diffuse the feeling-tone through the sentence, their paucity helps to bring out the separate qualities of the substantives. Yet when the poet does accumulate verbs, what effects he attains! Take the last stanza of the *Noche oscura*, depicting that moment in a love-affair when time seems arrested, which Donne has elaborated in his *Ecstasie*:

Quedéme y olvidéme,
el rostro recliné sobre el Amado;

116

cesó todo, y dejéme,
dejando mi cuidado
entre las azucenas olvidado.

Here we see the sharp accented *é* and *ó* sounds of the preterite tense (the *é*s higher in tone than any other in Spanish) acting as so many full stops to bring to an end the action of the love drama and prepare the way for the last phase of *Nirvana*-like abandonment.

Adjectives too are rare. Dámaso Alonso, comparing the *Cántico* with Garcilaso's poem in the same type of stanza, has found that San Juan uses only one adjective for three used by the earlier poet. It is this, of course, that gives his poems their lightness and speed of movement: things pass by rapidly. But when he does use adjectives he masses them:

Mi Amado, las montañas,
los valles solitarios nemorosos,
las ínsulas extrañas,
los ríos sonorosos,
el silbo de los aires amorosos;

La noche sosegada,
en par de los levantes de la aurora,
la música callada,
la soledad sonora,
la cena que recrea y enamora.

It should be noted that all these adjectives follow the noun. As Dámaso Alonso explains, adjectives in this position extend its meaning, whereas adjectives that precede the noun have an analytical function and qualify it.

San Juan de la Cruz is a great coiner of images that can, as it were, be picked and stored in the mind without withering. In part this is due to his rhythmical mastery, in part to his powers of condensing different elements of thought or feeling into a single phrase, which thus acquires an extra vitality of its own. In the stanzas quoted above there are, I think, at least three instances of such unforgettable combinations. He frequently too writes lines that suggest by their sound the things they are describing – a proceeding much rarer in Spanish poetry than it is in English. How expressive, for example, of haste is this line in the *Cántico* with its rustle of sibilants:

117

Pasó por estos sotos con presura.

And how expressive of stuttering and stammering is:

Un no sé qué que quedan balbuciendo.

Or, as Professor Allison Peers has pointed out, how well the idea of the ineffable lovers' union is suggested by the chain of deep vowels that culminate in these two lines from the *Noche oscura*:

> Amado con amada,
> amada en el Amado transformada.

We need not multiply instances. Enough, I think, has been said to show that there is a density and complexity of allusion in these poems that prove the absurdity of supposing that San Juan de la Cruz was merely an 'inspired' poet who wrote his poems in ecstasies. A long period of preparation, both conscious and unconscious, preceded their composition, and if the ease and sureness with which they spring up show that many of them owe their birth to effortless moments, they were no doubt followed by careful correction and adjustment. Indeed the poet has told us so himself. Asked by a nun whether the words of the *Cántico* had been 'given him by God', he replied, 'Sometimes God gave them to me and at other times I looked for them myself.' And one may note that the poem he wrote after coming out of an ecstasy, *Entréme donde no supe*, is not one of his better productions.

Interpretations

San Juan de la Cruz's poems were written to express his mystical experiences. It follows, since we cannot form for ourselves any notion of these, that they are obscure. We shall not be able to go so far as to meet them with our own experience as we can in the case of most other poetry. We are thus really in the position of Conde Arnaldos, of the famous *romance* or ballad, who when riding on the sea shore with a falcon on his wrist, heard a mariner on a ship singing a magic song that made the winds drop, the sea become calm, the fish rise to the surface and the birds perch on the mast. But when he begged the mariner to teach him that song, the man replied:

> *Yo no digo esta canción sino a quien conmigo va.*
> 'I will only tell that song to him who sails with me.'

However there are different degrees and kinds of obscurity in poetry; although one cannot hope to interpret these poems in any complete sense, for even San Juan was not able to do that, let us try to see what meanings can be got out of them.

I think it will help us in our endeavour to do so if we first look at the plot of one of the poems. The *Cántico espiritual* is the one that presents the greatest difficulties, so I will begin by giving a brief *précis* of it. That in itself will provide a preliminary elucidation:

The poem is written in the form of a dialogue between a Lover and his Beloved. It starts off with a cry of anguish in which the Beloved complains that her Lover has wounded her and then deserted her. Setting out to seek him, she enquires of the woods and flower-enamelled fields if they have seen him pass. They answer that he went by hurriedly, leaving them clothed in his beauty as he looked at them. She then in another cry, recalling an Andalusian *saeta* in its intensity, complains once more of her abandonment, declares that everything in nature reminds her of him and begs him to show himself and kill her with his presence and beauty. If only his eyes, she exclaims, could be reflected in that crystal fount! The eyes appear and she is transported in a *vuelo* or ecstasy.

The Lover now speaks, telling her that her yearnings have refreshed the wounded stag – that is, himself. The Beloved answers him, declaring in the two wonderful stanzas which I have just quoted that her Lover *is* the mountains, valleys, strange islands, rivers, nights, music, silence and refreshing feast.

Up to this moment the general drift of the poem has been clear enough, but from now on it becomes harder to follow. The reason for this is that the Beloved in her irresistible flight towards her Lover has, as the prose commentary tells us, reached that 'union of love' with him which is known as the spiritual betrothal or espousal and the marriage-bed makes its appearance. But this is premature: the spiritual nuptials which will confirm this union are still twelve stanzas away so that the hitherto rapid action of the poem is slowed down and the momentum is lost. San Juan was evidently aware of this for in making his second prose commentary to the poem he changed the order of the next eighteen stanzas. The effect of this new arrangement is to postpone the appearance of the marriage-bed, which is certainly an improvement, but at the same time to bring the nuptials forward so that most of the courtship scenes occur after it. This is unfortunate. The natural order of events as well as the impetus of the poem are broken, which leads me to agree with Dámaso Alonso and most other critics that the first arrangement is greatly to be preferred to the second one. I shall therefore follow it here.

To continue: the Beloved, in a passage full of reminiscences of the *Song of Songs*, describes the various incidents of the courtship. The Lover leads her into his inner wine cellar (*in cellam vinariam*, in the Vulgate) and gives her to drink. He takes her in his arms and teaches her a *ciencia muy sabrosa*. She promises to be his spouse and, going out into the fields drunk with love, loses the sheep she had been tending. (This is a common occurrence with enamoured shepherdesses in pastoral poetry.) From now on, she declares, love will be her only occupation. Some stanzas follow, describing the simple pastimes of country lovers, and the Beloved then calls on the south wind to blow through her garden, that her Lover may feed among its flowers.

The Lover then speaks and his words denote that the consummation of the nuptials has taken place. After an allusion to the apple tree where her mother (Eve) was lost, in the shade of whose wood (the Cross) he had betrothed himself to her, he conjures the birds, lions, stags, mountains, valleys, river banks, water, airs and wakeful fears of night not to disturb his Beloved, who is sleeping in his arms.

The Beloved in her turn commands 'the nymphs of Judaea' not to disturb them and makes an obscure request to her Lover. In two evocative stanzas, full of echoes of Spanish folk poetry and of the Bible, the Lover replies to her, announcing that the white dove has returned to her mate and made her nest alone with him in solitude.

After this the Beloved begs him to take her to see by the light of his beauty the hills and forests where the pure water gushes out and to go deeper with her into the thickets and rocky caverns. There he must show her what she longs to behold and give her 'what the other day he gave her'. The freshness of the breeze, the song of the nightingale, the charm of the poplar grove, the clear night, with the flame of love that consumes but does not give pain. No one to see. Aminadab (the Enemy) away, the siege (passions of the soul) relaxed and the horsemen (the senses) descending to the waters (to be purified in them).

Such is the plot of the *Cántico*. Its general message is clear enough. We scarcely need the Argument, which the poet gives us at the beginning of his second version of the Commentary, to gather that it is an allegory representing the journey of the soul to union with the Godhead. Let us see what the programme that he sets out here has to tell us. According to it, the first twelve stanzas represent the purgative stage of the *vía mística* and express the misery and restlessness of the soul that is filled with unsatisfied love for God. After this comes the illuminative stage, which begins with the reflection of the Lover's eyes in the water and moves immediately to the spiritual betrothal or espousals. This is followed thirteen stanzas later by the unitive stage, introduced by the line *Entrádose ha la Esposa*, which announced that the spiritual marriage or nuptials has taken place. The last two stanzas represent the Beatific Vision, granted only to the perfect.

It will be seen that the poem does not fit the programme at all closely. The too early placing of 'the betrothal' does not accord with the later development of the courtship. The commentary places it in Stanza 13, yet five stanzas later we find the Beloved, drinking in the interior tavern with her Lover and promising to be his bride. Then how is it that no place is found in the poem for the very severe spiritual purgation that, as we are told in the *Dark Night of the Soul*, intermittently accompanies the illuminative stage, which also, we are told, begins in Stanza 13? One explanation of this could be that, although a large part of San Juan's prose works are devoted to the purgative process, he treats this very briefly in his poetry and hurries on to the later and more rewarding stages. Yet none of these things, which from the formal point of view can be called a defect, detract from our enjoyment of the poem. Just as the ambiguity and confusion which we find in the *Song of Songs* serve to heighten its poetic effect, so a certain looseness and uncertainty in parts of the development of the *Cántico* release it from the tyranny of too tight an allegorical interpretation and give it an appropriate air of mystery.

Let us now turn from the brief scheme of the Argument and look at the detailed prose commentary. Here, if anywhere, we ought to be able to discover what the hidden meanings are, for in it San Juan takes his poem and interprets it line by line often at considerable length. Yet the result is deeply disappointing. Although now and then we come on something that throws light on a passage, most of the interpretations drag down the text of the poem and destroy its reverberations. It does not add, for example to the significance of the line, *Iré por esos montes y riberas* to learn that the *montes*, being high, represent the virtues and the *riberas,* being low, mortifications and penances. Nor do we find it easy to believe that meanings of this sort were in the poet's mind at the time of his composing the poem. Slowly, as we read on, we discover that the reason why San Juan's interpretations have the effect of eviscerating the poem is that he is treating it down to its smallest details as an allegory in which every important word or image must have some precise concept that corresponds to it and 'explains' it. But the very failure of his explanation proves to us what we had already guessed – that the *Cántico* is only allegorical in a very loose sense: its intimate structure is both deeper and more complex.

Indeed the poet himself admits this. In the prologue to his second prose commentary he tells us that no gloss can fully explain the stanzas and that we need not feel bound to accept the interpretation that he offers. *Los dichos de amor en abundante inteligencia mística,* inspired as they are by the Spirit of the Lord, cannot be properly explained in words, any more than can the divine verses of Solomon's poem. That is to say, he felt before them the same thrilled surprise that other poets have felt on looking on the following morning at their miraculous overnight productions. He must have experienced this with particular force because he knew that these verses contained little incidental ornament or embellishment: every word, every image, something told him, had its roots deep in the real nature of things and was packed with esoteric significance. Those which he had taken from the *Song of Songs* had long been meditated by him and interpreted to fit his mystical experience, so that he would have had many of their meanings in his head before he began to write. But in his prose commentary he was not attempting a true elucidation of his poem, for that was beyond his powers. His aim, as in his other commentaries, was to produce a guide-book for the use of the small circle of *almas enamoradas* whom he was directing, which should instruct them in the various landmarks and hazards of the contemplative's road and encourage them to persevere in it by showing them the rewards which it offered. He had written it at the request of the nuns of Beas in the form of a *declaración* or commentary on his poem, instead of, as Santa Teresa had done in her two works on the same subject, in that of a treatise or textbook. While therefore we can learn much from this commentary that will help us if we wish to understand the *Cántico* better (which is not the same thing as to enjoy it better), we must not attempt to use it slavishly.

Perhaps the best way to get the full feeling and flavour of the *Cántico espiritual* is before beginning to read it to make oneself familiar with the *Song of Songs*. That oriental work with its exotic imagery provides San Juan's poem with a continual reinforcement. One senses its presence everywhere even when one cannot recall the precise allusion. So far as I know there is nothing else quite like this in literature. Milton's poetry is saturated with classical and biblical reminiscences, yet these are brought in mainly as learned references to confirm the fact that he is writing at the end of a long and complex tradition. Eliot's quotations in *The Waste Land* are there to provide a contrast between the sordid present and the lost world of beauty and significance that lies in the past. San Juan's poem on the other hand rises out of another and distinct poetic plane, bearing a number of deeply suggestive yet elusive meanings with it. Yet in doing so its tone has been totally changed and sublimated. The *Song of Songs* is a sensual poem dealing with sexual love, whereas in the *Cántico* everything is pure and delicate, most of all the acts of the lovers.

But there is nothing vaporous or imprecise in its language or imagery. Its energy is maintained by that process of 'condensation' which I have described and which provides a close web of hidden tissue linking all the words and images together. Although as we read we are not consciously aware of its ramifications, they provide the inner consistency we feel and also the extraordinary intensity. For few if any of the words in San Juan's poetry are adventitious or ornamental. Almost every one of them has been deeply fed and nourished from the poet's psychic stores and that is why, borne in on us as they are by his very personal rhythms, they move us so deeply. That *íntima viveza* which he declared to be a quality of mystical experiences is to some extent conveyed to us.

I must now leave the *Cántico espiritual* and speak of the other poems. I will take first that in the same stanza form, the *lira*, which begins *En una noche oscura*. We come here to the most comprehensive of San Juan's symbolic themes – that of the Dark Night. It is characteristic that he took the term from a not very striking passage in Garcilaso. In that poet's *Second Eclogue* the despairing lover Albanio goes out to seek death:

> La quinta noche, en fin, mi cruda suerte,
> queriéndome llevar do se rompiese
> aquesta tela de la vida fuerte,

123

hizo que de mi choza me saliese
por el silencio de la noche oscura
a buscar un lugar donde muriese.
Y caminando do por mi ventura . . .

'At last on the fifth night my hard fate, wishing to bear me to where the strong web of my life might be broken, made me leave my hut in the silence of the dark night, to find a place where I might die. And travelling where my lot led me . . .'

Compare this now with the opening stanza of the *Noche oscura*, where the soul sets out to seek union with God – a state which implies death to this world:

En una *noche oscura*,
con ansias en amores inflamada,
¡oh dichosa *ventura*!
salí sin ser notada,
estando ya mi *casa* sosegada.

As one can see, five of these words correspond either in form or in meaning to five of those in the passage quoted from Garcilaso, while the second line in San Juan's stanza perfectly represents the state of mind in which Albanio left his hut. This is just one more instance of how our poet altered everything that struck him in his reading to fit his inner experience. This passage from the *Second Eclogue* must have indeed made a strong impression on him for he had in his mind the line *aquesta tela de la vida fuerte* when, in the *Llama de amor viva*, he wrote *rompe la tela de este dulce encuentro*.

The *Song of Songs* also has a significant nocturnal passage: 'By night on my bed I sought him whom my soul loveth: I sought him and found him not.' And this search leads the Shulamite maiden out into the streets till at last she finds him and brings him home. Two chapters further on there is another passage of the same kind – what folklorists call a double – which is even more poignant. She dreams that she hears her lover knocking on the door, wakes to find he has gone and hurries after him. One can see how these two passages from the most thrilling of all love poems must have affected the poet as he lay in the darkness of his prison, where he was writing another poem on night. One may call them the starting-off point of both the *Noche oscura* and the *Cántico*. Only the *Noche oscura* was written after his escape as one may see from his Com-

124

mentary (*Ascent of Mount Carmel* I, 15) where he clearly alludes to it, though the prison here is not of course a material one.

The structure of the *Noche oscura* is a very simple one. In eight stanzas it takes us through the long purgation of the senses and of the spirit to the state of union with God. By the darkness of night is meant the darkness of faith, which, as we shall explain later, leads and guides the soul on its journey. The first stanza describes it as setting out, filled with burning love, safe and assured because it has conquered its sensual appetites. This is the meaning of the line *Estando ya mi casa sosegada* while the stanza that follows it and repeats it represents the purgation of the spirit. After this, trusting to the dark light of faith, it travels on till it reaches the ineffable moment when it is transformed into its Lover – *amada en el Amado transformada*. Three stanzas, shot through with the exotic imagery of the *Song of Songs*, represent the effects of that union which, as San Juan says, in a passage I have already quoted, it is quite impossible either to understand or to convey in ordinary language. Yet the climactic moment of these stanzas, the love scene by night on the battlements, was derived not from the Hebrew poem but from a very lame passage by Sebastián de Córdoba in which, to suit the requirements of his sacred theme, he deviated from Garcilaso's account of Albanio's lovesick meditation. This tells us something of the way in which San Juan's mind worked. What he extracted from a poetic text was not its power of evocation as poetry, but an image or episode which had a special significance for him because it accorded with those images he had collected to express his central mystical theme of the road to union. No poet borrowed more from other poets, yet none was more original because before he began to write all the work of transmutation into his own categories had been accomplished. These three stanzas, which are among the most magical that he wrote, provide a good example of his creative processes.

It will be remembered that one of the poems that San Juan brought with him out of prison is the *villancico* written in hendecasyllables that begins *Que bien sé yo la fonte que mana y corre* and which has for a refrain the line *Aunque es de noche*. I have already spoken of its spring or water symbolism and said that the theme of the poem was probably suggested to him by two Franciscan writers who represented the Trinity under the triple symbol of fountain, river and sea. The *fonte* thus stands for the Three-Personed God, but the *noche* or night through which he is dimly perceived is, as always in San Juan's writings, the symbol of Faith. He tells us this in the title he gave the poem – 'A song of the soul which delights in knowing God by Faith'. It is one of the most mysterious and beautiful of his poems, suggesting with its unfolding movement and its *sotto voce* refrain the early parallelistic poetry of Galicia, and one is tempted to see in it the influence of his prison surroundings – the darkness of his cell and the insistent sound of the Tagus flowing invisible in its trough below. But to San Juan the darkness and the river were both changed into symbols of his inner obsession. In all probability it was the first of his poems to be written in prison and he seems to have later added two more stanzas to bring out more clearly the meaning of its symbolism. But they do not improve it.

Another short but moving poem by San Juan is that which begins *Un Pastorcico, solo, está penado.* It is a pastoral poem in hendeca-syllables in the Renaissance manner with the refrain *Y el pecho del amor muy lastimado* and it tells the story of a shepherd who, abandoned and forgotten by his love, hangs himself on a tree with his arms stretched out and dies. It is clear that the shepherd is Christ. The tone of the poem is languid and tender – that is, not at all in San Juan's usual style – so that until recently it was thought to be an early production. But in 1949 a short article appeared in the *Revista de Filología Española* by José Manuel Blecua which showed that it was to be found without any attribution of authorship in a manuscript collection of the time in the form of an ordinary love poem. San Juan had taken it, made a few small emendations and added the last verse, by doing which he converted it from being a simple and rather charming pastoral into a religious poem express-ing deep feeling. Characteristically, as Dámaso Alonso has shown, it had another source in the expansion of a line of Garcilaso's by Sebastián de Córdoba. Since it was not likely that after leaving Salamanca San Juan ever looked at profane love poetry, one wonders whether some other person had not written a version of it *a lo divino* which he had seen.

The last poem but one that San Juan de la Cruz wrote was the *Llama de amor viva*, or *Living flame of Love*. As I have said, he took the form of its stanzas from the opening to Garcilaso's *Canción Segunda*, where it figures as a semi-strophe. The first line, *Oh, llama de amor viva* would seem to have been suggested by a line from Sebastián de Córdoba's pastiche of Garcilaso, which runs *El fuego de amor vivo*, and there are three other borrowings from Garcilaso in it. This, in a short poem expressing the summit of the mystical road, is surely extraordinary. Its subject, as he tells us in the prologue to his Commentary, is 'the highest degree of perfection which can be attained in this life, which is the transformation in God'. This state is known in the literature of mysticism as the state of union, but, as San Juan goes on to say, although it is not possible in this life to pass beyond it, it is possible with time and practice to increase the degree of the love that nourishes that union, just as when a fire, after taking hold of wood and transforming it by its heat into itself, still has the capacity to burn more fiercely. So this poem, 'written in the intimate and delicate sweetness of love and burning in its flames', expresses the summit of the poet's mystical ascent. But what exactly is meant by union? According to Catholic doctrine it consists in the union of the human will with the divine will, that being the only kind of union possible in this life between Man and God, and in one passage (*Ascent of Mount Carmel* I 11, 3) San Juan assents to this. But as a rule he speaks of it in much warmer terms as a complete transformation of the soul into God and of God into the soul by means of love so that 'the one gives possession of himself to the other and each abandons himself to the other and exchanges himself for the other, and thus each lives in the other, and the one is the other, and both are one by the transformation of love' (*Spiritual Canticle* 12, 7). Seen from another angle it is a state of great aloofness, punctuated by trance or ecstasy.

In the *Llama* the act of union is described in three stanzas as being brought about by a flame, by a delicate touch and by a lamp – burning, renewing and enlightening. The fourth and last stanza is written in a quiet key. In Dámaso Alonso's opinion this is the most sublime of all San Juan's poems, but with all respect for his authority I must disagree because it lacks the rapid, air-borne movement of the *Cántico* and the *Noche oscura* with their complex, many-levelled imagery as well as the strangely insistent quality of *Que bien sé yo la fonte*. Its tone is more literary than it is in his other poems and in spite of all its exclamation marks it is static. One reason for this may be that the form of its stanzas does not suit the lyrical intention. Or had the conjunction of events that led to San Juan's brief poetic phase already passed?

The last poems that I have to speak of are the three *villancicos* in octosyllabic measure and the *romances*. There is nothing I need add to what I have already written about the *villancico* he wrote on a theme that had been previously used by Santa Teresa except to say that the two paradoxical lines of the third verse – *Vivo sin vivir en mí* and *Que muero porque no muero* – have a long history in the song books of the century where they are used to express profane love. In the one that begins *Tras de un amoroso lance* the lover on his flight to union with God is compared to a falcon that flies 'so high, so high' and then swoops low to reach its prey. This was a conceit frequently employed in love songs at the beginning of the century and in the essay Dámaso Alonso gives on San Juan's poetry in *Poesía Española* he quotes a *villancico* on profane love that he had recently discovered in manuscript and which has the same initial verse. San Juan changed two words of it and gave it a much longer and completely independent development. For the *villancico* that begins *Entréme donde no supe*, there are no popular antecedents. It offers a good example of those contradictory and paradoxical statements that were so favoured by devotional writers in that age and that opened the way to the Baroque poetry of conceits that began to flourish towards the end of the century.

There remain the *romances*. That on the psalm *By the waters of Babylon* has a certain moving quality, though it cannot be compared to the poem by Camoens on the same subject. Of the nine *romances* on the Trinity and Incarnation it is harder to speak. They are certainly remarkable productions, but as their theme is doctrinal they belong to quite another class from the rest of San Juan's poems. They are written without images in a simple style that sometimes becomes 'metaphysical', but how much merit they have as poetry is another matter. I can only say that they are admired by some Spanish poets. Perhaps what is most interesting about them is the light they throw on San Juan's ideas. The first section – for since the same rhyme runs through all of them they must be considered as one poem or *romance* – describes the interrelations of the Three Persons of the Trinity. Like the Phoenix and the Turtle, though distinct in substance they are made one by love, and it is this love, which in the manner of an electric generator they manufacture among themselves, that spills over and manifests itself in the creation of the world. As the poem puts it, the Father, out of his immense love for his Son, offers to give him an *esposa* or bride and on his acceptance the Creation takes place. This is envisaged in the form of two compartments, a higher one in which are set the Angels and a lower one 'full of infinite differences' which is assigned to Man because by his nature or *compostura* he is necessarily inferior. Here we arrive at an explanation of San Juan's so-called pantheism. The whole of Creation from the Angels to Man make up the body of the *esposa* or bride of Christ since their love for Him makes them one. Yet there is a distinction, for whereas those in the upper compartment possess the *Esposo* in *alegría* or joy, those in the lower one possess him only in hope. The rest of the poem develops the long history of this hope until with the Incarnation, when the Son takes on manhood by entering the womb of his *esposa* – another source of paradoxes – it is fulfilled. The *romance* ends with the weeping of the infant Christ and the rejoicing of his mother – a reversal of the usual rules of God and Mankind.

It will be noticed that there is no mention in this strange poem of Eve's sin which led to the Fall. Man was from the beginning created inferior, but endowed with a hope and faith which would, or could, ultimately raise him to the level of his Spouse. While we are not told why Man had to be created inferior, the sole cause of the Creation and of the long history in time that followed it is shown to be the love that existed from the beginning between the Three Persons of the Godhead.

Two of the *villancicos* that are usually included among San Juan's poems have been omitted from this book, because, since they are not in the Sanlúcar codex and bear no trace of his characteristic diction, there is great doubt as to whether they are by him. The first of these is that which begins *Sin arrimo y con arrimo* and is a very poor poem, while the second starts off with a beautiful theme verse:

Por toda la hermosura
nunca yo me perderé,
sino por un no sé qué
que se alcanza por ventura.

This would seem to be pure San Juan, but in fact, as Dámaso Alonso has pointed out, it appears in an anthology of poems published in 1580 by Pedro de Padilla, where it is followed by a development that might refer either to a profane or to a heavenly love. The development attributed to San Juan is quite different and so poor that, even if he wrote it – and it is not in his usual style or diction – it seems better to omit it.

The themes

San Juan de la Cruz's poetry springs from his experience as a practising mystic. This is a region very remote from the experience of almost everyone today and of which I am quite unqualified to speak. But there are two themes that appear in his poetry of which something ought to be said. One of them is his attitude to Nature and the other is his great symbolic conception of the Dark Night.

It will have been noted what a large part the beauty of natural objects plays in two of his poems, the *Cántico* and the *Noche oscura*. Mountains, valleys, trees, flowers and water are all celebrated in them as well as beasts, birds and the sonorous, insect-humming silence that fills the ears in Mediterranean countries. We know too that he delighted in spending whole hours in the open air, under trees, by water, or looking out towards distant horizons, and that he would take his friars with him to share in his contemplation. For was it not God who had created the things of Nature as a reflection of his own beauty and taught them to sing his praises? It was for that reason that the soul was so greatly moved to love him by considering them. So San Juan says in his Commentary to the *Cántico* and it was a view for which he had ample authority. In a famous chapter of his *Confessions* (Book IV, 10) St Augustine speaks of the beauty of created things as deriving from God and adjures his soul to praise their Creator through them, though not to let itself be fastened to them by 'the glue of the senses'. Again St Thomas Aquinas, in a passage quoted by San Juan, speaks of the creatures as being substantially united to God because he had made them. Yet we are met with the apparent inconsistency that in his prose works San Juan's attitude to them is usually disparaging. 'All the being of the creatures', he says, 'compared to the infinite being of God, is nothing. . . . All the beauty of the creatures, compared to the infinite beauty of God, is the height of deformity. . . . All the grace and charm of the creatures, compared to the grace of God, is disgrace and insipidity' (*Ascent of Mount Carmel* I, 4, 4). Again: 'All the creatures are no more than crumbs that have fallen from God's table, wherefore he that feeds regularly upon them is rightly called a dog' (*Ascent of Mount Carmel* I, 6, 3). Since two contraries, he asserts, cannot live together in one soul, the love of the creatures (by which he meant both the love of Nature and that of human beings) must be eradicated and destroyed so that God can fill it. Such are the sacrifices demanded by the purgation of the senses.

But the *Cántico espiritual* and its Commentary both speak a different language. In the first stanzas the forsaken soul is searching for her Lover. She sees the woods and thickets, the flowers and meadows which he had planted and implores them to tell her where he has gone, and they reply that he passed by in haste, leaving them clothed with his beauty as he looked at them. In haste, because they belonged to the lower order of Creation and a glance was sufficient to stamp his image on them. In his Commentary San Juan explains that when on his Incarnation Christ put on our humanity he also put on the whole of Nature and gave it supernatural graces in addition to the natural ones which God the Father had given it at the Creation. A little further on the Spiritual Betrothal is announced by the Beloved in two rapturous stanzas which assert that her Lover *is* the mountains, valleys, rivers, islands, music, night and so forth, both in himself and for her. In this apparently pantheistic statement the Beloved, in one of those brief foretastes that are given in the illuminative stage, is anticipating the state of union and the Beatific Vision, which are represented in the last stanzas of the poem when the soul, purified of all imperfections, sees the whole of Creation flooded with God's presence. As in Dante's *Paradiso* the poet's powers of apprehending beauty increase as he approaches the source of it.

In his prose commentary San Juan does not for once spoil this passage for us by telling us that the mountains, valleys, rivers and so forth signify the virtues, mortifications and higher states of the soul, but merely says, in a passage of impressive prose, 'These mountains' (and so forth) 'are my Beloved to me.' After that he reverts to his usual allegorical interpretations, following those rationalizing tendencies of the early centuries of Christianity according to which everything in the visible world must owe its virtue and meaning to being the manifestation of some invisible higher entity. But in a few cases at least this passion for precise and detailed interpretation has added something to the poetry. For example the *Cántico* twice mentions *las ínsulas extrañas*. These, we are told, are those remote islands, suggested no doubt by the newly discovered Pacific isles and the Indies, which are set apart from communication with other men and in which are found things that are very different from those that grow or are born here. For this reason they represent those attributes of God which are strange and unknown to men and even to the angels. Later, in the commentary on Stanza 32, they stand for those mysterious ways, foreign both to the reason and the senses, by which the soul communicates with God. In both cases they emphasize the incomprehensibility of God and of his ways with men.

The ambiguity in San Juan's attitude to Nature can, I think, be explained in this way. Since it is a creation of God and a reflection of his beauty, beginners can find it useful to meditate upon as a first step to raising their thoughts to the infinite being of the Deity. But after that these meditations must be given up. Like many Spaniards, he is a man of *todo o nada*, everything or nothing. The senses must be purged and emptied so that God alone may fill the soul. All he will allow is that certain places can be better suited than others to pray in because 'by the agreeable appearance of their differences, now of the lie of the land, now of trees, now of solitary quiet, they naturally incline to devotion'. But then the features of the place must be forgotten and the mind turned inwards. That, he declares, is what the anchorites of old did, choosing the smallest place they could find, a cave or an exiguous cell, and shutting themselves up in it, while all around them stretched the wide and delightful waste (*Ascent of Mount Carmel* III, 42, 1–2).

Yet in the end, after the state of union has been reached, the delight that the senses once found in Nature is given back in a different form. The soul is then able to see how all the creatures have their life and strength in God. That is, 'it learns to know the creatures through God and not God through the creatures, which is to know the effects by their cause and not the cause by its effects, thus substituting secondary knowledge for an essential one' (*Living Flame of Love* 4, 5). However this delight is not given back as a delight of the senses, but by the *via contemplativa* or way of contemplation, where it is accompanied by an intellectual understanding of their life and of their relations with one another. This is the bearing of San Juan's commentary on the line *el soto y su donaire* in the *Cántico* where the *soto* or grove stands for all the creatures, both celestial and terrestrial that have their root and life in God. Finally in the last stanza he speaks of the purification of the sensual part of the soul in the waters as meaning that by a certain redundancy of the spirit the pleasure that would naturally be felt by the senses is transmuted into a purely spiritual 'recreation and delight'. The state of union evidently brings with it a great detachment.

In the Dark Night we come to the deepest and most comprehensive of San Juan de la Cruz's symbolic themes. As we have said, he took the words that express it from Garcilaso de la Vega. What then was the meaning he gave to them? To explain this we must go back to the starting point of his mystical philosophy. In the *Ascent of Mount Carmel*, where we find the best account of it, he lays it down as an axiom that, compared to the infinite being of God, all the being of the creatures is *nothing*. From this it follows that those who put their affections in them are nothing and less than nothing. Man can only be *something* by allowing God, who alone has real existence, to fill him, but for this to happen he must first have emptied himself of every attachment to the creatures. Two contraries cannot exist together in the same person, said Aristotle, and so, if the choice is to be God, the senses, imagination, understanding and will, must all be torn up and uprooted from their usual functions, in order that the mind and soul may be free to receive God alone. It is this process of tearing up, known as purgation, which is the first meaning given to the term 'Dark Night'. For since night is a deprivation of light, so the deprivation of its ordinary faculties can be called night to the soul.

In an impressive doggerel (*Ascent of Mount Carmel* I, 13) San Juan has expressed the antithesis between *todo*, everything, and *nada*, nothing, that lies at the root of his thinking and feeling and led to his being called *el doctor de la nada*:

> Para venir a gustarlo todo,
> no quieras tener gusto en nada;
> para venir a poseerlo todo,
> no quieras poseer algo en nada;
> para venir a serlo todo,
> no quieras ser algo en nada;
> para venir a saberlo todo,
> no quieras saber algo en nada;
> para venir a lo que no gustas,
> has de ir por donde no gustas;
> para venir a lo que no sabes,
> has de ir por donde no sabes;
> para venir a lo que no posees,
> has de ir por donde no posees;
> para venir a lo que no eres,
> has de ir por donde no eres.

In order to arrive at pleasure in everything,
you must seek pleasure in nothing.

133

In order to arrive at possessing everything,
you must seek to possess nothing.
In order to arrive at being everything,
you must seek to be nothing.
In order to arrive at knowing everything,
you must seek to know nothing.
In order to arrive at that in which you find no pleasure,
you must go by a way in which there is no pleasure.
In order to arrive at that which you do not know,
you must go by a way you do not know.
In order to arrive at that which you do not possess,
you must go by a way of dispossession.
In order to arrive at what you are not,
you must go by a way in which you are not.

San Juan wrote these lines, which T. S. Eliot drew on in *East Coker*, at El Calvario and sent them to the nuns at Beas together with a drawing of Mount Carmel in which one finds written on the summit of the first ridge, at the end of the *via purgativa*, the words *Y en este monte nada*: 'And on this summit nothing.' Thus we see that he was at his most severe and negative at a time when he was engaged in writing the ecstatic stanzas of the *Cántico*.

'Less than all cannot satisfy Man,' said William Blake, and in order to attain this all San Juan was prepared to follow the road of renunciation and mortification, as prescribed by the teaching of his day, to the very end. For him no compromise was possible and the account he has given in his best known book, the *Dark Night of the Soul*, of the trials and sufferings experienced during the period of purgation has helped, even among Catholics, to throw a harsh and forbidding light on his character. Both William James and Huysmans, for example, speak of him with horror as a sort of *fakir*.

Yet without seeking in any way to attenuate the severity of the course he prescribed or the enormous, obsessionary nature of the whole undertaking we should note that there is nothing punitive in San Juan's ascesis. He did not hate the world or the senses, as so many religious persons have done, but sought rather to escape from them and to leave them behind him. His career, therefore, appears less as a struggle than as a flight – a vertiginous ascent away from everything and towards God. *Hay almas*, he says, *que vuelan como las aves que en el aire se purifican y limpian*: 'There are souls who fly like the birds which purify and clean themselves in the air.' And in one of his poems he compares the soul to a falcon flying at a heron:

> Volé tan alto, tan alto
> que dí a la caza alcance.

'I flew so high, so high that I reached my quarry.'

But one can only rise by throwing off ballast and so the first images associated with the Dark Night are those that express deprivation – solitude, silence, *desnudez*, poverty, emptiness, forgetfulness, ignorance, detachment from self and from all things. These words have no painful associations. The sufferings of the Dark Night, especially during its second stage of the purification of the spirit, which he describes as *horrenda y espantable*, are derived from the sense of unsatisfied love, mixed with self-doubts, aridity and the fear of being abandoned, which increase in intensity as the state of union draws near. They are the reverse side of the coin of love, corresponding to what are in ordinary lovers anxiety, jealousy and loneliness, and it would not be possible to endure them unless the soul was so filled with longings for God that, as he says, 'the very bones seem to be dried up, the natural powers to be fading away, their warmth and strength to be perishing through the intensity of that thirst of love' (*Dark Night* I, 11, 1). Yet much of the work of purgation gives peace. In the detachment that accompanies it, 'the soul finds its rest and repose for, since it desires nothing, nothing fatigues it' (*Ascent of Mount Carmel* I, 13, 13). This night is then *pacífica, dichosa*, peaceful and happy, and that is why, throughout most of his prose works, the words expressing abstinence and mortification have an aura of happiness and peace.

But the theme or symbol of the Dark Night has other meanings besides those associated with the purgative process. It also signifies Faith. Now Faith is the conative aspect of the triple impulse that leads the soul towards God, but it is dark because God is incomprehensible to the reason and understanding. Even at the end of the polar journey, when, on the attainment of union, the magnetic needle points downwards, it remains 'dark night to the soul in this life' (*Ascent of Mount Carmel* I, 2, 1). But why should God's light and message appear as dark? San Juan borrowed here an idea from Dionysius the Areopagite, the father of Catholic mystical theology, who spoke of the rays of light that emanate from the Divine Presence as appearing to the soul as rays of darkness because, living as it did by the light of existing things, which is knowledge and reason, it was not attuned to receiving them. San Juan employs the simile of a moth or an owl to explain this; their eyes being adjusted to the dusk, they cannot see when the light becomes too strong. Thus the sun or a lamp can be said to look dark to them because it makes their sight useless. In the same way God will appear dark to the human intelligence because it lacks the organs to apprehend him. It is here that the purgation of the senses and of the reason comes in. Being useless for the purpose of perceiving the true light, they must be discarded and new organs developed in their place. While this is happening, the soul lives in a double obscurity, without either its new faculties or its old ones. Night has delivered it from the anarchy of apparent existence, while there has only just begun to seep in from the deep darkness around an obscure apprehension of the true.

But the symbol of the Dark Night will not be properly understood unless it is felt to represent a state that precedes and heralds the day. A note of suppressed excitement and exhilaration runs under the surface, recalling in a quieter key the vibrant tones of Donne's poem on his sickness. *Esta noche*, San Juan says, *encubridora de las esperanzas de la luz del día*: 'This night, accomplice of the hopes of the light of day.' And although the two greatest of his prose works describe the Night, with its hushed suspense and its sharp stabs of longing, it is chiefly the coming of the Day that the lyrics celebrate. The poet, emerging from the dim states that precede the ecstasy of composition, finds in the illumination given by that ecstasy his best subject matter.

The end of the Night meant the satisfaction of the longings that had carried him forward – the final accomplishment of the work of love. 'To this end of love,' he says, 'we were created.' 'The one means by which the soul and all its faculties is moved is love.' In a passage on Mary Magdalene he speaks of 'that inebriating and daring force of love . . . which thinks all things possible'. Such a love could not be satisfied by anything short of union, for that alone gives calm and aloofness. On reaching it the moral values wither away because they have become useless and 'the soul returns in a certain sense to the innocence of Adam and can no longer distinguish between good and evil' (*Spiritual Canticle* 26, 14). Other values, more transcendent, now take their place. As in earthly-love unions, the lovers become two mirrors reflecting one another's beauty. Or so at least San Juan describes their state in his commentary on the line in the *Cántico* – *Y vámonos a ver en tu hermosura*:

'So I shall see thee in thy beauty, and thou me in thy beauty, and thou shalt see thyself in me in thy beauty and I shall see myself in thee in thy beauty and thou shalt appear to be me in thy beauty and my beauty will be thy beauty and thy beauty my beauty; and I shall be thee in thy beauty and thou shalt be me in my beauty, because thine own beauty will be my beauty.'

For beauty is the flowering of love and love is the criterion of everything. As he said, *A la tarde te examinarán en el amor.*

10

The Prose Works

The subject of this book is San Juan de la Cruz's life and poetry and although in the course of writing it I have found it necessary to give some account of his doctrine I have said no more on this than an interpretation of his poetry seemed to require. But I have often had occasion to refer to and quote from his prose works, which he wrote as commentaries on his poems. It may therefore be useful if I give a brief account of the genesis and scope of each of these and say a few words upon their language and style.

The *Ascent of Mount Carmel* and the *Dark Night of the Soul* in reality make up one book. In the *Living Flame of Love* (i, 25) San Juan brackets them together under the title of *The Dark Night of the Ascent of Mount Carmel*, which leads us to suppose that he intended to call them that. Both of these works deal with the purgation of the senses and of the spirit. The *Ascent*, which is divided into three books, describes their active purgation, whereas the *Dark Night*, which is divided into two books, describes their passive purgation. Both are written in the form of commentaries on his poem *En una noche oscura*, but the *Ascent* does not get beyond the exposition of the last line of the second stanza, while the *Dark Night* stops suddenly one line further on. Thus the six stanzas of the poem which describe the illuminative stage and the state of union receive no commentary at all.

There has been much discussion on why these two works have come down to us in this unfinished or mutilated state. Both of them break off abruptly, the *Dark Night* in the middle of an exposition. Yet we know that he intended to continue his commentary to the end of the poem because both in the Argument to the *Ascent* and in the Prologue to the *Dark Night* he tells us so. In the latter case he is quite definite about it. 'In the first two stanzas,' he writes, 'are expounded the effects of the two purgations of the sensual and spiritual parts of man. In the other six are expounded the various and admirable effects of the spiritual illumination and union of love with God.'

Why then do we not have his commentary on the last six stanzas? Is it possible that, in spite of his declaration in the Prologue, he never found time to write it? Against that it can be said that elsewhere in his books he alludes to subjects that he had treated, but of which we find no mention in his extant works. Yet if he did write it, he failed to follow his usual practice of having copies made to distribute to the Discalced convents and priories, since the manuscripts we possess all break off at the same point. Or could he have written it and then destroyed it? It would be very unlike him to do this, for he treasured everything that he wrote and spent his last years in revising his manuscripts. The only remaining hypothesis is that his commentary to these last stanzas had been written, at least in part, but vanished after his death. We know that two of his works, one on true and false miracles and the other entitled *Propriedades del pájaro solitario*, or 'Properties of the solitary bird', have not come down to us. Either he burned them on his death bed with his correspondence, or in the disgrace that accompanied the last months of his life they were destroyed. My own opinion, for what it is worth, is that he never finished writing his commentary on this poem, for if he had done so he would have had it copied and distributed. The same can be said of his other missing works.

San Juan began to write the *Ascent of Mount Carmel* in the spring of 1579 at El Calvario, apparently in the form of short passages. and sent some of these, including the famous doggerel verses which I have already quoted, to the nuns of Beas early in that year. With them went his drawing of Mount Carmel (see plate 4 above), showing the steep and narrow road up it, which he afterwards made much use of in teaching his friars and nuns. The book clearly came out of his work of spiritual direction and was written as a guide to his penitents to supplement his personal instruction. From the *Ascent* he went on to write the *Dark Night*, finishing them both at Granada in 1583 or 1584. These two books which, as I have said, are really one make up the most rigorous and logical of San Juan's prose works, and since they deal with the earlier stages of the *via mística* and not with the heights of union, which are reached by very few, they are those which are most read and known. They are also those which best bring out his gift of psychological insight and discrimination.

Of the *Spiritual Canticle* I have already written at some length.

San Juan did not provide titles for his poems and for some time the poem of this name was known simply as *Canciones* or *Stanzas*, and his prose commentary to it as the *Declaración de las Canciones*. It was his biographer and editor, Jerónimo de San José, who first gave both the poem and its commentary the title of *Cántico espiritual* in his 1630 edition of his works, and it has been called by that name ever since. San Juan began to write it in 1579 at El Calvario in response to Ana de Jesús' request for an explanation of the poem, which had deeply moved her and her nuns by its freshness and subtlety. He was thus working on it intermittently during the same period in which he was writing the *Ascent of Mount Carmel* and the *Dark Night*. He finished it at Granada in, there is some reason for thinking, 1584 and dedicated it to Ana de Jesús. It was written in short snatches, apparently with some difficulty, and, out of respect for such a sublime subject, on his knees. But, as we have already explained, the confused arrangement of the poem did not lend itself easily to a theoretical exposition of the road to union, so he rewrote it almost immediately afterwards, lengthening the commentary and altering the order of the stanzas. This new recension was apparently completed in 1586 and is known as the Jaén version, whereas the first one is known as the Sanlúcar version.

The *Living Flame of Love* was written at Granada in either 1585 or 1586. According to his companion Juan Evangelista he wrote it in fifteen days while he was vicar-provincial of the Discalced in Andalusia and busy over many other things. It had been undertaken at the request of his penitent, Doña Ana de Peñalosa, as a commentary to his short poem of the same name and was dedicated to her. Probably on account of the haste in which it had been put down he was not satisfied with it and made a second and longer redaction of it during the last years of his life. Most people would agree that it is the least interesting of his prose works.

In addition to these four treatises by San Juan we have two short collections of aphorisms or maxims. These are *Cautelas* or 'Cautions' and *Dichos de luz y amor* or 'Sayings of Light and Love', both of which he wrote at El Calvario for the nuns of Beas. Some of them were written for a particular nun and addressed to her needs and when he left the convent to return to his priory he would say, 'If I do not come back, imitate the sheep and ruminate on what I have taught you while I have been here.' One of these collections, 'Sayings of Light and Love', has been preserved in his own handwriting and is to be seen at the parish church at Andújar: it is the only one of his works that we possess in autograph. Thirty-two of his letters have also come down to us, some of them mere extracts because they were cut up to be placed in reliquaries.

San Juan's prose style is plain and direct and entirely lacking in the rhetorical tropes and latinisms which abound in most of the devotional books of that age. He keeps as a rule to straightforward statement and his comparisons and similes are of a homely kind and drawn from daily life. Since he was dealing mostly with states of mind, he is given to fine distinctions and analyses, in which he shows great precision. Quotations from the Bible are frequent, by far the greater number being rather surprisingly from the Old Testament. Yet his books are tedious to read at any length because, as his translator Professor Allison Peers has complained, of his involved and cumbrous parentheses. A single sentence will often run on till it has filled a paragraph. He is also, like most Spanish writers, inclined to prolixity and repetition and will wander off his subject for pages on end. He was well aware of these defects and in a passage in the *Ascent of Mount Carmel* (ii, 14, 14) excuses himself by the difficulty he had of making his meaning on 'such an extraordinary and obscure subject' sufficiently clear to his readers. At its best, however, his prose crystallizes out into brief, telling aphorisms and in fact it was through the maxims and aphorisms that he wrote for the nuns of Beas, and before that for those of the convent of the Encarnación at Avila, that he initiated his career as a prose-writer. Then occasionally he will break out into a passage of elevated prose, as in his comment on the stanzas from the *Cántico espiritual* that begins *Mi Amado, las montañas*:

'Las montañas tienen alturas, son abundantes, anchas, hermosas, graciosas, floridas y olorosas. Estas montañas es mi Amado para mi.

'Los valles solitarios son quietos, amenos, frescos, umbrosos, de dulces aguas llenos, y en la variedad de sus arboledas y suave canto de aves hacen gran recreación y deleite al sentido, dan refrigerio y descanso en su soledad y silencio. Estos valles es mi Amado para mi.'

PART THREE

THE POEMS

*Canciones del alma que se goza de haber llegado al alto
estado de la perfección, que es la unión con Dios, por el
camino de la negación espiritual*

En una noche oscura,[1]
con ansias en amores inflamada,
¡oh dichosa ventura!
salí sin ser notada,
estando ya mi casa sosegada.

A oscuras, y segura,
por la secreta escala disfrazada,
¡oh dichosa ventura!
a oscuras y en celada,
estando ya mi casa sosegada.

En la noche dichosa,
en secreto, que nadie me veía
ni yo miraba cosa,
sin otra luz y guía
sino la que en el corazón ardía.

Aquesta me guiaba
más cierto que la luz del mediodía,
adonde me esperaba
quien yo bien me sabía,
en parte donde nadie parecía.

¡Oh noche, que guiaste,
oh noche amable más que el alborada:
oh noche, que juntaste
amado con amada,
amada en el Amado transformada!

En mi pecho florido,
que entero para él solo se guardaba,
allí quedó dormido

THE DARK NIGHT

*Songs of the soul that rejoices at having reached
the high state of perfection, which is union with God,
by the path of spiritual negation*

On a night of darkness,
In love's anxiety of longing kindled,
O blessed chance!
I left by none beheld,
My house in sleep and silence stilled.

In darkness and secure,
By the secret ladder and disguised,
O blessed venture!
In darkness and concealed,
My house in sleep and silence stilled.

By dark of blessed night,
In secrecy, for no one saw me
And I regarded nothing,
My only light and guide
The one that in my heart was burning.

This guided, led me on
More surely than the radiance of noon
To where there waited one
Who was to me well known,
And in a place where no one came in view.

O night, you were the guide!
O night more desirable than dawn!
O dark of night you joined
Belovèd with belov'd one,
Belov'd one in Belovèd now transformed!

Upon my flowering breast,
Entirely kept for him and him alone,
There he stayed and slept

y yo le regalaba,
y el ventalle de cedros aire daba.

El aire de la almena,
cuando yo sus cabellos esparcía,[2]
con su mano serena
en mi cuello hería,
y todos mis sentidos suspendía.

Quedéme y olvidéme,
el rostro recliné sobre el Amado;
cesó todo, y dejéme,
dejando mi cuidado
entre las azucenas olvidado.

And I caressed him
In breezes from the fan of cedars blown.

Breezes on the battlements –
As I was spreading out his hair,
With his unhurried hand
He wounded my neck
And all my senses left suspended there.

I stayed, myself forgotten,
My countenance against my love reclined;
All ceased, and self forsaken
I left my care behind
Among the lilies, unremembered.

EL CÁNTICO ESPIRITUAL
Canciones entre el alma y el Esposo
(The Sanlúcar version)

ESPOSA

¿Adónde te escondiste,
Amado, y me dejaste con gemido?
Como el ciervo huiste,
habiéndome herido;
salí tras ti clamando, y eras ido.

Pastores, los que fuerdes
allá por las majadas al otero,
si por ventura vierdes
aquel que yo más quiero,
decidle que adolezco, peno y muero.

Buscando mis amores,
iré por esos montes y riberas,
ni cogeré las flores,
ni temeré las fieras,
y pasaré los fuertes y fronteras.

PREGUNTA A LAS CRIATURAS

Oh bosques y espesuras,
plantadas por la mano del Amado,
oh prado de verduras,
de flores esmaltado,
decid si por vosotros ha pasado.

RESPUESTA DE LAS CRIATURAS

Mil gracias derramando,
pasó por estos sotos con presura,
y, yéndolos mirando,
con sola su figura
vestidos los dejó de hermosura.

THE SPIRITUAL CANTICLE
Songs between the soul and the Bridegroom
(The Sanlúcar version)

BRIDE

Where have you hidden away,
Belovèd, and left me here to mourn?
Having wounded me you fled
Like the hart; I followed on
Behind you, crying out, calling – and you
were gone.

Shepherds, you who wander
There by sheepfolds to the mountain height,
If you should chance to see
The one I most desire,
Tell him I am sick, I suffer and I die.

Searching, I shall cover
Those hills and river shores for my most dear,
Nor stop to pick the flowers,
Nor fear the beasts of prey,
And I shall pass each fortress and frontier.

QUESTION TO THE CREATURES

O woods and crowded thickets,
By the hand of the Belovèd raised,
O meadow spread with verdure,
With sheen of blossoms glazed,
Speak, tell me if he has passed your way.

THE CREATURES' REPLY

Scattering a thousand graces,
He passed in swiftness through these groves,
And gazing in his going,
With his countenance alone
In garments of beauty he left them clothed.

ESPOSA

¡Ay, quién podrá sanarme!
Acaba de entregarte ya de vero;
no quieras enviarme
de hoy más ya mensajero,
que no saben decirme lo que quiero.

Y todos cuantos vagan
de ti me van mil gracias refiriendo,
y todos más me llagan,
y déjame muriendo
un no sé qué que quedan balbuciendo.

Mas, ¿cómo perseveras,
o, vida, no viviendo donde vives,
y haciendo porque mueras
las flechas que recibes
de lo que del Amado en ti concibes?

¿Por qué, pues has llagado
aqueste corazón, no le sanaste?
y, pues me le has robado
¿por qué así le dejaste,
y no tomas el robo que robaste?

Apaga mis enojos,
pues que ninguno basta a deshacellos,
y véante mis ojos,
pues eres lumbre dellos,
y sólo para ti quiero tenellos.

Descubre tu presencia,
y máteme tu vista y hermosura;
mira que la dolencia
de amor, que no se cura
sino con la presencia y la figura.[3]

¡Oh, cristalina fuente,
si en esos tus semblantes plateados

BRIDE

Ah – who can cure me?
Now make an end and yield yourself completely;
I beg you, send no more
Messengers from today,
For what I yearn to know they cannot tell me.

All those who come and go
And of your thousand beauties bring me rumour,
All wound me even more,
And there leaves me dying
A something – something – that they stay and
stammer.

O life, how is it you endure,
Not living where your life is – how continue,
Since close to death you draw
As you receive each arrow
Begotten of the Loved One deep within you?

Why then did you assault
And wound this heart, but not appease it?
You rob me of my heart
And yet you leave it;
The plunder you have stolen – why not seize it?

Extinguish all my sorrows,
For no other is able to relieve them,
And let my eyes behold you,
You who are their light;
For you alone do I desire to keep them.

Reveal your presence to me
And kill me with the sight of you, your beauty,
For see how nothing heals
Love's sickness and its grief
Except love's presence and the living being.

O fountain, crystal clear,
If in those your shining silvered faces

151

formases de repente
los ojos deseados
que tengo en mis entrañas dibujados!

Apártalos, Amado,
que voy de vuelo.

ESPOSO
Vuélvete, paloma,
que el ciervo vulnerado
por el otero asoma
al aire de tu vuelo, y fresco toma.

ESPOSA
Mi Amado, las montañas,
los valles solitarios nemorosos,
las ínsulas extrañas,
los ríos sonorosos,
el silbo de los aires amorosos;

La noche sosegada
en par de los levantes de la aurora,
la música callada,
la soledad sonora,
la cena que recrea y enamora.

Nuestro lecho florido,
de cuevas de leones enlazado,
en púrpura tendido,
de paz edificado,
de mil escudos de oro coronado.

A zaga de tu huella
las jóvenes discurren al camino,
al toque de centella,
al adobado vino,
emisiones de bálsamo divino.

En la interior bodega
de mi Amado bebí, y cuando salía

Could suddenly appear
The eyes so long awaited
And pictured in my heart's most inward places.

Turn them away, my love,
For I take wing.

BRIDEGROOM
                    Return, dove and alight,
For on the hill above
Appears the wounded hart
And drinks the wind and freshness of your flight.

BRIDE
My Belovèd is the mountains,
The wooded valleys, lonely and sequestered,
The strange and distant islands,
The loud resounding rivers,
The loving breezes with their gentle whispers.

The still and tranquil night
As it kindles with the coming dawn,
The music that is silent,
The ringing solitude,
The supper that refreshes and awakens love.

Our flowering bed
By lions' dens encompassed round,
With royal purple spread,
Raised up in peace profound,
And by a thousand golden scutcheons crowned.

Behind you in your tracks
Young maidens run along the path, drawn by
The spark's inspiring touch,
The spiced and seasoned wine,
Emanations of a balm that is divine.

In the deepest wine-vault
Of my Belovèd I drank, and going out

por toda aquesta vega
ya cosa no sabía,
y el ganado perdí que antes seguía.

Allí me dió su pecho,
allí me enseñó ciencia muy sabrosa,
y yo le di de hecho
a mí, sin dejar cosa;
allí le prometí de ser su esposa.

Mi alma se ha empleado
y todo mi caudal en su servicio;
ya no guardo ganado,
ni ya tengo otro oficio;
que ya sólo en amar es mi ejercicio.

Pues ya si en el ejido
de hoy más no fuere vista ni hallada,
diréis que me he perdido;
que andando enamorada,
me hice perdidiza, y fuí ganada.

De flores y esmeraldas
en las frescas mañanas escogidas,
haremos las guirnaldas,
en tu amor florecidas,
y en un cabello mío entretejidas.

En solo aquel cabello
que en mi cuello volar consideraste,
mirástele en mi cuello
y en él preso quedaste,
y en uno de mis ojos te llagaste.

Cuando tú me mirabas,
tu gracia en mí tus ojos imprimían:
por eso me adamabas,
y en eso merecían
los míos adorar lo que en ti vían.

On all this open plain
I knew no place or thing
And lost the flock I followed once before.

His heart he gave me there,
There knowledge of great sweetness he revealed;
To him I gave myself,
Gave all, without reserve;
There to be his bride I sealed my word.

My soul is now employed
To serve him, as well as all the goods I own;
I have no flock to tend,
No other office hold,
For now I practise love and love alone.

If then, from today,
I am no longer seen on village ground,
Then say I went astray,
That lost in love I roamed,
That I was lost on purpose, and was found.

With emeralds and flowers
Gathered in freshness of early morning air,
Garlands we will wreathe us
That blossomed in your care
And bound together with a thread of my hair.

In that one thread of hair
You heeded as about my neck it blew,
As you looked upon it there,
A prisoner it held you,
And by one of my eyes were you wounded through.

When you were looking on me,
Your grace was printed in me by your eyes;
This made you love me doubly
And gave the worth to mine
For adoring all they saw in you to prize.

No quieras despreciarme;
que si color moreno en mí hallaste,
ya bien puedes mirarme
después que me miraste,
que gracia y hermosura en mí dejaste.

Cogednos las raposas,[4]
que está ya florecida nuestra viña,
en tanto que de rosas
hacemos una piña,
y no parezca nadie en la montiña.

Detente, cierzo muerto;
ven, austro, que recuerdas los amores,
aspira por mi huerto
y corran sus olores,
y pacerá el Amado entre las flores.

ESPOSO
Entrádose ha la Esposa
en el ameno huerto deseado,
y a su sabor reposa,
el cuello reclinado
sobre los dulces brazos del Amado.

Debajo del manzano,
allí conmigo fuiste desposada;
allí te dí la mano,
y fuiste reparada
donde tu madre fuera violada.

A las aves ligeras,
leones, ciervos, gamos saltadores,
montes, valles, riberas,
aguas, aires, ardores,
y miedos de las noches veladores:

Por las amenas liras
y canto de serenas os conjuro

Forbear then to despise me;
Although at first you found me darkly coloured,
Now you may rest your gaze
For you have looked on me
And left your grace and comeliness behind.

Catch us the little foxes,
For now our vineyard opens into flower,
And whilst we make a cluster
Of roses bound together,
Let no one on the mountain-side appear.

Cease, death winds of the North.
Come, Southern winds, love's memories arouse,
And through my garden breathe
That its fragrance may flow out
And the Well-Beloved feed among the flowers.

BRIDEGROOM
She has entered in, the bride,
To the long desired and pleasant garden,
And at her ease she lies,
Her neck reclined
To rest upon the Loved One's gentle arms.

Beneath the apple tree,
There was your betrothal to me sealed.
There I gave my hand to you
And you were healed
Where once before your mother was defiled.

You, the light-winged birds,
Lions, stags, and leaping deer,
Highlands, valleys, river strands,
Water, air and burning fire,
And watchman of the darkness, wakeful fear:

By the sweet-stringed lyres
And by the sirens' song, I charge you

157

que cesen vuestras iras
y no toquéis al muro,
porque la Esposa duerma más seguro.

ESPOSA

O ninfas de Judea,
en tanto que en las flores y rosales
el ámbar perfumea,
morá en los arrabales
y no queráis tocar nuestros umbrales.

Escóndete, Carillo,
y mira con tu haz a las montañas,
y no quieras decillo;
mas mira las compañas
de la que va por ínsulas extrañas.

ESPOSO

La blanca palomica
al arca con el ramo se ha tornado,
y ya la tortolica
al socio deseado
en las riberas verdes ha hallado.

En soledad vivía,
y en soledad ha puesto ya su nido,
y en soledad la guía
a solas su querido,
también en soledad de amor herido.

ESPOSA

Gocémenos, Amado,
y vámonos a ver en tu hermosura
al monte u al collado,
do mana el agua pura;
entremos más adentro en la espesura.

Y luego a las subidas
cavernas de la piedra nos iremos,

To cease your raging ires
Nor sound against the wall,
That the Bride into surer sleep may fall.

BRIDE

O daughters of Judaea,
While that the flower and the briared rose
Still breathe their fragrant amber,
On the outskirts keep repose,
Nor stir upon the thresholds of our doors.

Hide, my love, be covered,
And turn your countenance towards the mountains,
And let it not be uttered,
But look on those companions
Of her who travels by the unknown islands.

BRIDEGROOM

Bearing an olive branch,
The white dove to the ark has now returned,
And on the verdant river banks
The turtle dove has found
The mate and spouse for whom she so long yearned.

In solitude she bided
And in solitude she built her nest,
In solitude is guided
By her dear one, him alone,
He, in solitude also, wounded by love.

BRIDE

My love, let us delight,
Let us see ourselves reflected in your beauty
And go to hill or mountain height
Where flows the purest water;
Let us pierce the thicket close more deeply.

And then go further,
To lofty caverns of the rock retire,

que están bien escondidas,
y allí nos entraremos
y el mosto de granadas gustaremos.

Allí me mostrarías
aquello que mi alma pretendía,
y luego me darías
allí tú, vida mía,
aquello que me diste el otro día.

El aspirar del aire,
el canto de la dulce Philomena,
el soto y su donaire
en la noche serena,
con llama que consume y no da pena.

Que nadie lo miraba,
Aminadab tampoco parecía;[5]
y el cerco sosegaba,
y la caballería
a vista de las aguas descendía.

Well sealed away and hidden;
We both shall enter there
And new wine of the pomegranate savour.

There will you reveal
That which my soul had sought for on the way,
Then you will give to me –
You, my very life –
That which you gave to me the other day.

The breathing of the air,
The nightingale's sweet song, the glade,
Its grace and splendour
In the silent night, with flame
That burns away yet brings no pain.

And there was no one watching,
Neither did Aminadab appear;
The siege was being raised,
And the horsemen,
At the sight of the waters, were riding down.

Canciones que hace el alma en la íntima
unión en Dios

¡Oh, llama de amor viva,
que tiernamente hieres
de mi alma en el más profundo centro!
Pues ya no eres esquiva,
acaba ya, si quieres;
rompe la tela deste dulce encuentro.

¡Oh cauterio suave!
¡Oh regalada llaga!
¡Oh mano blanda! ¡Oh toque delicado!
que a vida eterna sabe,
y toda deuda paga;
matando, muerte en vida la has trocado.

¡Oh lámparas de fuego,
en cuyos resplandores
las profundas cavernas del sentido,
que estaba oscuro y ciego,
con extraños primores
calor y luz dan junto a su querido!

¡Cuán manso y amoroso
recuerdas en mi seno
donde secretamente solo moras,
y en tu aspirar sabroso
de bien y gloria lleno
cuán delicadamente me enamoras!

THE LIVING FLAME OF LOVE
Songs of the soul in intimate union with **God**

O living flame of love,
How tenderly you wound
And sear my soul's most inward centre!
No longer so elusive,
Now, if you will, conclude
And rend the veil from this most sweet encounter.

O cautery that heals!
O consummating wound!
O soothing hand! O touch so fine and light
That savours of eternity
And satisfies all dues!
Slaying, you have converted death to life.

O lamps of burning fire
In whose translucent glow
The mind's profoundest caverns shine with splendour
Before in blindness and obscure,
With unearthly beauty now
Regale their love with heat and light together.

With what love and sweetness
You waken in my breast
Where in secrecy and solitude you move:
Suffused with joy and goodness
In the fragrance of your breath,
How delicately you kindle me with love!

Cantar del alma que se huelga de conoscer a
Dios por fe

Que bien sé yo la fonte que mana y corre,[6]
    aunque es de noche.

Aquella eterna fonte está escondida,
que bien sé yo do tiene su manida,
    aunque es de noche.

Su origen no lo sé, pues no le tiene,
Mas sé que todo origen de ella viene,
    aunque es de noche.

Sé que no puede ser cosa tan bella
y que cielos y tierra beben de ella,
    aunque es de noche.

Bien sé que suelo en ella no se halla
y que ninguno puede vadealla,
    aunque es de noche.

Su claridad nunca es escurecida,
y sé que toda luz de ella es venida,
    aunque es de noche.

Sé ser tan caudalosas sus corrientes,
que infiernos, cielos riegan, y las gentes,
    aunque es de noche.

El corriente que nace desta fuente,
bien sé que es tan capaz y omnipotente,
    aunque es de noche.

El corriente que de estas dos procede,
Sé que ninguna de ellas le precede,
    Aunque es de noche.

ALTHOUGH BY NIGHT
Song of the soul that delights in knowing
God by faith

How well I know the spring that brims and flows,
  Although by night.

This eternal spring is hidden deep,
How well I know the course its waters keep,
  Although by night.

Its source I do not know because it has none
And yet from this, I know, all sources come,
  Although by night.

I know that no created thing could be so fair
And that both earth and heaven drink from there,
  Although by night.

I know its depths possess no bed to fathom
And that none may ford across or sound them,
  Although by night.

Its radiance is never clouded and in this
I know that all light has its genesis,
  Although by night.

I know its currents carry such abundance
They water hell and heaven and all nations,
  Although by night.

The current welling from this fountain's source
I know to be as mighty in its force,
  Although by night.

And from these two proceeds another stream.
I know that neither over this one reigns supreme,
  Although by night.

Aquesta eterna fonte está escondida
en este vivo pan por darnos vida,
   aunque es de noche.

Aquí se está llamando a las criaturas,
y de esta agua se hartan, aunque a oscuras
   porque es de noche.

Aquesta viva fuente, que deseo,
en este pan de vida yo la veo,
   aunque de noche.

This eternal fountain is concealed from sight
Within this living bread to give us life,
  Although by night.

And here is calling out to all the creatures.
These waters quench their thirst, although by darkness,
  Because they lie in night.

I long for this, the living fountain-head.
I see it here within the living bread,
  Although by night.

Canciones a lo divino de Cristo y el alma

Un pastorcico, solo, está penado,
ajeno de placer y de contento,
y en su pastora puesto el pensamiento,
y el pecho del amor muy lastimado.

No llora por haberle amor llagado,
que no le pena verse así afligido,
aunque en el corazón está herido;
mas llora por pensar que está olvidado.

Que sólo de pensar que está olvidado
de su bella pastora, con gran pena
se deja maltratar en tierra ajena,
el pecho del amor muy lastimado.

Y dice el pastorcico ¡ Ay, desdichado
de aquel que de mi amor ha hecho ausencia,
y no quiere gozar la mi presencia,
y el pecho por su amor muy lastimado!

Y a cabo de un gran rato se ha encumbrado
sobre un árbol, do abrió sus brazos bellos,
y muerto se ha quedado, asido de ellos,
el pecho del amor muy lastimado.

A PASTORAL
Verses on Christ and the soul

A young shepherd was mourning in solitude
Far removed from all pleasure and joy,
Every thought on his shepherdess lay
And by love was his heart deeply injured.

Not in grief for the wound love had given
Nor distressed by the pain that it brought,
Although pierced by his wound to the heart,
He grieved more to think he was forgotten.

But the thought he was no more remembered
By his shepherdess sent him afar
To an alien land, its abuses to suffer,
For by love was his heart deeply injured.

'Ah woe to the one,' the young shepherd said,
'Who has stolen my dearest away.
She does not wish to know me or stay
By this heart for her love deeply injured.'

Time passed. Then mounting a tree high above
He opened his arms full and wide.
Held by them he stayed there, and died
With his heart deeply injured by love.

Coplas del alma que pena por ver a Dios

Vivo sin vivir en mí,
y de tal manera espero,
que muero porque no muero.

En mí yo no vivo ya,
y sin Dios vivir no puedo;
pues sin él y sin mí quedo,
este vivir ¿qué será?
Mil muertes se me hará,
pues mi misma vida espero,
muriendo porque no muero.

Esta vida que yo vivo
es privación de vivir;
y así, es contino morir
hasta que viva contigo.
Oye, mi Dios, lo que digo,
que esta vida no la quiero;
que muero porque no muero.

Estando absente de ti,
¿qué vida puedo tener,
sino muerte padescer,
la mayor que nunca vi?
Lástima tengo de mí,
pues de suerte persevero,
que muero porque no muero.

El pez que del agua sale
aun de alivio no caresce,
que en la muerte que padesce
al fin la muerte le vale.
¿Qué muerte habrá que se iguale
a mi vivir lastimero,
pues si más vivo, más muero?

DYING BECAUSE I DO NOT DIE
Verses of the soul that yearns to see God

Not living in myself I live
And wait with such expectancy
I die because I do not die.

I live within myself no longer,
Deprived of God I cannot live;
Lacking Him and self I'm left.
So such a life – what will it be?
It will deal a thousand deaths to me
Since I await my very life,
Dying because I do not die.

This life I live in such a way
Is nothing but life's deprivation,
One prolonged annihilation
Till at last I live with Thee.
Hear, my God, hear what I say,
I do not want this life of mine;
I die because I do not die.

Being absent and apart from Thee
What kind of life can I possess
But one that bears the pangs of death,
The worst of deaths I've ever seen?
I have some pity for myself
Since by living I continue
To die because I do not die.

Even the fish drawn out of water
Does not lack alleviation;
Death comes at last, the termination
Of the death-throes that it suffers.
What death is there to equal this,
This sad, despairing life I live?
The more I live the more I die.

Cuando me pienso aliviar
de verte en el Sacramento,
háceme más sentimiento
el no te poder gozar;
todo es para más penar
por no verte como quiero,
y muero porque no muero.

Y si me gozo, Señor,
con esperanza de verte,
en ver que puedo perderte
se me dobla mi dolor;
viviendo en tanto pavor
y esperando como espero,
muérome porque no muero.

Sácame de aquesta muerte,
mi Dios, y dame la vida;
no me tengas impedida
en este lazo tan fuerte;
mira que peno por verte,
y mi mal es tan entero
que muero porque no muero.

Lloraré mi muerte ya
y lamentaré mi vida,
en tanto que detenida
por mis pecados está.
¡Oh mi Dios! ¿Cuándo será
cuando yo diga de vero:
vivo ya porque no muero?

When thinking it will bring relief
To see Thee in the Sacrament,
My grief and pain are only deepened
To find that I cannot enjoy Thee.
All brings me greater misery
Not to see Thee as I long to
And I die because I do not die.

And if I take delight, my Lord,
In the hope of seeing Thee,
On seeing I can lose Thee
My agony is doubled.
Living in so great a dread
And waiting, yearning as I do,
I die because I do not die.

Lift me from this death, release me,
Give me living life, my God,
Not keep me in so strong a bond
To cripple and impede me;
For look, I long, I grieve to see Thee,
My sickness fills me so completely
That I die because I do not die.

I will mourn my death already,
Lament the life I live, as long
As misdeed, sin and wrong
Detain it in captivity.
O my God, when will it be?
The time when I can say for sure,
At last I live: I die no more.

Coplas a lo divino

Tras de un amoroso lance,
Y no de esperanza falto,
Volé tan alto, tan alto,
Que le di a la caza alcance.

Para que yo alcance diese
a aqueste lance divino,
tanto volar me convino
que de vista me perdiese;
y con todo, en este trance
en el vuelo quedé falto;
mas el amor fué tan alto,
que le di a la caza alcance.

Cuando más alto subía
deslumbróseme la vista,
y la más fuerte conquista
en escuro se hacía;
mas por ser de amor el lance
di un ciego y oscuro salto,
y fuí tan alto, tan alto,
que le di a la caza alcance.

Cuanto más alto llegaba
de este lance tan subido,
tanto más bajo y rendido
y abatido me hallaba;
dije: No habrá quien alcance;
y abatíme tanto, tanto
que fuí tan alto, tan alto,
que le di a la caza alcance.

Por una extraña manera
mil vuelos pasé de un vuelo,

A QUARRY OF LOVE
Verses with a divine meaning

Bent on an enterprise of love,
And not in lack of hope,
I flew so high, so high above
I caught my quarry on the wing.

In order that I might succeed
On that celestial enterprise,
So high in flight I had to rise
I lost myself from view;
Yet even in this last extreme
My pitch of flight was not enough,
But love moved on so high above
I caught my quarry on the wing.

As I rose to higher reaches
Dazzled, blinded was my vision,
And in an utter darkness won
The hardest of my victories;
I took a blind, unknowing plunge
Because the venture was for love,
And went so high, so high above
I caught my quarry on the wing.

The greater was the height I reached
On this exalted quest,
The more I found myself oppressed,
Exhausted and defeated;
I said, 'It can be reached by none,'
Which cast me down so much
That I flew high, so high above,
I caught my quarry on the wing.

By a course, obscure and strange,
I flew a thousand flights in one;

porque esperanza de cielo
tanto alcanza cuanto espera;
esperé solo este lance,
y en esperar no fuí falto,
pues fuí tan alto, tan alto,
que le di a la caza alcance.

When hope is hope of heaven
Reach is measured to its range;
I hoped for this one prize alone
And hope I had sufficient of,
For I soared high, so high above,
I caught my quarry on the wing.

Coplas hechas sobre un éxtasis de harta
contemplación

Entréme donde no supe,
y quedéme no sabiendo,
toda sciencia trascendiendo.

Yo no supe dónde entraba,
pero, cuando allí me vi,
sin saber dónde me estaba,
grandes cosas entendí;
no diré lo que sentí,
que me quedé no sabiendo,
toda sciencia trascendiendo.

De paz y de piedad
era la sciencia perfecta,
en profunda soledad
entendida (vía recta);
era cosa tan secreta,
que me quedé balbuciendo,
toda sciencia trascendiendo.

Estaba tan embebido,
tan absorto y ajenado,
que se quedó mi sentido
de todo sentir privado;
y el espíritu dotado
de un entender no entendiendo,
toda sciencia trascendiendo.

El que allí llega de vero,
de sí mismo desfallesce;
cuanto sabía primero
mucho bajo le paresce;
y su sciencia tanto cresce,
que se queda no sabiendo,
toda sciencia trascendiendo.

VERSES WRITTEN ON AN ECSTASY

I entered in, not knowing where,
And there remained uncomprehending,
All knowledge transcending.

I entered – where – I did not know,
Yet when I found that I was there,
Though where I was I did not know,
Profound and subtle things I learned;
Nor can I say what I discerned,
For I remained uncomprehending,
All knowledge transcending.

Of peace and holy truth
It was knowledge to perfection,
Within the depths of solitude
The narrow path of wisdom;
A secret so profoundly hidden
That I was left there stammering,
All knowledge transcending.

I was so caught up and rapt away,
In such oblivion immersed,
That every sense and feeling lay
Of sense and feeling dispossessed;
And so my mind and soul were blessed
To understand not understanding,
All knowledge transcending.

The one who truly reaches there
No longer in himself remains,
And all that he had known at first
Seems base and mean to him, and wanes;
So great a knowledge then he gains
That he is left uncomprehending,
All knowledge transcending.

Cuanto más alto se sube,
tanto menos se entendía,
que es la tenebrosa nube
que a la noche esclarecía;
por eso quien la sabía
queda siempre no sabiendo
toda sciencia trascendiendo.

Este saber no sabiendo
es de tan alto poder,
que los sabios arguyendo
jamás le pueden vencer;
que no llega su saber
a no entender entendiendo,
toda sciencia trascendiendo.

Y es de tan alta excelencia
aqueste sumo saber,
que no hay facultad ni sciencia
que le puedan emprender;
quien se supiere vencer
con un no saber sabiendo
irá siempre trascendiendo.

Y si lo queréis oir,
consiste esta suma sciencia
en un subido sentir
de la divinal Esencia;
es obra de su clemencia
hacer quedar no entendiendo,
toda sciencia trascendiendo.

His understanding is the less endowed –
The more he climbs to greater heights –
To understand the shadowed cloud
Which there illuminates the night;
Thus he who comprehends this sight
Will always stay not understanding,
All knowledge transcending.

This knowledge through uncomprehending
Is of such supreme dominion
That by learned men contending
It is never grasped or won;
Their learning never lights upon
The knowledge of unknowing,
Beyond all knowledge going.

And that exalted wisdom
Is of such a high degree,
It can be undertaken
By no art or faculty;
Who knows the way to mastery
By a knowledge that unknows
Transcending ever goes.

And if you wish to hear,
This highest knowledge is conceived
In a sense, sublime and clear
Of the essence of the Deity;
It is an act of His great Clemency
That keeps us there uncomprehending,
All knowledge transcending.

ROMANCE QUE VA POR 'SUPER FLUMINA BABYLONIS'

Encima de las corrientes[7]
que en Babilonia hallaba,
allí me senté llorando
allí la tierra regaba,
accordándome de ti,
oh Sión, a quien amaba;
era dulce tu memoria,
y con ella más lloraba.
Dejé los trajes de fiesta,
los de trabajo tomaba,
y colgué en los verdes sauces
la música que llevaba,
poniéndola en esperanza
de aquello que en ti esperaba.
Allí me hirió el amor,
y el corazón me sacaba.
Díjele que me matase,
pues de tal suerte llagaba;
yo me metía en su fuego,
sabiendo que me abrasaba,
desculpando el avecica
que en el fuego se acababa;
estábame en mí muriendo,
y en ti solo respiraba;
en mí por ti me moría,
y por ti resucitaba,
que la memoria de ti,
daba vida y la quitaba.

BALLAD ON THE PSALM
'BY THE WATERS OF BABYLON'

Beside the flowing river
That in Babylon I found
I sat and there with weeping
I watered foreign ground,

Recalling thee, O Zion,
Beloved by me so well;
The sweetness of thy memory
Increased the tears that fell.

I put aside my festive clothes
And those of labour wore
And on the verdant willows hung
The music that I bore.

Placing it in trust to wait
For all I hoped in thee;
There love struck me, wounding,
And took my heart away.

I entreated him to kill me –
I was so wounded through –
And in his burning furnace plunged,
To be consumed, I knew.

And so I was extinguished
Like the phoenix in the fire,
In myself to fail and perish,
In thee alone respire.

For thee my own life dying
And through thee newly born,
Since by the memory of thee
Life is given and withdrawn.

Gozábanse los extraños
entre quien cautivo estaba.
Preguntábanme cantares
de lo que en Sión cantaba:
'Canta de Sión un himno,
veamos cómo sonaba.'
Decid: ¿Cómo en tierra ajena,
donde por Sión lloraba,
cantaré yo la alegría
que en Sión se me quedaba?
Echaríala en olvido
si en la ajena me gozaba.
Con mi paladar se junte
la lengua con que hablaba,
si de ti yo me olvidare,
en la tierra do moraba.
Sión, por los verdes ramos
que Babilonia me daba,
de mí se olvide mi diestra,
que es lo que en ti más amaba;
si de ti no me acordare,
en lo que más me gozaba
y si yo tuviere fiesta,
y sin ti la festejaba.
¡Oh hija de Babilonia,
Mísera y desventurada!
Bienaventurado era
aquel en quien confiaba,
que te ha de dar el castigo
que de tu mano llevaba;
y juntará sus pequeños,
y a mí, porque en ti lloraba,
a la piedra que era Cristo,
por el cual yo te dejaba.

In revelry the strangers
Whose captive I was bound
Required of me the songs of mirth
I sang in Zion's land;
'Sing us one of Zion's songs,
Let's hear how well they sound.'

In strangers' lands, I answered,
Where I grieve for my own land,
How shall I sing of gladness
Left in Zion far behind?
If I rejoiced in exile here
I would cast it from my mind.

Let this tongue with which I utter
To my palate fast be tied,
If of thee I am forgetful
In this land where I bide.

O Zion, by these green boughs above me,
By this Babylonian tree,
Let my own right hand forget me
Which most I prized in thee,

If of thee I am forgetful,
In whom I used to most rejoice,
If on feast days I should revel
And without thee raise my voice.

O daughter of Babylon,
Ill-fated and despised.
Blest and fortunate the one
In whom I placed my trust;
The curse that your hand brought
By his will be chastised.

He will unite his little ones,
I with them, since in you I grieved,
And join us to the rock of Christ
For whom I cast you from me.

I

En el principio moraba[7]
el Verbo, y en Dios vivía,
en quien su felicidad
infinita poseía.
El mismo Verbo Dios era,
que el principio se decía.
El moraba en el principio,
y principio no tenía.
El era el mismo principio;
por eso de él carecía;
el Verbo se llama Hijo
que del principio nacía.
Hale siempre concebido,
y siempre le concebía,
dale siempre su substancia,
y siempre se la tenía.
Y así, la gloria del Hijo
es la que en el Padre había,
y toda su gloria el Padre
en el Hijo poseía.
Como amado en el amante
uno en otro residía,
y aquese amor que los une,
en lo mismo convenía
con el uno y con el otro
en igualdad y valía.
Tres Personas y un amado
entre todos tres había;

I

In the beginning abided
The Word, and in God he dwelled;
In Him was his happiness
Eternally held.

It was called the beginning,
This same Word which was God;
He dwelled in the beginning,
Himself unbegotten.

He was that same beginning,
Thus He Himself had none;
There was born of this beginning
The Word we call the Son.

He always has conceived him
And so conceives him always,
Always giving him His substance
Which always has been his.

And so the Son's great glory
From the Father had arisen;
All His glory then the Father
Possessed within the Son.

Each dwelled within the other
As Lover and Belovèd dwell,
And the self-same love that joined them
Resided there as well

With the one as with the other
In worth and in degree:
Three persons, one Belovèd,
Together they were three.

187

y un amor en todas ellas
y un amante las hacía;
y el amante es el amado
en que cada cual vivía;
que el ser que los tres poseen,
cada cual le poseía,
y cada cual de ellos ama
a la que este ser tenía.
Este ser es cada una,
y éste sólo las unía
en un inefable nudo
que decir no se sabía.
Por lo cual era infinito
el amor que las unía,
porque un solo amor tres tienen,
que su esencia se decía;
que el amor, cuanto más uno,
tanto más amor hacía.

II

De la comunicación de las tres Personas

En aquel amor inmenso
que de los dos procedía,
palabras de gran regalo
el Padre al Hijo decía,
de tan profundo deleite,
que nadie las entendía;
sólo el Hijo lo gozaba,
que es a quien pertenecía.
Pero aquello que se entiende
desta manera decía:
Nada me contenta, Hijo,
fuera de tu compañía.

A single love dwelled in them all,
One Lover all provided;
And the Lover is the Loved One
In whom they each resided.

For the Being all three possessed
To each alone belonged,
And what belonged to this one Being
By each one was beloved.

This Being was each single one
And they were tied by this alone
In an inexpressible union
For which no name is known.

For it was infinite, the love
Which wrought their unity,
And this is called their essence,
The single love possessed by three;
And the more love grows to oneness
The more it is increased.

II

The Communication of the Three Persons

From that unbounded, mighty love
Between the two arisen,
Words of deep content and joy
The Father uttered to the Son;

Words of such profound delight
That no one comprehended;
The son alone possessed their joy,
For him they were intended.

But what is fathomed of their sense
Was spoken in this way:
    My Son, nothing brings content to me
Beyond your company.

Y si algo me contenta,
en ti mismo lo quería;
el que a ti más se parece,
a mí más satisfacía.
Y el que en nada te semeja,
en mí nada hallaría;
en ti sólo me he agradado,
¡oh vida de vida mía!
Eres lumbre de mi lumbre,
eres mi sabiduría,
figura de mi substancia,
en quien bien me complacía.
Al que a ti te amare, Hijo,
a mí mismo le daría,
y el amor que yo en ti tengo,
ese mismo en él pondría,
en razón de haber amado
a quien yo tanto quería.

III

De la Creación

Una esposa que te ame,
mi Hijo, darte quería,
que por tu valor merezca
tener nuestra compañía
y comer pan a una mesa,
de el mismo que yo comía;
porque conozca los bienes
que en tal Hijo yo tenía;
y se congracie conmigo
de tu gracia y lozanía.
Mucho lo agradezco, Padre,
el Hijo le respondía;
a la esposa que me dieres,
yo mi claridad daría,

And if anything content me
In you do I desire it;
By him who most resembles you
Am I most satisfied.

And who resembles you in nothing
Nothing in me will he find;
By you alone have I been pleased,
O life of my own life.

You are Light of my Light,
My wisdom and my knowledge,
The form and figure of my substance,
In whom I am well pleased.

My Son, unto the one who loves you,
Of myself shall I give freely,
And place in him the self-same love
That I possess for you,
Because he also loves the one
Whom I have loved so dearly.

III
The Creation

My Son, it is my wish to give you
A bride for you to love,
Who through your worth will well deserve
To live as our companion,

And eat her bread at our table.
The bread on which I fare;
That she may know in such a son
The wealth of good I bear;
And she will join with me in praising
Your grace and glowing splendour.

I am deeply grateful, Father,
The son said in reply,
And to the bride you give me
I will add my clarity.

191

para que por ella vea
cuánto mi Padre valía,
y cómo el ser que poseo,
de su ser le recibía.
Reclinarla he yo en mi brazo
y en tu amor se abrasaría,
y con eterno deleite
tu bondad sublimaría.

IV

Hágase, pues, dijo el Padre,
que tu amor lo merecía;
y en este dicho que dijo,
el mundo criado había:
palacio para la esposa,
hecho en gran sabiduría;
el cual, en dos aposentos,
alto y bajo, dividía.
El bajo de diferencias
infinitas componía;
mas el alto hermoseaba
de admirable pedrería,
porque conozca la esposa
el esposo que tenía.
En el alto colocaba
la angélica jerarquía;
pero la natura humana
en el bajo la ponía,
por ser en su compostura
algo de menor valía.
Y aunque el ser y los lugares
de esta suerte los partía,

That with its light my Father's worth
By her may be perceived,
And how this nature I possess
Was from His own received.

And I shall hold her in my arms,
To burn there in your love,
And she will glorify your goodness
In eternal celebration.

IV

So let it be done, the Father said,
For so your love deserves;
And this sentence that He uttered
Was the making of the world:

Creating in surpassing wisdom
A palace for the Bride,
Which into two apartments,
High and low, He did divide.

And of an infinite variety
The lower He composed,
But beautified the one on high
With rare and precious stones.

That the Bride may know the Bridegroom
Whom she possessed in love,
He stationed choirs of angels
In hierarchy above.

But to the chamber down below
Human nature He assigned,
For being in its composition
A somewhat lesser kind.

And though their nature and their station
He chose so to divide,

pero todos son un cuerpo
de la esposa que decía:
que el amor de un mismo Esposo
una Esposa los hacía.
Los de arriba poseían
el Esposo en alegría;
los de abajo en esperanza
de fe que les infundía,
diciéndoles que algún tiempo
él los engrandecería;
y que aquella su bajeza
él se la levantaría,
de manera que ninguno
ya la vituperaría,
porque en todo semejante
él a ellos se haría,
y se vendría con ellos,
y con ellos moraría;
y que Dios sería hombre,
y que el hombre Dios sería,
y trataría con ellos,
comería y bebería;
y que con ellos contino
Él mismo se quedaría,
hasta que se consumase
este siglo que corría,
cuando se gozaran juntos
en eterna melodía;
porque él era la cabeza
de la esposa que tenía;
a la cual todos los miembros
de los justos juntaría,

They were all the single body
Of one beloved Bride.

For by the love of one sole Bridegroom
They formed a single Bride;
Those above possessed their Spouse
In fullness of delight;

Those below in expectation
With faith that He inspired
Through saying that by Him, one day,
They would be magnified.

And that the lowness of their nature
He would raise up and exalt,
In such a way that no one then
Could scorn it or find fault.

For He would make himself like them
And resemble them in all,
He would walk with them in friendship
And among them He would dwell,

And God would then be man
And man then God would be;
In their dealings He would mingle,
He would eat and drink as they,

And at their side unceasingly
He Himself would stay,
Until this age that now prevails
Is closed and passed away.

When in eternal harmony
They would rejoice as one,
For of the bride whom He possessed
He was the head and crown.

To her He would unite and join
The members of the just;

7-2

que son cuerpo de la esposa,
a la cual él tomaría
en sus brazos tiernamente,
y allí su amor la daría;
y que así juntos en uno
al Padre la llevaría,
donde del mismo deleite
que Dios goza, gozaría;
que, como el Padre y el Hijo,
y el que de ellos procedía,
el uno vive en el otro;
así la esposa sería,
que dentro de Dios absorta,
vida de Dios viviría.

v

Con esta buena esperanza
que de arriba les venía,
el tedio de sus trabajos
más leve se les hacía;
pero la esperanza larga
y el deseo que crecía
de gozarse con su Esposo
contino les afligía.
Por lo cual con oraciones,
con suspiros y agonía,
con lágrimas y gemidos
le rogaban noche y día
que ya se determinase
a les dar su compañía.
Unos decían: ¡Oh, si fuese
en mi tiempo el alegría!

They formed the body of the Bride
Whom He would gather up

Tenderly into His arms,
There give to her His love;
And thus would bear her to the Father,
United into one.

Where she would joy with that same joy
Possessed by God Himself;
For as the Father and the Son
And He who issues from them

All live within each other,
So also would the Bride;
Absorbed, immersed within her God
She would live His very life.

V

And this happy expectation
Coming to them from on high
Made the dullness of their labours
Seem easier to bear.

But the length of endless waiting
And the heightening desire
For possession of their Bridegroom
Made them constantly despair.

And so with supplications
With sighs of grief and pain,
With tears and lamentations,
They begged Him night and day

That to give them His companionship
He would at last decide,
Some said: 'If only this great joy
Could happen in my time!'

otros: Acaba, Señor;
al que has de enviar envía;
otros: ¡Oh si ya rompieses
esos cielos, y vería
con mis ojos, que bajases,
y mi llanto cesaría!
Regad, nubes de lo alto,
que la tierra lo pedía;
y ábrase ya la tierra,
que espinas nos producía,
y produzca aquella flor
con que ella florecería.
Otros decían: ¡Oh dichoso
el que en tal tiempo sería,
que merezca ver a Dios
con los ojos que tenía,
y tratarle con sus manos,
y andar en su compañía,
y gozar de los misterios
que entonces ordenaría!

VI

En aquestos y otros ruegos
gran tiempo pasado había;
pero en los postreros años
el fervor mucho crecía,
cuando el viejo Simeón
en deseo se encendía,
rogando a Dios que quisiese
dejalle ver este día.
Y así, el Espíritu Santo
al buen viejo respondía

'O Lord, have done,' said others,
'Send Him whom you decreed.'
Others: 'O if you broke those Heavens
Open so that I could see

You descend before my eyes,
Then I would cease my weeping.
O clouds above, send down your rain,
The dry land is beseeching,

And bring fertility to earth –
But thorns has she produced –
Set her budding with that blossom
Through which she will bear fruit!'

Others said: 'O fortunate is he
Who lives at such a time,
With worth enough to look upon
Our God with his own eyes,

And touch Him with his hands,
And share His company,
And rejoice in Sacred Mysteries
Which He will then decree.'

VI

With these and other prayers
A span of time ran by;
But in later years the fervour
Strengthened and rose high.

It was then that aged Simeon,
With longing set aflame,
Entreated God to spare his life
And let him see that day.

And so the Holy Spirit
To the good old man replied

que le daba su palabra
que la muerte no vería
hasta que la vida viese,
que de arriba descendía,
y que él en sus mismas manos
al mismo Dios tomaría,
y le tendría en sus brazos,
y consigo abrazaría.

VII
Prosigue la Encarnación

Ya que el tiempo era llegado
en que hacerse convenía
el rescate de la esposa
que en duro yugo servía,
debajo de aquella ley
que Moisés dado le había,
el Padre con amor tierno
de esta manera decía:
    Ya ves, Hijo, que a tu esposa
a tu imagen hecho había,
y en lo que a ti se parece
contigo bien convenía;
pero difiere en la carne,
que en tu simple ser no había.
En los amores perfectos
esta ley se requería,
que se haga semejante
el amante a quien quería,
que la mayor semejanza
más deleite contenía;
el cual sin duda en tu esposa
grandemente crecería

And gave his word in promise
That he should never die

Until he saw the very Life,
Descended from above,
And would take in his own hands
That self-same living God,
And would hold him in his arms,
And clasp Him to himself.

VII
Continuing the Incarnation

Now that the season had arrived
Appointed long ago
For the ransom of the Bride, who served
Beneath a heavy yoke,

According to the ancient law
Which Moses laid upon her,
The Father moved with tender love
To this effect then spoke:

My Son, you see now that your Bride
In your image has been formed,
And where she most resembles you,
You both are in accord.

But she differs through the flesh,
Not found in your pure soul;
There is, for love's perfection,
A law of love to know:

That the lover take on likeness
To the loved one of his heart,
And the closer the resemblance
The greater the delight.

And this delight within your Bride
Would greatly be increased,

201

si te viere semejante
en la carne que tenía.
Mi voluntad es la tuya,
el Hijo le respondía,
y la gloria que yo tengo
es tu voluntad ser mía;
y a mí me conviene, Padre,
lo que tu Alteza decía,
porque por esta manera
tu bondad más se vería;
veráse tu gran potencia,
justicia y sabiduría;
irélo a decir al mundo,
y noticia le daría
de tu belleza y dulzura
y de tu soberanía.
Iré a buscar a mi esposa,
y sobre mí tomaría
sus fatigas y trabajos,
en que tanto padescía;
y porque ella vida tenga,
yo por ella moriría,
y sacándola del lago,
a ti te la volvería.

VIII

Entonces llamó a un arcángel,
que San Gabriel se decía,
y enviólo a una doncella
que se llamaba María,
de cuyo consentimiento
el misterio se hacía;
en la cual la Trinidad
de carne al Verbo vestía;

If the flesh she is endowed with
She saw you also shared.

   My will is yours and yours alone,
The Son to him replied,
The sovereign glory I possess
Is that your will be mine.

So I accord with you, my Father,
In everything you say.
Your loving kindness will be seen
More clearly in this way.

Your mightiness and wisdom
And justice will be shown.
I shall go and tell the world
And make the tidings known
Of your graciousness and beauty
And of your sovereign throne.

I shall go and seek my Bride,
And I myself will bear
The weariness and hardship
That submerge her life in care.

And so that she may have life
I shall die for her sake,
And to you again restore her,
Lifted from the lake.

VIII

Then He summoned an archangel;
Saint Gabriel came,
And He sent him to a maiden,
Mary was her name,

Whose consent and acquiescence
Gave the mystery its birth;
It was the Trinity that clothed
With flesh the living Word.

y aunque tres hacen la obra,
en el uno se hacía;
y quedó el Verbo encarnado
en el vientre de María.
Y el que tenía sólo Padre,
ya también Madre tenía,
aunque no como cualquiera
que de varón concebía;
que de las entrañas de ella
él su carne recibía;
por lo cual Hijo de Dios
y del hombre se decía.

IX
Del Nacimiento

Ya que era llegado el tiempo
en que de nacer había,
así como desposado
de su tálamo salía,
abrazado con su esposa,
que en sus brazos la traía,
al cual la graciosa Madre
en un pesebre ponía,
entre unos animales
que a la sazón allí había.
Los hombres decían cantares,
los ángeles melodía,
festejando el desposorio
que entre tales dos había.
Pero Dios en el pesebre
allí lloraba y gemía;

Though the three had worked the wonder
It was wrought in but this one,
And the incarnated Word
Was left in Mary's womb.

And He who had a father only
Now possessed a mother,
Though not of man was He conceived
But unlike any other.

And deep within her body
His life of flesh began:
For this reason He is called
The Son of God and Man.

IX

The Birth of Christ

Now that the time of His birth
Had finally come
He emerged from His chamber
Like a newly wed groom,

His arms embraced closely
The Bride He brought in,
Whom the radiant mother
Laid down in a crib,

Among some of the creatures
There at that season.
Men singing songs
And angels in anthem

Rejoiced in the nuptials –
Such a pair were allied –
But God in the manger
Whimpered and cried.

que eran joyas que la esposa
al desposorio traía;
y la Madre estaba en pasmo
de que tal trueque veía;
el llanto del hombre en Dios,
y en el hombre la alegría,
lo cual del uno y del otro
tan ajeno ser solía.

These were the jewels
The bride brought in marriage,
The mother in wonder
To witness such change:

Man's grieving in God
And the gladness in man,
Which to either before
Had been so unknown.

EL CÁNTICO ESPIRITUAL
Canciones entre el alma y el esposo
(The Jaén Version)

ESPOSA

¿Adónde te escondiste,
Amado, y me dejaste con gemido?
Como el ciervo huiste,
habiéndome herido;
salí tras ti clamando, y eras ido.

Pastores, los que fuerdes
allá por las majadas al otero,
si por ventura vierdes
aquel que yo más quiero,
decidle que adolezco, peno y muero.

Buscando mis amores,
iré por esos montes y riberas,
ni cogeré las flores,
ni temeré las fieras,
y pasaré los fuertes y fronteras.

PREGUNTA A LAS CRIATURAS

Oh, bosques y espesuras,
plantadas por la mano del Amado,
oh, prado de verduras,
de flores esmaltado,
decid si por vosotros ha pasado.

RESPUESTA DE LAS CRIATURAS

Mil gracias derramando,
pasó por estos sotos con presura,
y yéndolos mirando,
con sola su figura
vestidos los dejó de hermosura.

ESPOSA

¡Ay, quién podrá sanarme!
Acaba de entregarte ya de vero;

THE SPIRITUAL CANTICLE
Songs between the soul and the Bridegroom
(The Jaén version)

BRIDE

Where have you hidden away,
Belovèd, and left me here to mourn?
Having wounded me you fled
Like the hart; I followed on
Behind you, crying out, calling – and you were gone.

Shepherds, you who wander
There by sheepfolds to the mountain height,
If you should chance to see
The one I most desire,
Tell him I am sick, I suffer and I die.

Searching I shall cover
Those hills and river shores for my most dear,
Nor stop to pick the flowers,
Nor fear the beasts of prey,
And I shall pass each fortress and frontier.

QUESTION TO THE CREATURES
O woods and crowded thickets,
By the hand of the Belovèd raised,
O meadow spread with verdure,
With sheen of blossoms glazed,
Speak, tell me if he has passed your way.

THE CREATURES' REPLY
Scattering a thousand graces
He passed in swiftness through these groves,
And gazing in his going,
With his countenance alone
In garments of beauty he left them clothed.

BRIDE
Ah – who can cure me!
Now make an end and yield yourself completely;

no quieras enviarme
de hoy más ya mensajero,
que no saben decirme lo que quiero.

Y todos cuantos vagan
de ti me van mil gracias refiriendo,
y todos más me llagan,
y déjame muriendo
un no sé qué que quedan balbuciendo.

Mas, ¿cómo perseveras,
oh vida, no viviendo donde vives,
y haciendo porque mueras
las flechas que recibes
de lo que del Amado en ti concibes?

¿Por qué, pues has llagado
aqueste corazón, no le sanaste?
y pues me le has robado
¿por qué así le dejaste,
y no tomas el robo que robaste?

Apaga mis enojos,
pues que ninguno basta a deshacellos,
y véante mis ojos,
pues eres lumbre dellos,
y sólo para ti quiero tenellos.

Descubre tu presencia,
y máteme tu vista y hermosura;
mira que la dolencia
de amor, que no se cura
sino con la presencia y la figura.

¡Oh, cristalina fuente,
si en esos tus semblantes plateados
formases de repente

I beg you, send no more
Messengers from today,
For what I yearn to know they cannot tell me.

All those who come and go
And of your thousand beauties bring me rumour,
All wound me even more,
And there leaves me dying
A something – something – that they stay and
stammer.

O life, how is it you endure,
Not living where your life is – how continue,
Since close to death you draw
As you receive each arrow
Begotten of the Loved One deep within you?

Why then did you assault
And wound this heart but not appease it?
You rob me of my heart
And yet you leave it;
The plunder you have stolen – why not seize it?

Extinguish all my sorrows,
For no other is able to relieve them,
And let my eyes behold you,
You who are their light;
For you alone do I desire to keep them.

Reveal your presence to me
And kill me with the sight of you, your beauty,
For see how nothing heals
Love's sickness and its grief
Except love's presence and the living being.

O fountain, crystal clear,
If in those your shining silvered faces
Could suddenly appear

los ojos deseados
que tengo en mis entrañas dibujados!

Apártalos, Amado,
que voy de vuelo.

ESPOSO
Vuélvete, paloma,
que el ciervo vulnerado
por el otero asoma
al aire de tu vuelo, y fresco toma.

ESPOSA
Mi Amado, las montañas,
los valles solitarios nemorosos,
las ínsulas extrañas,
los ríos sonorosos,
el silbo de los aires amorosos;

La noche sosegada
en par de los levantes del aurora,
la música callada,
la soledad sonora,
la cena que recrea y enamora.

Cazadnos las raposas,
que está ya florecida nuestra viña,
en tanto que de rosas
hacemos una piña
y no parezca nadie en la montiña.

Detente, Cierzo muerto;
ven, Austro, que recuerdas los amores,
aspira por mi huerto
y corran sus olores,
y pacerá el Amado entre las flores

Oh, ninfas de Judea,
en tanto que en las flores y rosa e

The eyes so long awaited
And pictured in my heart's most inward places.

Turn them away, my love,
For I take wing.

BRIDEGROOM

                    Return, dove and alight,
For on the hill above
Appears the wounded hart
And drinks the wind and freshness of your flight.

BRIDE

   My Belovèd is the mountains,
The wooded valleys, lonely and sequestered,
The strange and distant islands,
The loud resounding rivers,
The loving breezes with their gentle whispers.

   The still and tranquil night
As it kindles with the coming dawn,
The music that is silent,
The ringing solitude,
The supper that refreshes and awakens love.

   Catch us the little foxes,
For now our vineyard opens into flower,
And whilst we make a cluster
Of roses bound together,
Let no one on the mountainside appear.

   Cease, death winds of the North.
Come, Southern winds, love's memories arouse,
And through my garden breathe
That its fragrance may flow out
And the Well-Beloved feed among the flowers.

   O daughters of Judaea,
While that the flower and the briared rose

213

el ámbar perfumea,
morá en los arrabales
y no queráis tocar nuestros umbrales.

Escóndete, Carillo,
y mira con tu haz a las montañas,
y no quieras decillo;
mas mira las compañas
de la que va por ínsulas extrañas.

ESPOSO
A las aves ligeras,
leones, ciervos, gamos saltadores,
montes, valles, riberas,
aguas, aires, ardores
y miedos de las noches veladores:

Por las amenas liras
y canto de serenas os conjuro
que cesen vuestras iras
y no toquéis al muro,
porque la Esposa duerma más seguro.

Entrádose ha la Esposa
en el ameno huerto deseado,
y a su sabor reposa,
el cuello reclinado
sobre los dulces brazos del Amado.

Debajo del manzano,
allí conmigo fuiste desposada;
allí te di la mano,
y fuiste reparada
donde tu madre fuera violada.

ESPOSA
Nuestro lecho florido
de cuevas de leones enlazado,
en púrpura tendido,

Still breathe their fragrant amber,
On the outskirts keep repose,
Nor stir upon the thresholds of our doors.

Hide, my love, be covered,
And turn your countenance towards the mountains,
And let it not be uttered,
But look on those companions
Of her who travels by the unknown islands.

BRIDEGROOM
You, the light-winged birds,
Lions, stags, and leaping deer,
Highlands, valleys, river-strands,
Water, air and burning fire,
And watchman of the darkness, wakeful fear:

By the sweet-stringed lyres
And by the sirens' song, I charge you
To cease your raging ires
Nor sound against the wall,
That the bride into surer sleep may fall.

She has entered in, the Bride,
To the long desired and pleasant garden,
And at her ease she lies,
Her neck reclined
To rest upon the Loved One's gentle arms.

Beneath the apple tree,
There was your betrothal to me sealed.
There I gave my hand to you
And you were healed
Where once before your mother was defiled.

BRIDE
Our flowering bed
By lions' dens encompassed round,
With royal purple spread,

de paz edificado,
de mil escudos de oro coronado.

A zaga de tu huella
las jóvenes discurren al camino,
al toque de centella,
al adobado vino,
emisiones de bálsamo divino.

En la interior bodega
de mi Amado bebí, y cuando salía
por toda aquesta vega
ya cosa no sabía
y el ganado perdí que antes seguía.

Allí me dió su pecho,
allí me enseñó ciencia muy sabrosa,
y yo le di de hecho
a mí, sin dejar cosa;
allí le prometí de ser su esposa.

Mi alma se ha empleado
y todo mi caudal en su servicio;
ya no guardo ganado,
ni ya tengo otro oficio;
que ya sólo en amar es mi ejercicio.

Pues ya si en el ejido
de hoy más no fuere vista ni hallada,
diréis que me he perdido;
que, andando enamorada,
me hice perdidiza, y fui ganada.

De flores y esmeraldas
en las frescas mañanas escogidas,
haremos las guirnaldas,
en tu amor floridas,
y en un cabello mío entretejidas.

Raised up in peace profound,
And by a thousand golden scutcheons crowned.

    Behind you in your tracks
Young maidens run along the path, drawn by
The spark's inspiring touch,
The spiced and seasoned wine
Emanations of a balm that is divine.

    In the deepest wine-vault
Of my Belovèd I drank, and going out
On all this open plain,
I knew no place or thing
And lost the flock I followed once before.

    His heart he gave me there,
There knowledge of great sweetness he revealed;
To him I gave myself,
Gave all, without reserve;
There to be his bride I sealed my word.

    My soul is now employed
To serve him, as well as all the goods I own,
I have no flock to tend,
No other office hold,
For now I practise love and love alone.

    If then, from today,
I am no longer seen on village ground,
Then say I went astray,
That lost in love I roamed,
That I was lost on purpose, and was found.

    With emeralds and flowers
Gathered in freshness of early morning air,
Garlands we will wreathe us
That blossomed in your care
And bound together with a thread of my hair.

En solo aquel cabello
que en mi cuello volar consideraste,
mirástele en mi cuello
y en él preso quedaste,
y en uno de mis ojos te llagaste.

Cuando tú me mirabas,
su gracia en mí tus ojos imprimían;
por eso me adamabas,
y en eso merecían
los míos adorar lo que en ti vían.

No quieras despreciarme,
que si color moreno en mí hallaste,
ya bien puedes mirarme
después que me miraste,
que gracia y hermosura en mí dejaste.

ESPOSO
La blanca palomica
al arca con el ramo se ha tornado,
y ya la tortolica
al socio deseado
en las riberas verdes ha hallado.

En soledad vivía,
y en soledad ha puesto ya su nido,
y en soledad la guía
a solas su querido,
también en soledad de amor herido.

ESPOSA
Gocémonos, Amado,
y vámonos a ver en tu hermosura
al monte y al collado,
do mana el agua pura;
entremos más adentro en la espesura.

In that one thread of hair
You heeded as about my neck it blew,
As you looked upon it there,
A prisoner it held you,
And by one of my eyes were you wounded through.

When you were looking on me;
Your grace was printed in me by your eyes;
This made you love me doubly,
And gave the worth to mine
For adoring all they saw in you to prize.

Forbear then to despise me;
Although at first you found me darkly coloured,
Now you may rest your gaze
For you have looked on me
And left your grace and comeliness behind.

BRIDEGROOM
Bearing an olive branch,
The white dove to the ark has now returned,
And on the verdant river banks
The turtle dove has found
The mate and spouse for whom she so long yearned.

In solitude she bided
And in solitude she built her nest,
In solitude is guided
By her dear one, him alone,
He, in solitude also, wounded by love.

BRIDE
My love, let us delight,
Let us see ourselves reflected in your beauty
And go to hill or mountain height
Where flows the purest water;
Let us pierce the thicket close more deeply.

Y luego a las subidas
cavernas de la piedra nos iremos,
que están bien escondidas,
y allí nos entraremos
y el mosto de granadas gustaremos.

Allí me mostrarías
aquello que mi alma pretendía,
y luego me darías
allí tú, vida mía,
aquello que me diste el otro día.

El aspirar del aire,
el canto de la dulce Filomena,
el soto y su donaire
en la noche serena,
con llama que consume y no da pena.

Que nadie lo miraba,
Aminadab tampoco parecía;[5]
y el cerco sosegaba,
y la caballería
a vista de las aguas descendía.

And then go further,
To lofty caverns of the rock retire,
Well sealed away and hidden,
We both shall enter there
And new wine of the pomegranate savour.

There will you reveal
That which my soul had sought for on the way,
Then you will give to me –
You, my very life –
That which you gave to me the other day.

The breathing of the air,
The nightingale's sweet song, the glade
Its grace and splendour
In the silent night, with flame
That burns away yet brings no pain.

And there was no one watching,
Neither did Aminadab appear,
The siege was being raised,
And the horsemen,
At the sight of the waters, were riding down.

Notes to the Poems

The spelling and punctuation have been modernized to make the poems more easily accessible to readers. In this I have followed the text of Padre Silverio's edition. The Sanlúcar manuscript, which John Nims has reproduced in his edition and translation, contains no punctuation marks except the full stop.

PAGE 144

1 The spellings *oscuro*, *obscuro* and *escuro* all occur in various manuscripts. I have used *oscuro* throughout.

PAGE 146

2 *Cuando yo sus cabellos esparcía.*
The Hispalense MS gives *ya* for *yo* and this reading was followed in *The Oxford Book of Spanish Verse*. It completely alters the sense of the stanzas for if *ya* is preferred it is the breeze and not the Lover who scatters the Beloved's hair and strikes her neck. The same MS gives *la mano* in the following stanza in place of *el Amado*. These emendations seem to have been intended to weaken the erotic imagery in the poem, for in the Sanlúcar MS which San Juan himself corrected, the reading is *yo*.

PAGE 150

3 *Descubre tu presencia*
This stanza is lacking in the Sanlúcar version but was added in the Jaén version. I have given it here because it improves the poem, whereas the changes in the order of the stanzas which the Jaén version provides weaken it.

PAGE 156

4 *Cogednos las raposas*
The Jaén version gives *Cazadnos* (see p. 212).

PAGE 160 (and see also p. 220).

5 *Aminadab tampoco parecía*
The name Aminadab appears three times in the Bible: once in Exodus 6. 23 in a list of genealogies, once in the Song of Songs, 6.12, and once in Matthew 1.4 in the genealogy of Jesus Christ, where it comes halfway between Abraham and David. The reference in the *Song of Songs*, as the Vulgate gives it, is: *Nescivi: anima mea conturbavit me propter quadrigas Aminadab*, which one may translate: 'I became confused: my soul troubled me on account of the chariots of Aminadab.' The Authorized English Bible has 'like the chariots of Amminadab', while the Revised version prefers the reading 'among the chariots of my princely people'. All we know therefore

of Aminadáb, as the word is pronounced in Spanish, is that his name in Hebrew means 'is noble', that he possessed chariots and that he was one of the remote ancestors of Jesus Christ. San Juan, however, tells us in his commentary that according to Holy Scripture Aminadab is another name for the Devil, that adversary of the soul who fought with the Beloved continually and set before her temptations and traps so that she should not enter into intimate communication with her Lover.

In one of the early MSS of the poem the copyist wrote instead of Aminadab *A mi nada.*

PAGE 164

6 *Que bien sé yo la fonte que mana y corre*
The Sacro Monte MS gives two stanzas which are omitted from the Sanlúcar MS. They may well have been added at a later date by San Juan in order to clarify the meaning of the passage, but there is no proof of this and since by general agreement they detract from the beauty and flow of the poem I have omitted them. Here, however, I give them. After the first three-lined stanza comes:

> En esta noche oscura de esta vida
> que bien sé yo por fe la fonte frida,
> aunque es de noche.

and after the eighth stanza:

> Bien sé que tres en sola una agua viva
> residen, y una de otra se deriva,
> aunque es de noche.

PAGES 182–206

7 In *romances* the verbs which come at the end of the line must as a rule be in either the imperfect or the conditional tense in order to produce a rhyme. This allows a certain amount of poetic licence, which in this poem San Juan takes full advantage of. To grasp the meaning another tense must often be substituted for the one he uses.

A Select Bibliography

The material for the life of San Juan de la Cruz is very abundant, but of unequal value. It consists mainly of the sworn depositions made for the process of his beatification by friars and nuns who had known him. The collection of these began in 1614 and continued till 1627, but some of the best of this information is earlier, having been drawn from short memoirs or notes made either during the last years of San Juan's life or immediately after his death by persons who had been intimate with him. These depositions, which number well over two thousand, written in a handwriting that is difficult to read, are preserved in the Biblioteca Nacional at Madrid, while there are other documents which bear on his life in the Vatican library or in various Discalced Carmelite priories and convents.

The work of reading and sifting this huge mass of papers and of drawing from them reliable materials for a biography has been undertaken by a succession of Discalced Carmelite friars, beginning in the seventeenth century and continuing to the present day. The earlier of these biographies give the feeling of the age and contain details of interest that have been omitted for reasons of propriety by the modern biographers, but they have a strong tendency to hagiography and record miracles for which there is no good authority. The recent biographies not only deal with the often conflicting evidence in a more critical spirit, but contain many new facts obtained by patient comparison and research.

Fray José de Velasco: *Vida y virtudes del Venerable Varón Francisco de Yepes, que murió en Medina del Campo, año de 1607.* Valladolid, 1616.

This is a biography of San Juan's brother and contains valuable information on the early life of the saint taken from Francisco's lips by his confessor and confirmed and amplified by other persons at Medina.

José de Jesús María (Quiroga), o.c.d.: *Historia de la vida y virtudes del Venerable P. Fray Juan de la Cruz* . . . Brussels, 1628.

The first biography of San Juan, but laying the emphasis chiefly on his interior life.

Jerónimo de San José, o.c.d.: *Historia del Venerable Padre Fray Juan de la Cruz* . . . Madrid, 1641.

Jerónimo de San José was responsible for collecting many of the depositions for San Juan's beatification and so had great opportunities for learning about his life and cross-questioning the various witnesses. He was a cultivated man who had read the Latin historians and the medieval mystics and his book is thus by far the best and fullest of the early biographers, even though his tone is strongly inclined to hagiography as was inevitable in that age.

Francisco de Santa María (Pulgar), o.c.d.: *Reforma de los Descalzos de N.S. del Carmen de la Primitiva Observancia, hecha por Santa Teresa de Jesus.* Madrid, 1655: 2 vols.

This book contains 37 chapters on the life of San Juan de la Cruz, but gives little that is not to be found in Jerónimo de San José.

Bruno de Jésus Marie, o.c.d.: *Saint Jean de la Croix.* Paris, 1929. (With a preface by Jacques Maritain and 21 illustrations. English translation, 1932.)

Based on research into the documents. An excellent book.

Gerardo de San Juan de la Cruz, o.c.d.: *Obras del místico doctor San Juan de la Cruz. Edición crítica.* Toledo, 1912–14: 3 vols.

This is the first modern edition of San Juan's works but it has been superseded by other better ones.

Silverio de Santa Teresa, o.c.d.: *Obras de San Juan de la Cruz, Doctor de la Iglesia. Editadas y anotadas.* Burgos, 1929–31: 5 vols.

Silverio de Santa Teresa, o.c.d.: *Historia del Carmen Descalzo en España, Portugal y America.* Vol. V: *San Juan de la Cruz.* Burgos, 1936.

This is a very full biography, giving the texts of many of the depositions made for San Juan's beatification.

Crisógono de Jesús, o.c.d.: *Vida y obras completas de San Juan de la Cruz.* Biblioteca de Autores Cristianos, Madrid, 1964.

This is the most recent and exact of the biographies of San Juan and I have followed it closely, though sometimes adding particulars given in other biographies, chiefly those by Jerónimo de San José, Bruno de Jésus Marie and Silverio de Santa Teresa. This book also contains the fullest and most exact text of his works.

San Juan de la Cruz: *Obras completas.* Editorial Seneca, Mexico, 1942: 1 vol.

An attractive edition with good print and few notes.

E. Allison Peers: *The Works of Saint John of the Cross.* London, 1934–5: 3 vols.

The best English translation with good notes and introductory chapters. The third volume contains the text of some of the depositions made for San Juan's process of beatification, taken from Padre Silverio's biography.

E. Allison Peers: *Handbook to the Life and Times of St. Teresa and St. John of the Cross*. London, 1954.

An invaluable aid to the history of the Carmelite reform.

Jean Baruzi: *Saint Jean de la Croix et le problème de l'expérience mystique*. Paris, 1924.

A book of 788 pages by a French intellectual dealing principally with San Juan's doctrine.

Crisógono de Jesús, o.c.d.: *San Juan de la Cruz, su obra científica y su obra literaria*. Avila, 1929: 2 vols.

Roy Campbell: *The Poems of St. John of the Cross*. London, 1952.

The Spanish text with a translation in verse.

John Frederick Nims: *The poems of St. John of the Cross*, New York, 1959.

The Spanish text with a translation in verse. A revised edition came out in 1968.

Efrén de la Madre de Dios, o.c.d.: *Tiempo y Vida de Santa Teresa*. Biblioteca de Autores Cristianos. Madrid, 1968.

By far the best and fullest life.

Santa Teresa de Jesús: *Obras completas*. Ed. Aguilar, Madrid, 1948: 1 vol.

Santa Teresa de Jesús: *Obras completas*. Biblioteca de Autores Cristianos, Madrid, 1951–4: 3 vols.

E. Allison Peers: *The Complete Works of Saint Teresa of Jesus*, London, 1950: 3 vols.

E. Allison Peers: *The Letters of Saint Teresa of Jesus*. London, 1951: 2 vols.

Both these last books are well translated and provided with valuable footnotes and introductions.

Marcelle Auclair: *Saint Teresa of Avila*. Translated from the French edition of 1950. London, 1953.

The best biography in English.

Dámaso Alonso: *La Poesía de San Juan de la Cruz*. Madrid, 1942. 4th edition, 1966.

A detailed study of San Juan's poetry by the most distinguished of living Spanish critics. I have made great use of this book.

Dámaso Alonso: *Poesía Española*. Madrid, 1950.

This book contains an essay on San Juan which amplifies his previous work.

J. M. Blecua: 'Los antecedentes del poema "El pastorcico" de San Juan de la Cruz', *Revista de Filología Española*, 33: 1949.

Marcel Bataillon: 'Sur la genèse poétique du Cantique Spirituel', *Boletín del Instituto Caro y Cuervo*, 3: 1949.

Marcel Bataillon: *Erasme et l'Espagne*. Paris, 1937.

A masterly work on the background of the religious life in Spain during the first half of the sixteenth century.

Friedrich von Hügel: *The Mystical Element in Religion as studied in Saint Catherine of Genoa and her friends*. London, 1908. Fourth impression, 1961: 2 vols.

This is perhaps the best book in English on Catholic mysticism.

Principal Dates in the Life of San Juan de la Cruz

1515 Santa Teresa's birth at Avila.

1542 Juan de Yepes is born at Fontiveros near Avila.

1548 His mother removes to Arévalo.

1551 His mother leaves Arévalo for Medina del Campo.

c. 1552 Juan is boarded out at an orphanage called the Colegio de le Doctrina.

c. 1557 He works as male nurse at the Hospital de las Bubas.

1559 He attends the college of the Society of Jesus.

1562 Foundation by Santa Teresa of the first reformed convent – San José at Avila.

1563 He takes the Carmelite habit at the priory of Santa Ana, Medina del Campo, under the name of Juan de San Matías.

1564 After making his profession at Santa Ana he enters Salamanca University in *November* for a three years' course in Arts.

1567 He receives priest's orders and in *September* meets Santa Teresa at Medina and agrees to join the Discalced reform.

In *October* he returns to Salamanca for a year's course in theology.

1568 In *August* he accompanies Santa Teresa to Valladolid and then goes to Duruelo to prepare the new priory.

On *28 November* he takes the vows of the reform with Antonio de Jesús (Heredia) before the provincial of Castile.

1569 *July.* Foundation of a Discalced priory at Pastrana.

1570 In *June* Juan moves with the Duruelo community to Mancera. He visits Pastrana to organize the training of the novices.

1571 He is appointed rector to the new Discalced college at Alcalá de Henares.

1572 In *May* he spends a few weeks at Pastrana to correct the excesses of the novice-master. While he is there Jerónimo Gracián takes the habit.

In *September* he goes as confessor to the Calced convent of the Encarnación at Avila, of which Santa Teresa is prioress. He remains there for five and a half years.

1573 In *July* Santa Teresa ceases to be prioress of the Encarnación and leaves Avila.

1574 In *March* he accompanies Santa Teresa to Segovia, where she founds a convent.

1576 In *January* he is kidnapped by the Calced priors and imprisoned at Medina, but is released soon after.

1577 In *June* the papal nuncio, Ormaneto, dies and is succeeded by Sega, who is hostile to the reform.

On *2 or 3 December* Juan is kidnapped by the Calced friars and imprisoned at Toledo.

1578 On *16 August* or a day or two later he escapes and is sheltered by Don Pedro González de Mendoza.

In *October* he attends the illegal chapter of the Discalced at Almodóvar del Río and is appointed vicar to the priory at El Calvario in Andalusia. He reaches Beas de Segura at the end of the month and rests for a few days at the convent of which Ana de Jesús is prioress, before continuing to El Calvario.

1579   After spending 8 months here he goes on *13 June* to Baeza to found a Discalced college, of which he becomes rector. Meanwhile the crisis in the reform has ended with the appointment of Ángel de Salazar to be their vicar-general.

1580   Death of his mother and severe illness of Santa Teresa in the influenza epidemic. The pope recognizes the Discalced as a separate province under the Carmelite general.

1581   In *March* Juan attends the 'Chapter of the Separation' at Alcalá de Henares at which Gracián is elected provincial. Juan is appointed third definitor and prior of Los Mártires at Granada, but remains for the time being rector of the college of Baeza.

In *November* he travels to Avila where he sees Santa Teresa for the last time and returns with two nuns to Beas.

1582   In *January* he founds a convent at Granada with Ana de Jesús as prioress and is elected prior of Los Mártires by the community. He remains here on and off for over 6 years.

4 October – death of Santa Teresa.

1583   Chapter of Almodóvar, which he attends.

1585   In *February* he founds a convent at Málaga.

In *May* he attends the chapter of Lisbon, at which Nicolás Doria succeeds Gracián as provincial. Juan is appointed second definitor while remaining prior of Los Mártires.

In *October* he attends the resumption of the Lisbon chapter at Pastrana, where he is appointed vicar-provincial of Andalusia. This gives him nearly two years of continual travelling.

1586   In *May* he founds a priory at Córdoba.

In *August* he falls seriously ill with pleurisy at Guadalcázar.

In *September* he assists at the foundation of a convent at Madrid with Ana de Jesús as prioress.

In *December* he founds a priory at Caravaca.

1587   At the chapter of Valladolid in *April* he ceases to be definitor and vicar-provincial, but is reappointed prior of Los Mártires.

In *July* Sixtus V authorizes the creation of a Discalced congregation with a new constitution drawn up by Doria.

1588   In *June* he attends the first chapter-general of the reform at Madrid at which Doria is elected vicar-general. Juan is appointed first definitor and a consiliario on the consulta.

In *August* he becomes prior of Segovia and deputy for Doria during his absences. He remains for nearly three years at Segovia.

1591   At the chapter-general held at Madrid in *June* he is deprived of all his offices and sent as a simple friar to La Peñuela, near Baeza.

He arrives there on *10 August* but soon falls ill.

On *28 September* he leaves for Úbeda, where, on *14 December* he dies.

1592   On *14 February* Gracián is expelled from the congregation. Ana de Jesús and María de San José are relieved of their offices and sentenced to close seclusion in convents.

1593   In *December* the congregation of the Discalced Carmelites becomes a separate order by a bull of Clement VIII and Doria is appointed interim general.

1594   Doria is taken ill on his way to the chapter-general at Madrid and dies on *9 May*. On *23 May* the chapter-general meets and elects Elías de San Martín general. A fortnight later Fray Diego Evangelista, Juan's bitter enemy and calumniator, dies suddenly on his way to take up his office of provincial of Upper Andalusia.

1675   Juan de la Cruz is beatified by Clement I.

1726   He is canonized by Benedict XIII.

1926   He is declared a doctor of the universal church by Pius XI.

Index

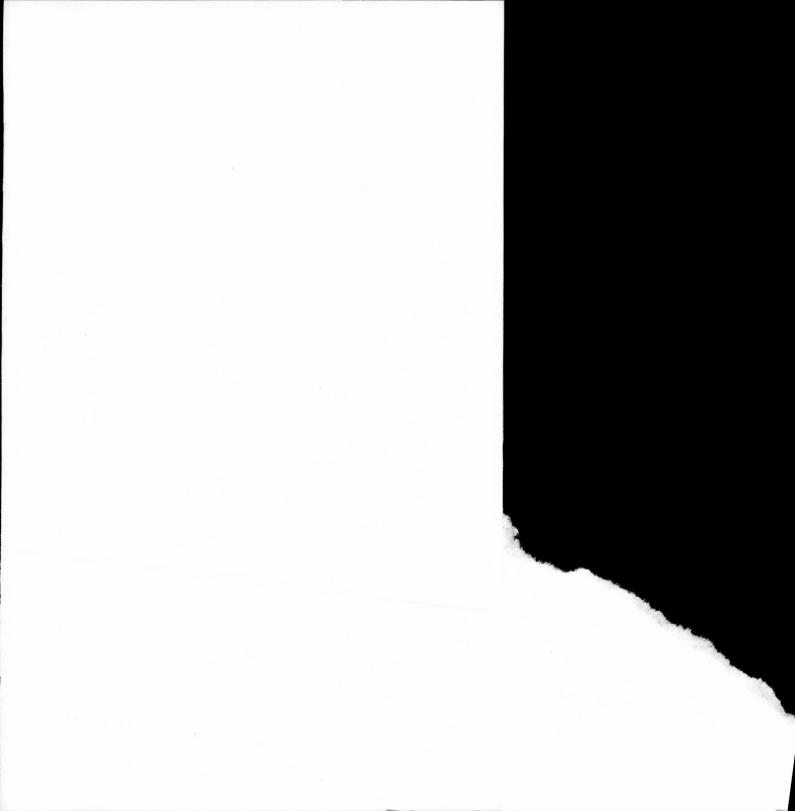